The making of orthodoxy
Essays in honour of Henry Chadwick

How did early Christianity arrive at a sense of what was and was not acceptable in its life and teaching? Scholarship in the last few decades has increasingly concluded that many non-theological factors were at work in this process, and that it was by no means as straightforward a story as was once thought. New discoveries and interpretations have overturned many textbook accounts of the story of the early church.

The essays in this book examine from a variety of viewpoints the problem of defining 'orthodoxy' in the first Christian centuries – from the New Testament era to the sixth century. They range from detailed studies on particular texts to general surveys of a whole area of research, and represent the work of some of the foremost experts in early Christian studies in the English-speaking world. They are dedicated to Henry Chadwick, who has for many years been recognized as a leader in this field, a scholar who, in his own researches and in his editorship of the *Journal of Theological Studies*, has long set the tone and standard for patristic studies in Britain and elsewhere. They are designed both to contribute to research and to offer fresh perspectives to students discovering the study of early Christianity for the first time.

Henry Chadwick, DD, FBA

The making of orthodoxy

Essays in honour of Henry Chadwick

EDITED BY ROWAN WILLIAMS

Lady Margaret Professor of Divinity, University of Oxford

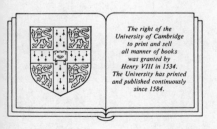

The right of the
University of Cambridge
to print and sell
all manner of books
was granted by
Henry VIII in 1534.
The University has printed
and published continuously
since 1584.

CAMBRIDGE UNIVERSITY PRESS

CAMBRIDGE

NEW YORK   PORT CHESTER   MELBOURNE   SYDNEY

Published by the Press Syndicate of the University of Cambridge
The Pitt Building, Trumpington Street, Cambridge CB2 1RP
40 West 20th Street, New York, NY 10011, USA
10 Stamford Road, Oakleigh, Melbourne 3166, Australia

First published 1989

Printed in Great Britain by the University Press, Cambridge

British Library cataloguing in publication data

The Making of orthodoxy: essays in honour of
Henry Chadwick.
1. Christian church, history
1. Williams, Rowan   11. Chadwick, Henry,
1920–
270

Library of Congress cataloguing in publication data

The Making of orthodoxy: essays in honour of Henry Chadwick / edited
by Rowan Williams.
    p.   cm.
Bibliography.
Includes index.
ISBN 0 521 35188 X
1. Theology, Doctrinal—History—Early church, ca. 30-600.
2. Chadwick, Henry, 1920–   1. Chadwick, Henry, 1920–
11. Williams, Rowan, 1950–
BT25.M3 1989
230'.11–dc19   88-29428   CIP

ISBN 0 521 35188 X

Contents

CONTENTS

vi

Preface

The range of Henry Chadwick's achievement is, of course, almost legendary – so much so that it was thought desirable to produce two volumes in his honour, one celebrating his continuing contribution to the work for unity between the Christian churches, the other concerned with his work as a patristic scholar over some four decades. The former volume, edited by Dr G. R. Evans and published by Oxford University Press, has already appeared. The present collection represents the tribute of fellow specialists to one who is perhaps uniquely a 'master in Israel' in the study of early Christian thought.

From the first, Henry Chadwick's researches have been concentrated on the question of how early Christianity developed an idiom of its own, especially in its long and fruitful (and often bad-tempered) conversation with the world of classical culture. Chadwick's first major production – in itself an achievement sufficient to guarantee his significance as a scholar – was a fully annotated translation of Origen's *Contra Celsum*, a work in which early Christianity's self-definition over against the religio-philosophical consensus of enlightened second-century minds has been decisively advanced, and the intellectual credibility of 'Catholic' Christianity defended at a new level of sophistication. In this translation, lately revised and reissued, some of the foundations are laid for the Cochrane lectures on *Christianity and Classical Culture*, and many shorter studies; and this concern for Christianity's critical absorption of the classical heritage finds its culmination in recent books on Boethius and Augustine – the former regarded by many scholars as Chadwick's finest work.

But the story of the early church is not by any means a history of the steady assimilation of intellectual disciplines. We are rightly wary these days of language that suggests an anachronistic clarity about where 'centre' and 'periphery' were to be found in the first Christian centuries, and Chadwick has given judicious and searching attention to forms of Christianity often regarded as marginal. There is a study of the theology of the *Odes of Solomon*, for instance, an article on the Messalians, and, above all, a ground-breaking monograph on Priscillian of Avila. Chadwick has never believed that the history of doctrine can simply be written as a history of (successful) ideas in a social vacuum; and an awareness of the complex interrelations of piety, politics, and theology appears in an early article – now justly regarded as a minor classic – on 'Eucharist and Christology in the Nestorian Controversy', and continues to be reflected in papers on 'Faith and Order at the Council of Nicaea' and 'The Role of the Christian Bishop in Ancient Society', to take two out of many possible examples.

Doctrinal history, then, is not to be written in abstraction from the discipline of 'ordinary' history. The patrologist is not exempt from the hard detail of assessing documentary sources, and settling chronologies and evaluating archaeological discoveries. Apart from some fundamentally important work on the Origen material in the Tura papyri, Chadwick has authoritatively established the presidency of the synod of Antioch in 325, with the help of a Syrian manuscript source, the date of Eustathius of Antioch's disgrace after Nicaea, and the authenticity of Boethius' theological *opuscula*. Attentive readers of bibliographies will also recall a tantalizing title alluding to a 'musical bishop of Ephesus'.

This is to pass over not only that supremely readable textbook on *The Early Church*, the various articles on New Testament topics (and a commentary on Ephesians) and studies of Philo, as well as essays on Pachomius and Philoponus, but the extraordinary corpus of reviews and notices, especially in the *Journal of Theological Studies*, year after year. These are anything but dutiful ephemera; many contain suggestions and *aperçus* worth an article in themselves, and it is much to be hoped that Professor John O'Neill's full catalogue of these will be published in its entirety to supplement the bibliography he has prepared for this volume. Even in the history of the *JThS*, there can seldom have been an editor so prolific in response to the flood of books in a dozen or more languages streaming in to the editorial desk.

As already suggested, the focus of Henry Chadwick's work might reasonably be seen as the process by which the early Christian mind found definition in its cultural setting. *The Making of Orthodoxy* thus seemed a proper subject for a volume such as this: a title which is meant to avoid the bland assumption that what we know as orthodox Christianity simply evolves in an uninterrupted movement of inner logic. Orthodoxy is *constructed*, in the processes of both theological and political conflict; which means that understanding it fully should involve understanding these conflicts. Few of the contributors to this volume would argue that orthodoxy is an empty or useless concept, historically or theologically, but all would agree that it is problematical. The editor's essay, taking up the theme of Chadwick's Oxford inaugural lecture, examines what was involved in being orthodox in the pre-Nicene period, attempting an assessment of both Walter Bauer and his critics. Professor Frend follows with a reminder of the variegated non-theological factors at work in debates over heresy and of the risks of an excessively text-dominated approach to the problem. Professor Osborn discusses the significance of the appeal to reason in anti-gnostic apologetic, and the importance of something like a concept of philosophical coherence in the development and defence of *regulae fidei*. These fairly general essays are followed by three more closely focussed studies. Dr Bammel discusses the interaction between Origen's speculative cosmology and his exegesis in relation to the figure of Adam; Professor Barnes shows how the new situation of the church under Constantine prompts a bold attempt at the fusion of literary genres to present the icon of an imperial saint, and in passing recalls the paradox that the peace of the church under Constantine is celebrated in quasi-eschatological terms by someone firmly committed to an 'orthodoxy' (anti-Nicene Trinitarianism) that would finally fail after decades of bitter strife; and Fr Green, examining Eusebius' witness to a variant of Matthew 28:19, raises some substantial questions about the role of doctrinal pressure in forming liturgy, not merely liturgy's role in shaping doctrine (often more readily taken for granted in patristic studies).

Nicaea must be a watershed in any survey of the growth of orthodoxy. Professors Hanson, Wiles and Heron deal with the aftermath of the council in various ways, Hanson examining the process by which specific terms come to be fixed as tests of orthodoxy, Wiles suggesting that we continue to underrate the spiritual seriousness of the opponents of Nicaea, Heron discussing one particular case in the formation of orthodox Trinitarian idiom, the work of Didymus the Blind. Professor Frances Young returns to a more general perspective, interpreting the tensions between Antioch and Alexandria which so dominated post-Nicene theology as shaped by the long-standing struggle between rhetoric and philosophy. Two papers, Dr Wickham's and Professor Markus', look at the aftermath of the Pelagian controversy in the

Eastern and Western churches respectively, examining both the degree to which it added fresh dimensions to the way orthodoxy was conceived and the degree to which it was associated with or absorbed in other struggles. Mr Bonner turns our attention to a seldom-studied aspect of Augustine's thought, his (changing) attitude to those who looked for a reign of the saints on earth: his response to this question looks forward into the world of mediaeval heterodoxies as well as back to the complex history of earlier Christian apocalyptic.

Three final essays offer perspectives upon issues frequently pushed to the margin of patristic studies, yet equally crucial to understanding orthodoxy. Professor Stead points out that the taking-over by theology from classical philosophy of an unreconstructed and often under-examined notion of God's simplicity made for major unclarities and confusions in the evolution of Trinitarian language; and he poses a challenge both to the concept of 'simplicity' and to conventional Trinitarianism. Dr Murray traces the interweaving of doctrinal themes and artistic development in early Christianity, reminding us that the communication of doctrine is not exclusively a verbal or conceptual affair. And Professor O'Neill questions prevailing views of what was normative *practice* in the early church by suggesting that monasticism, so far from being a development of the Constantinian era, is part of an apostolic and Jewish–Christian heritage; we should be asking what conditions us to read our material in terms of one particular 'story' of development (doctrinal or practical) rather than another.

This brief account of what the present volume offers should show the way in which Chadwick's sense of the range of study necessary to comprehend early Christianity has informed the enterprise. Several essays touch on the overlap with classical culture (Osborn, Young, Stead); others re-examine the context and effects of 'non-mainstream' currents (Wiles, Wickham, Markus, Bonner), and the broader issues of how definitions are created, both socially and intellectually (Williams, Frend, Hanson). There is attention paid to factors and movements rather neglected by textbook accounts of doctrinal development (O'Neill, Murray); and there is the indispensable close exegesis of particular texts (Bammel, Barnes, Green and Heron). In all these areas, Chadwick has set standards of professionalism which continue to be a stimulus to other scholars, and it is our hope that this book will be a tribute sufficiently apt to open doors into the world Henry Chadwick has made very particularly his own. There are signs, in the USA and in Britain, of a far more widespread interest in early Christianity among students of classics, history and philosophy, as well as theology, than prevailed a decade or so ago, and we trust that the issues opened up by Henry Chadwick and pursued here will be explored yet further and more fruitfully in the years ahead.

The number of distinguished scholars willing to acknowledge a debt to Henry Chadwick is so large that a *Festschrift* representing all of them would be a formidably huge volume. No principle of selection can be wholly rational and consistent; but, broadly, the present collection represents English-speaking scholars (outside the USA), colleagues from various epochs of Chadwick's teaching career, and British friends, collaborators and former research pupils. These names must stand for many more, of no less distinction, who look to Henry Chadwick, as teacher, writer and friend, with unqualified admiration and gratitude.

Thanks are due to the staff of Cambridge University Press for their constant help and encouragement, and to the Revd Peter Eaton for his work on the index to this volume. We have to record with great sadness the death of Professor R. P. C. Hanson while this volume was in preparation, and are grateful for his work on the proofs of his paper during the last months of his life.

Abbreviations

ACO	*Acta conciliorum oecumenicorum*, Berlin 1914–
ACW	*Ancient Christian Writers*, Westminster, Md. 1946–
AGPh	*Archiv für Geschichte der Philosophie und Soziologie*
AJAH	*American Journal of Ancient History*
AJP	*American Journal of Philology*
AöAWPH	*Anzeiger der österreichen Akademie der Wissenschaften: Philosophisch-historische Klasse*
ASTI	*Annual of the Swedish Theological Institute in Jerusalem*
Aug	*Augustinianum*
AugStud	*Augustinian Studies*
BAB	*Bulletin de l'académie royale de Belgique*
BALAC	*Bulletin d'ancienne littérature et d'archéologie chrétienne*
BASOR	*Bulletin of the American Schools of Oriental Research*
BEFAR	*Bibiotheque des écoles françaises d'Athènes et de Rome*
BFCT	*Beiträge zur Förderung christlicher Theologie*
BICS	*Bulletin of the Institute of Classical Studies of the University of London*
BJRL	*Bulletin of the John Rylands Library*
BLE	*Bulletin de littérature ecclésiastique*
BSNAF	*Bulletin de la Société Nationale des Antiquaires de France*
Byz	*Byzantion*
ByZ	*Byzantinische Zeitschrift*
CC	*Corpus Christianorum*, Turnhout 1953–
CCL	*Corpus Christianorum, series latina*
CP	*Classical Philology*
CQR	*Church Quarterly Review*
CRAI	*Comptes rendus des séances de l'académie des inscriptions et belles lettres*
CSEL	*Corpus Scriptorum ecclesiasticorum latinorum*, Vienna 1866–
CTh	*Cahiers théologiques*
DACL	*Dictionnaire d'archéologie chrétienne et liturgie*, Paris, 1905–53
DHGE	*Dictionnaire d'histoire et de géographie ecclésiastique*, Paris 1912–

Diels, *DG*	*Doxographi Graeci*, ed. H. Diels, Berlin 1879
DSp	*Dictionnaire de spiritualité, ascétique et mystique*, Paris, 1932–
DThC	*Dictionnaire de théologie catholique*, Paris 1903–
ERE	*Encyclopaedia of Religion and Ethics*, ed. J. Hastings, Edinburgh 1908–26
ET	*Expository Times*
EvTh	*Evangelische Theologie*
FGH	*Fragmente der griechischen Historiker*, Berlin 1923–
GCS	*Die griechischen christlichen Schriftsteller de ersten drei Jahrhunderte*, Berlin 1897–
GGA	*Göttingische gelehrte Anzeigen*
GRBS	*Greek, Roman and Byzantine Studies*
HThR	*Harvard Theological Review*
ILS	*Inscriptiones latinae selectae*, Berlin 1892–1916
JBL	*Journal of Biblical Literature*
JEH	*Journal of Ecclesiastical History*
JRS	*Journal of Roman Studies*
JSNT	*Journal for the Study of the New Testament*
JThS	*Journal of Theological Studies*
KpS	*Klassisch-philologische Studien*
MGH.AA	*Monumenta Germaniae historica. Auctores antiquissimi*, Hanover 1877–1919
MGH.SR.Merov.	*Monumenta Germaniae historica. Scriptores rerum Merovingicarum*, Hanover 1884–1920
NAWG	*Nachrichten der Akademie der Wissenschaften in Göttingen*
NPNF	*Nicene and Post-Nicene Fathers*
NTS	*New Testament Studies*
OrChrA	*Orientalia Christiana Analecta*
PBA	*Proceedings of the British Academy*
PG	Migne, *Patrologia Graeca*
PL	Migne, *Patrologia Latina*
PLRE	*Prosopography of the Later Roman Empire*, ed. A. H. M. Jones, J. R. Martindale and J. Morris, Cambridge 1971–
PO	*Patrologia Orientalis*
PS	*Patrologia Syriaca*
RechAug	*Recherches Augustiniennes*
RE	*Realencyklopädie für protestantische Theologie und Kirche*, 3rd edn., 1896–1913
RBen	*Revue Bénédictine*
REA	*Revue des études anciennes*
REAug	*Revue des études augustiniennes*
REL	*Revue des études latines*
RFIC	*Rivista di filologia e d'istruzione classica*
RHPhR	*Revue d'histoire et philosophie religieuse*

RMP	*Rheinisches Museum für Philologie*
RSR	*Recherches de sciences religieuses*
RSLR	*Rivista di Storia e Letteratura Religiosa*
RSPhTh	*Revue des sciences philosophiques et théologiques*
RThAM	*Recherches de théologie ancienne et médiévale*
SBAW.PPH	*Sitzungsberichte der bayerischen Akademie der Wissenschaften*, Philosophisch-philologisch und historische Klasse
SBL	*Society of Biblical Literature*
SC	*Sources chrétiennes*, Paris, 1941–
SE	*Sacris erudiri*
StEv	*Studia Evangelica*
StPatr	*Studia patristica.* Papers presented to the International Conference on Patristic Studies, Berlin 1957–
SPAW	*Sitzungsberichte der preussischen Akademie der Wissenschaften*
SVF	*Stoicorum Veterum Fragmenta*, ed. J. von Arnim
TRE	*Theologische Realencyklopädie*, Berlin 1974–
THQ	*Theologische Quartalschrift*
TU	*Texte und Untersuchungen zur Geschichte der altchristlichen Literatur*, Berlin 1882–
VetChr	*Vetera Christianorum*
VigChr	*Vigiliae Christianae*
ZKG	*Zeitschrift für Kirchengeschichte*
ZKTh	*Zeitschrift für katholische Theologie*
ZNW	*Zeitschrift für die neutestamentliche Wissenschaft und die Kunde der alteren Kirche*
ZThK	*Zeitschrift für Theologie und Kirche*

A bibliography of the books and articles of the Reverend Professor Henry Chadwick, DD, FBA

J. C. O'NEILL

HENRY CHADWICK

Born 23 June 1920

Regius Professor of Divinity, University of Oxford, 1959–69

Dean, Christ Church, Oxford, 1969–79

Regius Professor of Divinity, University of Cambridge, 1979–83

Master, Peterhouse, Cambridge, 1987–

Editor, *Journal of Theological Studies*, 1954–85

General editor, *A Library of Modern Religious Thought*

General Editor, Black's New Testament Commentaries

General Editor, Oxford Early Christian Texts

General Editor, with Owen Chadwick, *Oxford History of the Christian Church*

This bibliography was compiled with generous help from G. C. Stead and D. F. Wright, and revised in the light of G. R. Evans's Bibliography in *Christian Authority: Essays in Honour of Henry Chadwick*, Oxford, 1988, pp. 338–47.

1947 'Origen, Celsus, and the Stoa', *JThS*, 48, 34–49.
1948 'The Fall of Eustathius of Antioch', *JThS*, 49, 27–35. See 1982, no. 2.
'Athanasius, De Decretis xl.3', *JThS*, 49, 168–9.
'Origen, Celsus, and the Resurrection of the Body' *HThR*, 41, 83–102.
'The Episcopacy in the Second Century', *The Office of a Bishop: Four Essays.* Foreword by M. A. C. Warren. [First appearing in *The Churchman*, June, 1948], London, Church Book Room Press Ltd., pp. 15–24.

1950 'The Silence of Bishops in Ignatius', *HTL R*, 43, 169–72. See 1982, no. 2.

'1 Thess. 3.3: σαίνεσθαι', *JThS*, n.s. 1, 156–8.

1951 'Eucharist and Christology in the Nestorian Controversy', *JThS*, n.s. 2, 145–64. See 1982, no. 2.

1952 'An Attis from a Domestic Shrine' (with 3 plates), *JThS*, n.s. 3, 90–2.

1953 *Origen: Contra Celsum, Translated with an Introduction and Notes,* Cambridge, 1953; reprinted with corrections, 1965; 3rd printing with minor changes, 1980.

'Notes on the Text of Origen, *Contra Celsum*', *JTS* n.s. 4, 215–19.

1954 *Alexandrian Christianity, Selected Translations of Clement and Origen with Introductions and Notes* by John Ernest Leonard Oulton and Henry Chadwick, The Library of Christian Classics, vol. II, London (Clement: Introduction, *stromateis* II, revision of J. B. Mayor's translation of *Stromateis* VII; Origen: Exhortation to Martyrdom, Dialogue with Heraclides; Bibliography).

'de Sacramentis', *ET*, 66 (1954–5), 31.

1955 '"All Things to All Men" (1 Cor. ix.22)', *NTS*, 1 (1954–5), 261–75.

'The Exile and Death of Flavian of Constantinople: A Prologue to the Council of Chalcedon', *JThS*, n.s. 6, 17–34.

1956 'The Authorship of Egerton Papyrus No. 3', *HThR*, 49, 145–51.

Lessing's Theological Writings, Selections in Translation with an Introductory Essay, A Library of Modern Religious Thought, London.

G. L. Prestige, *St Basil the Great and Apollinaris of Laodicea*, edited from his papers, preface by H. Chadwick, London.

'The Quest of St Peter's Bones', review article of *De Pythagore aux Apôtres: Etudes sur la conversion du Monde Romain* by J. Carcopino; and of *The Shrine of St Peter and the Vatican Excavations* by J. Toynbee and J. W. Perkins, *The Cambridge Review*, 77 (1955–6), 680–2.

'Der Einfluss der deutschen protestantischen Theologie auf die englische Kirche im 19. Jahrhundert', *Evangelische Theologie*, 16, 556–71.

1957 Wilfred L. Knox, *The Sources of the Synoptic Gospels*, edited by

H. Chadwick, volume 2, *St Luke and St Matthew*, Cambridge
('Some rough outline comments on the problem of
Jesus' Messianic consciousness [by W. L. Knox] have been
made the basis of a brief discussion of the criteria of
authenticity': Epilogue, 'The Problem of Authenticity', pp.
138–48).

'The Evidences of Christianity in the Apologetic of Origen',
St Patr, vol. 2, Papers presented to the Second International
Conference on Patristic Studies held at Christ Church,
Oxford, 1955, part 2 edited by Kurt Aland and F. L. Cross,
TU, 64 (Berlin), pp. 331–9.

'St Peter and St Paul in Rome: The Problem of the *Memoria
Apostolorum ad Catacumbas*', *JThS*, n.s. 8, 31–52. See 1982,
no. 2.

'The New Edition of Hermas', *JThS*, n.s. 8, 274–80.

1958 'Ossius of Cordova and the Presidency of the Council of
Antioch, 325', *JThS*, n.s. 9, 292–304. See 1982, no. 2.

1959 *The Circle and the Ellipse, Rival Concepts of Authority in the Early
Church*, an inaugural lecture delivered before the University
of Oxford on 5 May 1959, Oxford, See 1982, no. 2.

*The Sentences of Sextus, A Contribution to the History of Early
Christian Ethics*, Texts and Studies, Contributions to Biblical
and Patristic Literature, New Series, 5, Cambridge.

'Rufinus and the Tura Papyrus of Origen's Commentary on
Romans', *JThS*, n.s. 10, 10–42. See 1982, no. 2.

1960 *Saint Ambrose, On the Sacraments, The Latin Text edited*, Studies
in Eucharistic Faith and Practice, London.

'Die Absicht des Epheserbriefes', *ZNW*, 51, 145–53.

The Vindication of Christianity in Westcott's Thought, Bishop
Westcott Memorial Lecture, 1960, Cambridge, 1961.

'A Latin Epitome of Melito's Homily on the Pascha', *JThS*,
n.s. 9, 76–82. See 1982, no. 2.

'The Sentences of Sextus and of the Pythagoreans', *JThS*, n.s.
9, 349.

'Faith and Order at the Council of Nicaea: A Note on the
Background of the Sixth Canon', *HThR*, 53, 171–95. See
1982, no. 2.

1961 'Justification by Faith and Hospitality', *StPatr*, Papers
presented to the Third International Conference on Patristic
Studies held at Christ Church, Oxford, 1959, part 2, *Biblica*,

Patres Apostolici, Historica, edited by F. L. Cross, *TU*, 79, Berlin, pp. 281–5.

'St Leo the Great', *Listener*, 16 Nov., 813–14, 819.

1962 'Enkrateia', *Reallexikon für Antike und Christentum*, edited by Theodor Klauser, Band 5, Stuttgart, col. 343–65. [Lieferung 35 issued August 1960.]

'Ephesians', *Peake's Commentary on the Bible*, edited by Matthew Black and H. H. Rowley, London, pp. 980–4.

'Soundings', review article (in place of an editorial) of *Soundings: Essays concerning Christian Understanding*, edited by A. R. Vidler, *Theology*, 65, 441–6.

'Pope Damasus and the Peculiar Claim of Rome to St Peter and St Paul', *Neotestamentica et patristica: Eine Freundesgabe, Herrn Professor Dr Oscar Cullmann zu seinem 60. Geburtstag überreicht*, supplements to *Novum Testamentum* 6, Leiden, pp. 313–18. See 1982, no. 2.

Syllabus of Lectures, The Gifford Lectures, University of St Andrews, Session 1962–3, 'Authority in the Early Church' [28 Nov., 5, 12 Dec. 1962; 27 Feb., 6, 13 Mar., 18, 25 Apr., 2, 9 May 1963].

1963 'The Ring of a Musical Bishop of Ephesus?', *ET*, 74 (1962–3), 213–14.

Syllabus of Lectures, The Gifford Lectures, University of St Andrews, Session 1963–4, 'Authority in Christian Theology' [27 Nov., 4, 11 Dec. 1963; 26 Feb., 4, 11 Mar., 8, 15, 22, 29 Apr. 1964].

'The Bible and the Greek Fathers', *The Church's Use of the Bible: Past and Present*, edited by D. E. Nineham, London, pp. 25–39.

'Arthur Darby Nock' (with E. R. Dodds), *Journal of Roman Studies*, 53, 168–9.

1964 'Celsus' [5.145–146]; 'Clement of Alexandria' [5.899–900]; 'Constantine (Constantius), the name of a pope and an antipope' [6.384]; 'Dionysius (The Areopagite)' [7.464–465]; 'Gregory, Saint (of Nyssa)' [10.906–907]; 'Hegesippus, Saint' [11.304]; 'John, Gospel According to and Epistles of Saint' [13.97–102], *Encyclopaedia Britannica*, Fourteenth Edition, Chicago.

1965 'Justin Martyr's Defence of Christianity', *BJRL*, 47, 275–97. See 1982, no. 2.

'Nestorius' Book of Heraclides.' A review of *Untersuchungen
zum 'Liber Heraclidis' des Nestorius*, by L. Abramowski, *JThS*,
n.s. 16, 214–18. See 1982, no. 2.

1966 *Early Christian Thought and the Classical Tradition: Studies in
Justin, Clement, and Origen,* Oxford, repr. 1971, 1984; Japanese
translation 1984.

'St Paul and Philo of Alexandria', T. W. Manson Memorial
Lecture, *BJRL*, 48, 286–307. See 1982, no. 2.

with H. von Campenhausen, *Jerusalem and Rome: The Problem of
Authority in the Early Church,* Philadelphia, pp. 21–36 = 1959,
no. 1.

'Les 318 Pères de Nicée', *Revue d'histoire ecclésiastique*, 61,
808–11.

1967 *The Early Church*, The Pelican History of the Church, vol. 1,
Harmondsworth = *Die Kirche in der antiken Welt*, translated
by G. May, Berlin 1972; provided with references, corrected
reissue 1985; translated into Portuguese and Korean.

'Lessing', *The Encyclopedia of Philosophy*, edited by Paul
Edwards, vol. 4, New York, pp. 443–6.

'Philo and the Beginnings of Christian Thought' (Philo – The
beginning of Christian philosophy: Justin: the Gnostics –
Clement of Alexandria – Origen), *The Cambridge History of
Later Greek and Early Medieval Philosophy*, edited by A. H.
Armstrong, Cambridge, pp. 133–92. See 1982, no. 2.

1968 'Ἀποστολικὴ παράδοσις, *The Treatise on the Apostolic Tradition of
St Hippolytus of Rome*, edited by G. Dix, reissued, with
corrections, preface, and bibliography, Church History
Society, London.

'La discussion au sujet des Ordres anglicans dans la théologie
anglicane actuelle', *Concilium*, 34, 127–34.

'The discussion on Anglican Orders in Modern Anglican
Theology', *Concilium*, 4, 72–6.

1969 The Enigma of St Paul, Ethel M. Wood Lecture, 1968,
London.

'Florilegium', *Reallexikon für Antike und Christentum* edited by
T. Klauser, vol. 7, Stuttgart, col. 1131–60.

'Some Reflections on Conscience: Greek, Jewish and
Christian', Robert Waley Cohen Memorial Lecture,
22 October 1968, Church House, Westminster, London:
Council for Christians and Jews.

'The "Finality" of the Christian Faith', *Lambeth Essays on Faith*, Essays written for the Lambeth Conference 1968, edited by the Archbishop of Canterbury [A. M. Ramsey], London, pp. 22–31.

'Romanticism and Religion', *The Future of the Modern Humanities*, Papers delivered at the Jubilee Congress of the Modern Humanities Research Association in August 1968, Publication of the M.H.R.A. 1, edited by J. C. Laidlaw, Cambridge, pp. 18–30.

1970 'Some Reflections on the Character and Theology of the Odes of Solomon', *Kyriakon, Festschrift Johannes Quasten*, edited by P. Granfield and J. A. Jungmann, vol. 1, Münster, pp. 266–70.

'Einigkeit in den fundamentalen Glaubensartikeln', *Theologische Quartalschrift*, 150, 396–403.

1972 'The Origin of the Title "Oecumenical Council"', *JThS*, n.s. 23, 132–5. See 1982, no. 2.

'Prayer at Midnight', *Epektasis, Mélanges patristiques offerts au Cardinal Jean Daniélou*, edited by J. Fontaine and C. Kannengiesser, Paris, pp. 47–9.

Norman H. Baynes, *Constantine the Great and the Christian Church*, with a preface by Henry Chadwick, 2nd edn, London.

'The Identity and date of Mark the Monk', *Eastern Churches Review*, 4, 125–30. See 1982, no. 2.

1973 'A Letter Ascribed to Peter of Alexandria', text edited by John Barns, Historical Introduction by H. Chadwick, *JThS*, n.s. 24, 443–(450)–455.

'The Status of Ecumenical Councils in Anglican Thought', *The Heritage of the Early Church: Essays in Honor of The Very Reverend Georges Vasilievich Florovsky, OrChrA,* 195, edited by D. Neiman and M. Schatkin, Rome, pp. 393–408.

1974 'John Moschus and his Friend Sophronius the Sophist', *JThS*, n.s. 25, 41–74. See 1982, no. 2.

'Betrachtungen über das Gewissen in der griechischen, jüdischen und christlichen Tradition', Rheinisch-Westfälische Akademie der Wissenschaften, Vorträge, G 197 [Düsseldorf, 28 February 1973], Opladen, 1974.

'Quelques réflexions sur le magisterium dans l'église', *Théologie:*

Le service théologique dans l'église, Mélanges Y. Congar, edited by G. Philips, Paris, pp. 163–76.

1975 Charles Gore and Roman Catholic Claims, Charles Gore Memorial Lecture, Westminster Abbey, 12 November 1974, *Theology*, 78, 68–75.

1976 *Priscillian of Avila: The Occult and the Charismatic in the Early Church,* Oxford; Spanish translation by J. L. López Muñoz, Madrid, 1978.

'The Etymology of Greek πάλαι', *Glotta*, 54, 68–71.

'Gervase Mathew OP', *New Blackfriars*, 57, 194–5, 239.

1977 'Episcopacy in the New Testament and Early Church', *Today's Church and Today's World with a Special Focus on the Ministry of Bishops*, The Lambeth Conference, 1978, preparatory articles edited by J. Howe, London, pp. 206–14.

Truth and Authority: A Commentary on the Agreed Statement of the Anglican–Roman Catholic International Commission, 'Authority in the Church', Venice 1976, by E. J. Yarnold and H. Chadwick, London, pp. 7–36.

'A Brief Apology for "Authority in the Church" (Venice 1976)', *Theology*, 80, 324–31.

'Anglikanische Kirche' (article 'Evangelische Kirchen'), *Konfessionskunde*, edited by F. Heyer, Berlin, pp. 575–94.

1978 'Gewissen', *Reallexikon für Antike und Christentum*, edited by T. Klauser, vol. 10, Stuttgart, col. 1025–107.

'Conversion in Constantine the Great', *Religious Motivation: Biographical and Sociological Problems for the Church Historian*, papers read at the sixteenth summer meeting and the seventeenth winter meeting of the Ecclesiastical History Society, edited by D. Baker, Oxford, pp. 1–13.

'Lambeth Conference 1978: Roman Catholic Relationships', *One in Christ*, 14, 376–80.

'Christianity before the Schism of 1054', 4.533–45 = 'The history of Christianity' (to 1054), 1985 printing, 16.275–86; 'John the Apostle, Saint' 10.241 = 1985 printing 6.585–6; 'Origen' 13.734–6 = 1985 printing 8.997–9 *The New Encyclopaedia Britannica*, Fifteenth Edition, Chicago.

1979 'The Relativity of Moral Codes: Rome and Persia in Late Antiquity', *Early Christian Literature and the Classical Intellectual Tradition, in Honorem Robert M. Grant*, Théologie

Historique 53, Paris, edited by W. R. Schoedel and R. L. Wilken, pp. 135–53.

'Messalianerne: En evangelisk bevegelse i det 4. århundre', *Tidsskrift for Teologi og Kirke*, 3, 161–72.

1980 'The Authenticity of Boethius' Fourth Tractate, De Fide Catholica', *JThS*, n.s. 31, 551–6.

'The Domestication of Gnosis', *The Rediscovery of Gnosticism*. Proceedings of the International Conference on Gnosticism at Yale, 1978, vol. 1, The School of Valentinus, ed. B. Layton, Supplements to *Numen* 41/1, Leiden, pp. 3–16.

'The Role of the Christian Bishop in Ancient Society', *Colloquy*, 35 (1980), The Center for Hermeneutical Studies, Graduate Theological Union, 2465 Leconte Ave., Berkeley, California 94709.

'Theta on Philosophy's Dress in Boethius', *Medium Aevum*, 49, 175–9.

1981 'Frontiers of Theology': An inaugural lecture delivered before the University of Cambridge, 5 May 1981, Cambridge.

Boethius: The Consolations of Music, Logic, Theology, and Philosophy, Oxford; translated into Italian, Bologna, 1986.

'Pachomios and the Idea of Sanctity', *The Byzantine Saint: University of Birmingham Fourteenth Spring Symposium of Byzantine Studies,* edited by S. Hackel, Studies Supplementary to Sobornost 5, pp. 11–24. See 1982, no. 2.

'Towards Unity in Truth.' A series of lectures given during Lent 1981 in Westminster Abbey, foreword by B. Hume. Herefordshire: The Church Literature Society.

Why Music in Church? Church Music Society Pamphlet, London.

'Introduction', *Boethius: His life, thought and influence*, edited by M. Gibson, Oxford, pp. 1–12.

'The Church of the Third Century in the West', *The Roman West in the Third Century: Contributions from archaeology and history,* British Archaeological Reports, International Series, 109, edited by A. King and M. Henig, Part 1, pp. 5–13.

'Full Communion with Other Episcopal Churches', *Churchman*, 95, 218–26.

1982 'Cambridge: The Patristic Greek Lexicon', *G. W. H. Lampe: Christian, Scholar, Churchman: A Memoir by Friends,* edited by C. F. D. Moule, London and Oxford, pp. 66–72.

History and Thought of the Early Church, Collected Studies Series

CS164, London: Variorum Reprints. Preface, i–v. Index,
1–6. See 1959 (no. 1), 1957 (no. 3), 1962 (no. 4), 1967 (no.
3), 1966 (no. 2), 1950 (no. 1), 1965 (no. 1), 1960 (no. 4),
1959 (no. 3), 1958 (no. 1), 1972 (no. 1), 1960 (no. 6), 1948
(no. 1), 1981 (no. 3), 1972 (no. 4), 1951 (no. 1), 1965 (no. 2),
1974 (no. 1).

'Priscilliano', *Dizionario Enciclopedico dei religiosi e degli istituti
secolari.*

1983 'New Letters of St Augustine', *JThS*, n.s. 34, 425–52.

'Freedom and Necessity in Early Christian Thought About
God', *Cosmology and Theology*, edited by D. Tracy and
N. Lash, *Concilium* 166, 8–13.

Preface to A.-J. Festugière, *Actes du concile de Chalcédoine, sessions
III–VI (La Définition de la Foi)*. Traduction française,
Geneva.

*An ARCIC Catechism: Questions and Answers on the Final Report
of the Anglican–Roman Catholic International Commission* by
E. J. Yarnold and H. Chadwick.

'Walter Ullmann, 1910–1983', *Cambridge Review*, 104, 212–13,
18 Nov.

'Canterbury and Rome: Progress and problems', Cardinal
Heenan Memorial Lecture, 1982, *The Month*, 245 (= Second
New Series 16), 149–54.

1984 'Origenes', *Gestalten der Kirchengeschichte*, Band 1, Alte Kirche 1,
ed. M. Greschat, Stuttgart, pp. 134–57.

'Oracles of the End in the Conflict of Paganism and
Christianity in the Fourth Century', *Mémorial André-Jean
Festugière. Antiquité païenne et chrétienne*, edited by E. Lucchesi
and H. D. Saffrey, Geneva, pp. 125–9.

'Lima, ARCIC and the Church of England', *Theology*, 87,
29–35.

Lima, ARCIC, and the Church of England, an address to the
General Synod of the Church of England at York on
13 July, 1983, *One in Christ: A Catholic Ecumenical Review*,
20, 31–7.

'Priscillian of Avila. Occult and Charisma in the Ancient
Church', *StPatr*, vol. 15, Papers Presented to the seventh
International Conference on Patristic Studies 1975, edited by
E. A. Livingstone, *TU* 128, Berlin, pp. 3–12.

'Justification by Faith: A Perspective', a paper written at the command of the second Anglican-RC Commission [ARCIC], *One in Christ: A Catholic Ecumenical Review*, 20, 191–225.

'†George Caird', preface to *JThS*, n.s. 35, part 2.

'History of the Oxford Movement: 150 Years On', Conference Paper, 1983, *Lift High the Cross: The Oxford Movement Sesquicentennial*, edited by J. Robert Wright, Cincinnati, Ohio, pp. 46–81.

'The Context of Faith and Theology in Anglicanism', *Theology in Anglicanism*, edited by Arthur A. Vogel, Anglican Study Series, Wilton, Conn., pp. 11–31.

'The Great Religions and the Environment', *Studies in the Archaeology of Jordan*, 2, Amman.

'Sir Arthur Armitage, 1916–1984', *Cambridge Review*, 105, 181–2, 20 Nov.

'The Oxford Movement and Church Music', *The World of Churc Music*, edited by L. Dakers, Royal School of Church Music, Croydon.

1985 'The Ascetic Ideal in the History of the Church', *Monks, Hermits and the Ascetic Tradition*, papers read at the 1984 summer meeting and the 1985 winter meeting of the Ecclesiastical History Society, edited by W. Sheils, Oxford, pp. 1–23.

'Augustine on Pagans and Christians: Reflections on Religious and Social Change', *History, Society and the Churches: Essays in honour of Owen Chadwick,* edited by D. Beales and G. Best, Cambridge, pp. 9–27.

'Christian Platonism in Origen and Augustine', *Origeniana tertia*, Papers of the Third International Colloquium for Origen Studies, 1981, edited by R. P. C. Hanson and H. Crouzel, Rome, pp. 217–230.

1986 *Augustine*, Past Masters, Oxford; translated into French, Paris, 1987; translated into German, Göttingen, 1987.

'Envoi: On Taking Leave of Antiquity', *The Oxford History of the Classical World* edited by John Boardman, Jasper Griffin and Oswyn Murray, Oxford, pp. 807–28.

'Priscillien', *Dictionnaire de spiritualité*, 12, coll. 2353–69.

'Unity and Pluralism'; 'The Petrine Office in the Church', *L'Altérité, vivre ensemble différents: approches pluridisciplinaires.* Actes du Colloque pluridisciplinaire du Collège dominicain de philosophie et de théologie (Ottawa, 4–5–6 octobre 1984), edited by M. Gourgues and G.-D. Mailhiot, Montréal and Paris, pp. 349–60; 369–75.

'Stanley Lawrence Greenslade, 1905–1977', *Proceedings of the British Academy*, 72, pp. 409–22.

987 Joint editor, *Atlas of the Christian Church*, with G. R. Evans, London and New York.

'Les deux Traités contre Appollinaire attribués à Athanase', *ΑΛΕΞΑΝΔΡΙΝΑ: Mélanges offerts à Claude Mondésert*, SJ, Paris, pp. 247–60.

'Some books on the sacraments', *Signs of Faith, Hope and Love: The Christian sacraments today*, edited by J. Greenhalgh and Elizabeth Russell, St Mary's, Bourne Street, London, pp. 112–14.

'Philoponus the Christian Theologian', *Philoponus and the Rejection of Aristotelian Science*, edited by R. Sorabji, London, pp. 41–56.

'Eusebius of Caesarea'; 'G. D. Mansi', *Dictionary of Historians*, Oxford.

1988 'Christian Doctrine', *The Cambridge History of Medieval Political Thought*, edited by J. H. Burns, Cambridge, pp. 11–20.

'Royal Supremacy', *John Fisher*, edited by B. Bradshaw and E. Duffy, Cambridge, pp. 169–203.

'Reflections on Tradition in Fact and Belief', Epilogue, *Scripture, Tradition and Reason: A Study in the Criteria of Christian Doctrine: Essays in Honour of Richard P. C. Hanson* edited by R. Bauckham and B. Drewery, Edinburgh, pp. 288–97.

Does it make sense to speak of pre-Nicene orthodoxy?

ROWAN WILLIAMS

I

Henry Chadwick's inaugural lecture as Regius Professor at Oxford sketched out,[1] economically and elegantly, some aspects of the problem confronting every historian of early Christian thought, the problem of how to discern and define the *self-perception* of the first Christian communities: how, with reference to what, did they define themselves? Chadwick portrays a tension between two models of authoritative self-identification, the 'circle' and the 'ellipse' – the unified institution with a definable centre providing a norm or touchstone for right belief, and the network of communities linked by their common origins in Jerusalem and the events transacted there at the navel of the earth.[2] In some sense, the narrative of Paul's career as set out in the Acts of the Apostles dramatizes this tension: the movement is necessarily and inevitably away from Jerusalem, itself originally the centre of a 'circle', the church of the circumcision (pp. 4–5), towards the administrative heart of the Roman civilized world (pp. 12–16); but Rome cannot replace Jerusalem or assert a unilateral sovereignty over the churches that stem from the events in Jerusalem. In spite of all temptations (and efforts), Rome never comes to be taken for granted as the sole standard of the church's self-definition; the circle model never quite triumphs (p. 12). In one way or another, the idea of the church as a family united in virtue of its ancestry rather than of its present organizational structure persists.

The Agreed Statements of the Anglican–Roman Catholic International Commission (ARCIC) seem to cast their shadow before them here: it is not hard to see how Henry Chadwick's influence came to be so weighty in this latter context. But the issues raised are in fact far more complex than the agenda of ARCIC. Chadwick in his lecture seems to be alluding, if only rather distantly, to the well-known thesis of Walter Bauer's essay on *Orthodoxy and Heresy in Earliest Christianity*:[3] all around the Mediterranean world and, even more, beyond the boundaries of the empire, in Syria, 'orthodoxy' tends to be a late growth. The prevailing early forms of Christianity are generally at odds with what later defined itself as normative; and only by the exertion of powerful pressure from the one church with a solid majority opposed to Marcionism and other 'deviations' did the churches of the Roman world gradually form a united 'orthodox' body. Practically and historically, it is indeed Rome that defines orthodoxy, and imposes its own order upon the chaos of interpretations prevailing elsewhere. Chadwick, in contrast, at least hints at a quite different reading: there are factors internal to the Christian enterprise – all, in fact, that is summed up by 'Jerusalem', the common origin, the 'mother of all churches' – which work towards a unified, if not uniform, orthodoxy not dependent upon a single central authority. There would have been orthodoxy without Rome – or, at least, Rome is *part* of the story of evolving orthodoxy, not its only begetter.

The present essay attempts to see whether Bauer's explicit or Chadwick's implicit schema better fits the facts – or whether, indeed, the discussion needs to enter a new phase altogether, with new questions asked. Does it make sense to think of a single and continuous Christian history, a steady movement towards the (nearly) universal dogmatic syntheses of the fourth and fifth centuries? Few scholars could be found to support such a thesis in those simple terms. Or is the orthodox consensus an historical accident? If the latter is true, considerable problems arise for the contemporary believer and the believer's delegate, the systematic theologian: is any version of Christianity as valid or 'authentic' as any other? if so, there can be little if any serious or productive *conflict* about goals and priorities between Christians *as* Christians – they have only a factitious common ground. Or can we at least say that Christianity is a set of competing claims about a certain definable cluster of issues, even if it is not a scheme of consistent and authoritative 'readings' of the human world? Or is that in itself an impossibly controversial redefinition of Christianity as it has *in fact* perceived itself? The question of whether there was an identifiable 'orthodoxy', a prevailing sense of the norms of Christian identity, prior to AD 300 has disturbingly wide repercussions. It also raises issues concerning methodological foundations in the study of religions overall – an area which theologians are liable to neglect: how, if at all, is one to identify the 'centre' of *any* religious tradition? At what point and why do we start speaking about 'a' religion, an interconnected pattern of symbolic resources with some kind of coherence? Or is the whole notion of looking for the essence of a particular religion, or the essence of what makes this or that tradition a *religion*, a mistake?

Bauer's case is interesting because, despite his hostility to the idea of doctrinal norms, he is not free from a certain kind of essentialism. The last chapter of his book makes it clear that he sees the Pauline mission as somehow basic to the Christian phenomenon. Paul's own move westwards dictates the shape and locus of Christian development, but his own distinctive perceptions are buried in that very process (pp. 232ff.). He is tolerant of purely doctrinal pluralism (pp. 234–5), and his general attitude rests upon a 'confidence that the Christian religion will again eliminate from itself whatever is alien to it' (p. 236). 'The Christian religion': Bauer assumes that such a category would make sense of Paul, perhaps even *to* Paul. There is a spiritual centre, after all, to the Christian phenomenon, with some kind of self-correcting, self-directing energy. Although Bauer does not himself endorse this 'Pauline' assumption, the entire tenor of this final chapter suggests that Bauer's is ultimately a history of *loss*, of the obscuring of some primitive and fundamental vision and life by ecclesiastical struggles and definitions. The idea of Christian religion in its Pauline integrity sits light to formulae and strictly doctrinal anathemas, and thus gives free play to distorting transformations by groups (such as Gnostics) concerned to domesticate and possess the original impulse in a variety of ambivalent ways. So subtly and precariously balanced is Paul's reflection on Christ and the believer's relation to Christ that it carries the seeds of wildly divergent theologies. Only by – to some extent – imitating the 'heretical' process of manipulation and definition does 'true' religion survive, undergoing a sea-change as it identifies itself over against what it is not. Heresy is the necessary precondition for orthodoxy, yet orthodoxy may be as much a metamorphosis (or pseudomorphosis) of the foundational religious idea as heresy.

Behind this it is possible to discern a version of the celebrated 'criterion of dissimilarity' applied in form-critical studies to the sayings of Jesus.[4] The indubitably authentic and distinctive is what cannot be generated reflectively out of what goes before (Judaism) or comes after (the church). So, in the history of Christian belief, the distinctive 'idea' of the Christian religion is an elusive spiritual possibility *not* present in Judaism or in gnosis or in merely ecclesiastical faith. The *novum* in Christianity is both utterly discontinuous with what goes before and

3

unrepeatable in what follows: as in Bultmann's vision,[5] it is a proclamation interrupting history, defining and authenticating itself, free therefore to defend, sustain and renew itself by its own inner energy, shaking off what is alien. The essentialism of Harnack's approach is refined and corrected in the crucible of something like a theology of the Word. Schneemelcher, in an important obituary tribute to Bauer,[6] emphasized the difference between Bauer and Harnack, in terms of Bauer's refusal to adopt Harnack's *Verfallstheorie* version of church history, which is simply a liberal Protestant reincarnation of the patristic idea of heresy as a *degeneration* from orthodoxy; for Bauer, so Schneemelcher claims, the primitive unity of the Christian community lay not in doctrine or in concordant apostolic testimony, but in relationship with the one Lord. Bauer does not state this with complete clarity, and much work still needs to be done on his own theological assumptions, but it is plain that he thinks in terms of a unity deeper and other than the visible unity of 'Organisation, Lehre und Kultus', which is the product simply of historical process.[7] The unity that matters is that of the (invisible?) body of Christ.[8] All other models are determined by or assimilated to the cultural circumstances of the day (the criterion of dissimilarity once more). The true uniqueness of Christian faith is grounded in the person of Jesus, while the empirical church 'steht unter vielfachen, von aussen in sie einströmenden Einflüssen' (p. 21). The gospel can never escape the necessity of such transmutations, but it remains in essence free of them.

What Schneemelcher does here, in fact, is to ascribe to Bauer (quite correctly, I think) a yet more radical form of *Verfallstheorie*. The Christian 'idea' in its purity is bound up with something not patient of articulation and definition, unity with Christ in his Body. In other words, a particular Pauline theologoumenon is identified as the heart of Christian identity; and, as we have seen, Paul's doctrinal tolerance – beyond this central insight – is implicitly commended, though acknowledged at the same time to be the seedbed for both 'heresy' and 'orthodoxy'. Not even Paul can find words for faith that will avoid ambiguity and the risk of betrayal. As indicated already, Bauer assumes that the essence of the Christian faith is a principle beyond history and speech: once this 'transcendental' reality is 'categorially' expressed and apprehended, it is *mis*apprehended, and the more thoroughgoing the articulation, the graver the distortion. Bauer is, indeed, not guilty of any kind of *historical* primitivism, not even Harnack's variety; but he is still bound up in a philosophical world where 'inner' truthfulness is perennially at odds with and at risk from the deceitfulness of material history, and still disposed to see the heart of Christianity as a supernatural – non-worldly, non-historical – still point, to which the contradictory and compromised phenomena of time (persons, words, institutions) are related in an inexpressible or inscrutable way. Hence the links of sympathy and understanding between Bauer and Bultmann.[9]

II

Such an understanding of the 'essence' of a religion has been challenged recently by Jonathan Z. Smith's learned and subtle essays in the anthropology of religion, especially 'In Comparison a Magic Dwells',[10] in which there is a pointed critique of religious taxonomies that seek to isolate a normative core in a religious tradition and which speak of the distinctive 'logic' of a tradition, as if it could be assumed to be a single *system*. Smith argues (pp. 31–5) that the most enormous questions are begged by the assumption that 'religions' are fundamentally self-contained *objects*, each with a timeless inner logic and homogeneity that excludes others. Rather, in any one tradition, there may be different systems, different 'logics', operating within different texts: the theoretical problem with which we are left is how our awareness of the *interplay* between such different texts might enable us to say anything about the *unity* between them. 'Comparison is, at base, never identity'; so, 'How am I to apply what the one thing shows me to the case of other things?' (p. 36).

If we are not permitted to speak of 'essences', how shall we define *a* religion at all? Perhaps we should begin by noting that the question itself is an odd one in many contexts. The 'religion' of classical Greece or Rome or modern India is simply the totality of cultic practices, mythology and speculation about the gods current among the people of a specific area or ethnic–linguistic unit or network of such units. Religious definition is inseparable from definition as a people or a city or whatever; the *de facto* context in which a person lives is assumed to be the source for 'meaning', the provider of a comprehensive pattern or map of the cosmos. This is mythologized in terms of there being a manifest and visible centre of the world within this environment – a shrine which acts as navel of the earth, as ultimate locus of sacred power and guarantor of the stability of things. Or else, in slightly more rationalized form, the same view may be expressed in terms of cultural and linguistic normativity (Greeks and barbarians).[11] Whatever the exact articulation, however, the basic point is that in such a setting the question of how a 'religion' identifies itself, let alone what its essence is, is meaningless: the search for coherence, for an organizing principle that would help us to locate this system in a typology of religions, is a waste of time, an attempt to answer questions that are not being (and cannot sensibly be) asked. Religious speech and behaviour here is bound to a sacral understanding of the world of immediate social and material experience: it is what Smith calls 'locative' in its emphasis – and is characteristically, though not 'essentially', linked with a hierarchy that guards and administers the loci of holiness and determines access to them.[12]

The problem of strictly *religious* definition arises only when irresoluble crises afflict the 'locative' religious life of a society, when it is no longer clear or credible that the *de facto* environment, cosmic and social, does provide meaning and pattern: the cosmos (including the sacred space secured in the social framework) is, in fact, no longer perceived as *cosmos*, as a givenness of order.[13] This may be the result of the destruction of a shrine, or the end of a monarchy, or the slower erosion of belief in cultic efficacy if it is seen to be too nakedly allied with dominant ideology in a situation of acute injustice, or the development of techniques of production that shift economic power and so alter supposedly immutable social relations, or any of these combining with any or all of the others.[14] It should perhaps be added that, unless one is the crudest kind of reductionist, none of this rules out the statement that we are dealing with crises about the experience of God or the gods; it merely reinforces the manifest truth that religious and social meanings or possibilities are not to be easily or glibly dissociated by the observer who starts from the voluntarist and privatized religious conventions of the post-Enlightenment West. The crises of 'locative' religion, however, represent a major factor in the history that leads to such conventions, because they provoke a radical separation between social and religious meaning; to borrow once more from Smith's analysis, we may speak of a 'utopian' or 'diasporic' religious speech and practice emerging, in which the moments of loss and liminality, inversion, contradiction, which had a specific, controlled, dialectical function in locative religion, become the moments of decisive insight. The existing order is to be rejected, history and cosmos are no longer to be trusted: we are aliens in the perceivable universe.

The question of definition and authenticity here arises for the first time as a distinctively religious issue. If the social context does not offer identity, a final and comprehensive identity, what is the context that replaces it? In Hannah Arendt's terminology, how are we 'to find a bond between people strong enough to replace the world'?[15] If there is to be a religious practice other than the locative, it must offer to those involved a definition or self-perception as strong as, or stronger than, that provided by the failed sacral society: that is to say, it cannot (from the point of view of the historian of religions) be identified simply with an incommunicable spiritual essence somehow present in the founder, or, as Bultmann might see it, the bare proclamation of the *Dass* of divine activity in the cross of Jesus. It will inevitably mean the construction of other sorts of social unities. We are faced with the question of what is definitive for a particular 'religion' precisely because the very concept of *a* religion results from there being a set of religious practices (cult, myth, doctrine, initiation, and so on) not catered for in the self-definition of the society in which they are set. But one obvious corollary of this is that, at the origins of a new, non-locative, tradition, we are bound to find debate and unclarity: we may see what the new phenomenon is *not* more clearly than what it is. A recent collection of essays on Buddhism – that supremely non-locative faith – observes that the Buddha 'saw himself as simply preaching the Dharma', that account of the world which presents the possibility of escape from the world, and that a 'Buddhist' is simply one who relies on this for liberation.[16] Since the Dharma cuts across the caste system of ancient India, a 'Buddhist' is paradigmatically one who opts out of that system: someone who belongs in no caste, who is not defined by brahminically dominated society and has no role in it – thus a mendicant, a monk or nun, a person without job or family. 'Buddhism' is, primitively, the Sangha, the monastic order, those voluntarily outside Indian society for the sake of Dharma.[17] Its identity as a developed system of thought, to which non-monastics may adhere, 'taking refuge' in the Buddha, the Dharma, and the Sangha, rests, as this formula implies, on the central fact of the repudiation of caste society in the name not of an alternative 'social programme' (the Sangha could co-exist with brahminical society) but of the vision of a way of salvation. The detail of early Buddhist theory is often obscure: it emerges as a *practice* of radical detachment, social and personal, and its clarity and definition as a religious phenomenon is to be found in the social reality of those performing such a practice.

No 'religion', no set of observable practices of a certain kind, can be wholly utopian or liminal – obviously not, since we are talking about what is, among other things, a social fact, something with a language and a memory. Smith notes that the figure of the charismatic magician could, in late antiquity, provide one way back to some of the values of the locative, in that his *presence* comes to be seen as the locus of holiness.[18] Some forms of Buddhism, notably in Tibet, have done the same thing on a large scale, by way of doctrines of the presence of a bodhisattva in a living holy man, and a highly sophisticated account of sacred succession in concrete monastic centres. It is also possible to carry through a paradoxical revaluation of the holy places of a parent tradition; so that (for example) Jerusalem, for the author of Luke-Acts, remains centrally significant in the new sacred narrative as the point to which and from which various lines lead, because it is the site of Jesus' *exodes* and vindication. Such borrowings or reworkings do not, however, modify the fundamental point that a counter-society is being created: what they do is to suggest that this counter-society's means of self-definition are not entirely discontinuous with those of the parent tradition – a significant claim, in contexts where novelty is suspect. There may still be a 'centre', a single focus of power and meaning, though one radically at odds with the structures of the parent tradition, and perhaps involving (as in the case of the magician) a reinterpretation of the very idea of holy place in terms of personal contact or proximity[19] – anthropology superseding cosmology, in Smith's language.[20] But there may also be a more drastic version of the possible criteria for belonging in the counter-society of a new religion. The primitive Sangha in Buddhism is the community of those sharing the perception of Dharma as the route to liberation: there is at least an element here of appeal to a common *experience*, though it is very muted. But it is not difficult to think of religious communities in which having the requisite initiatory experience is a crucial factor in determining belonging and not-belonging. Initiatory experience may be an aspect of locative religion,[21] but it will take on a different sort of weight in other religious styles. 'Charismatic' and 'prophet' churches in Christianity lay heavy stress upon this, and the New Testament itself indicates how important such an appeal was for many primitive Christian groups.[22] It seems reasonably clear that this was true of gnostic or gnosticizing communities in the second Christian century: to belong was to have received *ennoia*, enlightening insight.

The struggle over 'orthodoxy' in the pre-Nicene period is the struggle over which *kinds* of criteria will prevail in communities calling themselves Christian. H.-D. Altendorf, in a perceptive discussion of Bauer's categories and vocabulary, observes that the conflicts of the second Christian century are not usefully understood as a *case* of orthodox–heretical disagreement: they constitute a specific phenomenon in which the very possibility of such a disagreement, the terms in which an argument can be conducted, is being defined.[23] The primitive fact seems to be the existence around the Mediterranean, and further east in Syria, of groups manifestly dependent in certain respects upon the Jewish tradition, yet more or less alienated from it in virtue of some sort of commitment to or dependence on the figure of Jesus,[24] a dependence normally expressed by means of a distinctive initiation rite (baptism), widely seen as bestowing membership of a new 'race'.[25] It is a classically non-locative phenomenon, engaged in vigorous polemic against shrine and hierarchy in Jerusalem in its earliest years, assuming the radical dislocation or senselessness of the existing religious and political order, depending upon highly mobile teachers establishing new communities well outside the original sacral context. All these features breed particular tensions. Polemic against shrine and hierarchy may involve the rejection of the whole notion of sacred place, or a rival claim on the *same* place, or the transferring of shrine imagery to the new community itself, wherever it is. The first option is perhaps discernible in the Johannine literature,[26] and fuels some second-century argument (Justin's debate with Trypho);[27] in the next generation (Clement of Alexandria) it unites with a general Platonic relativizing of the contingent and particular.[28] The second can be seen in that narrative revaluation of Jerusalem already mentioned as characteristic of Luke, but perhaps also in the elusive, quasi-priestly figure of James at Jerusalem, and the community around him.[29] The third is present in 1 Peter, and perhaps in Revelation, and its imagery is foreshadowed in the Qumran literature, in which the community is itself a counter-temple.[30] As for the assumption of the meaninglessness of present order, this can appear as the apocalyptic hope of restoration or the gnostic repudiation of material creation as such.[31] And the mobility of teachers raises the question of how far they are answerable to each other, or share an identifiable point of reference, as well as the further problem of how the crisis of one locative system is to be induced and interpreted in another as something fundamentally the same (how the crucified Messiah becomes the crucified Logos).

'Early Christianity' is the field within which conflicts about these matters are fought out; its unity – like that of early Buddhism – is perceptible mostly in negative terms, in its tormentingly complex relation to the Jewish cult, law and scriptures,[32] but has some positive

9

content simply in the focussing of that new complexity upon the words and acts and fate of Jesus. At its most straightforward, this amounts to not much more than the belief that Jesus (like the Qumran Teacher of Righteousness) is both forerunner of and martyr for a renewed Israel, with its cult and hierarchy purged of corruption: the utopian or diasporic element in Christian identity is temporary and fortuitous. At its least straightforward, the relation to the Jewish world is something like symmetrical opposition: Christian belief is the reversed image of Jewish, Jesus the enemy of the God of the old covenant. Both the community and Jesus are discontinuous with the past; and there is also the sense that the community's connection with Jesus as himself an actual figure of the past is fragile. What he says, what he is, can be absorbed into the community's experience of enlightenment and liberation: *his* identity depends upon his role in the process of enlightenment. Hence the literary genre of *post-resurrection* dialogues between Jesus and his disciples, an ahistorical setting in which Jesus can be exclusively characterized as enlightener, and so identified in relation to the gnostic believer's experience.[33] In this account, the utopian wholly dominates, in that the idea of being at home in the universe, even to the extent of belonging in an historical continuity with the founder of faith, practically vanishes; definition is found only through common experience.

It is not surprising that not much of a consistent history can be plotted for groups with such views: the nature of their beliefs would effectively prevent their being in the mainstream of any institutional evolution.[34] The 'common experience' criterion for belonging does little to guarantee any socially durable unity: it is *not* 'strong enough to replace the world'. The creation of a new *genos* requires at least some of the features of a 'natural' society, and a significant dimension of what comes to constitute Christian orthodoxy is to do with this need. If the criteria that finally matter in determining where the true church is to be found move increasingly away from the narrowly experiential pole, this is partly for straightforward reasons of survival: what has staying power (and is *seen* as having staying power, and so pursued for that reason) is what offers a public, a social, identifying context for the believer – institutional, narrative and behavioural norms. But more than this, since the new *genos* is by definition not limited by geographical locality, continuities in space need to be preserved between scattered groups; identity with a kindred but spatially distant community must be affirmed and evidenced.

III

Here we touch upon a crucially important factor in the coming-together of a mainstream 'catholic' or 'orthodox' version of Christian belief. Groups regarded as heterodox had peripatetic teachers, moving from one Mediterranean city to another,[35] or crossing the eastern frontiers,[36] but we have no literary or archaeological evidence to suggest that there were regular and significant links between the congregations they established. In dramatic contrast, the Christianity of the New Testament documents and of the broadly non-gnostic churches of the second century presents us with an enormous amount of evidence for what can sometimes seem like an almost obsessional mutual interest and interchange. Paul's epistles established links not only between the apostle and his congregations but between the congregations them-selves. The whole of the Epistle to the Romans represents the opening of a new link between Pauline and other churches, and chapter 16 (whether or not it originally belongs in this context)[37] both reinforces existing connections between communities and, in its recommendation of Phoebe of Cenchreae, extends them. The celebrated 'collection for the saints' appears in 1 Corinthians 16 as a bond between Gentile churches as well as between them and Jerusalem; and here again, Paul's transmission of greetings between churches works towards the creation of a sense of shared identity. In 2 Corinthians 8 and 9, there is a blatant appeal to a number of unregenerate motives: surely Corinth will not let Paul down by failing to come up to the standard of generosity set by the Macedonian churches? especially when he has so sung the praises of the Corinthian believers. 1 Thessalonians points again to the significance of 'report' among the churches, the acquiring of a recognized name for hospitality and faithfulness. Colossians 4:7–18 may or may not be Pauline, but verse 16 establishes the existence of a convention among the Pauline churches of exchanging letters from the apostle.

However, it is not only the Pauline communities that operate in this way: 1 Peter[38] and 2 and 3 John presuppose networks of churches with epistolary links running through an 'apostolic' co-ordinator. 1 Peter has several features of interest: it lays particular emphasis on the gift of a new communal identity, membership of a 'people' (2:9–10) living as 'exiles' (1:1, 2:11) among the Gentiles (2:12, 4:3).[39] The imagery of the Jewish diaspora is deployed as a model for the self-understanding of Christian communities: common baptism, in which the 'word' of God's eternal election is appropriated (1:23, 3:21–2), substitutes for common ancestry; and in this ritually effected exile from the social order, a new 'household' is entered (4:17),[40] which 'throughout the world' (5:9) faces the same rejection and hostility. The proclamation of this shared vulnerability, the assurance that the local community's experience *vis-à-vis* the surrounding society is shared the world over, is a very weighty part of the epistle's construction of an identity for the baptized.

Discussion could be extended, but enough has been said to underline the importance, in at least a substantial number of first-century churches, of the sense of belonging with comparable communities and having a certain responsibility to them; the Pauline collection for the saints is a (doubtfully effective) attempt at binding Gentile churches to Jerusalem in a way similar to that in which they were – through Paul's mediation – bound to each other. The literary form which dominates the Christian canon is the letter in which the missionary creates in his clusters of proselytes a sense of a common world, and so creates the conditions for communication between them. Less emphasis is laid upon an identifiable *individual* core experience of inner enlightenment in virtue of which the members of the new *genos* are united than upon the manifest fact of belonging to communities with distinctive patterns of relation and behaviour, capable of a certain sort of exchange with each other, and facing the same problems of exposure and insecurity in the face of the two most firmly established modes of religious identity available: Mediterranean civic piety and ethnically determined Jewish practice. There are few if any analogues in the culture of the day to the enterprise represented by the canonical epistles;[41] and that we know them as 'canonical' says something about the constitutive part in the formation of orthodoxy played by this enterprise.

For it is not confined to the New Testament. Apart from Clement's letter to Corinth on behalf of the Roman church, and Ignatius' correspondence, we have an extensive record in Eusebius of the epistolary habit of Christian leaders. From the time of Ignatius onwards, the letter reinforcing the authority of the leader of another community by reaffirming fellowship is a widespread phenomenon; and for Eusebius, the stature of a bishop is evidently measured in part by the range of his recorded correspondence, the degree to which he activates the lines of communication between churches and participates in the debates of sister communities. Dionysius of Corinth is commended explicitly for his vigour in this regard,[42] and Dionysius of Alexandria, whose extensive correspondence is carefully itemized,[43] is said to have left a 'varied source of profit' to the churches, and is evidently regarded as a figure of special authority. Letters by such figures may carry accounts of local martyrdom or persecution, offering other churches a share, so to speak, in the grace bestowed on a particular congregation;[44] or they may carry an acknowledgment of a newly elected bishop in the recipient community, confirming the unbroken communication between the churches,[45] or they may either endorse or dispute a particular disciplinary ruling from a bishop or synod of bishops, affirming, whether negatively or positively, the principle of the mutual account-ability of physically distant churches.[46] In two cases recorded by Eusebius,[47] the bishop of Rome is censured for breaking communication over such issues: he is reminded by other bishops of the legitimate variety of inherited traditions in local churches, and, in the paschal controversy of the late second century, his attention is firmly drawn to the documentation of an earlier discussion in which this variety was accepted by the Roman pontiff. Disagreement may be sharp, it may even reach (as in the controversy over schismatic baptism) to quite fundamental points of practice; but the very expression of disagreement *within* the network of correspondence means that it remains a 'domestic' affair, a family quarrel. It is a misunderstanding of the nature of the 'catholic' network to move rapidly to an open break because of local divergences.

Eusebius, of course, has a consistent interest in representing the life of the church as essentially peaceful and harmonious; but this does not mean that he is to be mistrusted in these matters. On the contrary: consciously or not, he paints in his history a vivid picture of a catholic church whose unity is actually *articulated* in a steady flow of literary exchange between its parts, an exchange which is by no means always easy or harmonious, but whose continuance is crucial to the health and continuity of the whole, something not lightly to be broken by suspension of communion or of ministerial recognition. The atmosphere of the church as thus evoked can at times be claustrophobic to the reader of Eusebius, in just the way that the intense, warm, interfering mutuality of a set of letters between a Victorian family or circle of friends may be to the twentieth-century literary historian or biographer. But it is not quite the atmosphere suggested by Bauer, of the skilful manipulation by a single powerful church of the increasingly dependent relations to it of other churches. Nor is it quite, on the other hand, a climate in which the unity of the *local* church, the concrete eucharistic community in one particular place, is virtually the sole concern for the first century and a half of Christianity, with homogeneity in teaching and practice only assuming significance as theology acquired a more metaphysical tinge (the unity of the church as symbol of the unity of history and cosmos in the Logos).[48] It is an atmosphere which manifests something of the nature of the origins of local Christian communities in *mission*: they are planted or established by non-local agencies and so take on not only a *de facto* foreignness in their context, as 'resident aliens',[49] but also a sense of belonging to and with parent groups or personalities (or groups representing and identifying with personalities – 'Pauline' and 'Johannine' churches) elsewhere. Missionary foundation means that a particular church's existence is bound up with a history of personal contact: the greater the sense that the local church identifies itself in relation to its origins, the greater the significance of maintaining such contact; and the greater the connection between the idea of a 'normative' Christianity and the practices that maintain accountability between churches – correspondence, the sharing of both problems and achievements, travel,[50] ministerial recognition.[51] Only against such a fluid and complex background does the emergence of a canon of writings become possible and make sense. 'Orthodoxy', in short, depends heavily on the sheer mobility of believers as missionaries in the first generation and emissaries later on; it has a great deal to do with ease of communication in the Roman world, with all that – paradoxically – makes it possible to create and sustain a 'rival' world of interlocking and supportive communities.[52]

I have already suggested that, at the most pragmatic level, this is how 'non-locative' religious groups survive: the community whose identity is simply bound up in its members' claim to a single decisive religious experience is far more vulnerable. Yet, as we have seen, gnostic communities depended just as much as any others on the mobility of missionaries: why is there apparently no development comparable to the epistolary spider's web uniting what would become the catholic churches? The answer, or possible answer, to this may point us towards an account of orthodoxy less baldly sociological and pragmatic. Gnostic texts characteristically have a message, a point to be grasped: there is a sense in which the origins or process of gnostic conversion are irrelevant once it has happened. The experience is reproduceable, and the convert's relation to the teacher is not simply one of continuing unilateral dependence ('If you meet the Buddha, kill him' is an injunction many Gnostics would have understood) – though it would manifestly be wrong to suggest that the gnostic convert was a kind of spiritual monad, indifferent to membership in a group of like-minded 'proficients': if that were the case, there would be no gnostic literature. None the less, the strong gnostic emphasis on the recovery of an identity as a spiritual being, the discovery of one's true *genos*,[53] works against any differentiation between teacher and learner, any sense, that is, in which the historical *relation* of teacher and learner can have a constitutive role in the spiritual identity of either.

What we have to compare this with is the style of religious language and imagination represented by our canonical writings and by the kind of practice we have been examining in these last few pages. There *is* a single and decisive moment of transition from darkness to light, enacted in baptism; but the convert enters a new world in which, because conflict, constraint and uncertainty remain, learning and exchange must also continue, and progress needs to be checked against original inspiration, individually and collectively. The whole ethos takes rather more seriously the temporal nature of human knowing (and so too the risks of betrayal and forgetfulness). It generates, of course, its own, sometimes paralysing, mythology of 'primitive' truth and purity, its own variety of *Verfallstheorie*; but this reflects not simply a naivety about history, but the more significant capacity to question or distance oneself from the deliverances of a narrowly conceived present experience, from the merely local in time as well as space. This too is part of the heritage of the search for orthodox or normative faith in the first Christian centuries.

IV

But one further aspect should be mentioned. The Christian canon ended up containing gospels as well as epistles, a variegated set of narratives about Jesus. That the Jesus-tradition never finally systematized itself into a single coherent body of instruction in a single narrative framework is itself an important fact. The *way* in which the telling of the story of Jesus (especially of his death) functioned in producing conversion or enlightenment was clearly not readily assimilable to the transmission of a picture of the world or a model for behaviour, though the effort so to assimilate it was certainly made by many theologians. On the catholic side, we have hints (as in Irenaeus) of embarrassment at the existence of four gospels; on the gnostic side, the production of gospels in the conventional form of instruction discourses.[54] What the canonical narrative tradition suggests is a mode of preaching in which the priority is less the communication of principles and injunctions than the bringing

– of the hearer into 'dramatic' relation with the subject of the story –
– offering the hearer a new self-definition determined by his or her stance
– towards Jesus, offering a place within the story itself, as recipient of
– forgiveness and of judgment, as colluding with the betrayal of Jesus and
– sharing in the power of the risen Lord. As in the Deuteronomic
formulae of the Old Testament, the addressee of the words uttered in the
narrative past is the hearer in the actual present.

If this is what the canonical gospels presuppose, a community whose
origins lie in this kind of preaching and catechesis will be less likely to
sit light to the continuities of Christian practice in time and space –
however little these themes may be part of the *conscious* reflection of
second and third generations in the community. The transforming
encounter with the Christ is renewed and deepened in the repeated
hearing of the story, in words and in ritual enactment: there is more
growth to be undergone towards the stature of Christ, and the hearing
of the story is part of the work of Christ's 'spirit' generating that
growth. But for that hearing to go on being a hearing of the *same* story,
canons of authorization are necessary for those who tell it or enact it;
otherwise the story loses its distance or difference, and so its converting
power, by becoming simply a story I choose to tell to myself. It may be
that the very nature of the basic Christian narrative carries the notions
of canon and orthodoxy within it, in the sense that it resists
schematization into a plan of salvation that can be reduced to a simple
and isomorphic moment of self-recognition in response to illumination.
It is inescapably tied to a temporal account of faith, and so involved in
questions of legitimation and continuity.

J. D. Crossan, at the end of a speculative and controversial book on
non-canonical gospels, suggests that Jesus' own parabolic teaching (the
realistic secular narrative, inviting the hearer to 'find an identity' within
it) is the root of the non-gnostic option for narrative gospels. 'Is the
basic continuity between historical Jesus and ecclesiastical Christ
established not so much in discussions about orthodox and heterodox
contents as in the fictional realism with which Jesus spoke in parables
and with which they spoke about him as parable itself?'[55] If this is right,
then we could say that Bauer *was* largely correct in believing that the
unity of the earliest churches lay simply in 'relationship with the one
Lord';[56] correct too in supposing that this relationship is mediated
through a constant succession of cultural and religious variables (and
Drijvers[57] and Markus[58] are right in seeing what we call syncretism as
an unavoidable part of this mediation and articulation). His error is in

supposing that there is a hidden pre-categorial, ahistorical, 'authentic' dimension to this relationship which the very notion of normative faith subverts so gravely that we must suppose the latter to be alien to the very essence of the Christian enterprise, enforced only by the pressure of ecclesiastico-political developments. The relationship of believer to Lord in the most primitive Christianity is not to be conceived as a mysterious timeless interiority betrayed by language, history and community; even for the Gnostic, it is the result of specific historical activities in the shape of mission and conversion, and bears the marks of this. The 'catholic' insight is that it continues to be *constituted* by historical mediations – gospel and canon, sacrament, succession, communion, debate and exchange, with all the ambiguities involved in the life of historical and visible social realities, the problems of power and guilt and forgetfulness. The claim of this perspective to normative status has to do with the very nature of communication about Jesus as well as with the need of a 'non-locative' religious practice to establish a plausible social world. Smith, it will be remembered,[59] speaks of the reworking of locative ideas in terms of the presence of the holy teacher as sacred centre: early catholic Christianity, by allowing cultic access to an exalted Lord who was still identifiable and apprehensible as an individual of the human past, is a remarkable case of the *fusion* of anthropology with cosmology, rather than simply the replacement of the latter by the former, as defined by Smith.

If one final and more openly theological remark may be permitted: the implication of all this is that what is mysterious in Christian beginnings is not the *experience* of hearing the Christian kerygma but the record and image of Jesus himself.[60] His is conceived as a parabolic story, yet it is remembered in diverse and less than wholly coherent narrative forms, whose historical foundation is uncertain. To be introduced into relation with such a figure is to encounter what is not exhaustible in word or system – or so Christians have concluded: it is to step into *faith* (rather than a definitive enlightenment). In so far as certain features of the development of canon and orthodoxy paradoxically worked *against* the absorption of Jesus into a thematized religious subjectivity and a system of ideas, they preserved the possibility of preaching Jesus as a questioning and converting presence in ever more diverse cultures and periods, and the possibility of intelligible debate and self-criticism within Christianity. Drijvers has asked whether we should not see the critical disciplines of the history of religions as themselves 'a phenomenon of crisis *within* Christianity';[61] if we should, it is perhaps precisely because Christianity evolved into the network of human accountability, to the past and to the present, that we have been examining in this essay. It is right to acknowledge, with Bauer, the insuperable problems in supposing there to have been from the beginning a single, clearly identifiable 'mainstream', and the ease with which the inchoate structures we have observed can be conscripted into the service of authoritarian and centralizing impulses: the raw material for a good deal of the post-Nicene development of 'imperial' orthodoxy is already there before AD 300. But it is equally important to acknowledge with Chadwick that there are features *within* the most basic activity of communicating about Jesus that make for the precarious evolution of a 'normative' Christianity which is still an interwoven plurality of perspectives on what was transacted in Jerusalem. And the notion of a church whose unity lies primarily, if not absolutely and simply, in a shared attention to the questioning story of a crucified and resurrected Lord, *and* an attention to how that story is being assimilated in diverse and distant communities, culturally and historically strange, is not without relevance to our own day – as Henry Chadwick has himself demonstrated in so many ways.

NOTES

1 *The Circle and the Ellipse. Rival Concepts of Authority in the Early Church*, Oxford 1959 (= 1 in *History and Thought of the Early Church*, London 1982).

2 On the development of this and kindred themes in the 'mystique' of Jerusalem, see p. 7 of the lecture. It should be borne in mind, though, that Jerusalem as 'navel' and as 'mother of the churches' is essentially a fourth-century complex of ideas: earlier attitudes are more ambivalent. Peter Walker's Cambridge PhD thesis on 'Fourth Century Attitudes to Jerusalem and the Holy Land' (1986) is a fine survey of this subject. I take 'Jerusalem' in Chadwick's lecture to be something like a symbol for the church's *historical* roots in Palestine, rather than simply a designation for a specific place that was not all that significant for Christians between Paul and Constantine.

3 ET from the second edition of *Rechtgläubigkeit und Ketzerei im ältesten Christentum*, ed. Georg Strecker, Tübingen 1964 (the first edition was published in Tübingen in 1934). The English translation (Philadelphia 1971, London 1972) contains further additions and updating, notably an essay by R. A. Kraft on the book's reception. Further discussion of reaction to the work (mainly English language) during the 1970s may be found in D. J. Harrington, 'The Reception of Walter Bauer's *Orthodoxy and Heresy in*

Earliest Christianity During the Last Decade', *HThR*, 73 (1980), 289–98, and in Harrington's collection, *The Light of the Nations. Essays on the Church in New Testament Research*, Wilmington 1982, pp. 162–73.

4 Critically discussed in a celebrated essay by Morna Hooker, 'On Using the Wrong Tool', *Theology*, 75 (1972), 570–81.

5 Bultmann and Bauer admired and approved of each other's work; see Erich Fascher, 'Walter Bauer als Kommentator', *NTS*, 9 (1962), 23–38, esp. 32.

6 'Walter Bauer als Kirchenhistoriker', *NTS*, 9 (1962), 11–22; 12–13 on the difference between Bauer and Harnack.

7 Schneemelcher, *NTS*, 9 (1962), 20.

8 'Vielmehr scheint mir aus dem Arbeiten Bauers hervorzugehen, dass die Einheit der Kirche...als geglaubte Einheit des Leibes Christi zu verstehen ist, dass aber das, was gemeinhin unter Einheit verstanden wird, d.h. die *sichtbare* Einheit...das Ergebnis eines geschichtlichen Prozesses ist' (Schneemelcher, *NTS*, 9 (1962), 20; my italics).

9 Despite Bauer's un-Bultmannian and residually 'liberal' interest in the historical Jesus; see Schneemelcher, *NTS*, 9 (1962), 16–17.

10 *Imagining Religion. From Babylon to Jonestown*, Chicago 1982, pp. 19–35.

11 See Smith's essay, 'Earth and Gods', in his collection *Map is Not Territory. Studies in the History of Religions*, Leiden 1978 (pp. 104–28), pp. 117–18. On the notions of the 'centre' or 'mainstream' as tools of imperialistic control, compare the discussion in the title essay of the same volume ('Map is Not Territory', pp. 288–309, esp. pp. 292–5).

12 Smith, 'Map is Not Territory', pp. 308–9, gives a summary of the typology of the 'locative' and its mutations in religious practice, further discussed later on in the present essay; and compare the essays in the same volume on 'The Wobbling Pivot' (pp. 88–102, esp. p. 101), 'The Influence of Symbols on Social Change: A Place on Which to Stand' (pp. 129–46, esp. pp. 145–6), and 'The Temple and the Magician' (pp. 172–89, esp. pp. 185–6).

13 See, e.g., Smith, 'Birth Upside Down or Right Side Up?' (*Map is Not Territory*, pp. 147–71), and Kurt Rudolf, *Gnosis. The Nature and History of an Ancient Religion*, Edinburgh 1983, pp. 265–6, 286–92; some features of Rudolf's analysis are anachronistic and reductive, but there is much here of insight and importance on the social setting of new religious movements in late antiquity.

14 J. Z. Smith, 'Wisdom and Apocalyptic' (*Map is Not Territory*, pp. 67–87), p. 86, and 'The Temple and the Magician' (in the same volume, pp. 172–89), pp. 185–6, on the importance of the absence of a native king in the Near East after Alexander; and cf. the same author's 'A Pearl of Great Price and a Cargo of Yams: A Study in Situational Incongruity' (*Imagining Religion*, pp. 90–101), pp. 90–6. Kurt Rudolf enumerates some of the social and ideological factors in religious crises on pp. 332–4 of his valuable

essay, 'Einzige grundsätzliche Bemerkungen zum Thema "Schisma und Häresie" unter religionsvergleichenden Gesichtspunkt' (*Ex Orbe Religionum. Studia Geo Widengren*, Studies in the History of Religions/ Supplements to *Numen* 22, Leiden 1972, pp. 326–39). Rudolf's distinction here between cults interwoven with social life overall and *Stifter-religionen* or *Bekenntnisreligionen* (in which latter pair alone the concept of heresy makes sense, p. 328) adumbrates some features of Smith's more nuanced schema, and introduces some indispensable clarifications.

15 Hannah Arendt, *The Human Condition*, Chicago 1958, p. 53.

16 Richard Gombrich, 'Introduction: The Buddhist Way' (*The World of Buddhism. Buddhist Monks and Nuns in Society and Culture*, ed. Heinz Bechert and Richard Gombrich, London 1984, pp. 9–14), p. 13.

17 Erik Zürcher, '"Beyond the Jade Gate": Buddhism in China, Vietnam and Korea' (*The World of Buddhism*, pp. 193–211), notes (p. 199) the classical Chinese expression for joining the monastic order – 'leaving the household'.

18 Smith, 'The Temple and the Magician', pp. 186–9.

19 Rowan Williams, 'The Prophetic and the Mystical: Heiler Revisited' (*New Blackfriars*, 64, 757 (1983), 330–47), 337–9, 342–4, discusses the convergence of holy place and holy person in religious traditions which give some place to prophetic or shamanic ecstasy.

20 'The Temple and the Magician', p. 187.

21 E.g. Smith, *Map is Not Territory*, pp. 145, 156ff., 169–70, 300ff., on liminality *within* the structures of locative religion.

22 For a fine survey of such elements in New Testament Christianity, see J. D. G. Dunn, *Jesus and the Spirit*, London 1975. A more speculative and polemical re-reading of Christian origins in terms of magically induced experience of 'heavenly journeys' can be found in Morton Smith, *Clement of Alexandria and a Secret Gospel of Mark*, Harvard 1973; the evidence here adduced is still a matter of heated scholarly debate.

23 'Zum Stichwort: Rechtgläubigkeit und Ketzerei im ältesten Christentum', *ZKG*, 80 (1969), 61–74, esp. 72–4.

24 H. J. W. Drijvers characterizes early Syrian Christianity simply as 'die Gesamtheit aller Interpretationen Jesu von Nazareth durch Personen und Gruppen im kulturellen und geographischer Bereich den wir als "Syrien" bezeichnen' ('Rechtgläubigkeit und Ketzerei im ältesten Syrischen Christentum', *OrChrA*, 197 (1974) 291–308; = III in *East of Antioch. Studies in Early Syriac Christianity*, London 1984), pp. 291–2 – a judiciously and helpfully neutral definition that could be adapted to contexts other than Syria).

25 In the New Testament, see, e.g., 1 Corinthians 10:32, Galatians 6:16, Ephesians 2:19, Philippians 3:20, James 1:1 (possibly), 1 Peter 2:9–10. In later literature, compare the *Epistle to Diognetus* 5, and a number of gnostic

texts – though in these, the redeemed *already* belong to the spiritual race and need only to have this brought to light. See, e.g., the *Tripartite Tractate*, 118–19 (J. M. Robinson, *The Nag Hammadi Library*, Leiden 1977, p. 89), the *Apocalypse of Adam*, 82–3 (Robinson, *Nag Hammadi*, p. 263), the Books of Jeu (E. Hennecke/W. Schneemelcher, *New Testament Apocrypha*, vol. 1, London 1963, p. 261). Note in particular the reference in the *Apocalypse of Adam*, which describes the elect as a 'race with no king'. The whole idea is studied in G. Stroumsa, *Another Seed. Studies in Gnostic Mythology*, Nag Hammadi Studies 24, Leiden 1984.

26 John 2:19–21, perhaps, and 4:20–4.

27 E.g. *Dialogue* 22, 25–6, 52 (appealing to the present desolation of Jerusalem; cf. *Apology* 47); but it is worth noting that Justin also believes in an earthly reign of the saints in Jerusalem after the resurrection (80–1).

28 E.g. *Miscellanies* 7. 5–7.

29 Eusebius, *Ecclesiastical History* II. 23 (hereafter *HE*), preserves some of the relevant traditions.

30 1 Peter 2:5, Revelation 21:12–14, 22; the Qumran *Manual of Discipline*, VIII–IX. On this network of ideas, see B. Gärtner, *The Temple and the Community in Qumran and the New Testament*, Cambridge 1965.

31 J. Z. Smith, 'A Pearl of Great Price and a Cargo of Yams: A Study in Situational Incongruity' (*Imagining Religion*, pp. 90–101), p. 94 on the nature of the conceptual 'slippage' from apocalyptic to gnostic theodicy.

32 I avoid the term 'Judaism', which gives a misleading impression of the systematized coherence of *a* religion. See Smith's essay referred to in n. 11 above, and Jacob Neusner's two important books, *Judaism in the Beginning of Christianity*, Philadelphia 1984, and *Judaism in the Matrix of Christianity*, Philadelphia 1986, which stress the fact that 'Judaism' in the modern sense achieves definition largely in terms of confrontation with Christian polemic. See also H. J. W. Drijvers, *OrChrA*, 197 (1974), 295.

33 Non-gnostic Christians are accordingly charged with worshipping or following a dead man, as in the Second Tractate of the Great Seth and the *Apocalypse of Peter*; see Jacques E. Ménard, 'Normative Self-Definition in Gnosticism' (*Jewish and Christian Self-Definition*, vol. 1: *The Shaping of Christianity in the Second and Third Centuries*, ed. E. P. Sanders, London 1980, pp. 134–50), p. 144.

34 'The very nature of the Gnostic religion... would mitigate [*sic*] against the establishment of an institutionalized "normative" group self-identity': Birger Pearson, 'Jewish Elements in Gnosticism and the Development of Gnostic Self-Definition' (*Jewish and Christian Self-Definition*, vol. 1, pp. 151–60), p. 160.

35 The careers of Marcion and Valentinus illustrate this; cf., though with caution, Rudolf, *Gnosis*, pp. 217–18, on gnostic 'missionaries' (we do not, in fact, have hard evidence for the 'visitation' of gnostic communities by

their founders, or for a regular supervision by correspondence, apart from the rather special case of Mani), and H. J. W. Drijvers, 'The Origins of Gnosticism as a Religious and Historical Problem', *Nederlands Teologisk Tijdschrift*, 22 (1968), 321–51 = *East of Antioch* xv, pp. 330–1.

36 Classically, of course, the case of Edessa, so important to Bauer; cf. various of Drijvers' essays in *East of Antioch*, especially III, XII and XV.

37 For a good summary of the view that 16:1–16 is actually an independent letter of recommendation, see E. Käsemann, *Commentary on Romans*, Grand Rapids and London 1980, pp. 409–16; bibliography on p. 412.

38 Whether or not it was originally a letter in its entirety, it has taken on an epistolary form with some distinctive and interesting features.

39 J. H. Elliott, *A Home for the Homeless. A Sociological Exegesis of I Peter, its Situation and Strategy*, Philadelphia 1981, is a brilliant study of how the socially insignificant or displaced persons who are entering the Christian community receive their new location in the human world by means of learning this sort of self-description.

40 Cf. the Chinese phraseology (mentioned in n.17 above) for joining the Sangha, which supersedes the 'natural' household.

41 One such is mentioned by R. Lane Fox, *Pagans and Christians in the Mediterranean World from the Second Century A.D. to the Conversion of Constantine*, London 1986, p. 87; but it is a rare example of a network of worshippers with a world-wide extension, and there is no sense of belonging to an active interrelation within this network.

42 *HE*, IV.23.

43 VI.46, VII.2–9, 20–2, 26 etc.

44 E.g. IV.15, V.1–4, VI.11, 40–2, 43, 44, VII.10–11, VIII.10.

45 VI.11, 46.

46 V.19–20, 23–25 (esp. 25), VI.43–46, VII.2–9.

47 V.24, VII.5.

48 As suggested by, e.g., M. Elze, 'Häresie und einheit der Kirche im 2.Jahrhundert', *ZThK*, 71 (1974), 389–409, esp. 393–5, 404–5.

49 *Paroikeō, paroikia* and *paroikoi* occur not only in 1 Peter, but in Clement of Rome, the *Martyrdom of Polycarp* and the *Epistle to Diognetus*, as terms for the Christian community's experience.

50 The amount of travel in the early Christian period should not be underestimated. The well-known 'Epitaph of Avircius' records what seems to have been a journey made almost entirely for the sake of seeing the life of distant churches.

51 Though not interchangeability of ministries; the canons of Nicaea are typical in their hostility to the exercise of presbyteral or diaconal ministry outside the jurisdiction of the ordaining bishop or his successor.

52 R. Wilken, 'Diversity and Unity in Early Christianity', *The Second Century*, 1 (1981), 101–10, helpfully summarizes many of the factors briefly touched on here.

53 See above, n.25.
54 Cf. the remarks earlier in this paper on the post-resurrection dialogue as a gnostic convention.
55 J. D. Crossan, *Four Other Gospels. Shadows on the Contours of Canon*, Minneapolis 1985, p. 187.
56 See Schneemelcher's essay, *NTS*, 9 (1962), quoted above, nn. 6–9.
57 See the remark on the syncretistic features in all religious traditions in 'Bardaisan von Edessa als Repräsentant des syrischen Synkretismus im 2. Jahrhundert nach Christus' (*Synkretismus im syrisch-persischen Kulturgebiet*, ed. A. Dietrich, Göttingen 1977, pp. 111–22), p. 119.
58 'The Problem of Self-Definition: From Sect to Church' (*Jewish and Christian Self-Definition*, vol. 1, pp. 1–15), *passim*; and cf. Hans-Dieter Betz, 'Orthodoxy and Heresy in Primitive Christianity: Some Critical Remarks on Georg Strecker's Republication of Walter Bauer's *Rechtgläubigkeit und Ketzerei im ältesten Christentum*', *Interpretation*, 19 (1965), 299–311, where orthodoxy in several systems is described as the 'final stage of a syncretistic process' (310).
59 Smith, 'The Temple and the Magician', pp. 186–9.
60 Once again, Schneemelcher's discussion of Bauer moves in the same direction; but we need to move more decisively away from any residual focus on the teaching of the historical Jesus as a focus or norm in abstraction from the paschal story.
61 *Nederlands Teologisk Tijdschrift*, 22 (1968), 351 (my italics).

'And I have other sheep'—*John 10:16*

W. H. C. FREND

Patristic scholarship has always been one of the great strengths of the Anglican Communion. It has been represented by a long succession of able scholars, including J. B. Lightfoot (d. 1889), B. F. Westcott and F. J. Hort, Benjamin Kidd and G. L. Prestige. It has never been subjected to the constraints that beset Roman Catholic patristic scholars on the continent at the time of the imposition of the anti-Modernist oath by the Papacy in 1910. The critical study of the early Fathers has flourished in the United Kingdom as one of the hallmarks of 'sound learning' in the church, and in particular, the four-yearly patristic conferences at Oxford initiated by F. L. Cross in 1951 remain a memorial to the contribution by scholars of British universities in that field. For more than forty years Henry Chadwick has represented the outstanding quality of their achievement.

Patristics, however, are by definition concerned largely with the literary study of the orthodox tradition of early Christianity. The Fathers were educated men, belonging to the relatively small cultural élite that has left its ideas for posterity. They were conscious, also, of belonging to a tradition of Christian teaching that was the sole truth, and they were concerned to defend its message against heresies, false interpretations, and misunderstandings. Their vast output of works expounding and defending the orthodox position as defined by the precedent of tradition reinforced by church councils, and their commentaries on every book of the Bible fill the columns of Migne's *Patrologia*. These men represent the mainstream of early Christian teaching and their views still influence theology today.

For them, the history of the church was the history of the people of God, extending from creation until the end of the present age. As Eusebius of Caesarea wrote (*c.* 324), while this 'really fresh name of Christians was recently known among all nations, nevertheless our life

and method of conduct in accordance with the precepts of religion has
not been recently invented by us but [has existed] from the first creation
of man'.[1] In the West, Augustine wrote the *De civitate Dei* to demonstrate
the workings of the eternal providence of God in both secular and
sacred history, in which catholic Christians as sojourners in the world
were destined eventually to be numbered among the citizens of the City
of God.[2] The only thing that counted for man in this life was his relation
to God, and that could only be assured through obedience to the
universal or catholic church.

Thus, Eastern and Western Church Fathers wrote to defend catholic
truth, however differently they interpreted this. Those who disagreed
received short shrift. No epithet was too bad for any caught up in 'the
deadly disease' of heresy.[3] Indeed, one is often surprised by the
defensive and ill-tempered utterances that one finds even in the personal
letters of the Fathers of the fourth and fifth centuries, and their obvious
daily concern to hunt down and suppress any dissenting opinion. Basil
of Caesarea, writing to his friend Amphilochius of Iconium in *c.* 375,
defines the problem thus: '[The Ancients] called certain errors heresies,
others schisms, and others "parasynagogi"'.[4] The heresies included
those who were 'completely separate and are aliens to the faith; the
schismatics are those who are separated [from us] on [clearly] defined
ecclesiastical grounds that could not be solved through mutual
agreement, and the "parasynagogi", are factions formed by priests, or
rebellious bishops, or by undisciplined congregations' (*Epistula* 188.1).
Each category of dissent was precisely defined for condemnation,
complete with suggestions on how to deal with it. No wonder that the
writings of dissenters did not survive. Those of Nestorius were
proscribed by imperial decree, having been equated with the anti-
Christian apologetic of Porphyry of Tyre (*c.* 232–*c.* 304),[5] but even those
of Hosius of Cordoba (256–357) who had accompanied Constantine in
his campaign against Maxentius, and only lapsed from Nicene orthodoxy
in the final year of a century-long life, have failed to reach posterity.
There was neither forgiveness nor hope of salvation for those who died
'outside the church'.

Fortunately for later generations, wrong opinions that had to be
refuted had also to be quoted. Though sometimes the context may be
lost, most quotations seem to have been accurate, if selective. To an
extent therefore, the ideas of Petilian of Constantine, Faustus of Milevis,
and Julian of Eclanum, to mention three of Augustine's most effective
opponents, have survived through the works of their adversary. For

scholars, however, a foundation had been laid on which the study of the varied forms of opposition to orthodoxy could be based. The historian of the early church was never wholly bereft of sources whence to assess the claims of orthodoxy and its adversaries.

'Creeds, Councils and Controversies',[6] these dominate the story of the church in the age of the Fathers. The variety of opinions subject to anathema by the multitudinous councils of bishops indicate a diversity of interpretations of Christianity which anyone seeking to assess the impact made by the new religion on Greco-Roman society would need to study. Patristic scholarship alone, however, could only take him part of the way towards his goal.

The beginnings of an alternative approach to the study of Christianity, less beholden to orthodox interpretations, may be traced back to the Renaissance. The spirit of free enquiry which this produced was expressed at an early date by an interest in the material remains of Christianity. In the late fifteenth century the catacombs in Rome were becoming known to explorers as well as pilgrims. Among the explorers around 1475 were members of the Roman Academy who styled themselves 'perscrutatores antiquitatis', while one bold spirit called himself 'sacerdos Academiae Rom[anae]', and invented a 'Pope Pomponius' after Pomponius Letus, their leader.[7] Not surprisingly, they were arrested and tried on the charge of being pagans and conspiring against the pope. In a similar lay and somewhat anti-clerical spirit, other Renaissance scholars, such as Marsilio Ficino (1433–99) of Florence, were attempting to integrate Platonism and Christianity into a new religious synthesis, and extended their researches into the Corpus Hermeticum and the Sibylline oracles. They too, were abominated as 'atheists', but in the next century, in the background of the battles between reformers and catholics, they formed a third grouping whose contribution to the early comparative study of religion, including Zoroastrianism and the *Hermetica* is only in recent years being properly evaluated.[8]

The Enlightenment produced the first real attempts to write the history of the church as history, subject to the same critical disciplines as other aspects of the subject. The pioneer in this field was J. L. Mosheim, Chancellor of the University of Göttingen in the 1760s, who had close relations with the Hanoverian court.[9] He set out to explain, with as much impartiality as possible, the paradox 'of the religion of Jesus rising upon a benighted world, striking conviction into the hearts of mortals by the irresistible lustre of divine truths...and furnishing new supports to civil and social virtue', and 'the lamentable changes that have been introduced into the church in consequence of the corruption of men, the ambition of a licentious and despotic priesthood and the bigotry and tyranny of ignorant and wicked sovreigns' (vol. 1, p. vii). The history of the early church was divided simply between 'external' and 'internal' aspects, and praise and blame were distributed among orthodox and dissenters impartially. Augustine as well as Pelagius contributed, it is implied, to the 'unhappy disputes' associated with the latter.[10]

Mosheim provides a good example of the climate of opinion that was reflected by Gibbon fifteen years later. Gibbon's integration of the history of Christianity into the general history of the later Roman empire was as important as his strictures against 'Christianity and barbarism' as contributing to the empire's fall. An element of relativism had been introduced into the study of early Christianity. Orthodoxy and heresy were exposed to similar canons of criticism and, in addition, could not be divorced from the general history of the times and the pressures exerted on both by non-theological factors.

There was a limit, however, to what historians could learn about the early church so long as they were confined to existing literary sources. It was the discovery of quantities of material remains and their study that has made an historical and sociological approach to the subject possible. This has now taken its place alongside patristics as a means of understanding the development of Christianity in the Greco-Roman world as a separate culture as well as a new religion.

Exploration of the catacombs in Rome had been going on since the 1590s, thanks to Antonio Bosio (1576–1629), and Jewish as well as Christian catacombs had been discovered. Interest in archaeology and the information it could yield was growing steadily through the eighteenth century. 'At the call of the pick and shovel, the earth yields up her hidden treasures', such was the hopeful comment of an English traveller, George Dennis, after his visit to Bolsena in the 1840s.[11] In fact, the real archaeological revolution that made new assessments of orthodoxy and its opponents possible was the result of separate and unconnected events about this time. Renewed interest in the critical study of the New Testament associated with D. F. Strauss (1808–74) and Ernest Renan (1823–92) coincided first with the French conquest of Algeria (1830–47), and then with the expansion of European influence in the Turkish empire, not least in Asia Minor.

In North Africa, Roman civilization based upon the towns and villages of settled agricultural communities had been replaced by the nomadism of the Berber and Arab conquerors of the seventh and eighth centuries AD. Settlements, however, had seldom been destroyed. The Algerian high plains between the Aures and Atlas mountains had been traversed by nomadic tribes as a corridor linking the richer and more important parts of the Arab world of Tunis and Cordoba. In consequence, the Roman and Byzantine settlements had simply been bypassed and left in the same state as when they had been abandoned by their last inhabitants, skeletons of a dead civilization.

In large parts of Asia Minor and Syria similar developments had taken place. European settlers and explorers were therefore confronted with a mass of standing remains of the Roman and Byzantine eras and prominent among these gaunt reminders of the past were those of early Christianity. Fortunately for scholarship, the first generation of French settlers in Algeria included individuals of wide cultural interests who perceived at once the significance of the ruins they saw around them. In 1856 Adrien Berbrugger founded the Société Historique Algérienne with the object of 'conserving and making known the antiquities of the province', and preventing, incidentally, the removal of some of the more outstanding, such as the Triumphal Arch at Djemila, to France.[12]

Exploration, however, was not confined to urban sites and classical monuments. As their settlements progressed away from the Mediterranean coast, settlers came across very considerable evidences of early rural settlement extending from quantities of megalithic remains to farms and villages occupied down to the end of the Byzantine period These latter produced an abundance of Christian evidence. In 1893 and 1894 Henri Graillot and Stéphane Gsell published an account of archaeological surveys they had made in the countryside north of the Aures mountains.[13] The churches they found differed, however, from the large stone buildings being discovered in the towns. They were small, rustic apsidal buildings with traces of walls built of baked mud ('toub') and floors of beaten earth. Inscriptions found associated with them indicated a strictly biblical religion and some proclaimed the Donatist watch-word, 'Deo Laudes'. Art forms also owed more to the craft of the native woodcarver and even to reminiscences of the carving on false doorways of megalithic tombs than to classical motives.[14] Archaeology was bearing out the claims of Optatus of Milevis and Augustine that Donatism flourished most in Numidia. Here was evidence for an overwhelmingly Donatist rural culture. Archaeological and literary evidence corroborated each other.

Meanwhile, in Asia Minor, the discoveries of British scholars in the Phrygia of classical times were shedding new light on another regional movement of Christian dissent, namely Montanism. From the early fourth century onwards, Montanus' original movement of prophecy and apocalyptic had been dubbed by orthodox church historians the 'heresy of the Phrygians'.[15] The end of the world prophesied by Montanus and his women aides, Priscilla and Maximilla had not happened, but his church none the less continued and flourished. C. S. Sterrett and W. M. Ramsay, starting out as New Testament scholars with the aim of investigating and, if possible, proving the truth of Acts, came across inscriptions dateable on epigraphic grounds to the third century AD whose authors proclaimed their Christianity openly.[16] They addressed themselves as 'Christians for Christians' (*Christianoi Christianois*). The uncompromising call suggested Montanist identity, and the presence of plough, tools and weaving combs on the inscriptions indicated an agricultural background for the dedications, combined with a good knowledge of Greek. The discovery of more of these inscriptions on sites in the Tembris valley in northern Phrygia suggested the existence of rural Montanist communities, tenant farmers on imperial estates,[17] just as a similar distribution of Donatist remains on Numidian imperial estates suggested a strongly regional and rural basis for Donatism in that province.

Between the wars, further discoveries of Montanist inscriptions were made in Phrygia by Ramsay's pupil, W. M. Calder, but unfortunately no excavations of possible Montanist sites were carried out. In North Africa, however, the Donatists were being better served. From 1930 to 1940, a succession of students from the Ecole française de Rome were being given the task of working on a site, generally ecclesiastical, on the high plains of central Algeria, an area coinciding with southern Numidia. In addition, in Algeria itself the vigorous and scholarly curator of the Musée Gustave Mercier at Constantine, M. André Berthier initiated a survey of the Romano-Berber remains over an area some 110 km by 40 km south-west of Constantine.[18] The result of these combined activities was to demonstrate literally on the ground the reality of Donatist Numidia and confirm further the statements made by Optatus of Milevis in the 360s and Augustine of Hippo half a century later.

The outstanding single discovery by the scholars of the Ecole française de Rome was that of the church associated with the Donatist bishop and martyr, Marculus, the story of whose arrest, torture and execution at the time of the imposition of catholic unity in 347–8 had been preserved in Donatist *Acta martyrum*.[19] The church was a fine building, erected probably near the end of the fourth century when the Donatist church was at the height of its power in North Africa. It was an apsidal structure, measuring 26 m long by 12 m wide. The floor, however, was of beaten earth without cement or mosaics. But great care had been taken to honour the tomb of the martyr, with well-cut slabs of stone and rich decoration in geometric non-classical patterns, and plasterwork representing a Eucharistic chalice flanked by birds and fishes. On a keystone of the vault over the apse had been inscribed the words 'Deo laudes H[ic] omnes dicamu[s]', and, as the discoverer wrote, without wishing to exaggerate the significance of this last word, one can note that the stress placed on the unanimity of the faithful fits well with a sect that found in its collective enthusiasm the strength to sustain perpetual struggles against the powers of the existing world and the 'false church' of the African catholics.[20] This was confirmed by a further inscription found the next year which quoted Psalm 131 : 18 : 'De dono / [Dei] Inimicis / [conf]usionem / [fe]cit'. The martyr sustained by God's grace heaped confusion on his enemies.[21]

The discoveries by Berthier and his colleagues supported the conclusions reached by Cayrel and Courcelle. Actively assisted by the regional administration, they worked systematically over a broad strip of territory between the salt lakes north of the Aures mountains and the Constantine–St Arnaud (pre-1962 nomenclature) railway. This contained some 290 sites already known to Gsell and the compilers of the *Atlas archéologique de l' Algérie* in 1911, of which some 250 contained Roman or Byzantine-period remains. The result of eight years of energetic work between 1931 and 1939 was the survey of seventy-four separate rural sites and the establishment in some detail of how the inhabitants spent their lives in late-Roman and Byzantine times.[22]

One thing was clear: whereas down to *circa* AD 240 the ambition of many native African communities had been to become towns and acquire civic rights, nothing seems to have been further from the minds of their fourth-century successors. Archaeologists were confronted with large, rural communities sometimes extending to as much as fifty hectares in area, in which there was no evidence, except for a few small bath-buildings, of any public building. Instead, there were granaries native-type dwellings and above all, olive presses and churches.[23] These last attracted Berthier's particular attention. Every settlement contained more than one church, and some, such as Mechta Azrou, south of the

Garaet Ank Djemel salt lake, as many as seven. All were built on a similar basilican plan with an enclosure in front of the apse for the altar, and beneath the altar a reliquary housing martyrs' remains. Inscriptions proclaimed the names of martyrs and the day of their *redditio* and occasionally a biblical text and the Donatist watchword 'Deo Laudes'.[24] This was Donatist country. The impression left on those who worked on the sites was of a population identifying themselves with a uniform religion oriented towards the cult of martyrs, as one would expect in the Donatist church.[25] As in Phrygia, these archaeological surveys confirmed patristic texts pointing to the regional strength of a dissenting church whose members lived in a world of prophetic and apocalyptic hopes. With the Donatists, apocalyptic conviction took the form of violence towards landowners and the rich in general, as representatives of the present (Satan-dominated) age.[26] The economic background was provided by the imperial estates on which these villages were located and the high taxation and arbitrary rule to which they were often subjected. It was impossible henceforth to deny the existence of non-theological factors behind both schismatic movements and the historian and sociologist had a part to play alongside the patristic scholar in unravelling these factors.

Unfortunately, the Second World War and the disturbed aftermath in Algeria that led to the full-scale uprising in 1954 has prevented further work on the Numidian village sites. The writer has found, even, that many of his photographs and notes of sites he worked on in 1938 and 1939 are almost the sole surviving archaeological records of that time. Enough, however, had become known to stake the claims of fieldwork as an invaluable adjunct to literary research in furthering the study of early Christianity.

Donatists and Montanists were not the only non-Orthodox churches to benefit from archaeological research between the wars. Since the discovery of the Manichaean monastery and library in the oasis of Turfan in central Asia by Sir Aurel Stein in 1904, Manichaeism had also become a centre of scholarly interest. Why had this religion, apparently an amalgam of Zoroastrianism, Buddhism and gnostic Christianity, made such progress in North Africa during the fourth century and held the allegiance of a mind such as Augustine's for nine years? In 1930 a brilliant chance find by Carl Schmidt of the Pergamon Museum in Berlin, while on a visit to an antique dealer in Cairo, restored to the world some of the original works of Mani himself, as well as some 300 psalms and prayers used by his humble followers in Egypt.[27]

Manichaeism was shown to be not merely a dualistic sect with little Christian content and an unsocial way of life, but a gnostic-type religion whose emphasis on lifelong search for wisdom could inspire idealism and whose philosophy of life was well adapted to the ascetic inclinations of many Christians in the latter part of the fourth century.

> I have known my soul and the body that lies upon it.
> That they have been enemies since the creation of the world.[28]

Expressed thus, and associated with liturgical songs of great beauty, the attraction of Manichaeism to young men who were repelled from orthodox Christianity, not least by some of the crudities of the Old Testament, became easier to understand.

Post-war discoveries have added most to knowledge of the gnostic–Manichaean strain in early Christianity. Scholarship had also benefited from a greatly increased popular awareness of the value of archaeological discoveries and a deepening sense of history, which links individuals with their remote ancestors. Thus, despite unfavourable circumstances, including a blood feud involving the Egyptian peasants who had made the discovery in December 1945, nearly the whole of the gnostic library found at Nag Hammadi was eventually preserved for scholars, thanks very largely to the awareness of the discoverers and their friends of the importance of their find.[29] Up to then, only five gnostic texts had been published, though another three included in a Coptic text purchased by the British Museum in 1896 were being worked upon. Thirty-two years elapsed, however, between the discovery of the Nag Hammadi documents and the rendering of the complete collection in English. Every conceivable problem, from delays imposed by constant changes in Egyptian governments down to 1954, to unscrupulous acts by antique dealers and rivalries among scholars, kept the majority of the documents under wraps until the early 1970s. As published in 1977, the collection of twelve codices and fragments of a thirteenth included a complete version of the *Gospel of Thomas*, hitherto known only through papyrus fragments found at Oxyrhynchus in the 1890s,[30] as well as fifty-one other tracts or fragments of tracts. Some of these clearly precede the Christian period in origin. Completely new horizons had been opened up for the study of gnosticism. The different schools of gnosticism represented in the documents showed that the Gnostics derived their teaching very largely from Jewish traditions, including that of the school of Philo at Alexandria which mediated Platonism to Hellenistic Judaism. It was no accident that gnosticism blossomed in Alexandria itself. In addition, the new sources promise to bring nearer, as Kurt Rudolf claimed, a solution to the problem of the relation between the pre-Christian gnostic redeemer figure and the gnostic Christ.[31] The existence of the former, long asserted by scholars such as Reitzenstein of the *Religionsgeschichtliche Schule*, has proved to be correct. In addition, one can point to a developing gnostic polemic against Judaism itself and against the hierarchical system of the Great Church.[32]

It was argued that what distinguished the false and true church was not relationship to clergy but the level of understanding among its members. *The Gospel of Thomas*, while including much purely gnostic material, also seems to contain some very early Aramaic-derived versions of the authentic sayings of Jesus, in particular, the parables of the Kingdom, of the Great Supper, and of the Sower. These appear to be early, but independent, versions of the Synoptic parables.[33] Of special interest is the fact that the *Thomas* version of the Sower rather than the Synoptic is used by the writer of *I Clement*, before AD 100.[34]

Further light has also been thrown on the gnostic–Manichaean tradition of Christianity by the successful decipherment of the tiny Cologne Papyrus by Henrichs and Koenen, between 1970 and 1978.[35] Mani was shown to have been born in 216, a member of the Christian baptist sect of Elkesites near Basra. The sect had communities on both sides of the Roman–Parthian frontier. His origins were therefore Christian, but at the age of twenty-four he rejected the sect, largely through his dislike of what he considered excessive purificatory ablutions and concern for the body rather than the soul. He believed that a truly Christian life was that of an ascetic.[36] Christ did not send his disciples forth equipped with millstones and ovens, he commented.[37] He accepted and developed the dualistic teaching of Marcion and Bar-Daisan and the concept of the Docetic Christ taught in gnostic apocryphal gospels.[38] His aim was, however, to preach a universal religion adapted equally to the prevailing Buddhism he found in northern India and to the Christianity of 'the West', that is, Mesopotamia and Syria.[39] Manichaeism therefore takes its place as a continuation of the gnostic–Christian tradition and as the third religious force, a rival to orthodox Christianity and the religion of the immortal gods of Rome for the allegiance of the Greco-Roman world in the third century.

Finally, the international salvage projects in areas threatened by inundation or loss to urban sprawl produced astonishing evidence, respectively, for the spread of Monophysitism down the Nile valley from the sixth century onwards, and for the economic decline of Christian North Africa even before the Arab invasions of the seventh century. The Christian remains in the Nile valley in upper Egypt and Sudan had been fairly thoroughly surveyed from the time of the establishment of the Anglo-Egyptian condominium for the Sudan in 1899. The prospect of the whole area from Aswan to Wadi-el-Halfa, where many of the Christian remains were known to lie, being flooded as the result of the building of the High Dam, from 1965 onwards, brought together twenty-three international teams from East and West in a major piece of co-operative work. The frescoes from the cathedral at Faras and the liturgical documents found at the cathedral-fortress of Q'asr Ibrim have shown the splendour of the Monophysite Nubian kingdoms during the European Middle Ages.[40] They also show the development of a religious tradition which, while it was much beholden to its Coptic parent, was as self-supporting as those of other Monophysite kingdoms, such as Armenia and Ethiopia. Monophysitism itself was demonstrated to be not merely a sect but the religion of populations who between the seventh and thirteenth centuries covered a greater area than orthodox and much of Latin Christianity combined.

The expansion of material, mainly archaeological, concerning the non-orthodox interpretations of Christianity has been immense. But where does that leave us today? It is no longer possible to treat gnosticism, for instance, as an isolated phenomenon confined to the second century and deservedly extinguished by the arguments of Irenaeus, Tertullian, Clement, and Hippolytus. Its links with pre-Christian movements within Judaism seem to have been established through writings found among the Nag Hammadi texts, while the nature of its contribution to Mani's religion is now clearer than before. The criticisms of the Fathers can be tested against the accumulating evidence that enables the Manichees and other dissenters to speak for themselves.

All, however, is by no means on the debit side for orthodoxy. The existence of 'the Great Church', no doubt regarding itself as lineal descendant of 'the Great Congregation' in Israel (Psalm 22:25 and 40:9 and 10) is itself significant. To outside observers, such as Celsus, it stood on its own, contrasting with the multifarious sects that opposed it.[41] Its God, like the God of Israel, was a God of order and righteousness to be served by an ordered hierarchy and set services, the bases of which were inherited from the past. It represented tradition, the counterpart of 'one faith and baptism'.[42] As such it remains the major contributor to 'the pattern of Christian truth'.[43] But it must now share its throne with other traditions, notably that of the prophetic trend in early Christianity, whose representatives were the Montanists and Donatists. These could also claim a respectable Old Testament pedigree for the gathered community, whose ideal put purity and integrity before universality as the test of the true church. They could also point to the tradition of reform, for the benefit of the poor in Israel. The Psalmists and the writings of the Covenanters of the Dead Sea demonstrate that these ideals were very much alive at the time of Christ.[44] Montanism and Donatism both fit into the slot of prophetic and rural religion extending from the Old Israel to the New and beyond.

The historian and theologian working in the field of early Christianity is not, therefore, confronted primarily with issues of Truth versus Error, but with different traditions and ideas present from earliest Christian times. These often derived their origins from even earlier phases of Judaism. There are also proven non-theological factors to be understood in assessing the causes and development of theological disputes. Theologians have tended to fight shy of such notions, while historians of religion, such as Walter Bauer, have sought to interpret the history of primitive Christianity in the framework of 'orthodoxy' versus 'heresy', rather than the working out of divergencies that were making themselves felt within a few years of the Crucifixion. An instance is provided by attitudes prevalent among the Jews and Christians in the first half of the first century AD towards the Temple. The Covenanters rejected it: John the Baptist had harsh words for its emissaries who had come out from Jerusalem to see him (Matthew 3:7), but to Jesus and the disciples, the Temple was 'my father's house' (Luke 2:49, compare 19:45) and the meeting place for their earliest followers (Acts, 5:12). The old conflict, however, spilled over almost immediately into Christianity. Stephen, the first martyr, could also have found himself the first schismatic.

'That they all may be one' (John 17:21) and the Pauline 'one Lord, one faith, one baptism' (Ephesians 4:5) could be realistic only so long as the Christian name stretched to include all who accepted Jesus as Lord, and were baptized in His name. Even without the antinomians and the outright Judaism denounced in the Pastoral Epistles, in Paul's own time it is difficult to see how an organization based on a resident ministry headed by presbyters and deacons could have avoided clashing with the apostles and prophets declared in the Epistle to the Ephesians 2 : 20 to be 'the foundation of the household of God, of which Christ is the cornerstone'. Paul left behind too many loose ends relating to church organization, belief and worship for Christianity to develop as a unified structure. It is not surprising perhaps that by AD 100, along with several different gospels and collections of Jesus' sayings, there were also different forms of Eucharist and even separate versions of the Lord's Prayer.[45]

Early Christianity was not a monolithic movement but a kaleidoscope of varied traditions, beliefs, and hopes centred on the single figure of Jesus Christ. The endeavours of the patristic scholar need to be supplemented by those of the historian and the archaeologist in order to understand the nature and cause of these variations that added up to the wholeness of Christianity. Future teaching and research requires a far greater degree of interdisciplinary work than hitherto. It is sad to record that the outlook in Britain is less promising than it should be, granted the outstanding tradition established by scholars in the past both in patristic theology and historical scholarship. In addition, Roman Britain provides an unparalleled training ground for successive generations of archaeologists. The lack of any central institution, however, such as the Institut für Antike und Christentum in the University of Bonn, or the Institute for Antiquity and Christianity at Claremont Graduate School in the University of California, has been a serious disadvantage. The emphasis also, in schools of theology in the United Kingdom, has remained on doctrinal and patristic study, and forays across traditional interdepartmental boundaries that have divided theology from the other humanities have been few and beset with difficulty. As a result, historical theology has suffered, and chances for working in the field on early Christian sites, for instance during the 'Save Carthage' project, have been lost. The next generation of scholars may in consequence have to be content with commenting on the discoveries of others, instead, as in the past, of making discoveries themselves.

The balance between patristics and other branches of learning relating to early Christianity needs to be restored. The former has been served with great distinction by Henry Chadwick. It is now time for the complementary work of the historians of early Christianity to be brought out of the shadows. For the future, it must be realised that too great a concentration of authority in the hands of scholars of one discipline can have far-reaching and damaging effects on the situation of others. Is the study of early Christianity in all its wealth of diversity to be restored to its proper role in the United Kingdom? One trusts that it will. Much depends, not least for the future of the Anglican Communion, on the answer. For how else can the evolution of orthodoxy be understood and also the other sheep in the Lord's flock be fed?

NOTES

1 Eusebius of Caesarea, *Historia ecclesiastica*, ed. Kirsopp Lake (hereafter *HE*) 1.4.4 and compare 1.2.1, 'The real antiquity' of Christianity.

2 On earth the Christian is always a pilgrim, 'not yet home' but 'on his way'. Victory 'was still to come'. Augustine, *Enarratio in Ps.* 123.2.4. Life was 'one long trial', *Confessions*, x.28.39. See R. A. Markus, *Saeculum: History and Society in the Theology of St Augustine,* Cambridge 1970, ch. 7, pp. 166–86, and P. R. L. Brown, *Augustine of Hippo*, London 1967, pp. 177–81.

3 Thus Basil of Caesarea, *Epistula* 262.2, to the monk Urbicus, who reported that some members of the church in his area believed that 'God Himself was turned into flesh'. Ecclesiastical correctives should be meted out to such offenders. Compare also *Epistula* 125.

4 *ep.* 188.1. Montanists were 'heretics', but Cathari and Encratites were 'schismatics'. Basil is considering the validity or otherwise of baptism dispensed by each group. See B. Gain, 'L'Eglise de Cappadoce au IVe siècle d'après la correspondence de Basile de Cesarée', *OrChrA*, 225 (1985), 365–74. Augustine was, as is well known, even harder.

5 *Codex Theodosianus* 16. 5.66 of 3 August 435.

6 The title of J. Stevenson's second volume of documents illustrative of the history of the early church, London 1966.

7 Cited from J. Stevenson, *The Catacombs, Rediscovered Monuments of Early Christianity*, London 1978, 47–8.

8 See D. P. Walker, *The Ancient Theology, Studies in Christian Platonism from the Fifteenth to the Eighteenth Centuries*, ch. 2, London 1972.

9 J. L. Mosheim, *An Ecclesiastical History, Antient and Modern from the Birth of Christ to the Beginning of the Present Century*, 4 vols., tr. A. Maclaine, Dublin 1767.

10 Mosheim, *An Ecclesiastical History*, vol. 1, p. 435.

11 Cited from a review by John R. Patterson, *JRS*, 76 (1986), 308.

12 Recorded by G. Esquer, in *Centenaire de la Société historique algérienne, 1856–1956*: vol. C of *Revue Africaine*, 1956, pp. 194–5.

13 H. Graillot and S. Gsell, 'Exploration archéologique dans le département de Constantine', *Mélanges de l'Ecole française de Rome*, 13 (1893), 461–541 and 14 (1894), 17–86.

14 Discussed by the writer in 'The Revival of Berber Art', *Antiquity*, 16 (1942), 342–52.

15 Thus, Eusebius (*HE*, v.16.1) writing in *c.* 311, speaks of 'the so-called heresy according to the Phrygians'.

16 W. M. Ramsay, *Cities and Bishoprics in Phrygia*, 2 vols., Oxford 1895–7, vol. 1, p. 496, and see the present writer, 'Montanism: Research and Problems', *RSLR*, 30 (1984), 521–37.

17 W. M. Calder, 'Philadelphia and Montanism', *BJRL*, 7 (1923), 309–55. For later discussion, see Frend, *RSLR*, 30 (1984), 530–1.

18 André Berthier and colleagues, *Les Vestiges du Christianisme dans la Numidie centrale*, Algiers 1942.

19 Anon., *Passio Marculi* (*PL* 8. 760–6).

20 P. Cayrel, 'Une basilique donatiste de Numidie', *Mélanges de l'Ecole française de Rome*, 51 (1934), 114–42, at 132.

21 P. Courcelle, 'Une seconde campagne de fouilles à Ksar-el-Kelb', *Mélanges de l'Ecole française de Rome*, 52 (1936), 166–97, at 181.

22 Berthier, *Les Vestiges du Christianisme*, map.

23 Described by the writer, 'A Note on Religion and Life in a Numidian village in the later Roman Empire', *Bulletin archéologique du Comité des Travaux historiques et scientifiques*, n.s., fasc. 17B (1984), 261–71.

24 Berthier, *Les Vestiges du Christianisme*, p. 216. '*Deo Laudes*' inscription from Foum el Amba, p. 77.

25 Berthier, *Les Vestiges du Christianisme*, pp. 205ff.

26 As exemplified by Optatus of Milevis' description of Fasir and Axido as 'duces sanctorum', giving a religious pretext for their outrages, *De schismate Donatistarum*, ed. C. Ziwsa, *CSEL* 26 (Vienna 1895), III, 4, p. 82.

27 Described by C. Schmidt and H. J. Polotsky, 'Ein Mani/Fund in Aegypten. Orginalschriften des Mani und seiner Schüler', *SPAW*, Phil. Hist. Klasse (1933), 4–90.

28 Cited from C. R. C. Allberry, *A Manichaean Psalmbook*, Part II: Manichaean manuscripts in the Chester Beatty Collection, London, 1938, p. 56, and on Augustine and Manichaeism see Brown, *Augustine of Hippo*, ch. 5.

29 For the discovery see J. M. Robinson, *The Nag Hammadi Library in English*, New York 1977, Introduction, and for the story of the difficulties surrounding the acquisition and publication of the manuscripts, see John Dart, *The Laughing Savior*, New York 1976, Part I.

30 *Oxyrhynchus Papyri*, ed. B. P. Grenfell, A. S. Hunt *et al.*, London 1898–, I, 654 and 655, dating to mid-third century.

31 Kurt Rudolf, *Gnosis* (ET by R. McL. Wilson, Edinburgh 1983, pp. 51–2).

32 Especially in the Gnostic *Apocalypse of Peter*, ed. James M. Robinson, *The Nag Hammadi Library*, San Francisco 1977, pp. 340–5. See E. Pagels, *The Gnostic Gospels*, London 1979, p. 106.

33 See H. W. Montefiore, 'A comparison of the Parables of the Gospel of Thomas and of the Synoptic Gospels', *NTS*, 7 (1961), 220–48.

34 *1 Clement*, 24.4–5. Compare *Thomas* Logion 9 and Matthew 13:3–9. See the present writer, 'The Gospel of Thomas. Is Rehabilitation possible?', *JTS*, n.s. 18 (1967), 21–3.

35 A. Henrichs and L. Koenen, 'Ein griechischer Mani-Codex', in *Zeitschrift für Papyrologie und Epigraphik*, 5.2 (1970), 97–216, 19 (1975), 1–85, 32 (1978), 78–199, 44 (1981), 201–318, and 48 (1982), 319–77.

36 Henrichs and Koenen, *Zeitschrift für Papyrologie und Epigraphik* (1970), 133 and following.

37 Ibid., 141.

38 Thus, Ephraem Syrus, *Prose Refutations of Mani, Marcion and Bardaisan*, ed. C. W. Mitchell, 2 vols., London 1912–21, vol. 2, p. xxxii.

39 As he makes clear in *Kephalaion* 154, cited from J. Stevenson, *A New Eusebius*, London 1957, p. 282.

40 The best account of Christian Nubia as recovered by the excavations at Faras and elsewhere from 1964 onward is in *Kunst und Geschichte Nubiens in christlicher Zeit*, ed. E. Dinkler, Recklinghausen 1970.

41 Celsus cited by Origen, *Contra Celsum* (ed. and ET by Henry Chadwick, Cambridge 1953), v. 59–65.

42 Thus, *1 Clement*, 40.1.

43 The phrase is of course H. E. W. Turner's, and the title of his distinguished work published in 1954.

44 For instance, Ps. 41 and 74, and from the Scrolls, see Millar Burrows, *More Light on the Dead Sea Scrolls*, London 1955, p. 95. The tradition of 'Ebionism' ('the Poor') is another that crosses the boundary between the Old Israel and the New. The possible links between the Ebionite, Montanist and Donatist traditions would be worth further research.

45 See my analysis in *Saints and Sinners in the Early Church*, London 1985, ch. 1.

Reason and the rule of faith in the second century AD

ERIC F. OSBORN

INTRODUCTION

Kanon (*euklees kai semnos*)[1] and *kriterion* were kingly words which lived and reigned for four hundred years in the philosophy of the hellenistic period. For they answered the questions: is there objective truth? How can it be known? To Stoics and Epicureans, who gave an affirmative answer to the first question, the answer to the second question was 'by following the criterion or canon'. For the Sceptics who denied truth, its proposed canon was the target of their attack. *Regula* (*kanon*) also had a common legal application as a summary principle which governed any situation within a certain definition, but Cicero is the chief Latin source.[2] Since Tertullian has commonly been regarded as more of a lawyer than he was, the legal definition has seemed more useful than the philosophical; this is not the case and we shall find a strong philosophical interest in the Christian use of this concept.

The rule of truth or faith is central to the emergence of orthodoxy. It has been regarded either as restrictive to the use of reason (Celsus made it central in his attack) or (by nineteenth-century liberals) as the decline into intellectualism which reduced a gospel to a set of doctrines. In the hands of Tertullian it begins as a barrier to enquiry. Arguing about scripture is useless and uncertain; only the rule is decisive and apostolic. The rule is enough; after Christ there is no place for argument (*De praescriptione hereticorum*, hereafter *Praescr.*, (7). Clement demands the rule as a starting point but insists on inquiry, while Irenaeus regards the apostolic preaching as proved from scripture. There is no way of separating fideist from rationalist among these writers. Yet the question remains: was the chief concern to limit reason to make room for faith or to use faith to make room for reason? Both Clement and Tertullian argue for the place of reason in their debate against Gnostics, who opted out of reason at the beginning of their speculations instead of the end, when reason could go no further.

CANON AND CRITERION

Kriterion (a means of judging) is found in philosophers after Plato who had used it to explain Protagoras' man as the measure of all things 'having in himself the criterion for these things' (*Theaetetus* 178b; cf. also *Republic* 582a).[3] The *kanon* of Epicurus is probably the first work devoted to the exposition of the theory of criteria.[4] Elsewhere, in a fragment from *On Nature*,[5] Epicurus insists that without a canon which discriminates (*epikrinon*) opinions, no enquiry is possible and the foolish will be encouraged.

Kanon is a straight stick, used for testing straightness or measuring length. Aristotle explains: 'by means of the straight line we know both itself and the curved — the carpenter's rule enables us to test both — but what is curved does not enable us to distinguish either itself or the straight'.[6] Lucretius saw that a faulty rule produced disaster:

> denique et in fabrica, si pravast regula prima,
> normaque si fallax rectis regionibus exit
> et libella aliqua si ex parti claudicat hilum,
> omnia mendosa fieri atque obstipa necesse est (*De rerum natura*, 4.513–16)

Lucretius uses three words (*regula, norma, libella*) to explain the importance of the canon for building.[7] Without a canon there is no security (*De rerum natura* 4.505–6):

> et violare fidem primam et convellere tota
> fundamenta quibus nixatur vita salusque

Since a canon is a means of judging, legal terminology is frequently found in philosophical use. By means of sensations, one judges what is true and false. Judgment involves assessing testimony for and testimony against.[8] A dispute is to be settled by the sensations whose testimony is unshakeable.[9] The *kanon* of Epicurus is described by Seneca as *de iudicio et regula*,[10] and by Cicero (with a sarcasm later taken up by Plutarch) as if the rule had fallen from heaven, *ad quam omnia iudica rerum derigantur*.[11]

In his canon and criteria, Epicurus is less concerned with epistemology than with a theory of knowledge which can move from the known to further knowledge.[12] Stoicism with its grasping impressions,[13] offered a straightforward epistemology. If there is a *kataleptike phantasia* that p, then p is the case.[14] The relation between Zeno and Chrysippus on this question has been confused and the Stoic account absorbed the Epicurean account. Epictetus talks about *prolepseis* and *koinai ennoiai*, and makes much of the concept of *kanon*,[15] but does not speak of the first as criteria. The purpose of philosophy is to find the rule which distinguishes truth from appearance or to investigate and establish rules which, though apprehended directly, require rational clarification and application. An examination of Epicurus and the Stoics reveals three distinct ways of understanding canon and criteria.[16] The permanence of the theme is evident in Cicero and in Albinus, who begins his account of Platonic dialectic with a discussion of the *kriterion* (*Didaskalikon* 4).

It is wise not to claim too much for those who supported science against scepticism. Epicurus was attacked by Cicero (*De finibus* 1.6.18ff.) for his account of atomic swerve. The criticism was misguided because Epicurus was concerned with ethical questions rather than scientific explanation. Atomic swerve gave grounds for free will against determinism. Again, without making a choice, Epicurus offers multiple, inconsistent explanations of the same thing; he is concerned with moral indifference, with *ataraxia*, freedom from fear and necessity rather than pure science.[17] As the philosopher of the ordinary man, he found value in philosophy only if it relieved mental anguish, and in astronomy only if it bestowed tranquillity and confidence.[18]

A final contribution of Epicurus to the theme of *kanon* was his anticipation of the fourth century *stoicheiosis*, which required that teaching be presented concisely and memorably.[19] Proclus found in Euclid the necessary qualities: removal of superfluities, coherence conducive to a proposed end, clarity, conciseness, comprehensiveness through generalization.[20] The ten *stoicheiomata* of the *Letter to Herodotus* begin: 'Nothing comes into being out of nothing', and end 'Atoms share only three of the characteristics of sensible things: shape, weight, mass' (*Epistula ad Herodotum* 38.8–54.6).[21] Here again the purpose of Epicurus is to preserve his followers from destabilization – *ataraxia* is all.

RULE, BAPTISM AND TRUTH

The rule of faith, like many theological simplicities, is surrounded by an historical jungle which obscures its exact place and by a liturgical jungle which obscures its exact use. It has been argued that the church universal was governed by three norms, one of which was the rule of faith which developed out of the baptismal confession.[22] While the first claim has been overstated and justly criticized,[23] the three norms are treated in close proximity by Tertullian (*Praescr.* 21, 32 and 36). 'From the consideration of these three passages', argued Harnack, 'it directly follows that three standards are to be kept in view, viz., the apostolic doctrine, the apostolic canon of scripture, and the guarantee of apostolic authority, afforded by the organisation of the Church, that is, by the episcopate, and traced back to apostolic institution. It will be seen that the Church always adopted these three standards together, that is simultaneously.'[24] While the interdependence of the ideas is clear, their relation cannot be defined with precision. The baptismal hypothesis must be rejected; it was once confidently claimed that by the middle of the second century the Roman church had a fixed baptismal creed which was the source of the rule of faith.[25] This theory was based on two false assumptions – that the rule of faith was the same as the creed and that declaratory creeds were always used in baptism; but it is useless to look to the baptismal liturgy as the source for declaratory creeds at this time.[26]

With the rejection of documentary theories, several alternative approaches have emerged. One influential account has turned to the church as the fundamental reality.[27] Irenaeus includes under the rule the plain teaching of scripture, the doctrine preached by the apostles as transmitted by the succession and taught in the churches. It is the body of which the different doctrines are members (*Adversus haereses* 1.1.15, hereafter *AH*), the formula for the interpretation of scripture, in sum, the living doctrine of the churches (p. 291).

In Tertullian, also, the rule of faith is the doctrine itself and the genitive is subjective. In Clement the rule concerns the distinction between true believer and heretic, dividing truth of church from error of heretics. The norm is the church itself, which disposes sources of truth and preserves them intact (p. 314). The secondary questions and the discipline of the church are subordinate to the unchanging doctrines of one God, one revelation and one economy of salvation (p. 319). Irenaeus and his successors merely systematized ideas which were already present: 'l'église a simplement légitimé et renforcé des normes qu'elle possédait déjà; elle n'a pas eu à s'en créer de nouvelles'.[28] The difficulty of this view is that tension was not uncommon within the church between its government and its doctrine. Tertullian and Origen anticipate later differences.

A variant on this view looks to the catechumenate as the social locus of the rule to explain its importance and variations. Tertullian's rule of faith is identifiable, verbal, bipartite and verbally variable. It is an oral composition, performed by catechists, and 'chosen from old and familiar elements of Christian teaching' to combat the heresies of the second century.[29] All of which sounds reasonable, were it not for the variety of old and familiar elements in early Christian teaching. W. Bauer and A. le Boulluec have shown the great variety of early Christianity which makes these explanations hard to accept.[30]

The elusive nature of the evidence is evident in the attempt to identify a 'secret tradition' in Clement as often 'nothing else than an interpretation of the Scriptures', 'the church's rule of faith', 'the church's *kanon*', where every inspiration or intuition derived from teachers is a tradition.[31] Such vagueness supports the conclusion of another scholar that Clement does not withhold a secret tradition (p. 70), for Clement is concerned with a limited audience and not with a private secret. The decisive medical analogy is linked to the total truthfulness of the Gnostic even if he 'sometimes' therapeutically withholds information (*Stromateis*, 7.9.53, hereafter *S*). Granted that Clement may have intended and achieved some confusion in this area, when 'Clement has confused in his theory of secret tradition at least three separate things' (p. 71), it would be useful to speak of such a theory as a thing of straw.

As scholarly opinion moves towards the rule as a totality of truth, the relevance to baptism does not disappear. For a *narratio* or *exegesis* is integral to baptismal liturgy,[32] as a declaration of 'what is preached in the church'. The theme is God's care for man from creation to resurrection, a divine order against which life may be rightly lived. Gnostics and Sophists claimed that truth was determined by human opinion and not by an external order. Irenaeus attacks the Gnostics because they do not have an order and rule but emulate the indifference of the Cynics and boast of a teacher 'qui non solum a malis operibus avertit suos discipulos, sed etiam a sermonibus et cogitationibus' (*AH* 2.49.1) (p. 456). The last three chapters of the *Epideixis* declare that to follow the preaching of the truth is to follow the way of life which is the human response to the work of Father, Son and Holy Spirit.

The challenge of the sophistic movement was one cause of the rule of faith. Clement attacks Sophists persistently because they deny objective truth and deal in verbal tricks. This is borne out by recent discussion, in which the rule can be identified neither with baptismal symbol nor with any derivatives, but with the totality of Christian truth as set down in holy scripture.[33] For Irenaeus, the rule is the original truth which the church preserves as true and firm knowledge of God. With the truth itself and God's open testimony, there is no excuse for wandering into other opinions and questions (*AH* 2.28.1). For Irenaeus truth stands in the centre of all theology, one and absolute, over against the different 'truths' of the Gnostics. When he speaks of the *somation* of truth (*AH* 1.9.4) in contrast to the *plasma* of the heretics he is not referring to a book or collection of writings. The mosaic of a king which Gnostics have turned into a fox points to the coherence of the truth (*AH* 1.8.1). There is only one teaching and message of salvation and one reconciliation wrought in Christ who was truly incarnate. This truth is less a form of words than the events of creation and redemption. Its coherence is underlined by the metaphor of a melody which the harmony of different parts of scripture conveys to those who received the rule of baptism (*AH* 1.9.4). Irenaeus often refers to individual texts or books of the Bible as a 'rule of truth'. 'The concept of scripture and the *regula veritatis* really coincide' for scripture bears witness to the truth and to the order of creation.[34] This is what the apostles handed down (*AH* 3.4.1) and conserved. The rule of truth is the saving revelation of Father, Son and Holy Spirit in creation and redemption; to this truth baptismal confession, scripture and preaching bear witness.

For Tertullian the rule is a fixed form, unshakeable, irreformable, identical with the totality of revelation from God, and prior to all heresy. It runs straight back to the apostles and Christ. Heresy is secondary; truth is primary, total and the same in its many presentations.

Clement of Alexandria describes the rule of the church as truth in contrast to philosophy and heresy, as the *arche tes didaskalias* which leads back to the words and works of Jesus and on to true gnosis. It is both saving revelation of Christ and ultimate reality. The only first principle is Christ himself who speaks through prophets and apostles but the rule of the church leads to him through the agreement and harmony of law, prophets and gospel (*S* 6.15.125).[35]

The rule is defined by an objective truth which stands over against the endless mutability of human opinion. The rule of truth or faith has both a subjective and an objective genitive. Truth imposes its rule, for the power of the tradition (*AH* 1.10.1-2) is universal and those who receive it are passive in its transmission. The early teachers were concerned to guard the truth of the preaching *ten aletheian tou kerugmatos* (Eusebius, *Historia ecclesiastica* v.28.3, hereafter *HE*). The absence of declaratory creeds in the second and third centuries is less important than the constantly expressed conviction that there is one rule of truth.

ERIC F. OSBORN

All of which is confirmed by a still more recent study which sees the canon of truth as the ground, within the church, of all particular doctrines, and as the fullness of right belief found in scripture and tradition.[36] As for Clement, so for Irenaeus, it is the true gnosis (*AH* 4.33.7) (p. 166). Under the heading 'Ratio und Regula', Irenaeus is seen to present the rationality of the divine economy (*credibile, acceptabile, constans*) in contrast to the irrationality of the gnostic accounts (*incredibile, fatuum, impossibile, inconstans*) (p. 202).

NEW TESTAMENT, RULE AND TRUTH

'Ad quam regulam Galatae sint correcti' (Tertullian, *Adversus Marcionem* 4.5.1). Much has been written on credal formulae in the New Testament. What was the logical role of 'rule' and 'truth' in the exposition of Christian belief? Over against scepticism and sophistry, or against gnostic deconstruction, Christians could return to Paul's denunciation of the Galatians, the first upwardly mobile Christians to face the two persistent questions: what must I do to be saved? What must I do to be a superior Christian to my neighbour? The Galatians, who reasoned that *both–and* was superior to *either–or*, had to learn the axiom that there was one gospel, one rule of truth. No one in their right mind would try to improve on it. Commenting on Galatians 1:6, Theodore of Mopsuestia describes the astonishment of Paul that the Galatians had been carried over like lifeless objects 'non dixit *transducimini*, sed *transferimini*, quasi in exanimes aliquos, et qui animi motum non habeant'. While the place of transfer is called another gospel 'ut videatur plenaria pietatis', it is nothing of the kind, because it is not true. 'ut ostendat quoniam non illis praeponit se sed veritatem vindicat.' It does not matter who speaks or where on earth or heaven they come from; if they preach another gospel they are to be anathema. 'de caelo adiecit, ut neque loci dignitas, neque personae coniunctio *exaequari umquam veritati* posse existimetur.' Nothing is of any worth beside the truth which has been declared. Paul defends the violence of his anathema on the grounds that he was moved *pro veritate*. It is not a matter of persuading God or pleasing man; God revealed his Son to the most improbable persecutor, who then went into Arabia.[37]

Tertullian links the rule specifically to Galatians 6:16 (*Marc.* 4.5.1 and *Praescr.* 37.1). At the climax of the letter (Galatians 6:14–16) Paul gives a statement of the Christian canon: Christ crucified and the new creation. For good reason, says Theodore, he uses strong language; 'absit; quia qui devotat se, ne aliquando in aliud aliquid magnum sapiat cupit'. By his coming, Christ has renewed all things so that everything else is dissolved and Paul looks to the incorruptible and immortal, 'omnium illorum quae in lege sperantur erit renovatio. haec enim nobis Christus per suam providit crucem; in qua etiam magna semper superopto, non illam ignobilitatem quae videtur erubesci, sed illa lucra quae exinde adnascuntur considerans. et confidens magnitudini rerum, adicit: *et quicumque regulam hanc sectantur, pax super illos et misericordia, et super Israel Dei.*' He wants all who have chosen this rule to enjoy the benefits of peace and mercy which flow from it and his final reference to the Spirit is a provision for the resurrection in which the keeping of the law can have no place.[38]

For Paul there is no distinction between the gospel, the kerygma and the rule; it is concerned with the recital or proclamation of an event: Christ and him crucified. Verbal identity is impossible because words change, and inappropriate because truth is too big for words unless they too are seen as events.[39]

Augustine comments in similar terms on the autonomy of the gospel. There cannot be another gospel beyond that which the Lord gave. Trouble comes from those who *want* to pervert the gospel, which 'manet firmissimum: sed tamen convertere volunt'. That is why 'Paul does not say they pervert, but that they want to pervert.' The gospel is independent of any messenger, however angelic. 'Veritas propter seipsam diligenda est, non propter hominem, aut propter angelum, per quem annuntiatur. Qui enim propter annuntiatores diligit eam, potest etiam mendacia diligere si qua forte ipsi sua protulerint' (*Expositio epistolae ad Galatas = Ep. ad Gal.* 4). Paul goes on to speak of the folly of pleasing men, or persuading God whom no one persuades because everything is manifest to him; but he persuades men well 'qui non se illis placere vult, sed ipsam quam suadet veritatem'. An intricate piece of reasoning follows. He who pleases men for their salvation is actually pleasing God, so that it is one thing to please men and another to please God and men. Truth is all. 'Item qui hominibus propter veritatem placet non jam ipse illis sed veritas placet' (*Ep. ad Gal.* 5).

When Augustine comes to the statement of the rule, he sees it as a statement about reality and the order of things. The world is crucified to Paul so that it has no hold on him; Paul is crucified to the world so that he does not hold on to it. The new creature is what must be noted. 'Novam creaturam dicit novam per fidem Jesu Christi: et notandum verbum est. Difficile enim inveneris creaturam vocari etiam eos, qui iam credendo in adoptionem filiorum venerunt.' The future liberation of the creature will leave the old humanity behind and those who follow this rule are those who are truly being prepared for the vision of God (*Ep. ad Gal.* 62f.).

The Johannine account of divine truth is also an important element in the complex of ideas which surround the rule of faith or rule of truth. The exclusiveness and autonomy of the Christ who says 'I am truth' and 'All who came before me were thieves and robbers' derives from his uniqueness as the *monogenes* of the Father, the Word who was in the beginning and was God. The unknown God is seen by no man, the *monogenes* in the bosom of the Father has told his story. Exclusive truth leads to argument in the long disputations (chapters 7–10).

Truth is for John a reality of history, the revelation present in Jesus Christ and the divine economy. 'La vérité appartient à ce que les théologiens appellent "l'économie": la venue de la vérité est un *événement* fondamental dans l'histoire de la révélation, l'événement de grâce (Jn 1,17) qui ouvre les temps eschatologiques.'[40] Jesus is not the eternal truth who becomes incarnate, for it is only in his becoming man, in his flesh, that he is the truth. 'Cette *révélation du Christ*, cette *vérité*, devait atteindre son point culminant à la Croix' (p. 1011). In the man Jesus, his sonship and submission to the Father, are to be seen the image of the relation of the Father to the Son. For John, 'la vérité est ce dévoilement de la vie profonde de Jésus'.[41] It becomes a principle of new life for the believer, who does, knows and loves the truth in which he walks and in which he sanctifies himself.

It has been shown that the rule was a matter of logic and that Christian truth, because of its exclusive revelation, generated argument from the beginning. To abandon it was not merely wrong but unreasonable. However, it is only in the writings of the second-century fathers that argument moves to the centre. To establish this we must look at the function of the rule in an extended passage from each of three writers.

IRENAEUS: THE POWER OF PREACHING

The rule is a statement of what Christians believe and preach. Brevity is a distinctive quality of Christian truth. In contrast to the long-windedness of the law, God gave, in Christ, a short word[42] which summed up all that was needed for man's salvation. He was salvation *in compendio*,[43] and therefore his truth could be expressed in a *somation* in contrast to the *plasma* of the heretics.[44] Similarly, both Clement and Tertullian attack the verbosity of heretics and extol the simplicity of faith; Justin praises the terse brevity of the words of Jesus, who was no Sophist, but whose word was the power of God (*Apol.* 1.14) and defines right dogma at his trial: one God, who has existed from the beginning, maker and framer of all creation, and one Lord Jesus Christ, Son of God, promised by prophets as the bearer of salvation and the master of true disciples. Such a concise response is required by the circumstances of a trial. Brevity did not mean the avoidance of argument. Irenaeus wrote a *proof of the apostolic preaching*. In the third book of the *Against Heresies* he announces that he will bring proofs from the scriptures in the fight against falsehood and for the defence of the only true and life-giving faith. The preaching of the apostles declares one God and one Christ; to deny their preaching is to deny their Lord (3.1) Heretics claim a secret tradition which puts them above the apostles and alone leads to purity of truth (3.2.2). Such slippery opponents have to be handled with rigour. Argument is *for, by, and from* the rule of faith.

1. *Argument* for *the rule of faith is historical, scriptural and necessarily public*

The tradition of the apostles is public and open to the world; they would not have kept secrets from those to whom they committed the care of the churches. The successions of all churches cannot be listed, says Irenaeus, but Rome is the most important; its succession is clear, providing overwhelming proof that one life-giving faith, one apostolic truth, has been handed down (3.3). Other churches provide supporting historical evidence as proof of the truth which the apostles deposited for later transmission. The unlettered believer who receives this ancient tradition finds the highest wisdom and will reject the novelties of heretics who arrived too late for access to original truth (3.4.2). The truth of Christ can be proved from scripture. His disciples were concerned to impart this truth and not, as heretics suggest, to hide it and to send blind men along false paths (3.5.2). Law and prophets are insistent upon the first point of faith: that there is one God (3.6). Paul is explicit on the same central point; heretical objections, which are based on 2 Corinthians 4:5 and Matthew 6:24, receive a reasonable answer. It is proved that there is no reasonable ground for finding a second God anywhere in scripture. Many passages from the gospels prove the one unique God and Father, declared by prophets and true gospel (3.10). Actions speak as loudly as words: as when the Lord took

ERIC F. OSBORN

the bread or the wine supplied from creation and then made more of each, declaring the unity of creator and redeemer (3.11.5). Nor can the first-principles of the gospel be evaded by those who use only parts of the gospels; their errors can be demonstrated even within their limited scriptural base (3.11.7). There have to be four gospels because the gospel is universal and there are four winds, and because the gospel gives life and living creatures are tetramorphic; God creates with due proportion and harmonizes the outward aspect of the gospel with its true nature (3.11.8f.). Extended examination of other apostolic writings confirms the unicity of God (3.12). The claim that only Paul knew the truth is refuted: the Lord would not have come just to save one man, nor would God have been so ineffective as to produce only one apostle who understood the plan of salvation in Christ (3.13). It is equally unreasonable to suppose that Paul kept secrets to himself and denied them to Luke, his constant companion (3.14).

2. *Argument* by *the rule of faith is its internal coherence*

The summing up of all things in Christ, who is perfect God and perfect man, is the entirely consistent act of Him who does nothing incomplete or out of due time (3.16.6). The incarnation summed up the human race and provided salvation in a concise *compendium*, so that those who in Adam had lost the image and likeness of God, might regain it in Christ. Man was helpless to overcome his enemy, so the word incarnate came to complete the plan of salvation (3.18.2). Yet it was necessary for a man to conquer man's enemy, as it was necessary for salvation to come from God, the only source of incorruption (3.18.6f.). So Jesus, in whom man could find incorruption, had to be God (3.19.1). (Irenaeus is here following a straightforward logic of participation, as Justin had before him, when he insisted on the difference between life in itself and that which participates in life.) Further argument is used to defend Isaiah 7:14 against the interpretations of Theodotion, Aquila, Ebionites and Jews (3.21), before returning to the Pauline parallel of Adam and Christ and expanding the consequences which might be drawn from it (3.21.10). Still more argument is needed to defend these claims against Tatian (3.23).

3. *Argument* from *the rule of faith rejects the inconsistencies of heretics*

Irenaeus draws the argument of the book together. Heretics have been defeated by their own arguments which have been shown to point in the opposition direction to that which they desire. The preaching of the church has been proved entirely consistent with itself and with the whole testimony of prophets, apostles and disciples, so that saving faith is grounded on a sound system of proof. Meanwhile the heretics wallow in error, playing with words instead of following truth (3.24.1f.), so the closing words are given to a prayer, that they might be rescued from the pit which they dug for themselves, and might leave empty shadows behind for a knowledge of the only true God and Lord of all. In the next book, says Irenaeus, he will try again, using the very words of Christ to convince some of them and to persuade them to abandon error and blasphemy against the Father and the Lord Jesus Christ (3.25.7).

CLEMENT OF ALEXANDRIA: THE POWER OF TRUTH

Clement argues for a dialectic of faith and knowledge. There is no knowledge without faith; the only basis for knowledge is belief in the first principles contained in the rule of the church. There is no faith without knowledge for faith cannot stand still; it must grow into knowledge like the mustard seed of the gospel. Clement argues against those who want knowledge without faith (philosophers and Gnostics) and against those who want faith without knowledge (simple believers). His arguments for the necessity of faith include the need for an indemonstrable first principle to stop the infinite regress against which Irenaeus and Tertullian also warned. His arguments for knowledge include the necessity of philosophy, which would have to be used in order to prove its own redundancy. Clement talks about truth in two ways;[45] it can be the essential elements of Christian belief or it can be everything which is consistent with Christian belief. The first use is that which concerns the present study and is clearly presented in the case against heresy in *Stromateis* 7.15–18.89–111. In Clement as in Irenaeus there is argument for, by, and from faith.

1. *Argument* for *faith begins from the objection to Christian plurality*

The variety of its sects is a major objection against Christianity. Clement replies that Jews and philosophers who make this objection have just as many sects, that the Lord foretold tares among the wheat, and that every good thing is succeeded by a bad shadow. When others deny the confession which they have made in our presence, we are still bound to keep the rule of the church, the confession of the most important things. As no sick man denies himself treatment because there are different schools of medicine, so no idolater should deny himself health and conversion to God. Finally, heresies exist to test and develop the powers of *discernment* in those who are approved.

2. *Argument* by *faith is the critical distinction of true from false, of consistent from contradictory*

Truth is never easy to find and there is plenty of counterfeit coinage about; hard work and great care lead to the real truth about the true God. When real fruit and wax imitations are placed before us we make our choice by *kataleptike theoria* and *kuriotatos logismos*. Those who travel the safe and royal road will find out all they can about it. No gardener gives up because of the presence of weeds (!). There are many resources available to help find the *akolouthia* of truth and to distinguish what is contradictory, unseemly, contrary to nature and false from what is true, consistent, seemly and according to nature (*S* 7.15.91). All who wish may find the truth and those who make unreasonable excuses may be quickly dismissed. Most people will admit that proof is a possibility (Clement argues elsewhere against sceptical suspense of judgment) for total scepticism is senseless. Therefore we must get down to particular passages of scripture and find by demonstration that only in the truth and in the original church are the most accurate knowledge and the truly best *hairesis* (*S* 7.15.92). The many who disagree try to deceive themselves and sometimes their neighbours. Their pretensions are false because they cannot offer any proof and will not enter into logical discussion; yet they are clever enough to win followers through an effective mixture of plausibility and obscurity. None of which removes the fundamental distinction between plausibility and truth, a distinction which Sophists are pleased to ignore.

3. *Argument* from *faith toils at scripture to build a coherent account on the basis of faith's indemonstrable first principle*

Truth does not come easily but only after much mental toil at the scriptures, using rational procedures for separating true and false propositions. He who receives the gospel will not turn back from this toil and will receive truth from scriptures which remain barren to heretics. The lover of truth needs strength of soul, close adherence to the rule of truth, discrimination between true and false, and a critical awareness of what is essential. The Lord gives, through prophets, gospel and apostles, in different ways and at different times, all truth from beginning to end. If a more ultimate source be sought, then we should be caught in infinite regress. The only first principle is the voice of the Lord and from this all else is tested and proved. The methods of the heretics are *logically indefensible*: they do not use the whole of the scriptures but quote verses out of context, twisting ambiguous statements to suit their wishes, selecting random phrases, playing with words and changing the sense, preferring their own subjective judgment to the verdict of most of scripture and the plain arguments against their opinions. Heretics do not learn the mysteries of the church's knowledge (*S* 7.16.97), their minds are too small for the greatness of the truth and too lazy to ask fundamental questions. After superficial reading they put the scripture to one side and, starting from human opinion, compensate for their lack of truth and logic by strenuous verbosity. They are like eels in muddy water, easily trapped because they cannot see. They are like empty almond shells, because they do not contain the traditions of Christ. The believer does not desert the truth which has been assigned to him by the Word, but stands firm. When others are drawn into apostasy, they simply need the *akolouthia* of the testaments explained to them. The follower of the Lord becomes divine, so that deviation means falling from a great height.

The true Gnostic holds to the church's apostolic and right belief, grows old in the scripture, lives according to the gospel and discovers proofs in the law and the prophets. He must never, like the heretics, corrupt the truth or the canon of the church, but must always teach his neighbour to cling to the truth. The heretics (*S* 7.17.106) do not enter the church by the main door, which is the tradition of Christ, but cut a side door through the wall to constitute a human sect which denies the unity of the church. The church must be one because its God and Lord are one; when this unity is broken there can be no true church. Heretics are unclean animals because, despite their claim to part the hoof (i.e. to believe in Father and Son) they do not ruminate on the word and chew over the divine oracles (*S* 7.18.109). To the end Clement insists that the failure of the heretic is logical and intellectual; the rule of the church which guides the interpretation of scripture makes no sense apart from argument.

TERTULLIAN: THE POWER OF CHRIST; FINDING IS KEEPING

Tertullian, who is commonly classed as a fideist, argues more vigorously and persistently than any other writer of his time.

1. *Argument* for *faith insists on the need for a starting point*

Heretics have no fixed point in history or in logic from which to base their argument. For this reason they fail in two obvious ways: they regress infinitely in their argument, with a neurotic curiosity, and they divide incessantly into more and more sects which destroy the unity of the church. The rule of faith provides a basis for reasoning which limits the fantasy of heretics and unites the church universal.

Heresies should not surprise anyone, for they were predicted and they provide an essential test for the proving of faith (*Praescr.* 1). Like a fever they should be an object of loathing rather than of wonder which can bring those of weak faith to fall under their power (2). Only the Son of God has persevered sinless to the end, but this perseverance is now required of every Christian. There have always been traitors, from the time of Judas on, so no one should be shocked by the sight of deserters (3). The possibility of apostasy gives point to perseverance in the true faith (4). Heresies are linked by Paul with schisms because they are the greater evil and the cause of divisions; only where there is common thought and speech can the true community be found. There can be no church where there is no logical harmony of belief (5). Paul explains further that a heretic is a self-condemned man because his error is something chosen (*hairesis*) (6). There is no continuity between this world's wisdom and the truth of Christ. For the former is found in philosophy which, like heresy, *keeps turning over* the questions of evil and human origins. It consists, as Paul put it, in fictitious tales and endless genealogies, futile questions and words which spread like a cancer. Therefore philosophy must not be connected with Christ whose gospel is all-sufficient (7).

2. *Argument* by *faith both seeks and finds*

What then does the command 'Seek and you shall find' mean? For an answer, *logical analysis is necessary*, carefully determining the meaning of the words by the rational principle of all interpretation. No divine utterance is so incoherent and diffuse that its words can be considered apart from their logical context. The command makes sense if it means that Christ taught *one definite thing* (possessed by the church) which must be believed and which must be sought for the sole purpose of this clearly directed faith. This interpretation of the command is required by *the rule of reason*, for the command has *three parts*: matter, time and limit. These point to the three questions: what, when and how long we have to seek.

What is to be sought? Christ's teaching. When is it to be sought? Until it is found. When does seeking stop? When what is found is believed. The only point in seeking is to find and the only point in finding is to believe. Faith sets its own limit and there is no further point in seeking. If this limit is not accepted then sect after sect offers its invitation. 'Then I shall be nowhere and still be encountering the command "Seek and you shall find", just as if I had no resting-place, as if I had never found what Christ had taught, what it is proper to seek, what must be believed' (*Praescr* 10). The man without faith deserts nothing when he wanders away; his endless seeking, knocking and asking is the pathetic plight of one who has nothing to lose (11).

3. *Argument* from *faith continues to seek, but does not argue with heretics*

The believer continues to seek, but seeks within, from and about that which is his own, namely the church and its rule of faith (*Praescr.* 12). To know nothing against the rule is to know all things (14) and to be entitled to use scriptures which are forbidden to those who do not accept the correction of the community. Scripture warns against disputes with such heretics and argument over scripture can produce nothing but disorder of belly or of brain (16). For heretics either tamper with a text or pervert its interpretation by taking it out of context and mixing it with other texts which they have chosen for their ambiguity. Against this kind of biblicism, no one, however much they know about scripture, can make any progress (17). The only course is reference to the rule, the content of which was openly determined by the incarnate Lord, handed down by the apostles to the churches which they founded. 'Thus all are primitive, all are apostolic, all are one. Their unity is proved by their peaceful communion, title of brotherhood, token of hospitality – which rights no other reason directs than the one tradition of the same mystery' (20).

4. *Argument* from *faith derives from the existence of a universal church*

Here it might seem that Tertullian has abandoned his claim to reason for a tradition which is just as arbitrary as that of any gnostic sect. On the contrary he has turned to another argument which is based on the existence of a universal church; what is universal and undivided is the true church and its authenticity may be proved by its unity, communion, brotherhood and hospitality, signs which spring from the mystery which is its rule. From the present existence of a universal church he projects back a common faith to the beginning. 'It remains that we should demonstrate whether this our teaching, the rule of which we have given above, may be attributed to the tradition of the apostles, and for this reason, whether all other doctrines do not come from falsehood. We hold communion with apostolic churches because our doctrines do not differ: this is the attestation of our truth' (*Praescr.* 21). The argument is deceptive because it appears to be grounded on history; in fact it is grounded on the observable phenomenon of a universal church which believes itself to be descended from the apostles simply because it is universal and that is the kind of church which the apostles were told to establish. It is defended against two incompatible heretical objections to its universality: Jesus did not tell the apostles everything, and the omniscient apostles did not pass on all they knew to everyone. Both these objections are proved false from the text of scripture (22–5). The totality of truth was proclaimed by the apostles. A further objection – that the churches have wandered from the truth which the apostles taught their fathers – is answered by the argument that such errors would have produced many differences between the doctrines of the churches. It is impossible for all to have deviated into uniformity (28). The lateness of the heresies is evidence against their claim to the one truth; the good seed is sown first and the weeds come later, the tradition of the Lord is the original truth and the strange doctrines come later (31). There are episcopal lists in the older apostolic churches, but not in the sects. There is apostolic doctrine in recent churches which agrees with the doctrine of the whole church. These two tests are failed by the sects. Tertullian invites them to sift the evidence which he produces concerning the earliest churches – Corinth, Philippi, Thessalonica, Ephesus, Rome – and to note the unambiguous teaching which is found in all these places (36). Tertullian and his fellow Christians who walk according to the rule can claim this inheritance but heretics have no right to use the scriptures (37), which they misuse either by addition and subtraction or by rearrangement. Just as others have taken lines of Virgil and of Homer and stitched them together in a fantastic patchwork, so the heretics have done with scripture, which is easily manipulated in this way (39). Logic and church go together. Heretics have a lot to do with magicians, mountebanks, astrologers and philosophers because, without fear of God, they put no check of any sort on their curiosity. If there is no God, there is no truth, and if there is no truth there is no need of serious discipline. The wisdom that begins with the fear of God is marked by serious, thoughtful diligence, by fear and modesty. He who knows that truth will be revealed before the judgment seat of Christ will prove a more reliable source of truth than he who denies both truth and final judgment (43,44). Here the integrity of those to whom, in the beginning, was committed the gospel and the rule of faith, will be judged by him who is the beginning and the end.

So at every point Tertullian argues for the rationality of the rule and the irrationality of heresy. He argues for, by and from faith. In two other works he uses the rule of faith as part of the basis of his argument (*De virginibus velandis* 1; *Adversus Praxean* 2). In both cases there is development from the basic twofold structure which governs the rule.[46] In the first, the Paraclete is seen to be an essential addition to the law of faith, which does not change but needs the discipline of divine grace which moves forward to the end. Since the devil is always up to new tricks, the work of God must go on; so the Paraclete directs discipline, reveals scripture, remakes the mind and leads on to better things. Tertullian believes in one God even more now because of the better instruction of the Paraclete; his Montanist mind is not closed and restrained by the rule, he is moving on but not leaving the rule behind him.

CONCLUSION

The link of rule with argument has been established; the closer examination of that argument and its context will prove a rewarding study. The rule did not limit reason to make room for faith but used faith to make room for reason. Without a credible first principle, reason was lost in an infinite regress. Most heretics either played with sophistry or rejected discursive reason and indulged theosophical imagination, while sceptical Sophists believed it was better to travel hopelessly than to arrive. The chief exception was Marcion, who presented a clear case against the rule.

Since there are few aspects of theology which are not touched by the rule of faith, two comments must suffice. The failure of the quest lay in ecclesiology; the success lay in the concept of truth.

Limit, logic, definition, simplicity and truth were closely linked with the unity of a universal church which offered salvation. This unity derived from God through Christ, through the apostles and the tradition handed down within the churches. Irenaeus and Tertullian link the tradition unambiguously to the succession of bishops. For this they had little warrant in history,[47] but they projected back from the present reality of a church universal to the kind of history which could have produced it. Granted that they were wrong and that the primitive churches presented great variety, the question is whether the two standards of true preaching and episcopal authority were readily compatible. For Irenaeus, himself a bishop, there was no problem; but Tertullian and Origen found great difficulty. Within the last decade, the most effective Christian apologist, one of the few theologians to make an impact on secular Europe, has been disowned by custodians of tradition. His colleagues, who disagreed with him, pointed out, in an historic letter,[48] that Hans Küng had been able to reach far beyond them in his communication of Christian truth. Objections to his doctrine can be shown to have little substance, but it is easy to see why some bishops, with no Hegel, took them seriously. What was established by good logic (rule of faith) and bad history (episcopal succession) has been of value; but it has never provided the security which its founders wished.

The success of the second century was the affirmation that there was a true gospel; this was more important than any particular account of that gospel.[49] In an age when the truth of Christianity is still widely challenged, these writers recall the serious integrity of theology. While Irenaeus and Tertullian tell their jokes, they warn of the danger posed by any form of *theologia ludens*, Artemisian apologetic (sinking one's own ships) or that philosophy which is vain deceit. The recollection of humane integrity, which upholders of the rule preserved, is one reason for this essay dedicated, gratefully, to a teacher and friend.

NOTES

1 Clement of Rome, 1 Cor. 7:2 and Clement of Alexandria, *Stromateis*, 1.1.15.

2 P. Stein, *Regulae Iuris*, Edinburgh 1966, pp. 66f., cites Paul, *Ad Plautium* XVI: 'Regula est quae rem breviter enarrat. Non ex regula ius sumatur, sed ex iure quod est regula fiat.' For Cicero, see H. Oppel, KANON, *Philologus*, suppl. vol. 30 (1937), pp. 74f.

3 In this discussion I am indebted to G. Striker, *Kriterion tes aletheias*, *NAWG*: Phil. hist. Klasse, 1974, 1, pp. 47–110, and to the dissertation of Robin Jackson, of Ormond College, Melbourne, *Studies in the Epistemology of Greek Atomism*, Princeton 1982, especially pp. 238–49. Three collections of essays, *Doubt and Dogmatism* (Oxford 1980), *Science and Speculation* (Cambridge 1982), *The Norms of Nature* (Cambridge 1986), edited by M. Schofield and others, indicate the recent advances which have been made in understanding the philosophy of this period.

4 *peri kriteriou e kanon*. Listed tenth among the books of Epicurus, by Diogenes Laertius, *vitae* 10.28, and designated by the Epicureans as *peri*

kriteriou kai arches kai stoichiotaton, all words which explain the place of the canon (Diogenes Laertius, *vitae* 10.30). Diogenes Laertius says that the Epicureans regarded Canonice as the *ephodous* to their system.

5 Arrighetti fr. (34) 31, 11–27.

6 *De anima* 1.5, 41144, cited Jackson, p. 247.

7 Cf. H. Oppel, KANON, *Philologus*, 80f. and Jackson, *Studies*, p. 248.

8 Sextus Empiricus, M. VII 211–16.

9 Diogenes Laertius, *Vitae* 10.32.

10 *Epistulae morales* 89.11.

11 *De finibus* 1.19.61ff. Cf. Plutarch, *Adversus Colotem* 19, 1118. See C. Bailey, *The Greek Atomists and Epicurus*, Oxford 1928, p. 238, who notes that for Epicurus sensation was unquestionable because it was irrational and because there was no other criterion to test it. Diogenes Laertius, *Vitae*, 10.31.

12 Striker, *Kriterion tes aletheias*, p. 82.

13 Sextus Empiricus, M. VII 248, 426.

14 Striker, *Kriterion*, p. 90.

15 *Dissertationes* I. 28, 28–30; II. 11, 13–25; II. 20, 21; III. 3, 14–15; IV. 12, 12; *Enchiridion* 1.5.

16 Striker, *Kriterion*, p. 102.

17 A. Wasserstein, "Epicurean Science', *Hermes*, 106 (1978), 484–94.

18 *Epistula ad Pythoclem* 85; cf. *Epistula ad Herodotum* 37.81–4; *Epistula ad Menoeceum* 122. A. A. Long, "Aisthesis, Prolepsis and Linguistic Theory in Epicurus', *BICS*, 18 (1971), 114–34.

19 D. Clay, 'Epicurus' Last Will and Testament', *AGPh*, 55 (1973), 252–80.

20 Proclus, *In primum Euclidis elementorum commentarii*, 73.25–74.9. Cited D. Clay, *AGPh*, 55 (1973).

21 Ibid., 260f.

22 A. von Harnack, *History of Dogma*, vol. 2, London 1896, translated from the third German edition, p. 20.

23 H. von Campenhausen, *The Formation of the Christian Bible*, London 1972, p. 329.

24 A. von Harnack, *History of Dogma*, vol. 2, p. 19.

25 See C. P. Caspari, *Quellen zur Geschichte des Taufsymbols und des Glaubensregels*, 3 vols., 1866–75; *Alte und neue Quellen zur Geschichte des Taufsymbols und des Glaubensregels*, 1879. See also F. Kattenbusch, *Das Apostolische Symbol, vol. 2, Verbreitung und Bedeutung des Taufsymbols*, Leipzig 1900 and Hildesheim 1967.

26 J. N. D. Kelly, *Early Christian Creeds*, London 1952, pp. 63f.

27 D. van den Eynde, *Les normes de l'enseignement chrétien, dans la littérature patristique des trois premiers siècles*, Gembloux and Paris 1933.

28 Ibid., p. 322. The uniformity, it is claimed, which the church provided at this time covered ideas of revelation, scripture, tradition and their mutual relations, together with its understanding of itself and its bishops. Other

matters, like the development of faith and the primacy, were not yet fixed.

29   L. W. Countryman, 'Tertullian and the Regula Fidei', *The Second Century*, 2 (1982), 226.

30   W. Bauer, *Orthodoxy and Heresy in Earliest Christianity*, Philadelphia 1971; Alain le Boulluec, *La notion d'hérésie dans la littérature grecque IIe-IIIe siècles*, 2 vols., Paris 1985.

31   R. P. C. Hanson, *Origen's Doctrine of Tradition*, London 1954, pp. 58–70.

32   See V. Grossi, 'Regula veritatis e narratio battesimale in sant'Ireneo', *Aug*, 12 (1972), 437–63.

33   This is the thesis of B. Hägglund, 'Die Bedeutung der "regula fidei" als Grundlage theologischer Aussagen', *Studia Theologica*, 12 (1958), 1–44, whose argument is set out in the remainder of this paragraph. Hägglund acknowledges his debt to J. Kunze, *Glaubensregel, Heilige Schrift und Taufbekenntnis*, Leipzig 1899.

34   Hägglund, *Studia Theologica*, 12 (1958), 14.

35   Ibid.

36   N. Brox, *Offenbarung, Gnosis und gnostischer Mythos bei Irenäus von Lyon*, Salzburg and Munich 1966, pp. 105f.

37   *Theodori Episcopi Mopsuesteni in Epistolas B. Pauli Commentarii*, ed. H. B. Swete, Cambridge 1880, vol. 1, pp. 9–14.

38   Ibid., 108–11. On the significance of this passage for Tertullian see R. Braun, '*Deus Christianorum*'. *Recherches sur le vocabulaire doctrinal de Tertullien*, Paris 1962 pp. 447–51, 'Le prestige d'un énoncé scripturaire (Gal. 6.16) explique peut-être l'emploi absolu qu'il en fait' (p. 451).

39   These two points could be developed in a larger context. Logic of events has little to do with the mighty acts of God as understood in the 1950s. See U. Wilckens, *Der Brief an die Römer*, vol. 1, Zurich, Einsiedeln, Cologne 1978, pp. 330–7, for a starting point into 'das Wesen der christologischen Geschehens-Logik'.

40   I. de la Potterie, *La vérité dans Saint Jean* vol. 2, Rome 1977, p. 1010. This massive work discredits existentialist and Platonic accounts of John and shows the originality of his concept of truth. He refers to the interesting work of J. D. Zizioulas, whose recent *Being as Communion*, London 1985, sees Johannine truth as communion without logic, the key concept of the early fathers and the hope of the twentieth century. However, in the second century, communion without logic is a gnostic preserve.

41   Ibid. p. 1012. It is impossible to do justice to the richness of de la Potterie's work in this brief reference.

42   *epideixis* 87.

43   *AH* 3.18.1. For the seven formulae of the rule in this work, see pp. 209–16, A. Benoit, *Saint Irénée, Introduction à l'étude de sa théologie*, Paris 1960, and the conclusion. 'L'unité demeure sa note fondamentale; elle est comme Dieu, le Christ, l'Evangile, la Tradition et la foi, une et toujours la même.'

44 *AH* 1.9.4.

45 See E. F. Osborn, *The Philosophy of Clement of Alexandria*, Cambridge 1957, pp. 113–78.

46 See J. M. Restrepo-Jaramillo, 'La doble formula simbólica en Tertulliano', *Gregorianum* 15 (1934), 57f.

47 W. Telfer, *The Office of a Bishop*, London 1962, p. 119.

48 Letter to Bishop Moser from members of the Catholic faculty at Tübingen, 19 December 1979, see pp. 118f. of *Der Fall Küng, Eine Dokumentation*, ed. N. Greinacher and H. Haag, Munich 1980. On the relevance of truth, see also R. Nowell, *A Passion for Truth, Hans Küng and his Theology*, London 1981 and Walter Jens (ed.), *Um nichts als die Wahrheit, Deutsche Bischofskonferenz contra Hans Küng, Eine Dokumentation*, Munich 1978.

49 For limitations which turn into advantages see R. A. Greer, in J. L. Kugel and R. A. Greer, *Early Biblical Interpretation*, Philadelphia 1986, p. 198.

Adam in Origen

C. P. BAMMEL

Western discussion of the fall has been dominated by the views expressed by Augustine during the course of the Pelagian controversy. Just over a decade before the outbreak of this controversy, with the condemnation of Caelestius at Carthage for denying that Adam's sin injured the rest of the human race, the late fourth-century Origenist disputes had been terminated by the pronouncements of Theophilus of Alexandria and Anastasius of Rome against the heretical teachings attributed to Origen. Up to this date the rival theories on the origin of the human soul (creationism, traducianism or pre-existence) had been a matter for open discussion. Augustine himself had aired all three in his *De libero arbitrio* and sometimes speaks in his earlier writings of sin and the fall in terms that can best be understood of an individual fall in a previous existence.[1] Meanwhile opponents of Origenism were rejecting not only the theory of the fall of the pre-existent soul but also the suggestion that Adam's fall implicated the subsequent human race[2] and were propounding what seemed a naively optimistic view of the human condition. Pelagius himself, although strongly influenced by Origen's anti-gnostic emphasis on human free will, came to adopt this anti-Origenist optimism with regard to the fall, whereas Augustine in attacking Pelagianism retained Origen's view of the human condition in this life as a fallen one but, because of his rejection of the theory of pre-existence, placed the whole burden of responsibility for this condition on Adam's sin and condemnation.

Despite the fact, therefore, that Origen's views on the fall were not themselves adopted *in toto* by subsequent orthodoxy, they did play a very significant role in the development of that orthodoxy. Consideration of them only in relation to later controversy, however, is likely to result in over-simplification. In Origen's own time questions concerning not only the origin of the soul but also the significance of Adam's fall were wide open. Origen was faced with a confusing variety of earlier Jewish, Christian and gnostic views and of relevant texts in the Bible itself and in apocryphal literature.[3] It is not least because of the way that he attempts to do justice to this variety that a study of his own pronouncements on the subject of Adam is of interest.

The student who first encounters Origen and learns that he allegorized the story of Adam's fall in Genesis and at the same time that he believed that every soul has fallen before its entry into the body can easily gain the impression that Origen denied the existence of Adam as an individual and interpreted the story of his fall only as symbolizing the fall of every man's soul. This assumption is incorrect.[4]

In this paper the view will be presented that Origen did regard Adam as a historical figure, as the first man and the ancestor of the human race. The story of the garden of Eden and the fall does include details which cannot be taken literally even on the narrative level, but it none the less really happened, while at the same time, like other Old Testament stories, pointing to hidden mysteries and containing deeper levels of meaning as well.

The subject under consideration would more appropriately be examined in a book than in a brief paper. It involves questions which have been frequently debated by scholars and on which much has been written in recent years. These associated questions can only be touched on here with the utmost brevity. In view of the loss of the main source for Origen's views on Adam, his *Commentary on Genesis*, it would have been desirable to describe the interpretation of Adam's story in earlier and later writers likely to have influenced or been influenced by Origen. Here there is only room for a brief comparison with the relevant parts of the *Commentary on Genesis* of Didymus the Blind. It is also necessary to bear in mind that to ask the question 'What was Origen's teaching about Adam and his fall?' may be misconceived. In the majority of his works, Origen's aim is to expound scripture and to reflect the complexity of scripture. He discusses the problems raised by the biblical text and searches for parallel passages that may provide illumination, airs rival views and arguments, but does not provide dogmatic answers. In addition, corresponding to his view of the different levels of meaning in scripture, he may himself in expounding a biblical passage use language which can be understood on more than one level. A further problem is that the possibility must be taken into account that Origen altered his views between the composition of his *Commentary on Genesis* and the *De principiis* and his later works (although the fact that he refers back to his

Commentary on Genesis for the exegesis there of the account of the creation of the world and of man and of the story of Adam and the garden of Eden when writing the *Contra Celsum* in about AD 248–9 makes a significant change of view unlikely).[5] Another difficulty is the fact that of the surviving works of Origen only a small proportion is preserved in the original Greek. It will be necessary to refer also to catena extracts and the Latin translations, both sources which may be biassed in their selectivity[6] and whose reliability is open to question. The statements of Origen's views by his opponents provide valuable information, since they possessed writings which are now lost, but such statements must be used with caution, since they are likely to be influenced by the systematization of later Origenists. Bearing these caveats in mind and aiming to give some impression of the complexity and variety of Origen's treatment of the figure of Adam we will look at the evidence of the *De principiis* and of the charges made against Origen by fourth-century opponents in connection with his exegesis of Adam's story, and then, after outlining a tentative solution to the question of the relation of Adam's fall to that of the pre-existent soul, consider firstly how Origen may have dealt with the figure of Adam in the lost *Commentary on Genesis* and secondly how he refers to Adam in his surviving works.

Origen's account of the creation and fall of rational beings in *De principiis* is given without any reference to the Genesis story and indeed it is difficult to imagine how this version of the fall, in which all rational beings are created equal and fall a greater or lesser distance through neglect of the good,[7] could be identified with the story of Adam and Eve, which takes place in an environment in which there is already a differentiation of roles. Adam appears in *De principiis* as an historical figure.[8] In *De principiis* v.2, on biblical interpretation, Origen states that the historical narrative of scripture, beneath which the Spirit has hidden the symbolical meaning, includes the account of the visible works of creation, and of the creation of man and the descendants of the first men (IV.2.8, p.320.1–7). He states that the story of paradise and the fall provides clear examples of details (God planting a garden, the trees, God walking there, Adam hiding beneath the tree) which cannot be taken literally and demand a symbolic interpretation (IV.3.1, p. 323.7–324.4), but does not here state what that symbolic interpretation is. In IV.3.7 (p. 333.20–28) he states that Adam is said by Paul to be Christ and Eve to refer to the church. Christ is father of every soul, as Adam is of all men.

The accounts of Origen's false teaching given by late fourth-century opponents include both general accusations concerning the pre-existence and fall of the soul based primarily on *De principiis* and also, as a separate item, specific accusations concerning the allegorization of the story of Adam, based primarily on the lost *Commentary on Genesis*.[9] Jerome's summary lists Origen's interpretation of the coats of skin in Genesis 3:21 as human bodies;[10] his allegorization of paradise, understanding the trees as angels and the rivers as heavenly powers;[11] and his statement that the image and likeness of God, in which man was created, was lost by him.[12] Also derived from Origen's exegesis of Genesis is the accusation that he allegorized the waters above the firmament (Genesis 1:6ff.) as angelic powers and those below the firmament as hostile powers.[13] This last accusation is anticipated by Basil,[14] though without mentioning Origen's name, and the view that the coats of skin are bodies and that paradise is not on earth but in the third heaven is attacked by Methodius of Olympus,[15] who is quoted by Epiphanius.[16] A further accusation concerning Origen's treatment of the figure of Adam appears in the description by Photius of a lost anonymous *Apology for Origen* in five volumes,[17] namely that the soul of the saviour was that of Adam. According to Socrates (*Historia ecclesiastica* III.7) Pamphilus and Eusebius defended Origen on a charge of this kind on the grounds that he interpreted a mystical tradition of the church.[18]

The statements of Origen's critics are likely to be distorted by exaggeration, misrepresentation and the tendency to regard speculations aired or discussed by Origen as Origen's own viewpoint, or to attribute the views of later Origenists to Origen himself. It is clear, however, that their criticism of Origen's understanding of the story of Adam's fall concerns the allegorization of the various details of the story of Adam (whose individual existence is not denied), not any identification of Adam's fall with that of rational beings in general. How then, it may be asked, did Origen relate the fall of Adam to the fall of rational beings described in *De principiis*? The answer Jerome would give to this question is clear from the work just quoted. Before man was made in paradise, souls dwelt among rational creatures in the heavens.[19] According to Origen's teaching all rational creatures, being incorporeal and invisible, if they have become negligent, slip gradually downwards and take to themselves bodies according to the nature of the places to which they sink (16, 368A). Origen uses Jacob's ladder to expound this gradual descent, with as many changes of bodies as there are stopping places between heaven and earth, to the bottom rung, that is flesh and blood (19, 370B–C).[20] This gradual descent expounded by Jerome is able without difficulty to include the general fall of the rational creatures from the state in which they were created (as expounded in *De principiis*) as its first stage and the story of Adam as its second or last stage. Adam is clothed in a body already in paradise, but it is only after his fall there that he is clothed in mortal flesh and blood (thus in *Ancoratus* 62.1–2 Epiphanius identifies *to sarkōdes tou sōmatos* (*ē auto to sōma*) with the coats of skin).

A scheme of the kind that Jerome implies is attributed to 'the allegorists' by Procopius of Gaza, *Commentary on Genesis* (*PG* 87.221A), and related to the exposition of Genesis 1:27, 2:7, and 3:21. The view of these allegorists is 'that the man according to the image signifies the soul, the man moulded from the soil [*chous*] the body made of fine particles [*leptomeres*] worthy of life in paradise, which some have called luminous [*augoeides*], and the garments of skin [are referred to by] "you have clothed me in skin and flesh and entwined me with bones and sinews" (Job 10:11). They say the soul uses as a vehicle first the luminous [body] which later put on the garments of skin.'

The theory that Origen did indeed think in terms of a gradual descent of the rational creatures from their original condition involving the assumption of bodies of differing degrees of thickness can be supported from passages in Rufinus' translation of *De principiis*.[21]

In *Contra Celsum* v.29–32, Origen narrates a biblical story which fits the fall of pre-existent souls and the view that souls fall gradually and in differing degrees much better than does that of Adam. He emphasizes that this (the story of the tower of Babel) is a story which indicates a secret truth and that the account of how souls become bound to bodies should not be revealed indiscriminately (v.31 and 29, pp. 32.20-1 and 31.6ff.). According to his paraphrase of the story (v.30), those on the earth remain without moving from the east as long as they pay attention to the light and the effulgence of the everlasting light. When they move from the east and pay attention to things alien to the east they lose their source of nourishment, and desire to collect material things and conspire by means of material things ('making bricks') against immaterial things. Corresponding to whether they have moved a greater or lesser distance from the east and to their brick-making activity, they are handed over for punishment to angels of varying character and led to different parts of the earth. Those who remain in the east (v.31) become the Lord's portion and their sins are at first tolerable, later increasing, despite the application of remedies, so that eventually they too are dispersed among the rulers of other nations.[22]

In the *Commentary on Matthew* xv.31ff., Origen gives an interpretation of the parable of the workers in the vineyard which makes clear the role of Adam as the first of those sent to labour in the present age. The 'day' of the parable is the whole of the present age; the master went out early and hired Adam and Eve to work the vineyard of religion. Thus the first rank is that according to Adam contemporaneous with the creation of the world, the second rank that according to Noah and the covenant with him, and so on (p. 442.22ff., p. 446.23ff.).

Procopius' statement on the interpretation by the allegorists of Genesis 1:27, 2:7 and 3:21 must be taken with caution, since his allegorists may be later Origenists, rather than Origen himself.[23] Origen certainly distinguished between the body of this life, which Paul calls the body of humiliation (Philippians 3:21), and the resurrection body, which is like the bodies of angels 'ethereal and luminous light' (*hopoia esti ta tōn aggelōn sōmata, aitheria kai augoeides phōs*).[24] How exactly this picture is to be related to Genesis 1:27, 2:7 and 3:21 is not entirely clear, because Origen is far more concerned with man's present condition and future hope than with the stages by which he reached his present condition. His references to the verses from Genesis are often associated with Pauline quotations. Thus he frequently distinguishes between the inner and outer man (2 Corinthians 4:16), identifying the inner man with the man made according to the image of God in Genesis 1:26 and the outer man with the man which God moulded taking soil from the earth in Genesis 2:7.[25] According to the *Commentary on John* 11.23 (p. 79.3ff.), it is possible to understand the term 'man' (*anthrōpos*) in Genesis 1.26 of everything that has come to be in the image and likeness of God and thus as equally applicable to angels, since the rational beings are given their various names (men, angels, thrones, etc.) according to differences in rank, not in nature.

Commenting on Jeremiah 1:5 ('before I moulded you in the womb I know you') Origen states that the making (*poiēsis*) of Genesis 1:26 and the moulding (*plasis*) of Genesis 2:7 are to be distinguished. *Before* their *plasis* God knows those who are worthy of this knowledge.[26] The origin of this *plasis* or moulding is (according to Job 40:19) the serpent, who was the first of those who came to be in a body. When the saints were leading an immaterial and incorporeal life in blessedness, the so-called serpent fell from the pure life and deserved before all others to be bound in matter and a body.[27] He thus became the first 'choic'.[28] It is this 'choic', namely the devil, whose image we carry if we do his desires.[29] Being in heaven or on earth is not a matter of place but of disposition (*proairesis*). He who while still on the earth has his citizenship in heaven and lays up treasure in heaven, and has his heart in heaven, and bears the image of the heavenly, is no longer of the earth nor of the world below but of heaven and of the heavenly world, which is better than this one. The spiritual powers of wickedness (Ephesians 6:12) while in the heavens have their citizenship on earth and lay up treasure on earth, bearing the image of the choic.[30] It is noteworthy that Origen understands the 'choic' of 1 Corinthians 15:49 not of Adam but of the devil. Adam carried the image of the choic on account of his sin (*dia tēn hamartian*); both in Adam himself and in all men that which is according to the image of God is prior to the image of the evil one.[31] It is if one carries the image of the choic that the words addressed to Adam in Genesis 3:19, 'you are earth and unto earth you shall return', are rightly said to one.[32] If one carries the image of the heavenly, putting off the image of the choic, one is not earth.[33]

The evidence so far quoted is compatible with the view that Origen thought in terms of a first general fall of the rational beings as having preceded the moulding of man's bodily nature as described in Genesis 2:7 and a second fall of the protoplasts Adam and Eve, which resulted for them and their descendants in the conditions of life here on this earth. Scholars have tended, however, to be reluctant to think in this way in terms of 'two falls'. They have preferred either to think of Genesis 1:27 and 2:7 as referring to a double creation which happened simultaneously (therefore no fall before Genesis 2:7), or in terms of a fall before Genesis 2:7 which is symbolized by the story of Adam's fall (so that Adam's sin is identified with that of the pre-existent souls and there is no distinction between the bodily nature of Genesis 2:7 and human nature subsequent to Adam's fall).[34] A reason for the aversion to the theory of 'two falls' is no doubt the fear that, if combined with Procopius' suggestion of two stages of corporeality, it involves the implication that the first creation of Genesis 1:27 was incorporeal. Whether Origen thought it possible for rational creatures to exist in an incorporeal state is keenly disputed.[35] It may well, however, be an oversimplification to assume that Origen thought that there are only two possible kinds of corporeality (ethereal bodies and the gross material bodies of this life) and hence only two possible levels of corporeal existence. If one wishes to combine the theory of 'two falls' with the view that rational creatures cannot exist incorporeally, it may be necessary to think in terms of at least three levels of corporeality.[36]

The *Commentary on Genesis*, which would have made clear if not what view Origen held, then at least what views he aired and discussed and what speculations he put forward, is unfortunately lost. It was a lengthy and detailed work, consisting of thirteen volumes on Genesis 1–4, of which the first eight volumes were composed at Alexandria concurrently with *De principiis* (Origen refers back to the exposition of Genesis 1:1 in *De principiis* II.3.6, but had not yet expounded Genesis 1:26 when he wrote *De principiis* I.2.6). Only fragments survive and in speculating on the contents we depend on criticisms such as those listed above and on comparison with earlier and later writers on the same subjects. These include Philo, Basil of Caesarea, Gregory of Nyssa, Theodoret and Ambrose, as well as Procopius of Gaza's collection of extracts (preserved only in his own summarizing paraphrase). Particularly heavily indebted to Origen (but far briefer than Origen's lost Commentary) is Didymus' *Commentary on Genesis*, discovered at Tura in 1941 (the exposition of Genesis 1:1–6 survives only in a fragmentary state, that of 2.4–25 is lost).[37] The first of Origen's *Homilies on Genesis* translated by Rufinus gives a brief exposition of Genesis 1:1–30, concentrating chiefly on the 'moral' application. The commentary itself dealt with the early chapters of Genesis in great detail and it may be assumed that Origen discussed a variety of different possible interpretations of the verses concerned, without necessarily stating his own solutions. Furthermore it cannot be supposed that Origen saw the opening chapters of Genesis simply in terms of a chronological succession of events. Quite apart from the fact that 'before the world existed, time did not yet exist',[38] the narrative of the beginning of Genesis must be understood on more than one level, since it gives an account of the creation of the visible world beneath which deeper mysteries lie hidden. This means that to ask the question at what point or points in the Genesis account Origen would have located a fall or falls prior to that of Adam may well be to take an over-naive approach. None the less it is very probable that he did discuss the first general fall of the rational creatures at an early stage in his commentary. Light is thrown on this, as well as on the way in which the different levels of exegesis are related, by a comparison of Didymus' exposition of the waters above and below the firmament in Genesis 1.6–10 with that in the first *Homily on Genesis*.

Didymus supplements his literal interpretation of Genesis 1.6–10 with an allegorical interpretation clearly following the exegesis of Origen attacked by Basil, Epiphanius and Jerome (see above p. 65) and also linked to the 'Origenist' doctrine of the fall of rational creatures. After quoting biblical verses on good and bad spiritual waters (*SC* 233, 19.1–20.7), Didymus states that the rational creatures (*ta logika zō(i)a*) are indicated by the water (20.7–8) and that, whereas rational being, like water, is one in its substance (cf. 21.18–20), they have come to be in a state of either vice or virtue by means of their own impulse and will (20.8ff.; cf. also 28.14–16). In explaining what is meant by the firmament, Didymus speaks in terms of the individual soul. The firmament is the capacity of reason (*logos*) distinguishing good and evil placed in the commanding part of the soul (*hēgemonikon*) by God.[39] The waters beneath the firmament, or rational creatures which remained in a worse condition, are in different assemblies because evil is divisive, whereas virtue unifies, since he who has one virtue has all the virtues (26.11ff.). God wishes to benefit these scattered waters and orders that they be gathered together so that they may become like the water above the heavens, one not in number but in harmony. God's command in Genesis 1:9a, using the phrase *eis sunagōgēn mian*, refers to the final result aimed at; the statement of what happened in 1:9b, using the plural *eis tas sunagōgas autōn*, refers to progress on the way to this (28.11–29.22). The allegorical interpretation of Genesis 1:10 is applied to the individual soul. The soul, remaining the same in its substance, is freed from the waters covering it related to the abyss, and is called earth, receiving divine seed and bringing forth fruit (30.6ff.).

In Rufinus' translation of the first *Homily on Genesis* these verses are applied to the individual (pp.3–5). The first heaven (Genesis 1:1) is spiritual substance or our mind or spiritual man, who sees God. The firmament or corporeal heaven is our external man (later, however, p.10.10–11, 'nostrum firmamentum coeli' is explained as 'mentis nostrae uel cordis soliditas'). If man, when placed in the body, can distinguish the waters above and below the firmament, he will be called 'heaven' or 'heavenly man'. If he understands and shares in spiritual water, rivers of living water will flow from his belly (John 7:38, quoted also by Didymus, 19.4), and he will be separated from the water of the abyss below, where the prince of this world and his angels dwell. If we collect and disperse from ourselves the water beneath the heaven, that is, the sins and vices of our body, our 'dry land', our works done in the flesh, will appear, and our bodies will not remain 'dry' but be called 'earth', because they will be able to bear fruit to God.

The various levels of exegesis, literal (not included in the above summaries), allegorical and 'moral', are linked by the fact that the various levels of reality itself mirror one another, as also the microcosm man represents a reflection of the constitution of the macrocosm or universe. This latter point is stated explicitly in the first *Homily on Genesis*.[40] In the narrative of Genesis, the description of the creation of the visible world, referring allegorically to the microcosm man, is followed by the account of the creation of man (Genesis 1:26ff.), which may to some extent therefore be regarded as a doublet of what comes before.[41]

The exposition of Genesis 1:27 in the first *Homily on Genesis* utilizes the contrast between the inner incorporeal man made according to the image of God in this verse and the outer or corporeal man moulded from the earth in Genesis 2:7. It is in such qualities as his invisibility, incorporeality, incorruptibility, and immortality that the inner man is understood to be according to the image of God (p.15.7–14). 'Male and female' is specified already in Genesis 1:27, either in anticipation of the subsequent creation of woman, or because everything made by God is linked together, as heaven and earth, or as sun and moon, or (according to the allegorical interpretation) because our inner man consists of spirit (male) and soul (female), whose union produces good and useful attitudes and thoughts, which enable them to dominate the earth, that is, the flesh (pp. 18–19). There also survives an extract from the *Commentary on Genesis* on Genesis 1:26–7,[42] attacking the view that *to kat' eikona* is located in the body and arguing that the view that it is in the rational soul may be supported by a consideration of the capacities (*dunameis*) of the soul. That which in man is according to the image is characterized not by the form of the body but by actions, as is shown by St Paul's words in 1 Corinthians 15:49 and Colossians 3:10.

For the story of Adam, a number of extracts and quotations are preserved which may come from the lost commentary, perhaps in part also from the *Scholia on Genesis*.[43] Two sentences quoted with disapprobation by Eustathius of Antioch apparently introduce an allegorical interpretation of the trees in paradise (p. 56). Catena fragments include (pp. 56–7) an interpretation of *Edem* as *hēdu* together with the mention of a Hebrew tradition that Eden, where God planted paradise or the garden, is the centre of the world like the pupil of an eye, and that the river Phison is accordingly interpreted as *stoma korēs*; also a brief interpretation of Genesis 2:12 apparently on a 'moral' level (*chrusion kalon* refers to *kala dogmata*), and on 2:13 the information that the Hebrew for Ethiopia means *skotōsis*. A paragraph on Genesis 2:15

(pp. 57–8) refers God's placing Adam in paradise to the placing of those reborn in baptism in the church to work spiritual works. They receive a command to love all the brethren (Genesis 2:16). He who follows the arguments of the serpent and loves some and hates others disobeys the command. The resulting death is caused not by God but by the man who has hated his neighbour. These extracts give some idea of the variety of Origen's exegesis but are not informative on the relation of Adam's fall to the prehistory of the individual soul. More obviously relevant is the extract on the garments of skin in Genesis 3:21.[44] In this passage Origen rejects a literal interpretation as foolish and describes the interpretation of the garments as bodies as plausible but not clearly true, since Genesis 2:23, mentioning Adam's bones and flesh, then presents a problem. The view that they represent mortality (*nekrōsis*) is rejected on the grounds that in this case God and not sin would be the author of *nekrōsis* and flesh and bones would not on their own account be perishable. 'Moreover, if paradise is a divine place, let them say how each of the limbs performed its proper function there and was not created in vain.' With regard to the mention of a nostril (Aquila and Symmachus) or face (LXX) in Genesis 2:7, it must be said that one ought not to cling to the letter of scripture as being true but to seek the treasure hidden in the letter.

Origen does not here state his view explicitly, but his argument appears to deny that Adam and Eve had bodies of flesh and bones in paradise and hence to tend in the direction of the interpretation of which Epiphanius and Jerome accuse him (see above, p. 65). The problem is not just one of specifying the change undergone by Adam and Eve as a result of the fall but rather of identifying what exactly it is that is referred to in Genesis 3:21. Origen agrees with the view that mortality was a result of the fall (thus in the *Commentary on John* I.20 and XIII.34, pp. 25.2ff. and 259.34ff. he states that, but for the fall, man, 'having been made for incorruptibility', would have 'gained possession of incorruptibility', or 'would have remained immortal'), but he regards sin and not God as its author, and therefore rejects the identification of the garments with mortality. Two references in other works are equally non-committal, but not incompatible with an interpretation of the garments as the fleshly body of this life. In the *Contra Celsum* IV.40 (p. 313–25ff.), Origen states that the man thrown out with the woman from paradise, clothed in skin garments, which, because of human transgression, God made for those who had sinned, has a certain secret and mysterious meaning, superior to that of the descent of the soul in

Plato, when it loses its wings and is carried here until it finds some firm resting place. In *Homily on Leviticus* VI.2 (p. 362.11–22) he states that Adam after his sin was clothed in animal skins, to be a sign of the mortality which he had received for his sin and of that weakness which came from the corruption of the flesh.[45]

The question of the kind of body Adam had in paradise is related to that of the kind of place paradise is. In the extract on Genesis 3:21 Origen allows for the view that paradise is a 'divine place' (*theion ti chōrion*), hence a place superior to this earth but none the less a place and not simply a spiritual condition. To examine all Origen's references to paradise would be a major task, which cannot be undertaken here.[46] The question of its location is complicated by the fact that terms like world (*kosmos*), heaven, earth and dry land are used of more than one level of existence;[47] also that Origen sometimes distinguishes between 'paradise' and 'paradise of God' or 'paradise of luxury'[48] (the former is where the robber went with Jesus at the first hour (Luke 23:43), the latter is where he will have been if he received and ate from the tree of life and of all the trees which God did not prohibit; it is also where the devil fell from;[49] it is the destination of martyrs after death).[50] In *Homily on Numbers* XXVI.5 Origen distinguishes various meanings of the word 'earth' (p. 251.27ff.). The earth on which we live was originally called 'dry land' and received the name 'earth' afterwards. Adam was driven out into the place called 'dry land' from paradise, which is not on the 'dry land' but on the 'earth'. Similarly it is the 'earth' which is promised to the meek in Matthew 5:5. Very frequently Origen uses language of paradise that can be understood on a moral or spiritual level. The paradise of God may be planted in our hearts.[51] If we mortify our limbs on earth and bear fruits of the spirit, the Lord may walk in us as in a spiritual paradise.[52] It is this level of understanding which provides a solution to the problematic verse, Genesis 3:8, where God is described as walking in paradise and Adam and Eve as hiding. God walks in paradise as he does in the saints, whereas the sinner hides himself from God.[53] In the beginning God planted a paradise of luxury, that we might enjoy spiritual luxuries.[54] The transplanted tree of Psalm 1:3 may be understood as the soul of the Saviour, transplanted into paradise, so that those worthy to be with Christ may be enlightened by him by the illumination of knowledge.[55] It may be noted that whereas conditions in the paradise of luxury may be understood to represent the life enjoyed by the rational creatures before the first fall and that to be attained by the saints after the resurrection, Adam himself in Genesis 2 to 3 does not exist in these conditions, since he does not partake of the tree of life and the other trees which God did not prohibit.

Further evidence for Origen's treatment of the figure of Adam in his *Commentary on Genesis* is provided by ten fragments from a papyrus codex of the fourth or fifth century, containing parts of the exegesis of Genesis 3:11ff.[56] Most of the fragments consist of only a few letters from each line, allowing the identification of the biblical verses discussed or quoted and some individual words, but not much more. Fragment III^v contains references to the versions of Theodotion and (probably) Symmachus, and the better preserved fragment VI a discussion of Genesis 3:15 (the enmity between the seed of the serpent and the seed of the woman on VI^v, with a reference to Stoic theories of heredity on VI^r). The passage from Procopius (*PG* 87.1, 205Cf.) which Sanz (p. 99) quotes as providing a parallel to fragment VI^v turns out to be taken from Didymus, *Commentary on Genesis* 98.31ff. Other parallels provided by Didymus concern the greater strength of the man over against the woman as an adversary of the serpent,[57] and the kindness with which God questions the protoplasts in Genesis 3:9ff.[58] More importantly, a comparison with Didymus may be able to throw light on features which Sanz found obscure. The most interesting of these is the quotation of a number of verses concerning Christ's incarnation and sinlessness.[59] The most likely context for these quotations is a comparison of Adam and Eve with Christ and the church, such as recurs a number of times in Didymus' *Commentary* attributed at first to certain persons (83.25ff., 93.23ff.) and later repeated without qualification (100.4ff., 101.27ff., 105.7ff.). According to this exegesis, which utilizes Ephesians 5:32 and 1 Timothy 2:14, Adam followed Eve not in transgression but to help her, while Christ, himself without sin, emptied himself and took on the form of a servant to help the fallen human race of which the church consists (there is an allusion to Philippians 2:7 in 105.9 and a quotation in 105.15). In 101.24ff., Didymus contrasts the cursing of the serpent in Genesis 3:14 with the milder words spoken to Adam in Genesis 3:17. It may be that the same point is being made in fragment IIa^r 2–4. The references to the bridegroom and bride in fragment VI^{r}9–10 and IIb^r 1–2 (as restored by Sanz) may belong to the context of Christ as bridegroom of the church,[60] in which case the seed of the woman and that of the serpent in fragment VI is probably to be understood allegorically (as in Didymus 99.1ff., of teachings). That Origen did indeed interpret Adam as Christ and Eve as the church is confirmed by

Socrates, who states that he established this fully in volume 9 of the *Commentary on Genesis*, also that Origen there illuminated the mystery concerning Christ's human soul (*empsuchon ton enanthrōpēsanta*).[61]

In view of Didymus' dependence on Origen it is worth listing a few points from his treatment of the paradise story as an indication of the kind of themes Origen may have discussed in his commentary. Didymus' exegesis of Genesis 2:4–25 is lost, but there are some references back to it in that of Genesis 3. Paradise is a divine place, the dwelling place of blessed powers (102.9–10). Those who think it even now exists on earth can be refuted from Genesis 3:24 (114.21ff.). It is a transcendent place, where thick bodies cannot be worn (107.20–22, 108.5–15). The robber of Luke 23:43 entered paradise in his naked soul (ibid.). Didymus seems to envisage the body worn in paradise as an intermediate stage between the incorporeal creation according to the image of Genesis 1:27 and the dense mortal body of the present life (107.4–20). This intermediate body is referred to as *to geōdes skēnos* in Wisdom of Solomon 9:15 (ibid.) and as *chous* in Genesis 2:7, which indicates the corporeal substance of the body appropriate for life in paradise (118.13–16). The garments of skin are the bodies referred to as skin and flesh in Job 10:11 (106.8ff.). As a result of his faults, man received dry land instead of the earth of the meek, to which he will return in a spiritual body after the resurrection (104.17ff. on Genesis 3:19).

A different view of man's condition in paradise seems to be envisaged in the speculations expressed in connection with God's words 'Where are you?' in Genesis 3:9 (90.9–91.11). Here Didymus considers what is meant by place in this context. Is it the task to which Adam has been assigned and which he has deserted? Some exegetes think of incorporeal substance as the first substrate of the soul and therefore reckon that the soul should be outside all place but that, when it has of itself made trial of a body, it is admonished with the words 'Where are you?' Moreover he who has his heart in heaven is not in a place, being above the world.

The nature of the fall is such that it can be applied to sin in general, both that of the pre-existent soul and also to human sin in this world. The command given to Adam indicated that he should eat of the tree of the knowledge of good and evil together with all the other trees and not alone, since human aptitude without the practice of virtue is very harmful (92.26ff.). The serpent wished Adam and Eve to become wise for evil and their eyes inclining towards evil to be opened, eyes which are not opened when virtue is active (81.19–21; cf. 83.7–25). After the fall Adam is addressed with the words of Genesis 3:22, because he has become like the devil, who fell from heaven, knowing what is good and what is evil, but not distinguishing so as to choose the good and shun the evil (109.2ff.). 'Naked' in Genesis 3:7 is explained as stripped of their previous virtue (83.1–7, 84.20–28, 92.10–12), the girdles of fig-leaves as excuses (85.5–86.7). Before their transgression, God was with Adam and Eve and did not walk outside them, but after they abandoned God by turning away from virtue, he distanced himself from them but still made them aware of their sin by means of the universal notions[62] which he implanted in them (85.2–5, 87.1–21).

Interwoven with the above exegesis is an allegorical interpretation derived from Philo[63] according to which Adam represents the mind (*nous*), Eve sensation (*aisthēsis*) and the serpent pleasure (*hēdonē*, 95.18–21, 82.29–83.1). The allegorical interpretation according to which Adam represents Christ and Eve the church has already been mentioned (above, p. 74). Didymus emphasizes, however, that not everything said of Adam applies to Christ (104.28ff.).

So far we have considered the attacks on Origen's treatment of Adam and speculated on the themes included in his *Commentary on Genesis*. A fairer picture may, however, be obtained if we examine Origen's references to Adam in his other surviving works and fragments. Such an examination may show which features Origen himself considered of particular significance and worthy of frequent repetition. We shall look first at the references to the story of Adam, then at the interpretation of Adam as Christ and Eve as the church, and finally at the question of the connection between Adam's fall and the fallen state of every man in this life.

There are a number of references to the story of Adam and his fall, some of which appear to be more or less straightforward, while others are open also to interpretation either on a higher level of the first fall, or on a moral level of every man. These references will be listed or summarized here in the order of the events of the story.[64]

God placed the man he moulded in paradise to work it and guard it.[65] If the woman had not been deceived and Adam had not fallen and man made for incorruption had obtained incorruption, Christ would not have descended.[66] In Genesis God places man in the paradise of luxury, giving him laws about eating and not eating such and such things and man would have remained immortal if he had eaten from every tree in paradise and refrained from eating from the tree of the knowledge of good and evil.[67]

In the *Commentary on John* XIII.37, p. 262.5ff., Origen considers the question whether the rational creature created by God was incomplete (*ateles*) when placed in paradise. It would not, however, be reasonable to call him who was able to work the tree of life and everything which God planted and caused to spring up 'incomplete'. So perhaps he was complete in some way (*pōs*) and became incomplete through the transgression. Origen seems here to be thinking on more than one level, since his use of *to logikon* (p. 262.9ff.) suggests that he is talking of rational creatures in general, yet he goes on to state that not only man fell from completeness to being incomplete but also the 'sons of God seeing the daughters of men' (Genesis 6:2) and all those who 'leave their own habitation' and 'kept not their first estate' (*archē*, Jude 6), explaining that the *archē* of existence for man was in paradise and that each of those who have fallen have their own *archē*.

Adam is counted as a prophet, since he prophesied in Genesis 2:24.[68] The devil envied Adam and deceived him by means of food (and tried to do the same to Christ).[69] When God saw the devil reflecting 'if a serpent could speak, I would have approached by means of it for the deception of the protoplasts', he allowed this.[70] Eve's gullibility and the unsoundness of her reasoning did not arise when she disobeyed God and listened to the serpent, but existed previously and were shown up, since the serpent approached her for this reason and seized on her weakness with his own shrewdness.[71]

Before his transgression, man is described as able to see with one kind of eyes (in Genesis 3:6 'the woman saw') and unable to see with another (Genesis 3:5,7 'your eyes will be opened', 'their eyes were opened'). The eyes which were opened were the eyes of sense perception. Previously they had rightly shut these, so as not to be distracted or hindered from seeing with the eye of the soul. On account of their sin, however, they shut the eyes of the soul with which they previously saw and which rejoiced in God and his paradise[72] (a similar distinction is made in *Homily on Numbers* XVII.3, p. 157.6ff. between the 'eyes of the earth' or 'sense of the flesh' opened in Genesis 3:7 and the 'better eyes' referred to in Genesis 3:6).

In *Homily on Jeremiah* XVI.3 (p. 136.15ff.) Origen explains Genesis 3:8. Even though Adam sinned, his sin was not excessively bad. Therefore he hid from the face of God (thus showing a sense of shame), whereas Cain, being a greater sinner, went out from the face of God (a similar distinction is made in *Homily on Exodus* XI.5, p. 258.4ff.).[73]

In *Homily on Genesis* XV.2 (p. 128.24ff.) the death referred to in God's words to the first man in Genesis 2:17 is stated to be sin. He died as soon as he transgressed the commandment. The soul which has sinned is dead, and the serpent, who said 'You will not die', is proved to have lied. Comparing the deceit from the serpent with deceit from God, Origen states in *Homily on Jeremiah* XX.3 (p. 182.4ff.) that deceit from the serpent drove Adam and his wife out of the paradise of God. In the *Commentary on John* XX.25 (p. 360.18ff.), Origen summarizes the narrative of the fall before going on to explain the meaning of true life and death and its application to all men: Adam and Eve were not killed so far as they had not sinned, but on the day they ate from the forbidden tree they immediately died, killed by none other than the murderous devil, when he deceived Eve through the serpent and Eve gave to the man from the tree and the man ate.

Adam and Eve were the parents of all men.[74] In the *Commentary on John* XX.3ff. (p. 329.7ff.), Origen discusses spiritual and physical descent from Adam and other ancestors of the human race. According to the *Commentary on Matthew*,[75] there is a tradition that the body of Adam, the first man, is buried at Calvary, so that the head of the human race and father of all men may receive the benefit of resurrection together with his descendants.[76]

The interpretation of Adam as Christ and of Adam and Eve as Christ and the church is inspired by 1 Corinthians 15:45 and Ephesians 5:30–2. In expounding Romans 5:14,[77] Origen explains Adam as a type of Christ 'by opposites',[78] but elsewhere a positive parallelism appears. Often this applies to Christ incarnate and the church on earth.[79] In *Homily on Numbers* XXVIII.4 (p. 284.16ff.) the dispersion of the sons of Adam at the beginning of the world is compared with the distribution of the sons of the last Adam at the end of the world (here the element of contrast predominates, with a quotation of 1 Corinthians 15:22).

There are also hints of (and references which can be read in the light of) the exegesis according to which Adam symbolizes the unfallen soul of Christ and Eve the pre-existent church, whom he followed in his descent to this earth. Indeed it is possible that it was initially in this context that Origen regarded the story of Adam and Eve as symbolizing the first fall of the rational creatures. In the *Commentary on Matthew* XIV.17 (p. 325.27ff.) the word 'female' in Genesis 1:27 is applied to the church and Adam's words in Genesis 2:24 to the Lord's leaving the heavenly Jerusalem and cleaving to his fallen wife, the church which is his body.[80] In the *Commentary on John* XIX.4 (p. 302.17ff.), Origen explains that with respect to the knowledge of God the word 'knowing' in biblical usage implies 'being united with' and illustrates this point by the example of Adam and Eve, referring for its interpretation to Ephesians 5:32 and 1 Corinthians 6:16f.: Adam (= Christ) did not 'know' his wife when he made the statement of Genesis 2:23 but only when he clove to her (Genesis 4:1). In the *Commentary on the Song of Songs* II (p. 132.28ff.), Origen applies 1 Timothy 2:14–15 to the parallel of Adam and Eve with Christ and the church, prepared as his bride from the dispersion among the gentiles, a bride who was deceived and in transgression when he gave himself for her. Later in the same work (III, p.213.25ff.) it is stated that the serpent deceived Eve and infected all her descendants with the contagion of transgression.[81] In *Homily on Genesis* XV.5 (p. 133.23ff.) Adam's descent from paradise to the labours and troubles of this world to contend with the serpent is seen as parallel to that of the Lord, who descended to this world and became a great race (i.e. the church of the gentiles), in that both may be symbolized by Jacob's descent to Egypt. In the *Commentary on John* II.29ff. (pp. 86.1ff.), Adam's being sent from paradise to work the earth is compared with the sending of John the Baptist 'from heaven or from paradise or from wherever else' to this place on earth, and the guess is hazarded (p. 88.6ff.) that the Baptist may be one of the holy angels following the example of Christ's incarnation. In Book I of the *Commentary on John* Origen applies 1 Corinthians 15:45b to Christ as Adam, without making any contrast with the first Adam.[82] In *De principiis* IV.3.7 (p. 333.20–8) Christ as father of all souls is paralleled by Adam as father of all men, while Eve, interpreted as the church, includes fallen members among her offspring. The story of the woman being taken from Adam's rib while he slept and being 'built' by God is said to be an allegory in *Contra Celsum* IV.38 (p. 308.20ff.), but without further explanation. In a fragment on Proverbs 31:16 (*PG* 17.252A), however, it is stated that the church came forth from the side (*pleura*, rib) of Christ[83] (the preceding sentence seems to take not Eve but the garden of Eden as symbolizing 'the soul of the virtuous', which is identified with 'the church having the tree of knowledge and the tree of life; of knowledge as of the law, and of life as of the Logos').[84]

A different approach to the figure of Adam from that so far considered is taken in those passages where Adam is associated with the fallen condition of human life in this world. The reason for this association is that (whether or not a general fall of rational creatures symbolized by or previous to Adam's fall is envisaged) the terms under which man lives in his present life are those resulting from the expulsion of the protoplasts from paradise, as described in Genesis 3. In this connection, 'Adam' may be generalized to refer to fallen man or the bodily life of man. Origen frequently quotes in this context 1 Corinthians 15:22 ('in Adam all die') together with verses like Psalm 43:20 (LXX) and 26, Psalm 21:16 (LXX), Romans 7:24 and Philippians 3:21 (for example, *Commentary on John* XX.25, p. 361.7ff., on the devil as man's murderer and the subjection to him of this earthly region). These and other verses are cited in *Contra Celsum* VII.50 (p. 201.28ff.) together with the explanation that the 'place of affliction' referred to in Psalm 43:20 is the earthly region, to which Adam, which means 'man', came after being cast out of paradise for his sin (*dia tēn kakian*). In *Contra Celsum* IV.40 (p. 311.16ff.) Origen explains that, since Adam means 'man', the biblical texts stating that in Adam all die and are condemned in the likeness of Adam's transgression (an allusion to Romans 5:14, which Origen reads without the negative) are spoken of the whole race, also that the curses spoken against Adam and Eve apply to all men and women. Thus the words spoken in Genesis 3:17–19 mean that the whole earth is cursed; every man who has 'died in Adam' eats of it in grief all the days of his life, and it will bring forth thorns and thistles all the days of the life of the man who, in Adam, was cast out of paradise.[85] The sinner is called 'earth', since Adam is told 'You are earth and to earth you will go.'[86] We need the strength of God to apply to our own 'earth' (for Adam is told 'You are earth'), and without God's power we are unable to fulfil what is not according to the will of the flesh.[87]

The question how it can come about that all men 'die in Adam' and share the results of his transgression is considered by Origen in his exegesis of Romans 5:12ff., which survives only in the abbreviating paraphrase of Rufinus.[88] A number of solutions are aired, which need not be regarded as mutually exclusive. The simplest is that the devil gained power over men by means of the disobedience of the first man,[89] and it was because of Adam's sin that all men were condemned to mortality and that he was thrown out of paradise to this place of humiliation and vale of tears.[90]

In expounding Romans 5:12, Origen raises the question why sin entered 'through one man', when the woman sinned before Adam and the serpent before the woman.[91] The answer he suggests is that the succession of human descent which became subject to the death coming from sin is ascribed not to the woman but to the man. He compares the case of Levi, who was already present in the loins of Abraham when Melchizedek met him (Hebrews 7:9–10), and draws the conclusion that all men who are born or have been born in this world were in the loins of Adam when he was still in paradise, and thus that all men were driven out with him from paradise.[92] The idea of succession reappears, combined with that of inheritance of sin by the teaching of one's parents in the exegesis of Romans 5:14.[93] This succession from Adam is mentioned already in the exegesis of Romans 3:12, together with the idea of Adam as an example of decline from the right path.[94]

Outside the *Commentary on Romans* the most interesting discussion of the question of succession from Adam occurs in fragment 11 from the *Commentary on Matthew* (pp. 19–20, on Matthew 1:18, reading *gennēsis* ('birth') and contrasting this with *genesis* ('generation') in 1:1). According to this fragment, *genesis* is the first moulding by God and possesses incorruptibility and sinlessness, *gennēsis* is the succession from each other from the condemnation of death on account of transgression and possesses passibility and the tendency to sin. The Lord took the sinlessness but not the incorruptibility of *genesis*, and the passibility but not the tendency to sin of *gennēsis*, 'bearing the first Adam undiminished in his elements according to both'. In the case of Christ *genesis* is the path from being in the form of God to taking the form of a slave. His *gennēsis* was like ours, in that he was born from a woman, but superior to ours, in that it was not from the will of the flesh or of a man but from the Holy Spirit.

The idea of a sinful tendency inherited from Adam is not intended by Origen to replace the concept of a previous fall of the individual soul but is considered alongside it. The latter concept (and perhaps also the idea that subsequent to the first fall of rational creatures individual men may have suffered a further fall similar to that of Adam) is hinted at in the *Commentary on Romans*, at first cryptically (it is probably intended in the discussion of Romans 5:14, p. 342.11ff.: 'perhaps there were some who did something like what Adam is described as having done in paradise'; cf. 343.10ff., 352.6–8), then more obviously (p.355.1ff.: Paul says that each individual has sinned in the likeness of Adam's transgression, although he does not consider it safe to say openly where or when or how).[95] Since a choice is not made between these two explanations, it remains an open question whether it is because of its own previous fall or because of the taint of birth in succession from Adam (or rather it is probably for both these reasons)[96] that the soul is already polluted on arrival in this life and requires purification. In expounding Romans 6:6,[97] Origen quotes Pauline and Old Testament verses to show that the body of this life is the 'body of sin', 'body of death' and 'body of humiliation', and refers to the Old Testament sin offering for newly born babies and the Christian practice of infant baptism as evidence that all have the pollution of sin at birth. That succession from Adam plays a role in this pollution is suggested in this passage by the observations that it was only after his sin that Adam knew his wife and begat Cain and that it was because of the virgin birth that Christ only had the likeness of the flesh of sin and not the flesh of sin itself.[98]

Perhaps the most interesting exegesis of the death of all men in Adam or the entry of sin through one man (1 Corinthians 15:22, Romans 5:12) is that which interprets 'Adam' as the unregenerate individual in this life. Such an exposition, combined with a different use of 1 Corinthians 15:45ff. from that described above, appears immediately after the discussion of succession from Adam in the *Commentary on Romans* v.1 (p. 327.3ff.): if a man is not yet renewed in the inner man according to the image of God but is still in this world and is 'choic' and bears the image of the 'choic', it is of him that the words 'sin entered this world and through sin death' are said. Every man is first 'from the earth, choic', when he walks in the image of the 'choic' and thinks according to the flesh, and only with difficulty does he eventually turn to the Lord, accept the guidance of the Spirit of God and being made spiritual become 'the last Adam as a life-giving spirit' (1 Corinthians 15:47). In the *Commentary on Romans* v.9 (p. 394.1ff.), the 'old man' of Romans 6:6, Ephesians 4:22 and Colossians 3:9 is explained as the man who lives according to Adam, subject to transgression and death.[99]

In the context of the interpretation of 'Adam' as the individual it is possible to draw a parallel between St Paul's description of the human condition in Romans 7:7ff. and the story of Adam, by assimilating the law forbidding desire with the tree of the knowledge of good and evil or the command not to eat from it. Hints of such an interpretation appear in the *Commentary on Romans*. At VI.11 (pp. 65.15–66.1) it is suggested that the tree of the knowledge of good and evil symbolizes the law, because the law contains both the letter that kills and the life-giving spirit. At VI.8 (pp. 48.16–49.1), on the words 'sin deceived me by means of the commandment' (Romans 7:11), the suggestion is made that 'sin' refers to the author of sin, of whom the words 'the serpent deceived me' (Genesis 3:13) are written. The words 'I once lived without the law' in

Romans 7:9 are explained as referring to the fact that every man lives without the natural law until he reaches the age of reason. During this time sin is dormant, but when he reaches the age to be able to distinguish right and wrong sin revives.[100] The parallel is limited, however, because the condition of man before he reaches the age of reason is not seen as equivalent to that of Adam before the fall.[101] On the contrary, because of the fall death reigns in man from his birth until the age of reason and it is only then that he becomes capable of receiving the grace of Christ (v.2, p. 353.13ff.). Thus the situation of man in this life is seen not so much in parallel to Adam's fall as in terms of the exhortation to reverse the results of the fall by turning to Christ.

There is no need to suppose that the theory of a succession of sin handed down from Adam to his descendants is incompatible with that of the fall of the individual soul before entering the body, or that Origen 'changed his mind' on this subject.[102] A particular situation (in this case the human condition) can have more than one cause. The individual soul may enter human life as the result of its own previous fall and here be subjected to conditions which are the result of Adam's condemnation. If we wish to systematize Origen's scattered hints and tentative suggestions, we must think in terms of the story of Adam (the first event in human history) as having taken place subsequent to and at a lower level than the fall of rational creatures from their original state of contemplation, also of individual souls having descended through more than one level before their entry into human life.[103] It is not without significance, however, that Origen himself nowhere spells out such a scheme in his surviving works.[104] His aim was not to dogmatize or to force his biblical material into a straitjacket, but rather to do justice to the multiplicity, complexity and variety of the biblical pronouncements concerning Adam, human nature and the fall. Some of this variety and also the difficulty of gauging the 'level' at which Origen's language is to be understood has been illustrated in the above study. In particular, more emphasis than usual has been put on the interpretation of Adam as symbolizing Christ, who followed his bride in her descent to this world. It may well be that there were changes of emphasis in Origen's writings over the years and that his treatment of the figure of Adam varied according to the particular biblical text or book he was interpreting.[105] If his works had been preserved entire, we might hope to map such variations. A survey of what survives makes one aware of the tantalizing gaps but also of that richness of his exegesis which made it a quarry for subsequent generations.

C. P. BAMMEL

NOTES

1 The possibility of the pre-existence of the soul is aired in *De libero arbitrio* 1.24 and III.57–9. For an illuminating comparison of Origen and Augustine cf. H. Chadwick, 'Christian Platonism in Origen and in Augustine', in R. Hanson and H. Crouzel (ed.), *Origeniana Tertia*, Rome 1985, pp. 217–30, especially pp. 228–9 on the parallel between Origen and Augustine in their hierarchical view of the cosmos and their explanations of evil. At the time of his conversion, any influence of Origen on Augustine is likely to have come via Ambrose (later also via Hilary and the Latin translations of Origen's works, as these became available). Augustine's reflection of ideas on an individual fall of the soul however is primarily derived from Neoplatonism; cf. R. J. O'Connell, 'The Plotinian Fall of the Soul in St Augustine', *Traditio*, 19 (1963), 1–35.

2 Rufinus the Syrian, *De fide*, fiercely opposed to Origen, attacked the view that souls were made before bodies, that the garments of skin of Genesis 3:21 signify the human body, and that the transgression of Adam and Eve results in the punishment of their offspring or the subjection of the whole world to sin (ed. M. W. Miller, *Rufini Presbyteri Liber De Fide* (Catholic University of America Patristic Studies 96, Washington 1964), §§ 27, 36, 37–41, pp. 88, 108, 110–18). On this Rufinus cf. O. Wermelinger, *Rom und Pelagius*, Stuttgart 1975, pp. 11–15; also *JThS*, n.s. 28 (1977), 425–6

3 Cf. F. R. Tennant, *The Sources of the Doctrines of the Fall and Original Sin*, Cambridge 1903; N. P. Williams, *The Ideas of the Fall and of Original Sin*, London 1927. D. G. Bostock, 'The Sources of Origen's Doctrine of Pre-existence', in L. Lies (ed.), *Origeniana Quarta*, Innsbruck 1987, pp. 259–64, demonstrates the roots of Origen's doctrine of pre-existence in Jewish thought as found in the Bible, apocryphal writings and in Philo. For an excellent brief account of Philo, cf. H. Chadwick, 'Philo' in A. H. Armstrong (ed.), *The Cambridge History of Later Greek and Early Medieval Philosophy*, Cambridge 1967, pp. 137–57, especially p. 145 (fall of souls) and p. 146 (Adam and Eve and the 'coats of skins').

4 The distinguished scholar to whom this volume is dedicated would be the last to foster such a misconception and I hope that he will forgive my refuting it under his auspices (in his account of Origen in *Early Christian Thought and the Classical Tradition*, Oxford 1966, the discussion of the fall of rational beings (pp. 84–5, p. 115) is rightly kept separate from that of Adam's fall (pp. 90–1), as also, more recently, in 'Origenes' in M. Greschat (ed.), *Gestalten der Kirchengeschichte*: *Alte Kirche I*, Stuttgart 1984, pp. 136 and 143).

5 IV.37 (p. 308.7), 39 (p. 313.5–7), VI.49 (p. 120.18–27), 51 (p. 122.15–20), 60 (pp. 130.26–131.4). References to works of Origen are to the editions in the Berlin Corpus, where not otherwise specified. I have also used

84

H. Chadwick, *Origen: Contra Celsum*, Cambridge 1953. Old Testament references are to the Septuagint.

6 It is striking that the catena extracts on 1 Corinthians and Romans include nothing on the key passages 1 Corinthians 15:45–9 or Romans 5:12–21. The catena extracts on Ephesians make a much less 'Origenist' impression that Jerome's commentary on the same epistle.

7 II.9.2 and 6, pp. 165–6 and 169–70. On the nature of the first fall cf. H. Chadwick, *Early Christian Thought*, pp. 84–5, and 'Origen' in Armstrong (ed.), *The Cambridge History of Later Greek and Early Medieval Philosophy*, pp. 190–1; also M. Harl, 'Recherches sur l'origénisme d'Origène: la "satiété" (*koros*) de la contemplation comme motif de la chute des âmes', *TU*, 93 (1966), 373–405.

8 He is one of the just, along with Abel, Seth, etc., 1 *Praef.* 4, p. 9.15–16; he begat Seth according to his own image, 1.2.6, p. 34.21–3; he prophesied, 1.3.6, p. 58.5; if all worlds were the same, the story of Adam and Eve would be repeated, II.3.4, p. 119.6–7; the serpent described in Genesis as having misled Eve is said in the *Ascension of Moses* to have been inspired by the devil to cause the disobedience of Adam and Eve, III.2.1, p. 244.16–20.

9 Details of the specific accusations are given by Epiphanius in his *Ancoratus* (*GCS* 25 (1915)), *Panarion* (*GCS* 31 (1922)) and his letter against John of Jerusalem, which survives in Jerome's translation (Jerome, *Epistle* LI, *CSEL* 54 (1910), pp. 395ff.), and summarized by Jerome in his own work *Against John of Jerusalem* (7, *PL* 23.360B-D). Epiphanius' charges against Origen are discussed rather fully by J. F. Dechow, 'The Heresy Charges Against Origen', in Lies (ed.), *Origeniana Quarta*, pp. 112–22.

10 Cf. *Ancoratus* 62.1–2, p. 74, *Panarion* 64.4.9, p. 412, *Epistle* LI.5.2, p. 403.

11 Cf. *Ancoratus* 54.2ff., pp. 63f., attacking Origen for locating paradise not on earth but in the third heaven, *Panarion* 64.4.11, p. 413, *Epistle* LI.5.4f., p.404.

12 Cf. *Ancoratus* 55f., pp. 64ff. and *Epistle* LI.7, p. 409, attacking Origen and his followers for asking superfluous questions about the image of God in man, and *Panarion* 64.4.9, p. 412, and Epistle LI 6.5, p. 407.

13 Jerome, ibid., *Panarion* 64.4.11, p. 413, and *Epistle* LI.5.7, p. 405.

14 *Hexaemeron* Homily 3.9, *SC* 26, pp. 234–5.

15 *De resurrectione* I. 29 and 55, *GCS* 27 (1917), pp. 258 and 313–14.

16 *Panarion* 64.21 and 47, pp. 433 and 472–3.

17 *Bibliotheca* 117, ed. R. Henry, Paris 1960, vol. 2 pp. 88ff.

18 P. Nautin, *Origène. Sa vie et son oeuvre*, Paris 1977, p. 111 identifies the lost apology with that of Pamphilus; W. A. Bienert disagrees: 'Die älteste Apologie für Origenes?' in Lies (ed.), *Origeniana Quarta*, pp. 123–7.

19 *Against John of Jerusalem*, 7, 18, and 21, *PL* 23.360B, 369Cf., and 372A.

20 An interpretation of Jacob's dream along these lines is given by Philo, *De*

somniis 1.134ff. (cf. U. Früchtel, *Die kosmologischen Vorstellungen bei Philo von Alexandrien*, Leiden 1968, p. 63). Philo's interpretation is commended by Origen in *Contra Celsum* VI.21, p. 91.21–8.

21 1.3.8, p. 63.1ff., 'non arbitror quod ad subitum quis evacuetur ac decidat, sed paulatim et per partes defluere eum necesse est'; II.2.2, p. 112.22ff., 'materialis ista substantia...cum ad inferiores quosque trahitur, in crassiorem corporis statum solidioremque formatur...; cum uero perfectioribus ministrat et beatioribus, in fulgore caelestium corporum micat et spiritalis corporis indumentis vel angelos dei vel filios resurrectionis exornat'; see also *On Martyrdom* 45, p. 41.17ff., on the need of demons for suitable food to enable them to stay in this thick earthly atmosphere; *Contra Celsum* III.41–2, p. 237.15–16 and 24ff., Jesus' body changed to an ethereal and divine quality such as would be necessary for living in the aether and the regions above it, and VII.5, p. 156.22ff., contrasting the regions of the purer and ethereal bodies with the gross bodies here.

22 Another biblical verse applied to the descent of souls to bodies is Genesis 6:2; cf. Origen's references to such an interpretation in *Commentary on John* VI.42, p. 151.10ff., *Contra Celsum* V.55, p. 58.20–7.

23 In particular Didymus; cf. A. Henrichs, *Didymus der Blinde*: *Kommentar zu Hiob* I, Bonn 1968, pp. 313–14 n. 7.

24 *Commentary on Matthew* XVII.30, p. 671.10–21; cf. *Contra Celsum* V.19, p.20.27ff., where Origen, referring to 2 Corinthians 5:1–4, interprets the 'earthly house' as the body of this life, destroyed at death, and the 'tabernacle' (*skēnos*) as the corporeal nature which, though corruptible, is needed by the soul in order to pass from place to place, and which, in the resurrection, is not stripped off but clothed with a garment of incorruptibility on top. Cf. also *Contra Celsum* VII.32, p. 182.20ff., and H. Chadwick, 'Origen, Celsus, and the Resurrection of the Body', *HThR*, 41 (1948), 83–102.

25 Cf. *Dialogue with Heracleides* 11f., 15f., *SC* 67 (1960), pp. 78.16ff. and 88.28ff.; *Commentary on the Song of Songs* prol., p. 63.31ff. and p. liii; *Commentary on Romans* 1.19 (ed. Lommatzsch, VI. pp. 66.12–67.21) and II.13 (p. 142.1ff.). On the 'double creation' and the inner and outer man, cf. G. Sfameni Gasparro, *Origene*: *Studi di antropologia e di storia della tradizione*, Rome 1984, chapters 2–3, pp. 101–55. Cf.

26 *Homily on Jeremiah* 1.10, p. 8.28ff.

27 *Commentary on John* 1.17, p. 21.4ff.

28 *choikos*, *Commentary on John* XX.22, p. 355ff.

29 *Commentary on John* XX.22, p. 354.33ff.

30 *On Prayer* 26.5, p. 362.7ff.

31 *Homily on Jeremiah* II.1, p. 17.7–16; cf. *Homily on Luke* 39, p. 219.22ff.

32 *Fragment on Jeremiah* 22, *GCS* Origenes III, p. 208.11ff., *Homily on Jeremiah* II.9 and III.1, *GCS*. Origenes VIII, pp. 298.4–9, 26–9, 306.16–25.

33 *Homily on Jeremiah* XIV.8, p. 113.21–4; VIII.2, p. 57.30ff.

34 The latter view is taken by G. Bürke, 'Des Origenes Lehre vom Urstand des Menschen', *ZKTh* 72 (1950), 1–39, the former view by M. Simonetti, 'Alcune Osservazioni sull' Interpretazione Origeniana di Genesi 2, 7 e 3, 21', *Aevum*, 36 (1962), 370–81, and 'Didymiana', *VetChr*, 21 (1984), 129ff., followed by H. Crouzel in U. Bianchi and H. Crouzel (eds.), *Arché e Telos*, Milan 1981, pp. 42–5 and in *BLE*, 86 (1985), 137 (where he corrects his earlier view expressed in his *Théologie de l'image de Dieu chez Origène* (Paris 1956)). The treatment given to this question by these scholars, however, shows clearly that its solution is highly problematic. The possibility of two falls is raised briefly by H. Cornélis, 'Les Fondements cosmologiques de l'eschatologie d'Origène', *RSPhTh*, 43 (1959), 222 note 213; cf. also 217 note 193. A considerable advance is made in two contributions published in the proceedings of the fourth International Origen Congress, ed. L. Lies, *Origeniana Quarta* (Innsbruck 1987), of which I only received a copy after writing this paper: Paola Pisi, 'Peccato di Adamo e caduta dei NOES nell' esegesi origeniana', pp. 322–35, and M. Harl, 'La préexistence des âmes dans l'oeuvre d'Origène', pp. 238–58. (I was unfortunately unaware of the paper of P. Pisi until I received the proceedings and was unable to be present at the paper of M. Harl. I was, however, able to consult a summary provided by M. Harl for participants at the conference.) P. Pisi considers first the allegorical exegesis of Adam's fall in relation to the fall of the 'noes' and secondly the 'historical' reading and asks the question (pp. 326–7): 'Dobbiamo forse pensare ad una "protologia graduata", secondo cui la storia umana sarebbe segnata da due distinti e successivi momenti di caduta, rispettivamente la colpa precosmica dei *noes*, che porta all'assunzione di corpi pesanti, e posteriormente l'espulsione dei protoplasti dall'Eden, che inaugura il processo generativo, apportatore di una propria, e peculiarmente specifica, impurità?' – concluding, however, that there is a tension between the two fall accounts (that of the rational beings and that of the protoplasts) which remains fundamentally unresolved in Origen's thought. M. Harl devotes one section to the story of Adam (pp. 245–7), which she reads primarily on a historical level. She does not, however, place the account of the fall of rational beings and Adam's story in clear chronological succession, preferring to distinguish between different 'registers' of exegesis (p. 250).

35 Cf. *De principiis* I.6.4, II.2.2, pp. 85.14ff. and 112.15ff., and *Commentary on John* 1.17, p. 21.12ff. The question has been discussed most often in connection with the resurrection and final restoration; an excellent brief summary of the debate is provided by G. Dorival, 'Origène et la résurrection de la chair', in Lies (ed), *Origeniana Quarta*, pp. 312–15. Origen himself does not commit himself to a decision in his surviving writings; cf. H. Chadwick, *Early Christian Thought*, pp. 86–7.

36 If one takes the view that the first creation was corporeal, one does not necessarily have to think in terms of the body of Genesis 2:7 (or alternatively one might wish to understand this verse on more than one level), and again it may seem most probable that the body of Adam in paradise was identical neither with the resurrection body nor with the body of this life. In *Contra Celsum* v.19 (see above, p. 86, n. 24) Origen distinguishes on the basis of 2 Corinthians 5:1–4 the *epigeios oikia* of this life, the *skēnos* and the garment of immortality put on top of the *skēnos* in the resurrection. Didymus (see below, p. 75) regards the *chous* of Genesis 2:7 as being the same as the *skēnos*. In some passages, Origen seems to think of the body as able to occupy various positions on a scale of increasing grossness or subtlety. Cf. above, p. 86, n. 21 and D. G. Bostock, 'Quality and Corporeity in Origen' in H. Crouzel and A. Quacquarelli (eds.), *Origeniana Secunda = Quaderni di 'Vetera Christianorum'*, 15 (1980), 323–37, especially 334. On the philosophical background to such a view, cf. U. Bianchi, 'Origen's Treatment of the Soul and the Debate over Metensomatosis', in Lies (ed.), *Origeniana Quarta*, p. 279, and Bostock, 'Quality and Corporeity', following H. Chadwick, 'Origen, Celsus and the Resurrection of the Body', pp. 101–2, and *Early Christian Thought*, pp. 86–8. According to P. Pisi (p. 326) the difference between Adam's body and that of postlapsarian humanity is not that between a luminous body and a heavy body but between purity and impurity. M. Harl (p. 247) writes in terms of 'un corps de terre permettant d'abord une croissance facile, devenant ensuite, après la désobéissance, plus lourd, corruptible (les tuniques de peaux), entraînant les "peines" d'une éducation plus dure'. See also above, pp. 72–4 and 75.

37 P. Nautin and L. Doutreleau, *SC* 233 (Paris 1976).

38 *Homily on Genesis* 1.1, p. 2.17–18.

39 20.18ff., 21.2ff.; compare Origen on the *logos* in *On Martyrdom* 37, p. 34.22ff.

40 P. 13.18–23; cf. also *Homily on Leviticus* v.2, p. 336.22–24, and, most illuminatingly, *Fragment on Jeremiah* 22, p. 208.11–18, which summarizes an exposition similar to that just described.

41 The very detailed discussion of the allegorical interpretation of the waters above the firmament in Origen's first *Homily on Genesis* and in other sources by J. Pépin, *Théologie Cosmique et Théologie Chrétienne*, Paris 1964, pp. 390–417, was written before the publication of Didymus' *Commentary on Genesis*. Particularly illuminating for the interconnection between the interpretation applied to spiritual powers and that applied to the individual are his remarks about the triple meaning of the word *dunameis* (virtues of the human soul, attributes of the divine essence, or spirits distinct from God and man, pp. 374ff. and p. 391).

42 Ed. Lommatzsch, VIII, pp. 49–52 = Theodoret, *Quaestiones in Genesim* 20, *PG* 80.113A–117A.

43 Cf. Lommatzsch, VIII, pp. 48ff., *PG* 12.91ff. There also survive three
brief extracts in Latin on Genesis 2:25, 3:2–3 and 3:12, taken from an
otherwise unknown 'Epistula Origenis ad Gobarum'. These are quoted in
the catena of Johannes Diaconus on the Heptateuch as coming from
Victor of Capua. They discuss the verses on a historical level. It is suggested
by Nautin that the extracts were quoted in Pamphilus' *Apology for Origen* as
evidence that Origen did not reject a literal interpretation of Adam's story;
cf. J. B. Pitra, *Spicilegium Solesmense* I (Paris 1852), p. 267; P. Nautin, *Lettres
et écrivains chrétiens* (Paris 1961), pp. 248–9; Nautin, *Origène*, pp. 175–6.

44 P. 58 = Theodoret, *Quaestiones in Genesim* 39, *PG* 80.140C–141B.

45 All three passages are well discussed by Simonetti, 'Alcune Osservazioni',
Aevum, 36, 377. Cf. also H. Chadwick, *Origen: Contra Celsum*, p. 216 note 5
and *Early Christian Thought*, p. 90. G. Dorival, 'Origène et la résurrection
de la chair', in Lies (ed.), *Origeniana Quarta*, pp. 291–321, shows Origen's
caution in distinguishing the different biblical meanings of the word
'flesh'.

46 The ambiguity of Origen's references to paradise is reflected in the fact that
Bürke, 'Des Origenes Lehre', p. 27, is able to understand them solely on
a spiritual level as referring to 'der verklärte Urzustand der Schöpfung
überhaupt', whereas M. Rauer, 'Origenes über das Paradies', *TU*, 77
(1961), 253–9, argues that Origen thought of paradise as a 'real place'. It
should be noted that the catena fragment quoted by Rauer as evidence for
paradise as a place with real trees (pp. 258–9) is wrongly attributed to
Origen and is in fact part of Epiphanius' attack in *Ancoratus* 58.6–8, *GCS* 25,
pp. 68.13–69.2. Although it is true that many of Origen's mentions of
paradise as a place can simultaneously be understood as referring also
symbolically to a condition of the soul, it can none the less be argued against
Bürke (who tends to quote brief extracts of Origen out of context in a
manner which is sometimes misleading) that he regarded paradise as an
intermediate level where souls are trained in preparation for further
ascent.

47 Cf. *De principiis* II.3.6, pp. 121.22–123.18; *Contra Celsum* VII.28–9, pp.
179.12–181.2. On the question of the number of heavens, cf. *Contra Celsum*
VI.21, p. 91.15–28; Cornélis, 'Les Fondements cosmologiques', p. 224;
Pépin, *Théologie cosmique*, pp. 390ff.; P. Nautin, 'Genèse 1, 1–2, de Justin à
Origène', in *In Principio, Interprétations des premiers versets de la Genèse, Etudes
Augustiniennes*, Paris 1973, pp. 90–1.

48 Cf. Harl, 'La préexistence des âmes', pp. 245–6. This distinction needs to be
borne in mind if one attempts to apply the report of Procopius on the views
of the allegorists to Origen's thought.

49 *Homily on Ezechiel* XIII.2, pp. 447.23–448.10, *Contra Celsum* VI.44,
p. 115.13–20.

50 *On Martyrdom* 36 and 50, pp. 33.20ff. and 46.14–15; for the different orders
or levels of existence in the afterlife cf. *De principiis* II.11.6, p. 190.1ff., III.

6.8–9, pp. 289.23ff., *Homily on Numbers* III. 3, p. 17.11ff. and XXVIII.2, p. 281.34ff.

51 *Homily on Jeremiah* 1.16, p. 16.10, *Homily on Joshua* XIII.4, p. 374.6ff.

52 *On Prayer* 25.3, p. 359.2–3.

53 *On Prayer* 23.3–4, pp. 351.14–352.14, referring to the fuller treatment in the *Commentary on Genesis*.

54 *Homily on Psalm 36*, 1, *PG* 12.1326, *Excerpta in Ps.* 36.4, *PG* 17.121A; cf. *Commentary on the Song of Songs* 1, p. 104.17ff.

55 *Selecta in Psalm.* 1, *PG* 12.1088–9; cf. *Commentary on John* XX.36, p. 375.14ff., *On Prayer* 27.10, p. 369.23ff.

56 Papyrus Graecus Vindobonensis 29829, 29883, edited, discussed and assigned to Origen by P. Sanz, *Griechische literarische Papyri christlichen Inhaltes* I (Vienna 1946), pp. 87–104. The ascription to Origen is questioned by H. Crouzel, *Bibliographie critique d'Origène*, Steenbrugge 1971, p. 408, but he does not give detailed reasons or suggest a different author.

57 Fragment VI^v 7–9 on Genesis 3:15a; Didymus 99.31ff. on Genesis 3:15b.

58 Fragment I^r 3ff. on Genesis 3:11, Didymus 90.9ff.

59 Hebrews 2:2 and Philippians 2:7–8 in fragment I, John 14:30 in fragment IV, Hebrews 4:15 in fragment IIb.

60 Cf. Didymus 102.12ff., 106.1ff.; also 63.9ff., where the Logos is bridegroom of the rational nature.

61 *HE* III.7; see also above, p. 65.

62 The *koinai ennoiai*, a Stoic doctrine utilized also by Origen; cf. Nautin's notes SC 233 *ad loc.* and H. Chadwick's note on *Contra Celsum* 1.4.

63 *Legum allegoriae* II.xviii.73. It also appears in Ambrose, *De paradiso* 2.11 (*CSEL*, 32 (1896), p. 271).

64 The references in *De principiis* have already been listed above, p. pp. 64 and 85, n. 8.

65 *Homily on Jeremiah* 1.10, p. 9.2–5.

66 *Commentary on John* 1.20, p. 25.2ff.

67 *Commentary on John* XIII.32, p. 259.34ff.; this reference occurs in the context of a discussion of spiritual nourishment.

68 *Commentary on the Song of Songs* II, p. 157.23ff.

69 Fragment 62 on Matthew 4:3–10 (p. 40.1ff.), fragments 95–6 on Luke 4:1ff. and 4:4 (pp. 264.3 and 265.8ff.)

70 Fragment 95 on Luke 4:1ff., p. 264.6ff.; cf. fragment 62 on Matthew 4:3–10, p. 40.14–22.

71 *On Prayer* 29.18, p. 392.9ff.

72 *Contra Celsum* VII.39, p. 189.23ff.; cf. Philo, *Quaestiones in Genesim* 1.39 (quoted by H. Chadwick, *Origen: Contra Celsum*, pp. 426–7 note 8).

73 Cf. also *On Prayer* 23.3–4, quoted above, p. 73, and Philo, *Leg. all.* III.1.1.

74 Fragments 45 and 140 on John 3:29 and 17:11, pp. 520.20 and 574.7ff.

75 *Comm. Ser.* 126, p. 265.1ff.

76 Cf. fragment on Matthew 27:32–4, 551 III, p. 226.10ff., and *Commentary on Romans* v.2, ed. Lommatzsch, p. 352.8ff., where a quotation of Wisdom of Solomon 10:1 is used to show that Christ has saved Adam himself, together with the others to whom Adam was the cause of death.

77 *Commentary on Romans*, vol. 5, ed. Lommatzsch, pp. 322.9–14, 345.19ff., 349.13ff., 368.5ff.

78 Cf. also *Contra Celsum*, vi.36, p. 105.32ff.: 'through a tree came death and through a tree came life, death in Adam and life in Christ'; catena LXXXIV.82ff. on Ephesians 15:20–23 (*JThS*, 3 (1902), 48): Christ is the first fruits for life of those who will live, Adam became the first fruits of the death of men.

79 *Homily on Genesis* IX.2, p. 90.1–6: Genesis 1:28 is said of Christ and the church; fragment 45 on John 3:29, p. 520.13–22: Christ and the church are the parents of all good works, thoughts and words; *Commentary on Romans* v.1, ed. Lommatzsch, pp. 345.7–19: Christ came to unite the church with himself; and, without reference to Eve and the church, fragment 140 on John 17:11, p. 574.7–14: we have Adam as beginning and head of our birth and Christ of our rebirth; *Commentary on Romans* 1.13, ed. Lommatzsch p. 44.2ff.: both the first Adam, as vine and root of the human race, and Christ, the last Adam, bear both fruitful and unfruitful branches.

80 For this exegesis of Genesis 1:27 compare Didymus, *Commentary on Genesis* 62.21ff., especially 63.10–18, 'every rational nature occupies the position of female in relation to the Logos'.

81 Cf. also on the deception of Eve *Homily on Jeremiah* xx.3 and 8, pp. 182.5–8, 188.10–15, *On Prayer* 29.18, p. 392.9–13, *Contra Celsum* vi.43, p. 113.17–21: 'the serpent deceived the female race, which the man is said to have followed'.

82 1.18, p. 23.2–8: in that he became flesh he is Adam, which is interpreted 'man'; 1.31, p. 39.33ff.: Christ may be said to be beginning and end of the whole body of those who are saved, as for example 'beginning' in the man he assumed and 'end' in the last of the saints, or 'beginning' in Adam and 'end' in his sojourn on earth.

83 This parallel is elaborated by Methodius, *Symposium* III.8 (*GCS* 27 (1917), p. 35.9ff.).

84 Origen's understanding of Adam and Eve as Christ and the church needs to be seen in the whole context of his understanding of the church; cf. H. J. Vogt, *Das Kirchenverständnis des Origenes*, Cologne 1974, especially pp. 205ff.

85 *Contra Celsum* VII.28, p. 179.22ff.

86 *Homily on Ezechiel* IV.1, p. 359.23ff.

87 *Homily on Jeremiah* VIII.1, p. 55.10ff.; cf. also the passages referred to above, p. 68, on the image of the 'choic'.

88 Rufinus abbreviates the exposition of Romans 5:12ff. particularly heavily, partly no doubt because Origen's exegesis was very full here (cf. C. P. Bammel, *Der Römerbrieftext des Rufin und seine Origenes-Übersetzung*, Freiburg 1985, pp. 52 and 58–60), perhaps because he found some of the material unsuited to his intended readers. His selective approach may have resulted in some bias or distortion, but I see no reason to doubt that what he includes is derived from Origen.

89 Cf. *Commentary on Romans* v.1, Lommatzsch (ed.), pp. 339.5–340.6, and, for the word 'devil' as equivalent to sin and death, v.6, p. 373.10ff.; also *contra Celsum* 1.31, p. 83.3–5, on the devil's power over all human souls on earth.

90 *Commentary on Romans* v.4, pp. 363.15–364.5.

91 *Commentary on Romans* v.1, p. 324.17ff.

92 Ibid. p. 326.2–21, quoting 1 Corinthians 15:22; cf. also v.4, p. 364.5–7.

93 *Commentary on Romans* v.1, pp. 342.17ff.; cf. also v.2, p. 353.2ff., arguing that it is possible, when one reaches the age of reason, to turn away from the teaching of one's parents and to leave 'Adam', who engendered or taught one to death, and to follow Christ.

94 *Commentary on Romans* III.3, p. 181.5–15.

95 Cf. 356.9–13, 358.6ff.: the soul, created free by God, reduces itself to slavery by sin and, as it were, hands over to death the bond of its immortality, which it had received from its creator; p. 364.4–9: all are in this place of humiliation and vale of tears, whether because all born from Adam were in his loins and cast out with him, or that each individual is thought to have been driven out of paradise and received the condemnation in some other indescribable way that is known only to God.

96 I find unconvincing the suggestion tentatively put forward by C. Bigg, *The Christian Platonists of Alexandria*, Oxford 1886, pp. 202–3, and taken up by A. Harnack, *History of Dogma*, vol. 2, London 1896, p. 365 note 5, F. R. Tennant, *The Sources of the Doctrines of the Fall and Original Sin*, Cambridge 1903, pp. 298–9, and N. P. Williams, *The Ideas of the Fall and of Original Sin*, London 1927, pp. 223–4, that Origen first encountered the practice of infant baptism after his move to Caesarea and for this reason developed a doctrine of original sin.

97 *Commentary on Romans* v.9, p. 396.5ff.

98 Ibid. p. 397.5–7, p. 396.12–19; on the pollution of birth cf. also *Contra Celsum* VII.50, p. 200.21ff., *Homily on Leviticus* VIII.3, pp. 396.7–399.8, and *Homily on Luke XIV*, pp. 85.1ff., where it is argued that in putting on an earthly body, described as 'dirty garments' in Zechariah 3:3, Jesus put on pollution (*rhupos*) but not sin. On the pollution of life in the body cf. the full discussion by G. Sfameni Gasparro, *Origene*, pp. 193–252.

99 Cf. also, on the 'old' or 'choic' man, but without mention of Adam, *Commentary on Romans* IV.7, p. 281.15ff., *Homily on Genesis* IX.2, p. 89, *Homily on Judges* v.5, p. 495.9ff.

100 Cf. v.1, pp. 334.7–336.16; VI.8, p. 43.12ff. The parallel between Adam and a child not yet able to distinguish between good and evil is drawn in Ambrose, *De paradiso*, 6.31 (*CSEL* 32 (1896), 287.23ff.), where criticisms of the Genesis story made by the Marcionite Apelles and others are quoted (if ignorant of good and evil, Adam was no different from a child and ought not to have been blamed for his transgression). It is not possible here to examine Ambrose's use of Origen in this work; cf. A. Harnack, *Sieben neue Bruchstücke der Syllogismen des Apelles*, *TU*, 6.3 (1890), pp. 111ff.

101 In the *Commentary on John* XIII.37 (p. 261.32ff.) Origen discusses whether the rational creature was incomplete when placed in paradise and suggests rather than it became so through transgression. None the less his quotation of Hebrews 5:14 (p. 262.25ff.) suggests that the condition of the *teteleiōmenos* is different from that in paradise before the fall. (On this passage see above, p. 77, and the discussion by M. Harl, 'La préexistence des âmes', in Lies (ed.), *Origeniana Quarta*, p. 246.) In describing the final restoration (which will be similar to the beginning), Origen states that, when God is 'all in all', there will be no *mali bonique discretio*, since the mind will be aware of nothing except God (*De principiis* III.6.3, pp. 283.14–284.10).

102 The hypothesis of a 'change of mind' is implausible not least because the 'earlier' theory (re-)appears both in the *Commentary on Romans* itself and in the *Contra Celsum*; see above and Tennant, *The Sources of the Doctrines*, p. 302, Williams, *The Ideas of the Fall*, pp. 228–9. It may be noted that Didymus appears to have found no difficulty in accepting both the concept of the fall of the pre-existent soul and that of the succession (*diadochē*) of sin from Adam; cf. A. Henrichs, *Didymus der Blinde: Kommentar zu Hiob*, vol. 1, Bonn 1968, pp. 311–14.

103 If one does not think in terms of more than one stage in the descent, the uniqueness of the soul of Christ (as the only soul to have remained in union with God, *De principiis* II.6.3, p. 142) is jeopardized by the hypothesis, mentioned by Origen a number of times, that some souls have descended to this world, not because they deserved this as a result of their own fall, but in order to serve others (e.g. *De principiis* III.5.4, p. 275; *Commentary on John* II.31, p. 88). The problem of the apparent contradiction in *De principiis* on this question cannot be discussed here. Cf. Pisi, 'Peccato di Adamo', in Lies (ed.), *Origeniana Quarta*, p. 331, note 11.

104 Cf. the avoidance of so literal-minded an approach by M. Harl, 'La préexistence des âmes', in Lies (ed.), *Origeniana Quarta*, p. 250.

105 Thus we might surmise that he speculated more widely on the story of Adam in his *Commentary on Genesis* than in his later works, perhaps also that he moved in the direction of a more negative view of the figure of Adam himself (cf. *Commentary on John* XX.3, p. 329.25: it is still under investigation whether Adam is to be counted among the just or not).

Panegyric, history and hagiography in Eusebius' *Life of Constantine*

T. D. BARNES

Eusebius' *Life of Constantine* has an obvious relevance to the making of Christian orthodoxy. It has often seemed to be a peculiarly problematical text. I had the great good fortune to be introduced to the *Life* and its problems many years ago by Henry Chadwick, who pronounced, in that grave and rational tone of voice which all who have known him will recall so well, that Eusebius' authorship was the only plausible hypothesis – an opinion which he later reiterated in print.[1] At the time, I was wrestling with the problem of trying to understand Tertullian under Henry's temporary guidance, but I never forgot the remark. When I began to work seriously on the Constantinian period, I consciously adopted the transmitted and traditional attribution of the *Life* as a working hypothesis, which came to seem more strongly based the more I penetrated the period. Hence it is with deep gratitude and pleasure that I offer the following essay on the occasion of Henry Chadwick's seventieth birthday – all the more so since the first article which I wrote about Constantine was published in a volume celebrating the seventieth birthday of Sir Ronald Syme.[2] Debate has moved on since 1973: here I shall be less concerned to demonstrate partially novel interpretations of Constantine and Eusebius than to apply hypotheses which I have developed elsewhere to the work which has for ever linked their two names.[3]

The problems posed by the *Life of Constantine* are both literary and historical. The literary and historical problems are of course inextricably linked to each other, since proof of anachronisms would exclude Eusebius' authorship of the whole, while Eusebian authorship confers on the *Life* a certain status as evidence. Yet clarity demands that the literary and historical problems be considered separately – a procedure which reveals that the traditional 'problem of the *Life of Constantine*' in large part arose from confusing the two.[4] Progress has been made, and can still be made, when the two questions are asked separately: does the *Life* as transmitted in the manuscripts come entirely from the pen of Eusebius, or is it wholly or partly the work of a later hand? And what is the historical value of the extant *Life* as evidence for the actions and personality of Constantine? Even the former question, however, when posed in these terms, is misleading when the four books of the *Life* are considered as if they were designed to stand by themselves. Since its structure and literary genre are both problematical, the *Life* must not be considered apart from the three speeches appended to it, for Eusebius makes it clear that he intended them to stand as an integral complement to the *Life* (4.32,46), the four books and appended speeches forming a single literary whole.

The *Life* itself has a messy structure which can *prima facie* be analysed roughly as follows:

1.1–11 Introduction
1.12–19 Constantine at the court of Diocletian
1.20–5 Proclamation as emperor (306)
1.26–38 The war against Maxentius (311–12)
1.39–48 From Constantine's entry into Rome (29 October 312) to his *decennalia* (315/16)
1.49–2.18 War against Licinius: the two wars, of 316/17 and 324, are deliberately fused together as a single war
2.19–60 The consequences of Constantine's victory in 324 for Christians and pagans
2.61–3.23 The controversy over Arius and the Council of Nicaea (325), interrupted by comparison of Constantine with Licinius (3.1–3)
3.24–66 Actions of Constantine relating to Christianity and the Christian church
4.1–13 Constantine's qualities as emperor (1–6) and his fame beyond the empire (7), illustrated by his correspondence with the Persian King (8–13)
4.14–39 Constantine's Christianity and Christian legislation
4.40–52 Constantine's last years: introduced by an explicit reference to his *tricennalia* (40)
4.53–73 Death and burial
4.74/5 Epilogue

To this are appended three speeches:

1 Constantine's *Speech to the Assembly of the Saints*, styled Book v in two manuscripts. The authenticity of this speech has often been denied or disallowed, but it now seems certain that Constantine delivered it either shortly before or shortly after his defeat of Licinius in 324 in Thessalonica, Serdica, Nicomedia or possibly Antioch, and that what Eusebius preserves is an official (though not highly skilful) Greek translation of a Latin original which was often obscurely expressed.[5]

2 *Panegyric to Constantine*, delivered by Eusebius in Constantinople on the occasion of Constantine's *tricennalia*. Since the speech alludes to Dalmatius Caesar, who was not proclaimed a member of the imperial college until 18 September 335 (*Laus Constantini* 2.4, cf. *MGH.AA* 9.235), the date of delivery must be 25 July 336 (not July 335).[6]

3 *Treatise on the Church of the Holy Sepulchre*, delivered by Eusebius to the Council of Jerusalem in mid September 335 as part of the bishops' dedication of Constantine's magnificent new church.[7]

It would be unenlightening as well as depressing to describe yet again the history of the controversy over the authorship and authenticity of the *Life of Constantine*. Friedhelm Winkelmann's survey published in 1962 removes any necessity,[8] and it is clear that three turning points have now transformed the long and sterile debate. First, A. H. M. Jones (acting on a suggestion from C. E. Stevens) identified a fragmentary papyrus dated palaeographically between *c.* 320 and *c.* 340 as containing part of a document in the *Life* (2.24–42) which hostile critics had most confidently pounced upon as a manifest forgery.[9] Consequently, since the early 1950s the authenticity of all the documents has generally and correctly been conceded, as has Eusebius' authorship of the *Life*, despite some isolated denials.[10] Second, the first war between Constantine and Licinius has been convincingly re-dated from 314 to 316/17: on the traditional chronology, which held sway unchallenged from 1665 to 1953, Eusebius' account of the hostilities between the two emperors seemed to commit at least one gross error by putting the start of hostilities between them after Constantine's *decennalia* in 315 (1.49, cf. 48). The date of 316/17, which had prevailed before 1665,[11] was reinstated by Patrick Bruun in 1953 on the basis of the Constantinian coinage of Arelate:[12] when other numismatists demurred, Christian Habicht proved that the literary and documentary evidence also heavily favours 316, while Bruun demonstrated the same for the coinage of all the imperial mints.[13] The correct chronology not only removes the error in the *Life of Constantine*, but necessitates a fresh approach to Lactantius' *On the Death of the Persecutors*, which can now be used as a basis for writing the history of the Constantinian period.[14]

The third turning point is one whose importance was realized only slowly and is still sometimes denied. In 1910, Giorgio Pasquali demonstrated that the *Life of Constantine* is unfinished.[15] But other scholars exhibited a curious failure to understand Pasquali's thesis. His conclusions were totally misreported, not only at once by the French scholars Jules Maurice and Pierre Batiffol, but also in 1930 by Norman Baynes, in an influential study still regarded by many as the best introduction to the Constantinian period.[16] Baynes performed the agile feat of first refuting what he presented as Pasquali's thesis, then appropriating and arguing Pasquali's main conclusion as if in opposition to him. Henri Grégoire (it is amusing to observe) was not deceived, though he let the misrepresentation pass for tactical reasons.[17] Scholars who were more trusting (and perhaps too busy to read Pasquali for themselves) accepted Baynes' false report until 1962, when Winkelmann documented and exposed the misrepresentation. Since the reprint of Baynes' study of Constantine (published in 1972) charitably refrains from taxing Baynes with the error, a restatement of Pasquali's thesis will be apposite. Too much modern writing about Constantine has an air of unreality, as if the protagonists in the controversy prefer shadow-boxing to grappling with the real issues.

Pasquali began from Ivar Heikel's edition of the *Life of Constantine*, which he reviewed at length for the Göttingen Academy.[18] He therefore knew and accepted Heikel's demonstration, in the preface to his edition, that the language and style of the documents quoted in the *Life* is very different from that of the text – from which it follows that Eusebius himself cannot have invented them.[19] Pasquali then observed a curious, undeniable and significant phenomenon: the *Life* contains at least one clear and substantial doublet, since Book II first summarizes an edict of Constantine in some detail (20–1: more than twenty lines), then quotes the document just summarized verbatim and in full (24–42). Pasquali made a comparison of the quoted text and its preceding summary the cornerstone of a proof that, whatever the *Life* may be, it cannot be a finished literary product composed and articulated by Eusebius as a unitary composition. Accordingly, after identifying other indications that the *Life* contains 'two drafts or at least the remains of two drafts', Pasquali suggested an explanation in terms of two changes of plan and unfinished composition. On Pasquali's hypothesis, as soon as Eusebius learned that the emperor had died on 22 May 337 (i.e. in June), he composed a panegyric of the dead emperor in the style and manner deemed appropriate to a *basilikos logos* in Greek rhetorical handbooks.[20] However, when Eusebius discovered that his enemy Athanasius was being restored from exile, he began to remodel the encomium as more of a polemical pamphlet. Finally, when news came of the dynastic murders of the summer of 337 and the proclamation of Constantinus, Constantius and Constans as Augusti on 9 September, Eusebius revised the almost-finished work at the beginning and end to take account of the new political situation.

Pasquali argued that Eusebius died in May 338, before he had time to prepare the *Life* properly for publication. His concluding paragraph, tersely expressed in limpid German, deserves quotation:

Then someone came and published the work at once, as he found it: perhaps Acacius, Eusebius' successor in the see of Caesarea was the editor, but the name does not matter. The work was published with the same piety and the same lack of understanding as Plato's *Laws* were by Philippus of Opus. With the *Life*, political considerations too affected the publication.[21]

The analogy ought to have made the conclusion perfectly clear. Pasquali did not believe the *Life* to be interpolated in the normal sense, as Maurice, Batiffol and Baynes alleged: on the contrary, he held that the 'interpolations' which he identified were all inserted by Eusebius himself into his own earlier draft.

Pasquali's central thesis was never refuted, merely misreported or ignored. It cannot be refuted, for it corresponds to and explains the observable phenomena. Moreover, even though not all the doublets and inconsistencies which Pasquali identified really are what he claimed them to be, other features of the *Life* which he did not discuss support his central contention that a posthumous editor published the *Life* after Eusebius died. The following briefly annotated list includes passages adduced by Pasquali, by Winkelmann (in the preface to his edition of the *Life*)[22] and by the present writer:

Chapter headings Eusebius normally equipped his historical and
  apologetical works with chapter headings (*kephalaia*) before each
  chapter and lists of contents in the form of a consolidated list of
  the relevant chapter headings before each book (which it is
  convenient to style an 'index').[23] The chapter headings and index

to the *Life* use the third person (not the first) to describe the author's activity in composition (1.11 *keph.*: 'That he has now related only the god-loving actions of Constantine'; 4.33 *keph.*: 'How he stood to listen to the rhetorical display of Eusebius about the tomb of the Saviour').

1.11.1 Eusebius promises to omit Constantine's victories in war and his peaceful measures for the good of the whole commonwealth: in fact, the *Life* contains passages which depict the emperor with the traits of the traditional good ruler with little or no allusion to his Christianity (e.g. 1.25, on campaigns *c.* 307; 1.45, on campaigns *c.* 314; 4.1–7, on his generosity, his military prowess against the northern barbarians and his world-wide reputation). Moreover, these passages are matched by two others which denounce Licinius as a tyrant (1.54.2–55) and compare the two emperors point by point (3.1–3).

1.18.2 This passage praises Constantius, the father of Constantine, for surpassing other emperors in fertility by raising 'a large chorus of male and female children'. Eusebius is unlikely to have written that after the two surviving sons of Constantius were killed in the summer of 337,[24] though he may well have forgotten to delete the already written sentence. Everywhere else in the *Life*, Eusebius reflects the political realities of September 337 when the three sons of Constantine and Fausta were proclaimed Augusti after the elimination of their dynastic rivals, who included the Caesar Dalmatius.

1.23 Eusebius declares that he has decided to avoid sullying his work with accounts of the rulers who waged war on the church, but the first book of the *Life* closes with long accounts of the painful deaths of Galerius in 311 and Maximinus in 313, partly transcribed almost word for word from the *Ecclesiastical History* (1.57–9, cf. *HE* VII.16.3–4, 17.1; IX.10.2–3; X.14–15).

2.13 This is a clear insertion into its context: 14.1 (*tauta men oun*) follows on from 12.2, while 13.2 contradicts the closing sentence of 12.2, alleging that Constantine spared opposing soldiers even in the heat of battle, whereas the earlier passage boasts that his men slaughtered the enemy vigorously until victory was won.

2.20–1 These describe the document quoted in 24–42, and 23.1

follows on 19.3. As Pasquali showed, Eusebius cannot have
intended both passages to stand in the same work.[25]

3.1–3 This *synkrisis* of Constantine and Licinius interrupts a context
which moves from the Arian controversy (2.61–72) to the Council
of Nicaea (3.5–21).

3.4 This chapter repeats the last sentence of 2.72 and the substance
of 2.62, inelegantly introducing the Melitians for a second time. It
was (I believe) added by the editor of the *Life*, who betrays
himself by using a pastiche of phrases from elsewhere in the *Life*
with words Eusebius does not normally use.[26]

3.22 Eusebius speaks here about Constantine's letters from the
Council of Nicaea as if he had not already quoted one of them (as
he does in 17–20).

3.25 The chapter follows logically on the description of the Council
of Nicaea: 'These things being so, the god-lover began another
accomplishment worthy of memory in the province of Palestine.'
What immediately precedes (viz. 23–4) is intrusive to its present
context.

3.41–2 and 43.1–4 These form a doublet on Helena's foundation of
churches to mark the places of Christ's nativity in Bethlehem and
ascension from the Mount of Olives.

4.8 The introduction to Constantine's letter to Shapur (especially the
words *kai touto parastēsei*) implies that Eusebius has just quoted
another document, while the sentence which follows the letter
refers to Constantine's conquest of the East in 324 (14.1): Eusebius
surely intended this letter to follow those quoted in 2.24–60.

4.23 Eusebius summarizes in one brief sentence ('similarly a law
went to all provincial governors [ordering them] to honour the
Lord's day') an enactment which he has just paraphrased at length
(4.18–19: about twenty-five lines).

4.23–5 In this messy passage, two successive brief chapters
inelegantly begin with the same words (*enthen eikotōs*): of them,
4.24 seems to follow on the first sentence of 4.23, while 4.25 seems
to follow on the second sentence of the same chapter.

4.33–8 The abrupt changes of subject, from a speech which Eusebius

delivered before Constantine while the emperor insisted on
standing (33) to two letters of Constantine, the one thanking
Eusebius for a treatise on the date of Easter (35), the other asking
him to prepare copies of the scriptures for liturgical use in
Constantinople (36), may well indicate the lack of a final revision.
Moreover, 38 seems to be an alternative version of 37.

4.46 This chapter, describing two speeches which Eusebius intends
to append to the work, interrupts a context devoted to the Council
of Jerusalem in September 335, and the opening words of 47
('*tautēn megistēn hōn ismen sunodon deuteran*') read awkwardly after 46
and refer back to 45.

4.50 This is a doublet of 4.7.

4.54 This passage has a totally different tenor from any other passage
in the *Life*. It is angry, defensive and polemical, inspired (as
Pasquali saw) by the restoration of Eusebius' ecclesiastical enemies,
especially Athanasius, from exile in the summer of 337.[27]
   I suspect that the first sentence of 55 ('*alla tous men ouk eis makron
hē theia metērcheto dikē*') represents the editor's attempt to connect 54
to its context. The rest of 55 would follow on after the first lacuna
in 37.

Treatise on the Church of the Holy Sepulchre The hypothesis of
posthumous publication resolves the notorious conundrum posed
by the fact that the speech on the Church of the Holy Sepulchre
which stands in the manuscripts of the *Life* does not correspond to
the speech which the text of the *Life* promises to quote. For the
Life promises a speech describing the church and its costly
decoration (4.46.1), whereas the extant *Treatise* avoids physical
description in order to concentrate on Constantine's theological
motives in building the church. The discrepancy can most readily
be explained by the following hypothetical reconstruction:[28]

1 In September 335, Eusebius delivered the extant *Treatise* in
   Jerusalem (11.2) during the ceremonies marking the dedication
   of the Church of the Holy Sepulchre by the Council of Tyre
   (cf. *Life* 4.45.3).
2 In November 335, Eusebius delivered another speech on the same
   subject to Constantine in the imperial palace in Constantinople
   (4.33, 46.1).

3 Eusebius intended to append the later speech to the *Life* (4.46.1).

4 The editor of the *Life* attached the earlier speech, either through careless error or because he failed to find a copy of the later one among Eusebius' papers.

It is important to distinguish clearly between what Pasquali proved and what he did not. He demonstrated that the *Life of Constantine*, as extant, represents a conflation of two drafts and that someone else published the still unfinished work after Eusebius died. He did not, however, attempt to relate the *Life* to other works from the end of Eusebius' life, and he did not define precisely or accurately enough the nature of the two drafts which he distinguished.

Between the death of Constantine and his own, Eusebius was busy on works of contemporary polemic as well as on the *Life*, viz. *Against Marcellus* and *Ecclesiastical Theology*, which are both theological 'hatchet-jobs'.[29] The former was written to justify the deposition of Marcellus of Ancyra by the Council of Constantinople in 336, apparently when Marcellus returned from exile in 337: at all events, it refers to Constantine as dead and as having approved the condemnation of Marcellus.[30] The latter work (it seems) was designed to prepare the way for Marcellus' second deposition, which probably occurred at the Council of Antioch in 338/9 which deposed Athanasius as bishop of Alexandria and replaced him with the Cappadocian Gregory, probably under the presidency of Flaccillus the bishop of Antioch, the dedicatee of the *Ecclesiastical Theology*.[31]

The day of Eusebius' *depositio* or burial is certified as 30 May: it may be deduced, with something close to certainty, that the bishop of Caesarea died in late May 339.[32] This is very relevant to the *Life of Constantine*. Eusebius was not cut off as abruptly as Pasquali imagined (for he put his death in May 338). Moreover, the genesis of the *Life* may be more complicated than Pasquali believed. Even though the *Life* does indeed contain two different drafts or conceptions, of which one is a conventional commemoration of a dead monarch, it is not immediately obvious to which ancient literary genre the other belongs.

In what sense is the *Life of Constantine* a biography? Wilamowitz was characteristically forthright: it neither is nor claims to be a life.[33] For once Wilamowitz was correct as well as pungent, even though Averil Cameron has recently uttered a flat contradiction.[34] His verdict is strengthened by Pasquali's demonstration of posthumous publication.

The manuscripts present the title of the work in two forms. First, preceding the list of chapter headings:

kephalaia tou kata theon biou tou makariou Kōnstantinou basileōs.

Second, at the head of the text:

Eusebiou tou Pamphilou eis ton bion tou makariou Kōnstantinou basileōs.

Neither designation comes from Eusebius himself, and neither promises a proper biography. The phrase 'life according to God' echoes Eusebius' statement that he will record only Constantine's acts of piety (1.10.4), only what tends to produce a god-loving way of life (1.11.1). The preposition in the second title ('on the life of the blessed Emperor Constantine') may imply a partly non-biographical selection of material,[35] or could in theory be intended to suggest similarity to the *Life of Apollonius of Tyana*, a work certainly known to Eusebius, to which Philostratus give a similar title ('*ta eis ton Apollōnion ton Tuanea*').[36] But, whereas Philostratus described his work as a life of Apollonius,[37] the text of Eusebius' so-called *Life of Constantine* never uses the terms appropriate to a formal biography. It is wrong to claim that the work is 'at the same time a biography, a panegyric and an idealisation.'[38] As Wilamowitz saw, it is not a 'life' at all in the ancient sense of the term. It is equally mistaken to supply a noun and then construe the title as signifying 'Reflections of the Life of Constantine'.[39] On the contrary, Eusebius twice describes his work as a history: he protests that to collect and include all Constantine's correspondence with bishops and Christian congregations would interrupt 'the body of our present history' (3.24.2: '*hōs an mē to sōma tēs parousēs hēmin diakoptoito historias*'), and he refers to himself as 'the writer of this history' (3.51.2: '*hēmin de tois tēnde graphousi tēn historian*').

Literary analysis confirms. In his classic study of Greek and Roman biography as a literary genre, Friedrich Leo characterized the *Life* as 'an encomium in four books, with a half-biographical title, half-historical content, completely rhetorical style and ecclesiastical bias', in fact 'an ecclesiastical history of his time centred around the person of Constantine', in which 'the material and its depiction are a mixture of panegyric and history'. Nevertheless, Leo emphasized biographical elements in the *Life*, declaring that 'the thread is biographical' and detecting 'the Suetonian descriptive section' in the way Eusebius sums up Constantine's life before describing his death (4.53–5).[40] Leo's analysis is not quite subtle enough. In ancient writing, the line dividing biography from panegyric, especially encomiastic biography from large-scale panegyric, was narrow and frequently crossed.[41] It follows that what Leo identified as biographical elements may in fact be constituent pieces of the unfinished panegyric.

The arrangement of the *Life* in four books comes from the posthumous editor, not the author. It is necessary, therefore, before a detailed literary analysis can proceed, that passages of the abandoned panegyric be identified. On internal grounds, the following connected passages would be appropriate to a speech composed by Eusebius during 337, presumably begun when he heard of Constantine's death on 22 May but revised after news came that his sons alone had been proclaimed Augusti on 9 September:

1.1–9 Exordium in several sections, viz.

　1–3 Eusebius draws a parallel with the panegyrics of Constantine which he composed in 325 and 336 (1.1) and argues that Constantine alone of all Roman emperors became 'a shining example of a pious life to all men'.

　4–6 God was Constantine's protector.

　7–8 Comparison of Constantine with Cyrus and Alexander the Great.

　9 Summary of main themes and prayer for God's help in composition.

1.12–25 Constantine's origin, youth and accession as emperor, introduced by a comparison to Moses at the court of Pharaoh (12). Eusebius concentrates on Constantine's father, whom he presents as an ideal emperor, using a traditional story first found in Xenophon's *Cyropaideia* (14: he kept his treasury empty, but his friends supplied abundant funds as a gift when he needed them),[42] and as a Christian who refused to persecute his subjects in any way at all in 303 (13.3: disproved as exaggeration by Lactantius, *De mortibus persecutorum* 15.7). Moreover, he follows the advice of the rhetorical handbooks for a *basilikos logos*, ignoring both Constantine's birthplace and his low-born mother: since neither Naissus nor the ignoble Helena increased the emperor's glory, Eusebius simply omitted them.

1.47 God's preservation of Constantine against plots, first by Maximian in the summer of 310, then by other relatives, i.e. the alleged plot by Bassianus, the husband of Anastasia, in 316 (*Origo Constantini imperatoris* 15, cf. *Life* 1.50).[43]

The opening words of 47 ('*en toutois d'onti autōli*') follow on perfectly from 25, which refers to the emperor crossing to Britain – as Constantine in fact did both in 307 and late in 310.

3.1–3 A systematic comparison of the good and pious Constantine with Licinius, to whom Eusebius always applies a generalizing plural (*hoi men ... ho de*).

4.1–7 A panegyrical survey of Constantine as a good emperor in the traditional mould, with only a slight Christian colouring. Constantine showered *beneficia* on his subjects in the form of gifts of money, property and statues (1.2), he remitted taxes and assessed fairly (2–3), he compensated the losing parties in law-suits (4), he defeated the Goths and Sarmatians (5–6, with clear reference to campaigns waged in 332 and 334), and he received homage from the ends of the earth (7, describing the *tricennalia* of 336). The passage is a miniature *speculum principis*.[44]

In marked contrast to these flowing passages which observe the rules laid down in the handbooks for speeches in honour of rulers stand slabs of documentary history with a clear exposition of a theme:

2.24–60 The establishment of Christianity as the official religion of the Roman empire. Eusebius quotes documents in which Constantine repairs and restores the effects of Licinius' persecution in the East (24–42), provides for a massive programme of building churches (46) and defines his policy towards paganism (48–60), viz. to allow pagans to keep their 'shrines of falsehood' while implicitly reiterating the prohibition of sacrifice, consulting oracles and erecting new cult-statues which Eusebius records (45.1), along with a previous law forbidding magistrates and governors to sacrifice before performing public business (44).[45]

2.61–73 and 3.5–22 The Council of Nicaea. Eusebius introduces the theological controversy over the views of Arius allusively (2.61), for he is determined never to name Arius himself or to refer to him openly, and he lays more stress on the controversy over the date of Easter (3.5), though also alluding to the Melitian schism (2.62). The whole account was shown up as hopelessly lacunose, tendentious and self-serving by the discovery of a Syriac translation of the synodical letter of a Council of Antioch which met early in 325 and excommunicated Eusebius.[46]

In the present context, it need only be noted that Eusebius has
structured his account around two letters and a speech which he
had heard: he quotes Constantine's letter to Alexander and Arius
which was sent to Alexandria in the winter of 324/5 (2.64–72), his
opening speech to the Council of Nicaea (3.12) and his letter to the
churches on the correct date of Easter (3.17–20). In describing the
Council, Eusebius concentrates on ceremony (10, 15), Constantine's
personal behaviour (13–14, 16, 21–2) and the size and variety of
the assembly (7–9) – which matched the crowd at the first
Pentecost (Acts 2:5–11).

3.59–66 Constantine's beneficial interest in the affairs of the church,
illustrated by his letters concerning the election of a bishop to the
see of Antioch (60–2) and his letter or edict urging heretics to join
the catholic church (64–5).

To the same concept or draft belong five other passages:

1.10–11 A full and formal preface promising a work exclusively
devoted to these actions of Constantine that 'conduce to the life of
piety'.

1.26–46 Constantine's war against Maxentius and its consequences.
Eusebius presents Constantine's victories as the consequence of his
piety. First, needing superhuman aid against Maxentius,
Constantine decided to pray to the God of his father Constantius
(27), saw a vision in the sky, made the labarum, took theological
instruction – and prosecuted the war fortified with good hopes
(28–32). Maxentius' tyranny and Constantine's victory over him are
then described in a long passage which largely repeats the
Ecclesiastical History (33–41, cf. *HE* VIII.14.2, 17.3–6; IX.9.2–11).
Next comes Constantine's showering of benefits on the Christian
church (42–3) and his concern for its internal welfare, with clear
allusions to his presence at the Council of Arles in September 314
(44)[47] and to his subsequent attempts to compose the Donatist
schism in Africa (45.2–3).

1.48–2.19 Constantine and Licinius. Despite some intrusive passages
which belong to the panegyric proper (2.6.2, 11, 13), this section
of the *Life* falls into clearly articulated parts, viz:
1 Introduction: Constantine celebrated his *decennalia* in a Christian
fashion (1.48).

2 Licinius' treacherous treatment of Constantine (1.49–50).

3 Licinius' tyranny in the East (1.51–2.2).

4 Constantine's war against him (2.3–19).

The style of presentation is historical: Eusebius quotes a speech of Licinius to his troops, which he claims to know from those who heard it (2.5.2–5). But part 3 is badly arranged, with some incoherence as well as a large amount of repetition from the *Ecclesiastical History*: Eusebius passes from Licinius' anti-Christian legislation (1.51–4, cf. *HE* x.8.8, 10–11), to his fiscal and moral oppression of his subjects (55, cf. *HE* x.8.12–14), then back to his treatment of bishops (56) and his forgetfulness of the dreadful fates of Galerius and Maximinus, which are described (57–8), and back again to his persecution of bishops sympathetic to Constantine (2.1–2, expanding on 56.1).

An overlap with the panegyrical section which opens Book III is highly significant. Licinius' lust for money was insatiable:

apōdureto ptōcheian, Tantaleiō(i) pathei tēn psuchēn truchomenos (1.55.2);

chrēmatōn hēttous hupērchon Tantaleiō(i) pathei tēn psuchēn dedoulōmenoi (3.2.7).

Nothing could illustrate more clearly the fact that the two treatments of Licinius are alternative presentations of the same material, not designed to stand together in the same work.

4.8–14 Constantine's letter to Shapur (9–13), with its introduction and epilogue, stands between a panegyrical section (1–7) and a section of mixed character (15–55). Eusebius intended the letter closely to follow other documents (8).

4.56–75 A connected narrative of Constantine's last illness, death and burial, which begins with his preparations for an expedition against Persia during the winter of 336/7 (56: the lacuna between 56.3 and 58 is due to a purely accidental textual loss in transmission). There is no compelling evidence of two drafts here, one written before September 337, the other after:[48] here, as elsewhere, allowance must be made for Eusebius' normal and undoubted repetitiousness as a writer.

The one passage not so far classified (4.15–55) is a miscellany where fragments from the two drafts are jumbled together in some confusion. To the panegyric may be assigned the following:

15–17 The power of Constantine's faith in God.

21 The labarum (whose origin and power are described in the narrative sections 1.28–31, 2.7–9).

23, 25 Christian legislation (25.1 repeats 2.45.1).

27.3²–28 Constantine's generosity to the church.

31 Constantine's *philanthropia* (of a piece with the claim that he spared the lives of enemy soldiers in 2.13).

38–39 Examples of church building.

53 The length of Constantine's life and reign and his good health (with implicit reference back to 1.7–8)

Interspersed with these brief treatments of large themes are fragments of a more grandiose and detailed exposition and of connected narrative:

18–20 Legislation prescribing the observance of Sunday and prayers for the army.

22 Constantine's private devotions (the opening sentence follows on 20.2).

24 His respect for bishops as evidenced in a remark made at dinner.

26.2–6 Reform of Augustus' marriage legislation and of testamentary law.

27.1–3¹ Jews forbidden to own Christian slaves; decisions of church councils given legal force.

29–30 Constantine's study of Christian theology.

32 His speech *To the Assembly of the Saints* (this brief chapter belongs after 29, p. 131.26 Winkelmann).

33–37¹ Constantine and Eusebius.

37²: Constantine's treatment of Constantia in Palestine.

40–50 The Councils of Tyre and Jerusalem, set in the context of the celebration of the *tricennalia* in 335 (40) and in July 336 (49–50).

51–2 The territorial responsibilities and courts of Constantine's three sons as Caesars.

55 Constantine's readiness for death.

A more general question must now be raised. What familiarity did Eusebius possess with either the theory or the practice of ancient historiography? The question can be answered easily, since the contents of his library can be described with some precision. The library of Caesarea had been formed by Pamphilus, an intellectual disciple of Origen, and it reflects his interests, with a heavy emphasis on philosophy, especially Plato and the Platonic tradition.[49] The *Preparation for the*

Gospel and the *Proof of the Gospel*, composed on a vast scale between 313 and 324, deliberately flaunt Eusebius' erudition. Among the large array of philosophical authors quoted appear only a few historians, all of them adduced for very ancient history: Abydenos, Philo of Byblos on Phoenician religion, Alexander Polyhistor, Diodorus Siculus on Egyptian religion. The *Chronicle* admittedly displays a wider knowledge of historical or quasi-historical writers, but some of it is second-hand, cribbed from the Christian Julius Africanus.[50] Even here, however, the only imperial writers named are Phlegon of Tralles, Cassius Longinus and Porphyry.[51] There is no sign that Eusebius was familiar either with recent Greek historians of the Roman Empire such as Cassius Dio, Herodian and Dexippus or with the classics of Greek historiography such as Herodotus, Thucydides, Xenophon and Polybius.

It is as an outsider, therefore, that Eusebius comments on the contrast between his account of Constantine and traditional histories:

Would it not be disgraceful if, while the memory of Nero and certain impious and godless tyrants far worse than he wins bold writers who have beautified the accounts of base actions with pretty exposition and consecrated them in histories of many books, we should be silent whom God himself has deigned to bring together with such an emperor as the whole of history has never described, and to come to see, know and converse with him? Wherefore it would befit us above all others to proclaim the rich tidings of good to all in whom the imitation of virtue arouses a yearning for the love of God. For they (i.e. the historians of emperors like Nero), collecting lives of frivolous men and deeds unprofitable for moral improvement from favour or hatred towards individuals, and perhaps I suppose in order to display their own learning, have unnecessarily dignified the accounts of base affairs by pompous verbal rhetoric, becoming, for those fortunate enough through God not to have any part in the evil, instructors in deeds which are not good, but which deserve to be buried in oblivion, darkness and silence. Even if my skill as a writer (*ho tēs phraseōs logos*) is overawed by the magnificence of the facts described, let it nevertheless be joyful at the bare reporting of good deeds, and the recollection of a god-loving narrative will provide an acquaintance with them which is not unprofitable but extremely life-enhancing to those whose souls are well prepared. (1.10)

Despite some obvious points of contact with Greek and Roman historians (most obviously the accusations of bias and flashy writing),[52] Eusebius has strayed far from the paths of traditional historiography. Moreover, what he says about Nero indicates that he had either misremembered or else not read historical accounts of his reign, for Nero rapidly became a text-book example of a tyrant. The hostile Latin tradition given shape by Fabius Rusticus, Pliny the Elder and Cluvius Rufus is evident in the pages of Tacitus, Suetonius and Dio, and Josephus early observed that Nero's madness, murders and cavorting on the stage were hackneyed themes.[53] *A fortiori*, there is even less reason to imagine that Eusebius studied imperial biographies.

If the *Life of Constantine* is not a 'life' in the ancient sense, and if it was written without familiarity with Greek historiography, what then is its literary genre? Portions of the *Life*, it has been argued, belong to an imperial panegyric, a genre with which Eusebius was acquainted. What of the rest? The more historical design may perhaps be regarded as an experiment in hagiography. The fourth century saw a rapid proliferation of literary and semi-literary accounts of martyrs and lives of saints, which edified and entertained a new Christian reading and listening public. For this new hagiography, existing pagan literature could provide only partial models, not normative rules of composition. Hence the wide variation in the literary form of saints' lives, from the *Life of Antony*, originally written (it seems) in Coptic but soon adapted for a Greek audience in Alexandria, to Sulpicius Severus' biography of Martin of Tours and the letters and dialogues which supplemented it.[54] It is in a hagiographical sense that Eusebius surely intended readers to construe his statement that he would include only those actions of Constantine which conduce to the life of piety (1.11.1). Among Eusebius' voluminous writings, it is the *Martyrs of Palestine*, originally composed in 311 to commemorate friends who had died in persecution, that in some ways shows the closest thematic similarity to the *Life*. Both works are inspired by Eusebius' burning desire to leave a permanent record of important events for posterity.[55]

If the *Life of Constantine*, in its extant state, represents a conflation of a panegyric and a documentary history of a hagiographical nature, it must next be asked which of the two conceptions came first? It seems natural and obvious to suppose that Eusebius wrote the panegyric first, then abandoned it for the more grandiose design. So Pasquali, and (with divergences in detail) the present writer.[56] Another view of the genesis of the work is possible, preferable and perhaps imposed by Eusebius' choice of documents to quote. Scholarly discussion of the documents in the *Life* has concentrated on whether or not they are authentic. Since that controversy is now settled, attention should be transferred to the more revealing question of how Eusebius assembled them.

Besides speeches and brief quotations, the *Life* contains no fewer than fifteen letters and edicts of Constantine quoted entire.[57] A list of their dates and addressees reveals how personal is Eusebius' choice of what documents to quote:

1 2.24–42 To the provincials of Palestine in October 324, undoing the effects of Licinius' persecution. Since the letter closes with the instruction 'let it be posted up in our eastern territories' (42), a text was presumably posted publicly in Caesarea. Eusebius specifically states that he reproduces the text from an original copy with a *subscriptio* in the emperor's own hand 'preserved among us' (23.3).

2 2.46 To Eusebius, urging him to build churches (shortly after October 324).

3 2.48–60 To the eastern provincials, probably in 325 or 326, allowing them to retain their 'shrines of falsehood' but implicitly reaffirming the prohibition of sacrifice of 324/5 (45.1). Presumably also posted publicly in Caesarea.

4 2.64–72 To Alexander, the bishop of Alexandria, and Arius, urging them to treat their theological quarrel as a philosophical disagreement, not an occasion for schism. This letter was taken to Alexandria in the winter of 324/5 by a trusted envoy, and presumably circulated by each of the recipients among their allies as they prepared for the Council of Nicaea.[58]

5 3.17–20 Circular letter to all churches, written from Nicaea in June or July 325 to announce the Council's decisions about the date of Easter.

6 3.30–2 To Macarius, bishop of Jerusalem, instructing him to build the church of the Holy Sepulchre, dated to 326 or shortly thereafter by a reference to the *vicarius* Dracilianus (31.2).[59]

7 3.52–3 To Macarius and the other bishops of Palestine, instructing them to root out pagan ceremonies at the Oak of Mamre, where God appeared to Abraham, and build a church on the site. Eusebius received a copy of the letter (51.2), which was probably written *c.* 328.[60]

8–10 3.60–2 Three letters concerning the election of a bishop to the see of Antioch in 328: to the church of Antioch (60), to Eusebius (61), and to the bishops assembled at Antioch (62). The letter to

Eusebius implies that Constantine sent him copies of the other two letters (61.3).

11 3.64–5 To heretics excluding them from all benefits conferred on the catholic church: apparently an edict (65.3: 'let it be posted'), certainly issued before 25 September 326 (cf. *CTh* 16.5.2).

12 4.9–13 Letter to Shapur asserting Constantine's position as protector of the Christians of Persia, written *c.* 325.[61] Eusebius specifically states that Constantine wrote it in his own hand, and that he possessed a copy of the letter in Latin, but he leaves it unclear how he obtained a copy or who translated it.

13 4.35 To Eusebius, thanking him for his treatise on the date of Easter.[62] Eusebius dates this and the following letter to the time when he was returning to Palestine from his visit to Constantinople in November 335 (34).

14 4.36 To Eusebius requesting copies of the Bible for use in the churches of Constantinople.

15 4.42 Letter to the Council of Tyre, of which Eusebius was a member, brought by the *notarius* Marianus (4.44 *keph.*) and read at the opening session in August 335.

This is not a random collection of Constantine's letters and edicts. Two of the documents from the years 324–6 contain instructions for publication (nos. 1 and 11), which implies that they were posted in Caesarea and copied by Eusebius at the time, in exactly the same way as he had copied down letters of Galerius, Maximinus and Licinius in 311–13 for quotation in the *Ecclesiastical History*. Another four are letters addressed to Eusebius personally (nos. 2, 9, 13, 14) and it is known that he was sent a copy of two more (nos. 8, 10), while he belonged to the collective body addressed in another three (nos. 5, 7, 15). In addition, it is easy to see how Eusebius obtained a copy of Constantine's letter to Alexander and Arius (no. 4), while Macarius doubtless advertised his commission to build a splendid church in Jerusalem (no. 6). But what of Constantine's letter to Shapur? How did Eusebius obtain a copy, in Latin, of a diplomatic letter to a foreign ruler? The answer to that question may turn out to be the key to the genesis of the *Life of Constantine*. There are only two possibilities: either Constantine circulated the letter, or Eusebius obtained a copy for himself. The former hypothesis has historical plausibility: Constantine could have circulated the letter, in which he poses as the champion of the Christians of Persia, for purposes of propaganda in 336/7 as he prepared to mount an invasion of Mesopotamia.[63] But in that case Eusebius would surely have seen an official Greek translation specially made for the purpose. The fact that Eusebius possessed a copy of the letter in Latin suggests rather that he obtained one for himself.[64] Further, since Eusebius was not an habitué of the court, he either wrote to ask for a copy (which hardly seems plausible) or obtained one during one of his visits to the imperial court. Since Constantine wrote to Shapur *c.* 325, it may be suggested that Eusebius learned of the letter and obtained a copy in 325 while he was at court to attend the Council of Nicaea. Why then did he decide to request a copy from the emperor? Presumably because he was already thinking ahead to the day when he would compose a sequel to the *Ecclesiastical History* which he had recently brought down to 324, that is, a documented history of Constantine as a Christian emperor and protector of the Christian church.

That hypothesis will explain the odd chronological distribution of the letters and edicts quoted in the *Life* and the appended speeches. The majority of these documents belong to the first years of Constantine's rule of the East: eight were written between October 324 and 326 (nos. 1–6, 11, 12), and Constantine's *Speech to the Assembly of the Saints*, whatever its precise date of delivery, would have come into Eusebius' hands no later than 325. Of the remaining letters, six were sent to Eusebius himself, four *c.* 328 (nos. 7–10) and two in the winter of 335/6 (nos. 13, 14). The only other documents quoted are Constantine's letter to the Council of Tyre, read by the *notarius* Marianus in August 335 (no. 15), and Eusebius' two speeches, which he delivered in July 336 and September 335 respectively. Why are so few documents quoted from the central period of seven years during which Constantine ruled the East (from autumn 328 to summer 335)? It looks as if Eusebius collected letters and edicts of Constantine assiduously in 325 and 326, then stopped. Perhaps he decided that his *Commentary on Isaiah*, composed largely in these years, was a more appropriate medium for celebrating the Constantinian empire.[65] Perhaps he had some other reason. At all events, whatever his motive for dropping the project, it appears that Eusebius had begun to think about the work which eventually became the *Life of Constantine* as soon as the emperor conquered the East.[66] When Constantine died, Eusebius already had a preliminary collection of material on hand – and perhaps an inchoate narrative for the period down to 326.

The hypothesis just adumbrated receives confirmation from a well-known fact which seems never to have been exploited in this context. In three manuscripts of Eusebius' *Ecclesiastical History*, Constantine's letter to the provincials of Palestine in October 324 (no. 1) stands as an appendix to that work. It was certainly put there by Eusebius himself, since it is followed by the sentence:

Let this stand here; but come now let us assemble together, making a fresh beginning, all the laws and letters on behalf of true piety of our god-loving and most gentle emperor.[67]

Moreover, the text offered by the manuscripts of the *Ecclesiastical History* is superior in minor details to that in the manuscripts of the *Life*, which accordingly reveals itself as a secondary version.[68] That ought to count as a positive proof that the *Life of Constantine* originated as a continuation of or sequel to the final edition of the *Ecclesiastical History*. Book ix of that work provided the model for a narrative of an emperor's actions (there Maximinus in 311–13) centred around and illustrated by an array of documents quoted entire.[69]

A long scholarly tradition, whose recent representatives include Arnaldo Momigliano and Peter Brown, has presented Eusebius as a court writer, virtually an imperial propagandist.[70] Hence the *Life of Constantine* has been saluted as the only court biography still extant, a combination of 'Christian *Cyropaedeia* and novel', propounding the ideal of a Christian emperor for imitation by his successors and full of rhetorical and novelistic devices.[71] The exegetical premiss is totally false. Eusebius was no habitué of Constantine's court, which he visited only four times, always on ecclesiastical business in the company of other bishops.[72] He was a provincial bishop who resided at Caesarea in Palestine, far from the centre of political events. He was a scholar whose earlier historical works evince an honest desire to write a reliable history of his own day – an aspiration which the *Life* reiterates (2.23.2).[73]

No historian ever completely fulfils his aspirations to or professions of impartiality and fairness. How far short of the ideal does Eusebius fall? The traditional verdict on him has been harsh, and it is still argued that the *Life of Constantine* must be unreliable because it is 'a self-confessed panegyric'.[74] Recent research, however, has done much to rehabilitate the good faith of Eusebius. On issue after issue, Eusebius' testimony, so often dismissed or disregarded, either receives positive confirmation from other evidence or else deserves to be regarded as inherently plausible. Eusebius knew the precise date at which Constantine took the title *victor* (2.19.2),[75] and that Constantine instituted the office of *peraequator census* (4.3).[76] He presumably saw in Constantinople in 336 the Blemmyes whose presence there is incidentally attested by a papyrus (4.7.1, cf. 1.8.3).[77] And his reports that Constantine prohibited pagan sacrifice altogether in 324 (2.45.1, cf. 4.25.1) and forbade Jews to own Christian slaves (4.27.1) deserve credence: a constitution of Constans confirms the former,[78] while correct prosopography shows that the prohibition on Jews owning Christian slaves was indeed issued by Constantine, not under his sons.[79] Similarly, when Eusebius states that the new city of Constantinople contained no pagan cults (3.48), that should not be written off as one of his 'notorious distortions and falsehoods'.[80] A speech of the pagan Himerius, delivered in the city in 362, provides precise confirmation.[81]

On the other hand, gross tendentiousness in some areas cannot be denied. Eusebius consistently writes as if Constantine only had three sons and only proclaimed three Caesars: Crispus, Caesar from 317 until his execution in 326, and Dalmatius, who was appointed Caesar on 18 September 335 and killed in 337, are totally ignored. More serious, Eusebius totally misrepresents both the theological disputes and the ecclesiastical politics of the reign of Constantine in a partisan fashion. Yet his viewpoint can be defined, understood and discounted. Writing after September 337, he could avoid repeating the official view of Constantine's dynastic intentions only by writing a different sort of work. Nor did his contemporaries have any doubt where Eusebius stood within the church: he was instrumental in deposing such champions of Nicene orthodoxy as Eustathius of Antioch in 326 and Marcellus of Ancyra in 336.[82] The *Life* itself displayed its sympathy for Arius openly for all who could catch an allusion: when Eusebius complimented Constantine for a policy which brought back into the church in herds the ecclesiastical exiles who recognized their mother, the church (3.66.3), he echoed words used by Arius and Euzoius when requesting readmission to the catholic church in late 327[83] – a request granted by the Council of Nicomedia which Eusebius records and praises (3.23).[84]

The contrast between verifiable accuracy on many matters and flagrant bias on others prompts the question whether the *Life* contains hidden assumptions which pervade the work and impair its value as evidence for Constantine. That view has been argued recently with some subtlety.[85] Yet, as formulated, it relies upon dismissing as 'over-mechanical' (and therefore, presumably, erroneous) Pasquali's proof that the *Life* is a conflation of two generically different drafts. Perhaps a full literary analysis of the *Life* can restate the theory in a valid form. Certainly, there is need for structural analyses which will lay bare Eusebius' patterns of thought (note, for example, the schema of satanically inspired envy as the sudden cause of contemporary disputes within a peaceful church).[86] But such analyses must respect the observable phenomena. The so-called *Life of Constantine* is a combination of conventional panegyric and something daringly original which hovers between ecclesiastical history and hagiography. To treat it as a work cut from a single cloth is as misleading as it would be to suppose that Charles Dickens intended both endings of *Great Expectations* to stand side by side.[87]

NOTES

1 H. Chadwick, 'The Origin of the Title "Oecumenical Council"', *JThS*, n.s. 23 (1972), 132–5, at 133.

2 'Lactantius and Constantine', *JRS*, 63 (1973), 29–46.

3 Viz. in *Constantine and Eusebius*, Cambridge, Mass. 1981, henceforth referred to as *Constantine*, and *The New Empire of Diocletian and Constantine*, Cambridge, Mass. 1982, henceforth referred to as *New Empire*. For the sake of brevity, uncontested dates and facts documented there are not annotated here.

4 As was clearly stated by N. H. Baynes, *ByZ*, 39 (1939), 468, reviewing H. Grégoire, 'Eusèbe n'est pas l'auteur de la "Vita Constantini" dans sa forme actuelle et Constantin ne s'est pas "converti" en 312', *Byz*, 13 (1938), 561–83.

5 R. Lane Fox, *Pagans and Christians*, Harmondsworth 1986 pp. 627–35, argues for delivery in Antioch on Good Friday (i.e. 16 April) 325, against my arguments in favour of Serdica in 321 (*Constantine* 323 n. 115, modifying Barnes, 'The Emperor Constantine's Good Friday Sermon', *JThS*, n.s. 27 (1976), 414–23) or Thessalonica in 323 or 324 (as argued by A. Piganiol, 'Dates constantiniennes', *RHPhR*, 13 (1932), 360–72, at 370ff.). I am doubtful whether that hypothesis can be squared with what else is known about events preceding the Council of Nicaea which opened in June. The correct answer to the conundrum may be delivery on Good Friday 325 in Nicomedia, as argued in an unpublished doctoral thesis by D. Ison, 'The Constantinian Oration to the Saints – Authorship and Background', dissertation, University of London 1985, 207ff.

That the extant Greek is a translation from a Latin original was proved in a long series of articles by A. Kurfess: see now D. N. Wigtil, 'Towards a Date for the Greek Fourth Eclogue', *Classical Journal*, 76 (1981), 336–41.

Lane Fox, *Pagans and Christians*, p. 778 n. 9, cf. p. 630, promises a proof that Constantine both delivered and composed the *Speech* in Greek.

6 H. A. Drake, 'When was the *De Laudibus Constantini* delivered?', *Historia*, 24 (1975), 345–56.

7 'Two Speeches by Eusebius', *GRBS*, 18 (1977), 341–5. Although the two speeches precede the *Life* in the manuscripts, Eusebius intended them to follow it (4.46: '*meta tēn parousan tēs graphēs hupothesin ekthēsometha*').

8 F. Winkelmann, 'Zur Geschichte des Authentizitätsproblems der Vita Constantini', *Klio*, 40 (1962), 187–243.

9 A. H. M. Jones, 'Notes on the Genuineness of the Constantinian Documents in Eusebius' *Life of Constantine*', *JEH*, 5 (1954), 196–200. Jones had earlier presented his identification at the First International Patristic Conference in Oxford in 1951. For other discussions of the papyrus (*P. Lond*. 878), see T. C. Skeat, 'Britain and the Papyri', in *Aus Antike und Orient, Festschrift W. Schubart*, Leipzig 1950, pp. 126–32; W. Schubart, 'Zu Skeat: Britain and the Papyri', in *Festschrift für F. Zucker*, Berlin 1954, pp. 343–8. It had originally been identified as a 'literary fragment, perhaps of an oration' by F. G. Kenyon and H. I. Bell, *Greek Papyri in the British Museum* 3, London 1907, p. xlii.

The authenticity of the document in 2.24–42 had been denied by A. Crivellucci, *Della fede storica di Eusebio nella Vita di Constantino*, Livorno 1888, pp. 5off.; *Studi Storici*, 3 (1894), 369–84, 415–22: V. Schultze, 'Quellenuntersuchungen zur *Vita Constantini* des Eusebius', *ZKG*, 14 (1894), 503–55; A. Mancini, 'Osservazioni sulla Vita di Costantino d'Eusebio', *RFIC*, 33 (1905), 309–60: P. Batiffol, 'Les documents de la Vita Constantini', *BALAC*, 4 (1914), 81–95.

10 H. Grégoire, commenting on A. H. M. Jones' discussion of *P. Lond*. 878, in the 'Rapports des séances de la société "Theonoé"', *La nouvelle Clio*, 5 (1953), 215; 'L'authenticité et l'historicité de la *Vita Constantini* attribuée à Eusèbe de Césarée', *BAB*, Classe des Lettres' 5th Series, 39 (1953), 462–79; M. R. Cataudella, 'La "persecuzione" di Licinio e l'autenticità della "Vita Constantini"', *Athenaeum*, n.s. 48 (1970), 48–83, 229–50.

11 See C. Baronius, *Annales Ecclesiastici*, vol. 3, Antwerp 1623, p. 157: the erroneous date of 314 only became canonical with Gothofredus' prolegomena to his edition of the Theodosian Code (*Chronologia Codicis Theodosiani*, Lyons 1665, xiii).

12 P. Bruun, *The Constantinian Coinage of Arelate*, Finska Fornminnesföreningens Tidskrift, 52:2, 1953, pp. 17ff.

13 C. Habicht, 'Zur Geschichte des Kaisers Konstantin', *Hermes*, 86 (1958), 360–78; P. Bruun, *Studies in Constantinian Chronology*, Numismatic Notes and Monographs, 146, 1961, pp. 10ff.; *Roman Imperial Coinage*, vol. 7, London 1966, pp. 76ff.

14 As argued in Barnes, 'Lactantius and Constantine', *JRS*, 63 (1973), 29ff.;

Constantine, pp. 13f., cf. the recent commentary by J. L. Creed, *Lactantius: On the Deaths of the Persecutors*, Oxford 1985. However, the date of 314 continues to find defenders: so, recently, I. König, *Origo Constantini: Anonymus Valesianus*, Teil 1, *Trierer Historische Forschungen*, 11 (1987), 119–23.

15 G. Pasquali, 'Die Composition des Vita Constantini des Eusebius', *Hermes*, 46 (1910), 369–86.

16 J. Maurice, 'Sur la vie de Constantin d'Eusèbe', *BSNAF* (1913), 387–96, at 387f.; Batiffol, *BALAC*, 4 (1914), 94 n. 2; N. H. Baynes, *Constantine the Great and the Christian Church*, London 1931; 2nd edition, with preface by H. Chadwick, Oxford 1972, pp. 42ff. Baynes delivered the text of his paper as a lecture on 12 March 1930, then expanded it by the addition of 'a few bibliographical notes', amounting to some seventy-five pages, for publication in *PBA*, 15 (1929, published 1931), 341–442.

17 H. Grégoire, *Byz*, 13 (1938), 578.

18 Review of I. A. Heikel, *Eusebius Werke* 1 (Leipzig, 1902), *GGA*, 171 (1909) 259–86.

19 Heikel, *Eusebius Werke* 1 (*GCS* 7, 1902), pp. lxvi–lxxxii.

20 Heikel had detected the same model (ibid, pp. xlviff.).

21 Pasquali, *Hermes*, 46 (1910), 386 (my translation).

22 F. Winkelmann, *Eusebius Werke* 1.1.[2] (*GCS* 1975), pp. xlixff. The list omits cases where Pasquali and Winkelmann seem to me to fail to demonstrate doublets.

23 *JThS*, n.s. 27 (1976), 418–20, cf. R. T. Ridley, 'Anonymity in the Vita Constantini', *Byz*, 50 (1980), 241–58.

24 Viz. Flavius Dalmatius, consul in 333, and Julius Constantius, consul in 335 and *patricius*.

25 Pasquali, *Hermes*, 46 (1910), 369ff.

26 Eusebius nowhere uses the word *sumplēgas*; the verb *suntarattō* occurs only in quotations or where Eusebius is paraphrasing the Septuagint (*Praep. ev.* 6.8.23, from Diogenianus; *PG* 23.173, 560, 636, in the *Commentary on the Psalms*).

27 Pasquali, *Hermes*, 46 (1910), 383.

28 Proposed in Barnes, 'Two Speeches by Eusebius', *GRBS*, 18 (1977), 344f.

29 For a brief description of those works and their context, see *Constantine*, 264f.

30 *c. Marcellum* 2.4.29, cf. Barnes, 'Emperor and Bishops, A.D. 324–344: Some Problems', *AJAH*, 3 (1978), 53–75, at 64f.

31 See *Athanasius of Alexandria. Theology and Politics in the Constantinian Empire* (forthcoming), ch. 11.

32 *PO* 10.15, cf. Barnes, *Constantine*, p. 263.

33 U. von Wilamowitz-Moellendorf, 'Ein Bruchstück aus der Schrift des

Porphyrius gegen die Christen', *ZNW*, 1 (1900), 101–5, at 105 n. 1; 'die Schrift *eis Kōnstantinon*, die ein *bios* weder heisst noch ist'.

34 Averil Cameron, 'Eusebius of Caesarea and the Rethinking of History', *Tria Corda. Scritti in onore di Arnaldo Momigliano* (Como 1983) pp. 71–89, esp. pp. 82–3: 'not a straightforward panegyric but a *bios*, a *Life*, akin in some ways to the moralising *Lives* of classical authors, but with a very different purpose'. A footnote dismisses Pasquali's thesis as 'over-mechanical' (p. 83 n. 57, cf. pp. 71–2 n. 2).

35 Heikel, *Eusebius Werke* 1 (1902), p. xlv: 'nicht Vita Constantini (Das Leben Constantins), sondern De Vita Constantini (Über das Leben Constantins)'.

36 The testimony of the MSS. of the *Vita Apollonii* is confirmed by Philostratus, *Vitae sophistarum* 2.5.1. E. Schwartz, *RE*, 6 (1909), 1423, detected the influence of Philo in Eusebius' formulation of his aims (1.3.4) and his comparison of Constantine to Moses (1.12, 19–20; 2.12).

37 Philostratus, *Vita Apollonii* 1.9.1; Eunapius, *Vitae philosophorum* 2.1.2, p. 454; *Suda* A 3420 (1.307 Adler).

38 R. Farina, *L'impero e l'imperatore cristiano in Eusebio di Casarea*, Zürich 1966, p. 19.

39 W. Telfer, 'The Author's Purpose in the Vita Constantini', *Studia Patristica*, 1, *TU* 63, 1957, pp. 157–67. He asserts 'we clearly have to do with panegyric, not historical biography' appealing to Photius' description of the work as '*hē eis Kōnstantinon ton megan basilea egkōmiastikē tetrabiblos*' (*Bibliotheca* 127).

40 F. Leo, *Die griechisch-römische Biographie nach ihrer litterarischen Form*, Leipzig 1901, pp. 311–13.

41 H. Homeyer, 'Zu den hellenistischen Quellen der Plutarch-viten', *Klio*, 41 (1963), 145–57.

42 H. Kloft, 'Zur *Vita Constantini* I 14', *Historia*, 19 (1970), 509–14, adducing Xenophon, *Cyropaedia* 8.2.15–22. The story is also applied to Constantius in exactly the same way by Praxagoras (*FGH* 219), Libanius, *Orationes* 59.15 and Eutropius, *Breviarium ab urbe condita* 10.1.2.

43 So Habicht, *Hermes*, 86 (1958), 374 n. 5, correctly repudiating the allusion to Fausta and Crispus (i.e. to 326) postulated by other scholars (e.g. F. Vittinghoff, 'Eusebius als Verfasser der Vita Constantini', *RMP*, n.f. 96 (1953), 330–373, at 347ff.).

44 Note the use made of the passage by F. Millar, *The Emperor in the Roman World (31 B.C. – A.D. 337)*, London 1977, esp. 10, 117, 139, 278.

45 On this section of the *Life*, see recently C. Pietri, 'Constantin en 324: Propagande et théologie impériales d'après les documents de la *Vita Constantini*', *Crise et redressement dans les provinces européennes de l'Empire (milieu du IIIe – milieu du IVe siècle ap. J.-C)*, Strasbourg 1983, pp. 63–90; T. D. Barnes, 'Constantine's Prohibition of Pagan Sacrifice', *AJP*, 105 (1984), 69–72.

46 Published by E. Schwartz, 'Zur Geschichte des Athanasius', *NAWG*, hist. Klasse, 1905, 257–99, cf. L. Abramowski, 'Die Synode von Antiochien 324/25 und ihr Symbol', *ZKG*, 86 (1975), 356–66.

47 For other evidence attesting Constantine's presence at the Council, *New Empire*, pp. 72, 242.

48 Against Pasquali, *Hermes*, 46 (1910), 380–2, see N. H. Baynes, *Constantine the Great and the Christian Church*, London 1931, p. 44.

49 K. Mras, 'Die Stellung der "Praeparatio Evangelica" des Eusebius im antiken Schrifttum', *AöAWPH*, 209–17; Barnes, *Constantine*, pp. 93f., 182f.

50 On the sources used by Eusebius, see A. A. Mosshammer, *The 'Chronicle' of Eusebius and the Greek Chronographic Tradition*, Lewisburg, Pa. and London 1979, pp. 113ff. (not entirely convincing).

51 *Chronicle*, ed. J. Karst in *GCS* 20, 1911, p. 126, quoted and translated in Barnes, *Constantine*, 118.

52 For those motifs, G. Avenarius, *Lukians Schrift zur Geschichtschreibung*, Meisenheim/Glan 1956, pp. 40ff., 59ff.

53 Josephus, *BJ* ii.250/1. Josephus' later reference to those who were careless of the truth out of gratitude toward Nero (*AJ* xx.154) should be construed in a comparative rather than an absolute sense: Cluvius Rufus, who had been an habitué of Nero's court and to whom Josephus should here refer, provided a lurid enough account of the emperor's sexual escapades (Tacitus, *Annales* 14.2.1).

54 See, respectively, 'Angel of Light or Mystic Initiate? The Problem of the *Life of Antony*', *JThS*, n.s. 37 (1986), 353–68; C. Stancliffe, *St. Martin of Tours and his Hagiographer. History and Miracle in Sulpicius Severus*, Oxford 1983, pp. 86 ff.

55 On the nature of the *Martyrs* (which is often misunderstood), see Barnes, *Constantine*, pp. 154f.

56 Pasquali, *Hermes*, 46 (1910), 384–6; Barnes, *Constantine*, p. 265.

57 I. Daniele, *I documenti costantiniani della 'Vita Constantini' di Eusebio di Cesarea*, Analecta Gregoriana 13, 1938, pp. 5ff.

58 Neither the text of the *Life* nor the chapter headings name the envoy. Socrates, *HE* 1.7.1, identified him as Ossius of Cordoba, who certainly went to Alexandria during the winter of 324/5 (Athanasius, *Apologia contra Arianos* 74.4). Virtually all recent writers have accepted Socrates' identification. However, B. H. Warmington, 'The Sources of Some Constantinian Documents in Eusebius' *Ecclesiastical History* and *Life of Constantine*', *StPatr*, 18 (1986), 93–8, has argued from the similarities of *Life* 2.63, 73 to 4.44 that the envoy should instead be identified as the *notarius* Marianus, who performed similar duties in 335.

59 Barnes, *New Empire*, pp. 141, 246. Constantine alludes to the discovery of the 'true cross' (30.1). Eusebius' silence, which has puzzled so many

modern scholars, is due to his resentment towards Macarius, who undoubtedly used his discovery to bolster his claims to episcopal primacy within Palestine over the metropolitan bishop of Caesarea.

60 Constantine refers to the *comes* Acacius (53.2), who is attested in Macedonia on 21 February 327 (*Codex Theodosianus* 11.3.2) and in the East in 328 (*Life* 3.62.1).

61 'Constantine and the Christians of Persia', *JRS*, 75 (1985), 126–36.

62 A partial text is preserved by Nicetas of Heraclea (*PG* 24.693–706), but nothing in it fixes the date.

63 Wide distribution is assumed in Barnes, 'Constantine and the Christians of Persia', *JRS* 75 (1985), 131.

64 Warmington, *StPatr*, 18 (1986), 94f., suggests that Eusebius obtained both a copy of the letter and the information that the emperor wrote it in his own hand from the *notarius* Marianus. The hypothesis that Eusebius obtained his copy at court shortly after Constantine wrote the letter owes much to discussion with Mr John Harstone.

65 Published in full by K. Ziegler (*GCS*, 1975): see now M. Simonetti, 'L'Esegesi e ideologia nel Commento a Isaia di Eusebio', *RSLR*, 19 (1983), 3–44.

66 The notion that Eusebius began work before Constantine died goes back to P. Meyer, 'De vita Constantiniana Eusebiana', *Festschrift dem Gymnasium Adolfinum zu Moers* (1882), pp. 23–8. For a detailed argument that Eusebius conceived the *Life* in 335 and began composition in 336/7 see H. A. Drake, 'What Eusebius knew: the Genesis of the *Vita Constantini*', *CP*, 83 (1988), 20–38.

67 See E. Schwartz, *Eusebius Werke* 2.2 (*GCS* 9.2, 1908), p. 904. The passage is quoted by Daniele, *Documenti*, p. 32; F. Winkelmann, *Eusebius Werke* 1.1[2] (1975), p. xviii.

68 Heikel, *Eusebius Werke* 1 (1902), pp. xx–xxiv; F. Winkelmann, *Die Textbezeugung der Vita Constantini des Eusebius von Caesarea*, TU, 84 (1962), 121–31.

69 Pietri, *Crise et redressement*, p. 68, notes the similarity of the *Life* to the *History*; for the structure of Book IX see Barnes, *New Empire*, pp. 67f.

70 A. Momigliano, 'Pagan and Christian Historiography in the Fourth Century A.D.', *The Conflict between Paganism and Christianity in the Fourth Century*, Oxford 1963, p. 85; P. Brown, *The World of Late Antiquity*, London 1971, pp. 82, 86. The famous denunciation of Eusebius as 'the most objectionable of all eulogists' by J. Burckhardt, *Die Zeit Constantins des Grossen*, 2nd edn, Leipzig 1880, pp. 223ff., is more circumspect.

71 H. Peter, *Die geschichtliche Litteratur über die römische Kaiserzeit bis Theodosius I und ihre Quellen*, Leipzig 1897 1.405ff., 452; 2.279ff.

72 Viz. in the summer of 325, the winter of 327/8, November 335 and the summer of 336. H. A. Drake, *CP*, 83 (1988), 20–38, suggests that Eusebius

may have remained in Constantinople from the summer of 336 until at least Easter 337.

73 For the provincial viewpoint and basic honesty of Books VIII to X of the *Ecclesiastical History*, see Barnes, *Constantine*, pp. 155ff.

74 Averil Cameron, 'Constantinus Christianus', *JRS*, 73 (1983), 184–90.

75 For the inscriptional evidence, A. Chastagnol, 'Un gouverneur constantinien de Tripolitaine: Laenatius Romulus, *Praeses* en 324–326', *Latomus*, 25 (1966), 539–52, 543ff.; E. Guadagno and S. Panciera, 'Nuove testimonianze sul governo della Campania in età constantiniana', *Rendiconti della Accademia Nazionale dei Lincei*, 8th series, 25 (1970), 111–29, 111 ff.; G. Camodeca, 'Iscrizione inedite di Pozzuoli', *Atti dell'Accademia di Scienze Morali e Politiche, Napoli*, 82 (1971), 24–48, 30ff.

76 Probably in 321, cf. Barnes, *Constantine*, p. 69, adducing L. Aradius Valerius Proculus, consul in 340, who was *peraequator census provinciae Gallaeciae* shortly after 320 (*ILS*, 1240–2).

77 P. *Abinnaeus* 1, cf. Barnes, 'The Career of Abinnaeus', *Phoenix*, 39 (1985), 368–74.

78 *CTh* 16.10.1 (341), cf. Barnes *AJP*, 105 (1984), 69–72. The traditional view that Constantine issued no such prohibition is restated by P. Garnsey, 'Religious Toleration in Classical Antiquity', *Persecution and Toleration* (Studies in Church History 21, 1984), pp. 1–27, at p. 18, n. 39. The absence of the law reported by Eusebius from the Theodosian Code is in no way suspicious, cf. Pietri, *Crise et redressement*, p. 69.

79 *CTh* 16.9.2. is addressed to the praetorian prefect, Evagrius, on whom see *PLRE*, 1 (1971), 284f.; Barnes, *New Empire*, pp. 131f. O. Seeck, *Regesten der Kaiser und Päpste für die Jahre 311 bis 476 n. Chr.,* Stuttgart, 1919, p. 187 accepted the MSS. date of 339 for *CTh* 16.9.2, which is assumed to be correct by K. L. Noethlichs, *Die gesetzgeberischen Massnahmen der christlichen Kaiser des vierten Jahrhunderts gegen Häretiker, Heiden und Juden*, dissertation, Cologne 1971; Winkelmann, *Eusebius Werke* 1.1² (1975), note on p. 130.8ff.; M. Avi-Yonah, *The Jews of Palestine*, New York 1976, pp. 161ff., 174ff.; C. D. Reichardt, 'Die Judengesetzgebung im Codex Theodosianus', *Kairos*, 20 (1978), 16–39; F. Blanchetière, 'L'evolution du statut des Juifs sous la dynastie constantinienne', *Crise et redressement* (1983), pp. 127–41.

80 Cameron, *Tria Corda*, p. 85.

81 Himerius, *Orationes* 41.8: 'temenē men egeirōn theois, teletas de theias kathidruōn tē(i) polei xenas'. G. Dagron, *Naissance d'une capitale. Constantinople et ses institutions de 330 à 451*, Paris 1974, p. 376 translates: 'en relevant les temples des dieux, en instituant des initiations jusque'ici étrangères à cette cité'. That narrows considerably what Himerius is really saying, viz. that Julian introduced pagan religious rites into a city which was a Christian foundation.

82 On Eusebius' reputation, F. Winkelmann, *Byzantinische Beiträge*, ed. J. Irmscher, Berlin 1964, pp. 91–119.

83 H. G. Opitz, *Urkunden zur Geschichte des Arianischen Streites 318–328,
   Athanasius Werke* 3.1, Berlin/Leipzig, 1934, no. 30.
84 For this council (whose existence is often denied) and its context, see
   Barnes, *Constantine*, pp. 229–31. A full survey of the problem is given by
   R. Lorenz, 'Das Problem der Nach-synode von Nicäa (327)', *ZKG*, 90
   (1979), 22–40.
85 Cameron, *Tria Corda*, pp. 82ff.
86 Eusebius uses this pattern in his accounts of the Arian controversy (2.61.3,
   73; 3.4.1 (argued above to be an editorial addition)), the disputed election
   at Antioch in 328 (3.59.1), the Council of Tyre (4.41.1) – and of Licinius'
   disloyalty to Constantine (1.49.2; 3.1.1).
87 A preliminary version of the present essay was delivered as a lecture at the
   University of California in Santa Barbara in February 1987: the version
   published here owes much to the kind comments of Harold Drake who,
   through his courteous disagreements over many years, has taught me more
   than anyone else about the *Life of Constantine*.

Matthew 28:19, Eusebius, and the *lex orandi*

H. BENEDICT GREEN

La formule du baptême s'est enlargie et comprend sous une forme assez synthétique les trois mots sacramentales de la théologie du temps, le Père, le Fils, le Saint-Ésprit. Le germe du dogme de la Trinité est ainsi déposé dans un coin de la page sacrée, et deviendra fecond.[1]

Renan's comment on Matthew 28.19 revealed an insight into the part played by the *lex orandi* in the creation of this text, as well as by the text itself in the evolution of the *lex credendi*, that was well ahead of its time, and still remained so when F. C. Conybeare, a quarter of a century later,[2] proposed to advance on it in two respects. Renan had nowhere implied that the hand that planted the seed of Trinitarian dogma in the gospel, whatever its cultic background, was any but the evangelist's own; Conybeare found evidence in Eusebius' writings that suggested otherwise. And the extreme conclusions that he drew from that evidence about Eusebius' permanent ignorance of the received text were pressed into the service of an account of later dogmatic history that was not evolutionary so much as revolutionary.[3]

Iconoclasm invites overkill, and it was to be expected that conservative professionals like E. Riggenbach[4] and J. Lebreton[5] (who would have been little happier with Renan's position than with Conybeare's)[6] would apply themselves to crush the gentleman amateur on both counts. Of his wilder conclusions they were able to make short work. But while their systematic presentation of the Eusebian evidence (more professional than Conybeare's own) indicated that they took it seriously, their unconcealed determination to dispose it once and for all made clear that they were serious about it as a threat to the truth rather than as a possible clue to it. Contemporary radical students of Christian origins, among them Loisy, Lake, Bousset, Eduard Meyer, and Bultmann, were not readily impressed, and the weight of their influence continued to be felt down to the Second World War. The positions of the major commentaries produced during that period remained evenly balanced: Wellhausen, Allen, Loisy and Klostermann[7] on one side, against Zahn, McNeile, Lagrange and Schniewind on the other.

The reasons for the post-war eclipse[8] of the former position are nowhere fully spelled out.[9] They may be presumed to include: (1) long-term effects of the movement away from liberalism and towards neo-orthodoxy in the inter-war period; (2) the reluctance of textual critics even to consider the claims of a reading unrepresented in the MS. tradition;[10] (3) general acceptance of a relatively late date for the first gospel, which has eased the problem of a Trinitarian understanding of baptism that could antedate the Christological one evidenced in the Pauline letters; (4) the development of redaction criticism, which looks for and tends to assume the presence of both traditional and redactional elements in the final form of any gospel pericope.[11] What it clearly does not rest on is any fresh overall examination of the Eusebian evidence. Since Lebreton's work appeared in 1910 there have been only three attempts at this, and of these the first two have been too little known, and the third came too late, to be a formative influence on the trend. J. Lindblom's book,[12] to which I have not had access, has never been translated from the Swedish; references to it in other writings do not suggest that it broke new ground.[13] B. H. Cuneo's dissertation[14] owed far more to other writers, especially Lebreton, than it acknowledged, offering in addition only a more extended survey of Eusebius' habits in the quotation of scripture, for which, as Conybeare's posthumously published review complained,[15] its author was 'lamentably ill-equipped'.[16] B. J. Hubbard's monograph devotes an appendix (pp. 151–75) to the Eusebian evidence which still relies largely on Lebreton and Cuneo, though his conclusions, as we shall see, are more tentative than theirs.

The first task therefore is to re-examine the Eusebian material.

I

Matthew 28:19 (a favourite text of Eusebius, found no less than thirty times in his writings) is actually quoted by him not in two but in three forms:[17] (i) *poreuthentes...ethnē* (nine times);[18] (ii) *poreuthentes... ethnē en tō(i) onomati mou* (sixteen times, of which three are duplicates);[19] (iii) *poreuthentes...ethnē, baptizontes autous eis to onoma tou patros kai tou huiou kai tou hagiou pneumatos* (five times).[20]

Of these, (i) is on any showing an abbreviation of the full text; in some cases the quotation is simply cut short, in others it continues with some words evidently omitted. The three passages from the beginning of the *Demonstratio evangelica*, which fall in the latter category, are so similar to *Demonstratio evangelica* 3.6 (form (ii)) that it is reasonable to infer that the missing words here are *en tō(i) onomati mou*.[21]

But in general this group of texts offers no decisive grounds for preferring either of the other two forms. What its existence establishes is that where his argument was based on only part of a text of scripture, Eusebius was quite happy simply to omit the rest, without feeling obliged to offer a summary of what had been omitted.

Forms (ii) and (iii) (otherwise referred to as the 'shorter' (S) and the 'longer' (L) text) are, on the other hand, alternative versions of the missing clause, one of which has been substituted for the other. The word *onoma* is used in quite distinct ways in the two versions: in S it denotes the authority on which the missionary disciples are to act, making their converts disciples not of themselves but of the one true teacher;[22] in L the immediate reference seems to be to the form of words with which baptism is administered (see p. 135 below), though beyond that the triadic formula may serve either to distinguish Christian from other kinds of baptism or to convey the supernatural relationship into which the convert is introduced by it.[23] The two are not reducible to a single formula; S cannot be called a summary of L, nor L an expansion of S.

L, the only form of the text known to the MS. tradition, is confined within the Eusebian corpus to quotations of it in later and mostly controversial writings from the period when the Trinity had become the subject of intense debate: Eusebius' defence of his own orthodoxy after Nicaea, and his subsequent attack on that of Marcellus. The only non-controversial work in which it is found is the *Theophany*, where it occurs only once, alongside four instances of the S form (of which three have been lifted from the *Demonstratio*). Conybeare's rash attempt to dispose of this evidence by undermining the authenticity of *Contra Marcellum* and *De ecclesiastica theologia*[24] and the textual integrity of *Theophany* 4.8[25] was a failure, as he himself came to recognize, at any rate in the former instance.[26]

S, on the other hand, is by far the better attested form of the text in Eusebius' own writings. Though not, as Conybeare maintained, the only form known to him, it is the only one quoted by him before Nicaea, and the preferred version even in his later years.

These are the facts. How are they to be accounted for? Either L is original and Eusebius himself is responsible for S, or he had textual authority for S, in which case its authenticity cannot be ruled out.

To establish the first alternative it is necessary to offer (a) a convincing account of the genesis of S, and (b) a credible motive for its substitution. Riggenbach attempted both of these:[27] Eusebius suppressed the Trinitarian baptismal formula out of respect for the *disciplina arcani* and produced S as an equivalent for the benefit of uninitiated readers. The coherence of his explanation was shattered almost immediately by the refutation of its basic premiss:[28] Eusebius' S form is used in several works addressed to the initiated, to whom the *disciplina* would not have applied, while *Theophany* 4.8, which was written for the general public, reproduces and is followed by comment on the L text.[29] The hypothesis of Eusebian creation thus becomes an explanation in search of a motive; and nothing very plausible has been forthcoming. Lebreton argued that Eusebius varied the form of the text according to the drift of his argument: the passages in category (i) emphasize the expansion of Christianity, those in (ii) the supernatural source of its success, those in (iii) the Trinity or baptism. This would be more persuasive, as he himself half admitted,[30] if it were only a matter of partial or complete quotation of a single form of the text, as would be the case if only (i) and (iii) existed; it hardly accounts for the existence of an alternative text form for which Eusebius shows a marked preference. Furthermore, if, as Lebreton held, Eusebius' starting point was the L text, he could hardly have taken what it says of the use of the divine name in baptism to convey the idea of supernatural assistance for the apostolic missionaries. It would have been more natural for him to appeal to 28:20b, as he actually does in three places. The fact that he still quotes the S form of 28:19b in two of them,[31] as well as persistently elsewhere, suggests a different and more authoritative source for the latter than the requirements of his own arguments.

This is not adequately provided by the explanation (originally Riggenbach's) of S as the product of contamination of the text of Matthew with that of other synoptic versions of the final commission, in particular Luke 24:47. It must be conceded to Lebreton and Cuneo that Eusebius does in a number of places quote scripture inaccurately, doubtless from memory (though in some of the cases alleged, as Conybeare later showed,[32] the variant is known to have circulated in the textual tradition), and not infrequently, like most of the Fathers, combines two or more texts, usually on the basis of words they have in common, without indicating what he is doing. Nevertheless, as an argument against the genuineness of S, this explanation runs into a number of difficulties:

1 A text found thirteen times in identical wording is unlikely to be the product of casual or *ad hoc* combination.
2 In four cases out of the thirteen no other text (outside the context of Matthew 28:18–20) is cited, and for these no question of contamination arises.[33]
3 Where Eusebius goes on to quote other parts of 28.18–20, the S form of 28.19b is always placed in the correct sequence; that is, it is offered as part of the text of *Matthew*.
4 A conflation of Matthew 28:19 and Luke 24:47, as Crehan put it,[34] 'would involve the production of *en tō(i) onomati* out of *eis to onoma* and *epi tō(i) onomati*. Such a distillation of prepositions does not seem likely in a careful writer of Greek such as Eusebius'.

The alternative hypothesis of a Eusebian composition which its author would not have claimed as scripture fares no better. The most extended passage in which S figures, *Demonstratio evangelica* 3.7 (i) (*GCS*, 142), offers running commentary on it. It begins by quoting the command *poreuthentes...ethnē*. It then imagines the disciples asking how this could be possible for them, and answers their question by completing the quotation with emphasis on its final words *en tō(i) onomati mou*. Next it adduces Philippians 2:9f. as corroborative testimony to the power of the name; after which Matthew 28:19 is again quoted in full (in the S form), and 24:14 is appended. All three texts quoted are kept clearly distinct, and there is no possibility that the Pauline passage has influenced the form of the Matthaean (even if that were unattested elsewhere).[35] The latter is clearly quoted and commented on *as scripture*, and had it not already contained a reference to the name (of *Jesus*) the argument from Philippians would have had no bearing on it.[36]

We have therefore to consider seriously the alternative possibility that Eusebius had after all some MS. authority for the S text, and to find answers to the difficulties raised by it, the following in particular:

1 *The unanimity of the surviving MS. tradition in favour of L*

'Textual criticism', as Housman said,[37] 'is not a branch of mathematics, nor indeed an exact science at all...It is therefore not susceptible of hard-and-fast rules'. The regular practice among New Testament textual scholars of confining their options to readings attested by the MS. tradition is not exempt from this limitation. The 'eclectic' approach to textual criticism has urged in a number of cases that a reading represented by a single Greek MS. may nevertheless be original;[38] it cannot follow from this that no reading otherwise attested but not actually contained in a surviving MS. can possibly be original, but only that it is, as a general rule, less likely to be. In the present case we have, in the absence of papyri,[39] no MS. witness to the text earlier than the great fourth-century uncials, and of these Eusebius may be called a senior contemporary.

2 *The lack of any corroboration from Origen, despite his contribution to the establishment of the library at Caesarea*

The fact is that, with the relevant part of his commentary on Matthew lost, no extended treatment of this passage by Origen has come down to us. References to Matthew 28:19b (in the L form) are found in one or two places in his other commentaries, and those from fragments of the commentary on John are known to date from his Caesarean period.[40] But it is impossible to tell from this whether his reading reflects the Caesarean or the remembered Alexandrian tradition of the text, let alone whether he was aware of the existence of another form of it.

3 *The known antiquity of the L version*

Since L was known to Theodotus, Irenaeus and Tertullian, its external attestation is considerably earlier than that of S, which it must therefore have supplanted (if it did) at a very early date. How then can an isolated survival of S be accounted for? Conybeare's hypothesis,[41] that L arose in the West (like the Johannine comma) and only established itself in the East in the fourth century, founders on the fact that, Eusebius apart, the alternative to it seems to have been no more familiar in the East than in the West. A more plausible suggestion is that it originated fairly near the gospel's birthplace, but in a more influential church (Antioch?) and early enough to have affected its wider circulation from there. In that case it would have been from local circulation that any textual tradition preserving the original reading was likely to have been derived. Since the general consensus is that Matthew was written in Syria, and a number of scholars follow Kilpatrick in specifying the south-western coastal area, and since Caesarea is the nearest point to this where a systematic collection of scriptural MSS. is known to have been made, the possibility cannot be ruled out that one or more codices containing the S reading found their way there and were known to, or even discovered by, Eusebius (or, alternatively, his master Pamphilus). In his earlier years he would have used the reading with a scholar's confidence in his own judgment;[42] only latterly would he have discovered the difference between this and commanding a consensus in the Church.

This is of course conjecture. But so then is the hypothesis of 'abbreviation' by Eusebius. The evidence will not be accounted for without resort to conjecture. But the conjecture must still, nevertheless, be tested against the content of the gospel.

II

If the external evidence is held to be sufficient to establish the presence in the tradition of two genuinely alternative versions of Matthew 28:19b, which of the two, judging by the internal evidence of his gospel, is Matthew more likely to have written? This question presupposes a clear answer to another: was the evangelist working over traditional material or composing freely? A passage that is only a redaction of earlier material can more easily make room for a further, imperfectly assimilated item, such as a baptismal formula is bound to be (since the evangelist, or his source, would necessarily have derived it from, not imposed it upon, the liturgical practice of his church), than can a carefully wrought literary conclusion to a gospel. And, conversely, if the Matthaean commission can be shown to be a coherent composition, of a kind that can be convincingly attributed to Matthew himself, without including the command to baptize, then it is more likely that the addition of the latter took place at a stage subsequent to the completion of the gospel.

The redaction hypothesis, to be plausible, must postulate either a pre-existing continuous pericope or, at the least, an earlier form of the final commission itself. Less than this will not suffice to establish the case, unless any echo or reminiscence of what a writer has previously read automatically stamps his work as unoriginal; and that is not how real authors work. The reference to 'the mountain to which Jesus had directed them' (28:16), puzzling as it is, offers only precarious support for the first alternative,[43] and Hubbard's arguments for the second rely heavily on Luke's independence of Matthew and John's independence of both (to say nothing of pseudo-Mark's partial independence of all three) and collapse if these props are removed.[44] All in all the evidence of 'traditional' material in these verses alongside the abundance of Matthaean vocabulary and idiom is, as Friedrich says,[45] very thin.

If then the whole passage is treated, as in a number of recent studies,[46] as the evangelist's own composition, this raises more questions about L than most of them have so far recognized. Loisy[47] was the first modern scholar to remark on the awkwardness (unparalleled in the rest of the gospel)[48] of having two present participles, expressing successive actions, dependent on *mathēteusate*.[49] The problem disappears if what Matthew wrote was the S text. Much later Lohmeyer drew attention to the verse structure which is disclosed if the passage is read in the S form.[50] Having pointed it out, he then obscured its significance by theorizing about it in too narrowly form-critical a way; for him it was not the work of the evangelist, but was derived by him from the Aramaic stage of the oral tradition, in which it circulated in two forms corresponding to the two versions of our text, the shorter, which Matthew himself adopted, being associated with Jerusalem, and the longer, which eventually came to supplant it, with Galilee. It is hardly surprising that more attention was not paid to a hypothesis that had become involved with a Matthaean priorist position and with an idiosyncratic account of early Palestinian Christianity. H. Kosmala repeated the error in a different form;[51] although, unlike Lohmeyer, he began with a line-division of the (S) Greek text, he nevertheless presumed that it had been translated from Hebrew. This hardly did justice to the extensive evidence of Matthaean vocabulary in the commission. A short article by the present writer[52] arguing for composition in verse form and in Greek was missed by Hubbard, whose survey of attempts at a verse analysis of the passage (pp. 168–73) consequently included none that started from the Greek.[53] His conclusion 'We would be more convinced of the validity of the Semitic poetry theories if Matthew were in the habit of writing such poetry elsewhere in the gospel' (pp. 172f.) was, in the circumstances, a very fair challenge, and is taken up in what follows.

Let me begin by setting out the verse structure of Matthew 28:18–20 as I now see it:[54]

1a edo'thē moi *pá'sa* |
  b   exou'sia en oura'nō(i) kai epi gēs' ‖
2a poreu'thentes oun mathēteu'sate *pan'ta* |
  b   ta e'thnē en tō(i) ono'mati mou' ‖

3a didáskontes autous tḗrein *pánta* |
b hósa eneteíĺamēn humín ‖
4a kai ídou, egō-méth'-humōn eimi *pásas* |
b tas hēméras heōs tēs suntelèias tou aiōnos ‖

Formal characteristics to be noted are as follows:

1 An eight-line stanza divided into four couplets with a 3–3 stress in each (stresses indicated by ′).
2 Repetition of some form of *pas* at the end of the first line of each couplet; chiastic rhyming arrangement of these: *pasa – panta – panta – pasas*.
3 Emphasis on the personal pronouns, despite use of the Greek enclitic forms, with final *inclusio: egō meth' humōn*.
4 Pairing of longer words in corresponding positions on the basis of Greek quantitative scansion (though used very differently from the practice of classical Greek prosody): *pŏreūthēntĕs–dĭdāskōntĕs*.

These features are to be found in a whole series of passages, virtually all of them solemn pronouncements of Jesus, elsewhere in the gospel, to which I hope to give more extended treatment in a projected study of the Beatitudes. Here, since space is limited, I confine myself to (a) those with an eight-line structure, and (b) (since only a minority of readers is likely to share my resistance to the Q hypothesis) those peculiar, in whole or part, to Matthew.

(1) 11:28–30

The invitation to the yoke, of which both the content and the immediate context have been recognized as having affinities with 28:18–20,[55] is at the same time the closest to it in form:

1a deute-prós-me, pántes hoi kopíōntes |
b kai pephortíśmetoi kágō anapaúsō humas ‖
2a aráte ton zúgon mou′ |
b eph' húmas, kai máthete ap' émou ‖
3a hoti praüs eimi kai tapeínos tē(i) kárdia(i) |
b kai heúrēsete anapaúsin tais psúchais humōn ‖
4a ho gar zúgos mou′ chrēstos |
b kai to phórtion mou′ eláphron estin ‖

Here again we find an eight-line stanza with a basic 3–3 stress. This seems certain for 3 and 4; there is room for debate as to where the internal caesura should fall in 1 and 2, and even whether 1 should be treated as a 4–4 couplet; but the emphasis on the first-person pronoun, extending once more to the enclitic forms (note the parallelism in 4a–b), is in favour of a six-stress rhythm throughout (*kagō* in 1b would be superfluous if it were not stressed in preference to *humas*). It gives appropriate formal expression to the meaning of the invitation, in which Jesus points to himself, the fulfiller and the Messianic interpreter of Torah, as the alternative to the latter as enforced by the Pharisaic scribes.

(2) 5:3–10

The Matthaean Beatitudes are widely recognized to be verse, and are printed as such in, e.g., Nestle-Aland[26] or Aland's *Synopsis*, where they can be studied (though it must be insisted, against both arrangements, that the verse composition actually ends with the *inclusio* at 5.10; 5.11f., is, in Matthew at any rate, a specific application of what precedes it, and is prose).

Here the eight-line structure is doubled (probably on the model of Psalm 119).[56] Each of the two halves contains the same total number of words,[57] and, on my reckoning, of stresses. Among other formal characteristics that could be listed, the following are relevant to the argument here: the rhyming future passives in the apodoses of alternate Beatitudes are arranged chiastically; if the Beatitudes are numbered 1–8, they are found in 2, 4, 5, 7. This makes room for the *inclusio* between 8 and 1.

Words paired by quantity are: *ptōchōi–prāeīs*; *pēnthountĕs–pēinōntĕs*; and (in inverted form) *ĕlĕēmŏnĕs–eīrēnŏpŏiōi*.

(3) 1:20b–21

This dream-revelation, which G. H. Box identified as an eight-line stanza with a 3–2 rhythm,[58] is both lower key and structurally looser than those above, and other formal characteristics noted in them are missing here. Its content, however, like theirs, incorporates a tissue of Old Testament allusion and pastiche (here particularly Genesis 17:19, LXX), and it shares with 28:18–20 (assuming the S text) a preoccupation with the *name* of the Lord.

This makes an appropriate point at which to consider the relation of the gospel's ending to its beginning. That 28:20b echoes 1:23 is generally admitted. But the correspondences between the first chapter and the final commission do not end there, as H. Frankemölle[59] and B. J. Malina have independently shown.[60] Frankemölle's argument for a threefold reference to Father, Son and Holy Spirit in the former to correspond with the baptismal triad in the latter is, however, forced and unconvincing, since the Father is never named as such (contrast 11:27), and the Spirit (totally absent from the latter text) is only introduced, anarthrously and prior to the Son, as the agent of the latter's conception.[61] If on the other hand the S reading is adopted, there is a more direct and appropriate reference back from the name in which the eleven are to make disciples[62] to the names that are named by divine command and promise in the prologue, where the Son of God is called both Jesus, by the dream direction (1:21), and Emmanuel, in fulfilment of prophecy (1:23). 'Emmanuel' is taken up in 28:20, but 'Jesus' (= Joshua) is not absent from the commission either, as a glance at the LXX of Joshua 1:1–9 will confirm.[63]

The one so named in the prologue is also spoken of in its heading as son of David and son of Abraham. The first of these titles recalls the promise of God to David concerning his son Solomon (see especially the version in 1 Chronicles 22:6–13 LXX, and its verbal links with Joshua 1:1–9), the second his promise to Abraham concerning his son Isaac (Genesis 17:19), as well as the blessing bestowed through him on the nations of the earth (Genesis 12:3, 26:3; cf. Matthew 28:19a).

These texts are among the many collected by Hubbard in his attempt to isolate a commission genre in the Old Testament which could have served as a model for a proto-commission behind those in the gospels. That attempt, in the respectful and reluctant judgment of J. P. Meier,[64] was unsuccessful; Matthew's commission is *sui generis*. I concur; but that is not to say that much material from the evangelist's profound study of scripture according to the norms of contemporary Jewish exegesis did not go into its making. The links which Hubbard has disclosed between these passages, with characteristic words constantly recurring, are typical of the cross-referencing in which the scribal mind delighted; and of that mind Matthew was a notable Christian representative.

III

It remains to consider the roots of the interpolated words in the *lex orandi*, and their consequences for the *lex credendi*.

If, as seems now to be generally admitted, the triadic formula entered the gospel tradition, at whatever stage, from the current baptismal practice of a church, two things follow. First, that practice, for dominical authority to be claimed for it in the gospel itself, must antedate its adoption into the tradition by some years. If it were Matthew himself, writing around AD 85–90, who was responsible, it would be likely to go back to AD 70 or earlier; further still if the process had already taken place in the tradition behind him.[65] Secondly, the formula has to be seen as rubric rather than interpretation; it offers not an account of the meaning of the rite but, like the related passage at *Didache* 7.1, directions for performing it. Now it is something of a commonplace among liturgical scholars that the administration of baptism with an accompanying invocatory formula pronounced by the baptizer was, until a relatively late date, peculiar to Syrian Christianity.[66] There it can be traced backwards from its established position in the fourth and fifth centuries (for example, Chrysostom and Narsai) through the third (*Didascalia*; *Acts of Xanthippe and Polyxena*) to the second (*Didache*; *Acts of Paul and Thecla* – the only non-triadic example). G. Winkler, who has recently (1984)[67] drawn fresh attention to the distinctiveness of Syrian baptismal practice, shows also (pp. 435f.) that it saw the rite as uniting the candidate not with the death of Christ but with his baptism in Jordan. While she makes no explicit connection between this and the triadic formula, it is probable that they ought nevertheless to be connected. For the nearest that the New Testament comes to an *icon* of the Trinity (as distinct from a verbal triad) is the synoptic Baptism narrative – a much more credible background to the development of a threefold formula for use in baptism than the apocalyptic antecedents suggested by Schaberg.[68]

Now our earliest evidence (and Matthew's only identifiable source) for the Baptism is Mark's gospel (written *c.* AD 70); and Matthew's alterations of Mark at 3:6 and 20:22f. do not suggest that he saw a continuity between the baptism received by Jesus from John and that administered to Christian disciples.[69] We should therefore not suppose that because Matthew is in some sense Syrian it therefore represents an early stage of the Syrian baptismal tradition, but rather that it was affected by the latter after its completion.

With the Syrian practice we may compare that of Rome.[70] Here no formula of administration is attested before the seventh century. Previously to that, what accompanied the act of baptism was the candidate's own profession of faith in response to interrogation in the water, which is clearly Trinitarian by the time of Hippolytus, with slightly earlier attestation elsewhere in the west from Irenaeus and Tertullian.[71] At some point there will have been a transition from the Christological profession implicit in the Pauline letters and Acts.[72] It would be surprising if this had taken place in total independence of the gospel text elsewhere invoked in its support. An early date for the change would therefore imply early acquaintance with the L text, a later date probably a later discovery of it. But in the latter case it is so inherently unlikely that a gospel written by AD 90 and destined to become the second-century Church's favourite book did not reach the metropolis for several decades, that the alternative, that it originally reached Rome without the baptismal command and only incorporated it later, has to be taken seriously.

At this point the evidence of Justin is as crucial as it is puzzling. To quote what he says:

> Then we bring them to a place where there is water, where they are regenerated in the same way as we were; for they then make their ablution in the name of God the Father and Lord of all, and of our Saviour Jesus Christ, and of Holy Spirit.[73]

There is no citation of L here, explicit or implicit. Justin is describing current liturgical practice and justifying it not by scripture but by the experience of earlier initiates. Who then are the 'we' contrasted with the neophytes in this passage? If they are Roman Christians of longer standing, he can only mean that baptism in the name of the Trinity has been the practice in Rome as long as the bulk of Christians there can remember (thirty years, say). But why then should he go out of his way to mention such an internal matter to his readership – unless, that is, so far from being generally accepted, it had been the subject of recent comment?

On the other hand Justin may be using 'we' to distinguish himself from local initiates. We know that his own conversion took place not at Rome but somewhere in the east[74] – possibly in Asia Minor, but quite conceivably a place nearer his native city of Nablus. It is quite possible in the first case and highly likely in the second that he was baptized with the Syrian form. If so, he is not saying here that the church of Rome, whatever it did formerly, now conforms to the Syrian practice – for the witness of Hippolytus some sixty years later (with which his own description is entirely compatible)[75] shows that it did no such thing – but rather that the Trinitarian profession of faith that now accompanies the immersion is the Roman equivalent of the Syrian triadic formula, and as such is no innovation. But, again, there would be no call for him to defend the church of Rome against charges of innovation if it had not, fairly recently, made alterations in its own practice.

To cut short what could become a long story, I propose the following scenario: (1) the innovation, made around AD 140–50, was the introduction of the triple immersion with threefold profession of faith at baptism; (2) the immediate precipitating cause of it was the impact of Marcion (Justin's Trinitarian language here and elsewhere in the *Apology* has an anti-Marcionite ring); (3) the structure of the enlarged profession of faith, Trinitarian and not Binitarian, was modelled on the triad of Matthew 28:19, which was already associated with baptism and now circulating as part of the gospel.

That it was the gospel in this slightly enlarged form that was received into the Canon of the New Testament is not here contested. But if the foregoing arguments have any force, it was not the mind of the evangelist but the praxis of unknown Christians after him (or even maybe contemporary with him), inspired by gospel tradition, that produced the half-verse which contributed so signally to the genesis of credal forms in the post-apostolic church.

NOTES

1 E. Renan, *Histoire des origines du Christianisme: V. Les Evangiles et la seconde generation chrétienne*, Paris 1877, p. 197.

2 F. C. Conybeare, 'The Eusebian Form of the Text Matth. 28, 19,' *ZNW*, 2 (1901), 275–88.

3 See especially 'Three Early Modifications of the Text of the Gospels,' *Hibbert Journal*, 1 (1902), 96–113.

4 E. Riggenbach, *Der Trinitarische Taufbefehl*, BFCT 7, Gütersloh 1903.

5 J. Lebreton, *Histoire du dogme de la Trinité*, Paris 1910, 8th edn. 1927, note E, pp. 599–610.

6 The same goes for their less effective contemporary, F. H. Chase, 'The Lord's Command to Baptize,' *JThS*, 6 (1905), 481–517.

7 See E. Klostermann, *Das Matthäusevangelium* (Handbuch zum NT), Tübingen 1909, p. 357; 2nd edn. 1927, p. 232 (rewritten). Klostermann's judgment seems to have carried special weight, doubtless as that of a competent patristic scholar who had worked on the text of both Eusebius and Origen.

8 For a full (but not quite exhaustive or accurate) list of positions taken see G. Friedrich, 'Die formale Struktur von Mt 28, 18–20,' *ZThK*, 80 (1983), 172 n. 98. H. Fr. von Campenhausen, *Urchristliches und Altkirchliches*, Tübingen 1979, p. 208 n. 48, is a lone voice in Germany now.

9 O. Michel's influential study, 'The Conclusion of Matthew's Gospel' (ET from *EvTh*, 10 (1950–1), 16–26), in *The Interpretation of Matthew*, (ed. G. N. Stanton, pp. 30–41, London 1983), is particularly unsatisfactory in

this respect; cf. H. Kosmala, 'The Conclusion of Matthew', *ASTI*, 4 (1965), 133.

10 So, explicitly, F. Hahn, *Mission in the New Testament*, ET, London 1965, p. 67; K. Aland, 'Zur Vorgeschichte der christlichen Taufe', in *Neues Testament und Geschichte*, Festschrift O. Cullmann, ed. H. Bettensweiger and B. Reicke, Zurich/Tübingen 1972, p. 14, n. 1. The Eusebian reading, after featuring in previous editions of Nestle's Greek Testament from 1927 to 1963, disappeared from the apparatus in the Alands' recension of 1979 (Nestle-Aland[26]).

11 For a critical examination of this see H. Frankemölle, 'Evengelist und Gemeinde', *Biblica*, 60 (1979), 155–90.

12 *Jesus Missions–och Dophefallning Mt 28, 18–20*, Stockholm 1919.

13 See G. R. Beasley-Murray, *Baptism in the New Testament*, London 1962, pp. 81f.; W. Trilling, *Das Wahre Israel*, 3rd edn. Munich 1964, p. 35 n. 83.

14 *The Lord's Command to Baptise*, Catholic University of America NT Studies 5, Washington 1923.

15 Review of Cuneo in *JThS*, 25 (1924), 191–7.

16 More recent scholars who have drawn attention to Cuneo's work (notably Trilling, *Das Wahre Israel* and B. J. Hubbard, *The Matthean Redaction of a Primitive Apostolic Commissioning*, SBL Dissertation Series 19, Missoula 1974) would have done well to attend to this devastating, and by no means overstated, critique.

17 The classification is Lebreton's.

18 *Demonstratio evangelica* 1.3, 1.4, 1.6 (*GCS* 17.18–20, 20.11–12, 34.20–1); *In psalmos* 46.4, 95.3, 144.9 (*PG* 23.416A, 1221C; 24.60C); *In Isaiam* 41.10 (*GCS* 261.25–6); *Theoph.* 3.4 (*GCS* 129.10); *De ecclesiastica theologia* 3.3 (*GCS* 149.32–3) (omitted, perhaps inadvertently, by Lebreton – see note 5 above).

19 *Dem. ev.* 3.6, 3.7 *bis*, 9.11 (*GCS* 138.2–6, 142.6–28, 144.16–20, 429.28–33); *HE* III.5.2 (*GCS* 196.12); *In ps.* 59.9, 65.5, 67.34, 76.20 (*PG* 23.569C, 653D, 720C, 900C); *In Is.* 18.2, 34.16 (*GCS* 120.5–6, 226.12–13); *Laus Constantini* 16.8 (*GCS* 251.12); *Theoph.* 4.16 (*GCS* 189.28); 5.17, 46, 49 (228.27, 252.12, 255.9) (= *Dem. ev.* 3.6, 3.7 *bis*).

20 *Epistula ad Caesarienses* 3 (see *Athanasius Werke*, ed. Opitz, 3.1, p. 43.18–19); *Contra Marcellum* 1.1.9, 36 (*GCS* 3.7, 8.21); *De eccl. theol.* 3.5 (*GCS* 163.22); *Theoph.* 4.8 (*GCS* 177.2). (I exclude *In ps.* 117:1 (Pitra, *Analecta sacra* iii, 512) as doubtfully Eusebian.)

21 Conybeare's suggestion about these (*ZNW*, 2 (1901), 281) has force once the shorter text has been accepted on other grounds.

22 Cf. Matthew 23:8, and see n. 62 below.

23 For the former see L. Hartman, 'Into the Name of Jesus', *NTS*, 20 (1974), p. 439; for the latter E. Cothénet, 'La formule trinitaire baptismale de Matthieu 28, 19', in *Trinité et Liturgie*, ed. A. M. Triacca and A. Pistoia, Ephemerides Liturgicae: Subsidia 32, Rome 1984, pp. 70f.

24 F. C. Conybeare, 'The Authorship of the Contra Marcellum', *ZNW*, 4 (1903), 330–4; 6 (1905), 250–70.

25 *ZNW*, 2 (1901), 279f.

26 *JThS*, 25 (1924), 195–7, with acknowledgment to G. Loeschke, 'Contra Marcellum, eine Schrift des Eusebius von Caesarea', *ZNW*, 7 (1906) 69–76.

27 *Der Trinitarische Taufbefehl*, pp. 29–32.

28 Originally by Conybeare, *ZNW*, 6 (1905), 266f.; cf. K. Lake, art. 'Baptism (Early Christian)', in *ERE*, vol. 2, Edinburgh 1909, p. 380; Cuneo, *The Lord's Command to Baptise*, p. 71; G. Kretschmar, *Studien zur frühchristlichen Trinitätstheologie*, Tübingen 1956, p. 5 n. 1.

29 Ironically, it was Riggenbach himself (*Der Trinitarische Taufbefehl*, pp. 17–21) who had refuted Conybeare on this point.

30 See Lebreton, *Histoire du dogme de la Trinité*, p. 606.

31 *dem. ev.* 3.7 (ii); *In ps.* 76.20. The exception is *in Is.* 41.10 (category (i)).

32 Review of Cuneo, *JThS*, 25 (1924), 192f.

33 Hubbard, *Matthean Redaction*, p. 156, admits this, and with it the possibility of textual support for S, with reference to *HE* III.5.2, but is silent about the other instances (*Dem. ev.* 3.6; *in Ps.* 65.5; *In Is.* 34.16).

34 J. H. Crehan *Early Christian Baptism and the Creed*, London 1948, p. 25.

35 *Contra* Hubbard (p. 154).

36 Riggenbach, *Der Trinitarische Taufbefehl*, p. 26, admitted the force of these considerations, but declined to answer them. For E. Meyer, *Ursprung und Anfänge des Christentums*, 1, Stuttgart/Berlin 1924, p. 15 n. 1, they were decisive.

37 A. E. Housman, 'The Application of Thought to Textual Criticism', in *Selected Prose*, ed. J. Carter, Cambridge 1961, p. 132.

38 Including Luke 22:19f. where, if the shorter (Western) text is original (cf. now G. D. Kilpatrick, *The Eucharist in Bible and Liturgy*, Cambridge 1983, pp. 28–38), the longer (as here) would have made its appearance quite early and most likely have been influenced by liturgical practice.

39 There is evidence that the library of Caesarea was having to replace worn-out papyri at the end of the fourth century (see K. Lake, *The Text of the New Testament*, London 1953, p. 15, citing Lagrange). The survival prospects of a minority, and by then doctrinally suspect, reading would have been slight.

40 *In Joannem* 3.5, frs. 37, 79 (*GCS* iv. 512, 547, ed. Preuschen; see editor's introduction, pp. lxxviii–lxxx); cf. Conybeare, *ZNW*, 6 (1905), 268.

41 *ZNW*, 2 (1901), 288.

42 It is also conceivable that his confidence in preferring a minority reading was supported by the testimony of a much earlier commentator now lost to us. The name of Papias, the first commentator on a gospel text, suggests itself.

43 The immediate reference must be back to 28:10, itself secondary

development from 28:7 (cf. G. Strecker, *Der Weg der Gerechtigkeit*, Göttingen 1962, p. 208), which in turn is the Matthaean redaction of Mark 16:7. For the mountain as a Matthaean motif see J. Schaberg, *The Father, the Son and the Holy Spirit: The Triadic Phrase in Matt. 28:19b*, SBL Dissertation Series 61, Chico 1982, p. 59 n. 2, and T. L. Donaldson, *Jesus on the Mountain*, *JSNT* Supplement Series 8, Sheffield 1983 – though both favour a traditional *Vorlage* here.

44 Hubbard, *Matthean Redaction*, pp. 105ff. For dependence of John on the synoptics see now F. Neirynck, 'John and the Synoptics: The Empty Tomb Stories, *NTS*, 30 (1984), 161–87; for dependence of Luke on Matthew see, *inter alios*, H. B. Green, 'The Credibility of Luke's Transformation of Matthew,' in *Synoptic Studies*, ed. C. M. Tuckett, *JSNT* Supplement Series, 7, pp. 131–55, Sheffield 1984. On the latter hypothesis a fair case can be made for the S text of Matthew 28:19 as *Vorlage* for Luke 24:47.

45 *ZThK*, 80 (1983), 174.

46 cf. H. Frankemölle, *Jahwebund und Kirche Christi*, Neutestamentliche Abhandlungen, NF10, Münster 1973; J. Lange, *Das Erscheinen des Auferstandenen im Evangelium nach Matthäus*, Würzburg 1973; J. D. Kingsbury, 'The Composition and Christology of Matt. 28:16–20,' *JBL*, 93 (1974), 573–84; M. D. Goulder, *Midrash and Lection in Matthew*, London 1974; Friedrich, *ZTLK*, 80 (1983), 137–83.

47 A. Loisy, *Les Evangiles synoptiques*, vol. 1, Ceffonds 1907, pp. 751f.

48 The participles in 4:23, 9:35, claimed as parallels by Kingsbury, *JBL*, 93 (1974), 577, are not truly such, since they express *concurrent* actions.

49 The variant *baptisantes* in B D reflects an awareness of the problem, though the substitution of two aorist for two present participles really does nothing to resolve it. Cf. Michel, *The Interpretation of Matthew*, pp. 37f.

50 E. Lohmeyer, 'Mir ist gegeben alle Gewalt', in *In Memoriam Ernst Lohmeyer*, ed. W. Schmauch, Stuttgart 1951, pp. 22–49.

51 *ASTI*, 4 (1965), 132–47.

52 H. B. Green, 'The Command to Baptize and Other Matthaean Interpolations', *StEv*, 4 (1968), *TU* 102, 60–3.

53 Hubbard's own arrangement of the lines (pp. 171f.) anticipates the 'concentric' analysis proposed by H. Schieben, 'Konzentrik im Matthäusevangelium', *Kairos*, 19 (1977), 287f.; cf. Cothénet, *Trinité et Liturgie*, p. 65. Whatever else may be said of this, the result is prose and not verse.

54 The modifications of my earlier arrangement (*StEv*, 4 (1968), 60) reflect useful criticisms of it by G. Barth, *Die Taufe in frühchristlicher Zeit*, Biblisch-Theologische Studien, 4, Neukirche/Vluyn 1981, p. 14. But his argument that the form with the better rhythm could equally well be secondary is difficult to take seriously in this context. Can we imagine Eusebius (or anyone) excising and substituting for the command to baptize just for the sake of rhythmical improvement?

55 For content, cf. H. D. Betz, 'The Logion of the Easy Yoke and of Rest (Mt 11.28–30)', *JBL* 86 (1967), 24; for context, Lange, *Das Erscheinen des Auferstandenen*, pp. 152–67, 208–10.

56 See Goulder, *Midrash*, p. 186 n. 65.

57 Cf. J. Schniewind, *Das Evangelium nach Matthäus*, 7th edn, Göttingen 1956, p. 40.

58 G. H. Box, *St Matthew*, Century Bible, London 1926, p. 75; cf. Green, *StEv*, 4 (1968), 61.

59 Frankemölle, *Jahwebund und Kirche Christi*, pp. 321ff.

60 B. J. Malina, 'The Literary Structure and Form of Matt. xxviii. 16–20,' *NTS*, 17 (1970–1), 99ff.

61 J. D. Kingsbury *Matthew: Structure, Christology, Kingdom*, London 1976, pp. 77f., and Cothénet, *Trinité et Liturgie*, pp. 72, 76, look rather to 3.16f. as the prototype of Christian baptism. But see above, p. 135.

62 Cf. 7:22. For the equivalence of the Heb. *bᵉshem*, see H. Kosmala, 'In My Name,' *ASTI*, 5 (1967), pp. 89–92; Cothénet, *Trinité et Liturgie*, pp. 69f.

63 N.B.: '*pasas tas hēmeras, esomai meta sou, eneteilato, panta ta gegrammena, poreuē(i)*'.

64 J. P. Meier, 'Two Disputed Questions in Matt. 28:16–20', *JBL* 96 (1977), 424.

65 As argued by Strecker, *Der Weg*, p. 210 and Schaberg, *The Father, the Son and the Holy Spirit*, p. 321.

66 See Kretschmar, *Studien*, pp. 196–200; E. C. Whitaker, 'The Baptismal Formula in the Syrian Rite,' *CQR*, 161 (1960), 346–62; *idem*, 'The History of the Baptismal Formula,' *JEH*, 16 (1965), 1–12.

67 G. Winkler, *Das Armenische Initiationsrituel*, OrChrA 217, Rome 1984.

68 Schaberg, *The Father, the Son and the Holy Spirit*, pp. 183–7, 287–91, 322.

69 *Contra* Kingsbury and Cothénet (see n. 61 above).

70 See P. de Puniet, art. 'Baptême' in *DACL*, 2 (pt. i), pp. 251–346, Paris 1910, at pp. 337–43; Whitaker, *JEH*, 161 (1965), 4.

71 Hippolytus, *Traditio apostolica* xxi. 12–18, ed. G. Dix and H. Chadwick, London 1968 p. 36; Irenaeus, *Dem.* 3; Tertullian, *De corona* 3; *Adv. Prax.* 26.

72 The tenacity with which the later Roman tradition seems to have held to the sufficiency in principle of baptism in the name of Jesus only suggests that this transition was neither very early nor uncontroversial.

73 *Apology* 1, 61 (tr. H. Bettenson, *The Early Christian Fathers*, London 1956, p. 84).

74 See *Dialogue* 2.6, 3.1.

75 *Pace* Kretschmar, *Studien*, p. 207; Campenhausen, *Urchristliches und Altkirchliches*, p. 240.

The achievement of orthodoxy in the fourth century AD

RICHARD HANSON

I

The great majority of theological students in the English-speaking world can only read English. If such a one were to determine to investigate the critical development concerning Christian doctrine which took place in the fourth century of the Christian era, he would find himself very badly served. Recent books covering the whole story of the last stages of the formation of the doctrine of the Trinity are scarce, but they exist, and they are not in English. Much the best is Manlio Simonetti's *La Crisi Ariana nel Quarto Secolo*. There is also E. Boularand's *L'Hérésie d'Arius et la foi de Nicée*, which has some good points but generally is not satisfactory, if only because when Arius propounded his views they were not then formally heretical. In English the last full-scale book written on the whole Arian controversy was that of H. M. Gwatkin, *Studies of Arianism*, published in 1882. Twenty-seven years later he published the short *Arian Controversy* but in a note prefixed to it he says that this work is 'largely, though not entirely, an abridgement' of the earlier book. That book was a fine one in its day, but it is now almost completely out of date. The only other works that could be said to be comprehensive in approaching the subject are G. L. Prestige's *God in Patristic Thought* and J. N. D. Kelly's *Early Christian Doctrines*. The first suffers from two serious flaws: it is not an historical account, but a general treatment carried out thematically, and, like much of the work of Prestige, admirable though it was in its day, it suffers from the same assumptions which reduce the value of all work done on the Arian controversy (not least Newman's *Arians of the Fourth Century*) till very recently. And Kelly only deals with the period in a few chapters, as part of an ongoing development, and is consequently unable to enter into much detail. Otherwise the English-speaking student is left with general histories of the church, which by their nature cannot give a comprehensive account of the controversy. There are indeed some very good books dealing with single aspects of the period, such as G. C. Stead's *Divine Substance* and *Arianism* edited by R. Gregg, and E. J. Meijering's *Orthodoxy and Platonism in Athanasius* and T. A. Kopecek's *History of Neo-Arianism*, and there are several first-rate articles in English. But there is no other single full-length recent book giving a competent survey of the whole period during which the doctrine of the Trinity received its final form.[1]

The consequence is that the English-speaking theological student, if he studies the Arian controversy at all, is given quite a misleading impression of it. Of course, many students will avoid this misfortune by the simple device of totally ignoring the early history of doctrine, and jumping cheerfully from the New Testament to Schleiermacher (or even to Liberation theology). Early church history at the moment (whether of doctrine or of events) is given cavalier treatment in many theological colleges and university departments. But if he shows a desire to explore what is on any reckoning an extremely important and critical period in the formation of Christian doctrine, he will be given a picture which is neat and tidily schematized but which neither corresponds to the facts nor accounts for the evidence. He will be told that about the year 318 a wicked Alexandrian presbyter called Arius chose to propound a doctrine of the relation of the Son to the Father which was completely unorthodox and heretical, and which was in fact condemned by the first General Council of the church in Nicaea in 325, but that by various means the base and crafty supporters of this heretical doctrine managed to keep the orthodox out of influential positions and to continue to propagate their wicked ideas for nearly another sixty years after Nicaea, until, almost wholly through the selfless efforts of a noble and courageous champion of orthodoxy, Athanasius bishop of Alexandria, their politics were frustrated, their heterodoxy exposed, and the truth enshrined in the Nicaeno-Constantinopolitan Creed of 381.

This account is in many respects misleading. In the first place, on the central subject of the dispute, how divine is Jesus Christ, there was in the year 318 no universally recognized orthodox answer. This is one reason why the controversy lasted so long. It was a controversy which resulted in the determination of orthodoxy, not one consisting solely or even mainly in the defence of orthodoxy. By the year 318 Origen had given one answer to the question at issue, Tertullian another; nobody in the course of the dispute attempted to solve it on purely Origenist, and nobody on purely Tertullianic lines. Origen would no more have tolerated Tertullian's solution, which would have seemed to him scandalously materialist, than Tertullian could have accepted Origen's answer, for the doctrine of the eternal generation of the Son contradicted his 'economic' Trinity. Yet no theologian greater than these two was available in the year 318, and eventually both these were destined to provide material for those who were trying to think rationally about the central issue, but to provide it piecemeal, eclectically, as theologians drew on parts of the theology of these great men, and rejected parts. Again, even had orthodoxy on the subject existed, there was no common agreed vocabulary capable of being used in a clear sense by all schools of thought in which to conduct a general debate about so central and important a subject, either among the Greek-speakers or the Latin-speakers. The words *ousia* and *hypostasis* were for forty years and more after the controversy began used in different senses by different people who were not aware that the others were using these words differently, and the same applies to the word *substantia* in Latin. Until late in the controversy neither Greek-speakers nor Latin-speakers had a single term capable of being widely used to express what God is as Three in distinction from what he is as One, not even the word *persona*, which on the whole was, for reasons not easy to discern, avoided and by Marius Victorinus at least deliberately rejected. Athanasius is to be included in this generalization along with the others. In these circumstances, to maintain that the Arian controversy was a contest between known orthodoxy and manifest heresy is absurd. There were indeed certain extreme views which virtually everybody repudiated: that Jesus was a 'mere man' and nothing more (*psilos anthropos, purus homo*), that there were no distinctions within the Godhead but only one God in three different aspects (but Marcellus of Ancyra, a theologian never completely repudiated by Athanasius, came close to teaching this doctrine); that the doctrine of the Trinity meant that God was cut up, divided or diminished. But within these very broad limits no doctrine could properly be said to be heretical. Even Arius' views when they were first propounded could have been regarded (as Eusebius of Caesarea regarded them) as no more than a radical version of an acceptable tradition of theology.

The question at issue certainly had to be answered sooner or later. The work of the apologists, of Irenaeus, Tertullian, Hippolytus, Novatian, Origen and Eusebius of Caesarea, was all in fact a contribution, diverse and multifarious, towards the great task of finding an answer. Arius' theology was only peculiar in that it managed neither to give a satisfactory answer to the problem nor to be immediately and manifestly erroneous. There was one important aspect of the witness of the New Testament to the nature and activity of God which Arianism (and, I believe, Arius) grasped fully and courageously: this collection of documents witnessed to a suffering God. Arianism was carefully designed to enable Christians to believe just this. What remains of Arius' utterances is concerned almost solely with the metaphysical side of Arianism; but there was a soteriological side, to which recent research has paid much attention, and one cannot understand the former until one has grasped the latter. Now, the Arians believed that the only way to achieve a rational theology of a suffering God was to postulate the existence of a high God who was impassible and a lesser God who experienced the suffering for him. And there were certain traditions within existing Greek theology which were capable of being exploited for this end. The Arians were among the few theologians of the early church who seriously understood the scandal of the Cross. But the price which they thought it necessary to pay for this theology was too high.

When Athanasius began his life-work of refuting this doctrine, he had grasped clearly the danger and distortion which such a theology inevitably led to, and he continued to proclaim this unweariedly for more than twenty years. But the earliest point at which we can allow that he was writing anti-Arian works was about 339, twenty years after the Arian controversy had begun. And well before that he had behaved in such a way as to render any of his utterances of very little effect. The researches of British archaeologists in the 1920s turned up two papyri letters, which can be accurately dated and whose authorship is easily ascertained. They were written by enemies of Athanasius within his see of Alexandria, not theological adversaries, but lesser clergy, writing privately to each other, not for publication nor with a propagandist purpose. They make it clear beyond any doubt that Athanasius was using unscrupulous violence in his see of Alexandria in order to suppress and discourage people hostile to him, whose hostility arose from no doctrinal reason but was connected with a trouble (the Melitian affair) which predated his accession to the see. He was misusing his power disgracefully, even by the standards of the fourth century. When the Council of Tyre deposed him in the year 335 it did so for perfectly good reasons, well before he had made any written contribution to the theological dispute. When therefore he weighed in to the theological melée there were good reasons why nobody in the East should listen to him. And in fact, nobody did. For about twenty years almost no Eastern bishop, whatever his views, would have anything to do with Athanasius, and in this they were quite justified. Athanasius, in fact, brought a perfectly unnecessary complication into the theological debate, and one which tended to render his own contribution to it negligible. His actions shouted so loud that his words could not be heard.

The Council of Nicaea of 325, which was supposed to solve the dispute, nipping it in the bud at an early stage, in fact only added to the confusion. It declared that the Son was 'from the substance' (*ek tēs ousiās*) of the Father, that he was 'consubstantial' (*homoousios*) with him, and in a series of anathemas appended to its creed condemned anyone who taught that the Son was 'from another *hypostasis* or *ousia*' from the Father. It is difficult to know what these last two Greek words meant at the time; or rather, they must have meant different things to different people. But they were readily capable of being interpreted as meaning that what we would today call the Son's 'Person' was identical with the 'Person' of the Father. And there were present at the council theologians such as Eustathius of Antioch and Marcellus of Ancyra whose doctrine was not easily distinguishable from this. '*Homoousios*' was inserted in order to preclude Arians from agreeing to the creed; for Arius had specifically denied that this word should be applied to the Son. But it was not the precise, lucid concept which older scholars have made it out to be. It was a word of rather loose meaning, whose associations in the history of Christian doctrine before 325 had been gnostic and heterodox rather than otherwise. And 'from the substance' of the Father was an expression which Origen had explicitly refused, and which must have carried materialist overtones for many who read it at Nicaea. Because the pro-Christian Emperor Constantine wanted everybody to sign the Creed of Nicaea, almost everybody did. But as a contribution to solving the dispute it was a disastrous failure.

It can then be readily perceived why the conventional account of the Arian controversy, to be found in such authors as Newman, Gwatkin, Prestige and T. H. Bindley, is quite inaccurate and why the English-speaking theological student will be widely misled if he follows them.

II

If we discard the conventional account of how orthodoxy was achieved in the fourth century, we can if we choose fall back on the idea, which is not widely disseminated but which has had its champions in the past (for example, E. Schwartz), and still has them today, that the Arian controversy in fact consisted of a struggle for power within the church which was disguised under a theological dispute and that this theological dispute, if it had any serious meaning, was a competition between rival Greek philosophical theories with very little reference to the doctrines and assumptions of either the Old or the New Testament. Some evidence to support this view can be collected. It is undeniable that the dispute, which began as a theological debate, quite soon turned into a struggle for power by various groups, each of whom tried to obtain the emperor's ear and to gather the reins of ecclesiastical government into its hands. Emperors intervened again and again: Constantine, Constantius II, Valens, Gratian, Theodosius. Ecclesiastical depositions were almost invariably followed by imperial orders of banishment. Every party in a major dispute in the fourth century attempted to bring the emperor on to their side. And inasmuch as the peace and stability of the empire was to some extent by the fourth century bound up with the peace and stability of the church, it was virtually unavoidable that the emperor should become involved. But because the secular power was involved, it does not follow that the controversy was simply a story of men grasping at secular power under the mask of theology. We have no right to assume that Athanasius or Basil of Caesarea or Meletius of Antioch were mere power-seekers because they engaged in politics as well as in theology, any more than we have to make the same assumption about Thomas à Becket or Oliver Cromwell, both of whom were men of deep religious conviction engaged in politics which were the result of, rather than the real motive of, their theological ideas. And if we find, as we do, both that these men, and men like them, were prepared to risk or to endure exile and disgrace in defence of their views, and that when they express their theological views they do so with reasonableness and effectiveness, we have no right to assume that they were activated by unworthy motives. There were of course men like Valens of Mursa and Ursacius of Singidunum who were no more than theological weathercocks, responding to every wind of imperial favour. But against them we can set (even if we confine ourselves to the Western church) Hilary of Poitiers and Eusebius of Vercelli on the pro-Nicene side and Palladius of Ratiaria on the Arian, who refused to change their views to accord with those of the government and who suffered accordingly.

Again, it is certainly true that the controversy was carried on almost completely in the terms of Greek philosophy. All sides appealed to the

Bible, and all were convinced that the Bible was on their side, but as the Bible was a common quarry for all, so its vocabulary was of little use in determining the issue. All sides were driven to use non-biblical vocabulary while protesting strongly that the vocabulary of their opponents was non-biblical. One of the things which most people learnt as a result of the Arian controversy is a point which many people today still do not appreciate, that it is impossible to interpret the Bible in the vocabulary of the Bible. Anybody who does so is still faced with the old question, what does the Bible mean? The only alternative vocabulary open to the theologians of the Eastern Church was the vocabulary of what we today call late Greek philosophy, of late Stoicism, of Middle Platonism and of Neo-Platonism (and occasionally of the philosophy of Aristotle). There was no other available. Neither Indian philosophy nor Chinese philosophy (though no doubt both were then existent in some form) offered a practical alternative. So he who wishes to understand the controversy must perforce plunge into a jungle of Greek philosophical terms: *ousia, hypostasis, idiotēs, hyparxis, logos, enhypostatos, enousios, pathos, apatheia, gennētos, agennēsia, aïdios, ex ouk ontōn, homoousios, homoiousios, anhomoios, tautousios* and so on. Very often the debate seems to be remote from the vocabulary and the thought of the New Testament. Very often we seem to be in a thicket of obsolete philosophical language which has nothing to do with the living heart of Christianity.

But against this three points must be taken into consideration. First, the theologians of the fourth century were eclectic, not to say loose, in their use of Greek philosophical terms. They followed no system in their employment of philosophy as a handmaid to theology. *Homoousios*, for instance, was not a term much used in any form of ancient philosophy, though it appears sometimes. And the bewildering variety of the meanings attached to the word *ousia* shown in G. C. Stead's *Divine Substance* is a testimony to the looseness of the Fathers' use of their vocabulary. Even the expression 'beyond substance (or being)' (*epekeina tēs ousias*) has several different meanings. The same of course applies *mutatis mutandis* to those who wrote in Latin, because Roman culture never developed an independent philosophy of its own and simply used translations or even transliterations of Greek terms. A few, like Marius Victorinus and Gregory of Nyssa, knew pretty exactly what these terms meant in strict philosophical use. But even Gregory found his radical Arian opponent, Eunomius, absurdly wedded to philosophical terms, and castigated him accordingly. This looseness of use of Greek philosophical words suggests, not that the theologians of the fourth century were incompetent second-raters (though a few, such as Epiphanius and Lucifer of Calaris were), but that they were using this language for purposes other than that for which it had been coined, in fact for theological or religious ends rather than strictly philosophical.

This certainly was the case. The great majority of the theologians of the fourth century were bishops. Not one of them was a professional theologian. The early church did not know of the phenomenon of a professional theologian. Most of them might have agreed with Kierkegaard that to be a Professor of Theology was to crucify Christ. They all had pastoral responsibility. Behind them, and to some extent holding them to account, were their flocks, men and women, with whose spiritual welfare they were charged. They were conscious, much more than modern theologians are conscious, of a praying congregation and a worshipping church. Their theology, then, can never have been completely high and dry; it always had to be tested, as it were, along the pulses of the Christian community. The commonest words which they use for 'orthodox' and 'orthodoxy' are *eusebēs* and *eusebeia*, which means 'pious' or 'reverent' as well as 'true' or 'correct'. Their ideas of what is *eusebēs* of course differ. But it is quite mistaken to regard them as a collection of remote and ineffectual dons bickering with each other over empty words.

Above all, it must be conceded that though the theologians of the fourth century used the language of Greek philosophy, and were consequently to some extent influenced by the presuppositions and leading ideas of Greek philosophy, the great issue which they were debating was a live and real issue, as live and real today as it was fourteen centuries ago. The basic issue was not, are we to use *homoousios* or *homoeousios* to describe the relation of the Son to the Father, but, what is the Christian doctrine of God? From the beginning Christianity carried within its bosom two convictions: that there is only one God, and that Jesus Christ is divine. It had for three hundred years refused to compromise on the question of monotheism; it had steadfastly refused to make any concession to the tolerant polytheism of the culture of the late Roman empire in which it lived, and thousands of Christians had suffered and died because of this conviction. But just as deeply rooted in the heart of Christianity was the worship of Jesus Christ, not the cult of a deified man (which was common enough in the Roman empire), but the worship of the Son of God who had taken to himself human nature in the Incarnation. These two convictions had to be reconciled. It had been the task of Christian thinkers to reconcile them, ever since the

Fourth Gospel was written, ever since the first apologist had put pen to paper quite early in the second century. A rich tradition of theological discussion and discourse had in consequence been created, rich but diverse and by no means homogeneous. It was the task, and it was the achievement, of the theologians of the fourth century who inherited this tradition to mould it, to filter it, by choice, by trial, by discussion, by controversy, into a single comprehensive, flexible, satisfying doctrine which would be a recognizably Christian doctrine of God, neither a minor adaptation of the Jewish doctrine (much though they inherited from Judaism), nor a pale imitation of one or other form of Greek philosophy. It is not surprising perhaps that it took them rather more than sixty years to accomplish this, two whole generations; so that by 381 no single theologian who took part in the original debate which led to the Council of Nicaea survived, not even the long-lived Athanasius, Marcellus or Euzoius. To say that this controversy was a logomachy concerned only with the terms of Greek philosophy is not only erroneous; it is stupid.

The best proof of this is the treatment of the doctrine of the Holy Spirit in the controversy. There was no philosophical motive at all for including the Spirit in the Trinity. Theologians up to about the year 360 had freely used a philosophical model to describe the relation of the Son to the Father, a model drawn from Middle Platonism, which envisaged a Supreme Principle so abstract and metaphysically remote as to be virtually unknowable in himself, and a Second Principle who was capable of making the Supreme Principle known, and they tended to write in theistic terms rather than to speak of impersonal powers or entities. But part of the development of the doctrine of the Trinity in the second part of the fourth century was the virtual abandonment of this model. And though the type of Platonist philosophy widespread at that period in fact recognized three ultimate Principles or Realities, the One, the *Nous* or Mind, and the Soul, this Trinity was very different from the Christian Trinity of Father, Son and Holy Spirit and can have influenced it only marginally. The Holy Spirit figured very little in Christian theology till the second half of the fourth century, and when Christian theologians began to consider this subject seriously they recognized fairly soon that the Spirit must be regarded as a mode in which God subsists equally with the mode of Father and of Son. What persuaded them to this conclusion was not philosophical pressure at all but the evidence of the New Testament, and – no less important – the spiritual experience and the liturgical practice of the church. Philosophically the

Spirit might have been thought something of an encumbrance. But the genius of the Christian religion insisted that the Spirit cannot be omitted from the Godhead if revelation is to be taken seriously and if the career of Jesus Christ is not to be regarded as a closed incident in history, ever more widely divided from us as the centuries mount up, and if it is believed that God has not ceased being active in history. Here religion triumphed over philosophy.

III

If therefore we are to survey all these critical years from 318 to 381 candidly and then ask ourselves what was the process whereby orthodoxy was achieved during that period, we must abandon the old shibboleths. It is no use referring to a 'majestic pondering' on the part of the church. It is no use pretending that this was a story of orthodoxy being defended strenuously against the attacks of heretics. We must remember that the great majority of our sources for this period were written by people who belonged to the school of thought that finally triumphed, and that they are consequently infused by a bias for which we must make allowance. In these circumstances it is clear that the way in which orthodoxy was achieved was a *process of trial and error*. Though this conclusion is very different from that which historians of the period favoured till quite recently, it is not really surprising. This is, after all, the method by which human beings arrive at truth in any area of human knowledge and investigation, whether scientific, technical, literary, aesthetic or philosophical. It was indeed the method which had obtained in the history of Christian doctrine before the Arian controversy, and that controversy itself was no exception.

The process of trial and error of course included errors made by all schools of thought. Writers who are usually reckoned orthodox but who lived a century or two centuries before the outbreak of the Arian Controversy, such as Irenaeus and Tertullian and Novatian and Justin Martyr, held some views which would later, in the fourth century, have been branded as heretical. Justin appeared to believe that a kind of ichor, not blood, flowed in the veins of Jesus, and his presentation of God the Father comes dangerously near to suggesting that he is unknowable. Irenaeus and Tertullian both believed that God had not always been a Trinity but had at some point put forth the Son and the Spirit so as to be distinct from him. Tertullian, borrowing from Stoicism, believed that God was material (though only of a very refined material, a kind of thinking gas), so that his statement that Father, Son and Spirit were 'of one substance', beautifully orthodox though it sounds, was of a corporeality which would have profoundly shocked Origen, Athanasius and the Cappadocian theologians, had they known of it. Origen was in the sixth century to be declared a heretic by a general council, but without his doctrine of the eternal generation of the Son the fourth-century doctrine of the Trinity could never have been accomplished.

Even when we look at the participants themselves in the great sixty-year debate which led to the formation of the doctrine of the Trinity in its definitive shape, we cannot neatly divide them into orthodox and heretical. The side which supported Athanasius steadily, at least as steadily as possible, in the controversy also for a long time supported the doctrinal views of Marcellus of Ancyra, and his ideas were so near to Sabellianism (that is, a refusal to admit distinctions within God's being) as to be almost indistinguishable from it. And Marcellus had been acquitted of heresy by a pope and two councils. Athanasius himself may never have intended to eliminate or blur the distinctions within God's being, but at times he writes as if the 'Person' of the Son is identical with the being of the Father; he never, in fact, was able to envisage clearly what God is as Three in contradistinction to what he is as One. His account of the incarnate Son is intensely unsatisfactory; he articulates a kind of 'space-suit' Christology in which the humanity which the Son of God assumes is no closer to him than the space-suit to the astronaut, and in which the human mind of Jesus is completely ignored. His doctrine of the Incarnation wholly excludes the scandal of the Cross: God's Son can never have been really weak, really ignorant, really helpless; he only pretended to be so. Similarly when Hilary of Poitiers, the great upholder of orthodoxy in the West, attempts to deal with the Passion of Christ, he plunges heavily into Docetism (much to the embarrassment of the Migne editor of his works, who tries to exculpate him): Jesus felt the impact of the blow (*impetus*) but not its pain (*dolor*), and so on. Here at least the despised and reviled Arians are blameless. They accepted honestly the fact that God the Son suffered; they glimpsed the meaning of Paul's words about the weakness and the foolishness of God (even though they regularly denied that Christ had a human mind or soul). The people who were responsible for achieving the final stage of the formation of the doctrine of the Trinity were, of course, the three great Cappadocian theologians, Basil of Caesarea, Gregory of Nazianzus and Gregory of Nyssa. The school of thought from which they emerged, and upon whose ideas they built, was that headed by Basil of Ancyra, some of whose work survives. The Cappadocians of course knew much of the work of Athanasius, but it was from Basil of Ancyra's theology that the Cappadocians derived directly. This type of thought was called by the inept Epiphanius 'semi-Arian', and this quite unjust label has stuck to them, repeated by Newman, by Gwatkin and even by some contemporary writers. They in fact provided the first hope of a solution of the controversy, the first serious attempt to clarify the terms used, the first step towards the later doctrine of God as Three-in-One which was finally to win a consensus in the church. Yet even they were dominated by a strong tendency to subordinate the Son to the Father which Athanasius had already overcome and which the Cappadocians were later to discard. Indeed, until Athanasius began writing, every single theologian, East and West, had postulated some form of Subordinationism. It could, about the year 300, have been described as a fixed part of catholic theology. Further, these followers of Basil of Ancyra also demonstrated a tendency to teach a doctrine which was uncritically accepted by virtually every theologian until modern times, but which is surely incompatible with a full doctrine of the Incarnation; namely that the flesh which the Son of God assumed was human flesh indeed, but not human flesh like ours, because he was virginally conceived and we are not.

When, therefore, we maintain that orthodoxy in the fourth century was reached by a process of trial and error in which the error was not all on the side of the 'heretics', but was shared by the 'orthodox' too, we do not need even to invoke the well-known and much-used incident in which a bishop of Rome, Liberius, signed a manifestly unorthodox formula, nor the Council of Constantinople in the year 360 when the whole church after a general council formally committed itself to a creed which fell very far short of later orthodoxy. The pope later changed his views (or rather was able to revert to his genuine opinions), and the council was relegated to obscurity (except among the Arians, who continued to reverence it). It is, however, quite clear that the process was a process of trial and error. Almost everybody changed their ideas in some ways during it. A satisfactory vocabulary, a clear and constructive way of thinking, only gradually emerged. Men learnt by experience, by controversy, by seeing their own mistakes and the mistakes of others. This is how orthodoxy was reached in the fourth century. It is probable that this is the way that orthodoxy is always achieved. There must be a preliminary period of confusion, of groping, of uncertainty. Diverse and clashing views must be given expression.

Conference, conversation, perhaps even confrontation, are an unavoidable part of the process. Conceivably this observation may have a bearing on our own day.

IV

Finally, it is worth while casting a look at the end-product of the great controversy of the fourth century, the Nicene Creed itself, as we know it today. Of course it is not the creed of the original Council of Nicaea of 325, but that which is generally assumed to have been drawn up by the Council of Constantinople of 381, though the evidence that this council produced this creed is not unchallengeable. This Nicene Creed was, in the second half of the fifth century, appointed to be sung in the Eucharist by the Eastern church, and it was not very long before the Western church followed suit. Since then this creed has become the central ecumenical declaration of faith, and it is this creed, rather than simply the Bible, which is at the heart of the contemporary ecumenical movement. Eastern Orthodox, Roman Catholics and Anglicans at least are familiar with its words, translated into their various languages. For them it is the statement *par excellence* of what the church believes. There are in fact only parts of it which reflect this old controversy, of which the huge majority of those who repeat this creed regularly are completely unaware: 'eternally begotten of the Father, God from God, Light from Light, true God from true God, begotten, not made, of one Being with the Father...and his Kingdom will have no end. We believe in the Holy Spirit, the Lord, the giver of life, who proceeds from the Father [and the Son], with the Father and the Son he is worshipped and glorified. He has spoken through the prophets' (*Alternative Service Book* version). The anathemas of the original creed of 325 have been dropped, very much to the advantage of theological clarity, and the expression 'from the substance [*ek tēs ousias*] of the Father' has also disappeared, probably because it had material or corporeal suggestions about it (which is why Origen probably disliked it). The eternal existence of the Son with the Father and that he is not a creature is insisted upon. The word *homoousios* ('of one Being with') is retained, but for us today this word has lost almost all its force. We do not deal in philosophies which speak of the substance of God. We can no longer share many of the philosophical presuppositions which lie behind this creed, that God is one *ousia* but three *hypostases*, for instance. An eclectic composition of late Greek philosophy could not be expected to retain its full value and significance intact into the second millennium after it had first been produced. But we can and must take this language as stating, in the modes and thought-forms of the church of the latter part of the fourth century, that the Son is fully and unequivocally God, that the same applies, in a different mode, to the Holy Spirit, and that all three are distinct from each other while remaining one God. The little clause 'whose Kingdom shall have no end' was placed there originally to rebut what was thought to be the heresy of Marcellus of Ancyra. By 381 Marcellus was dead and his followers were anxious to assure everybody that they did not believe that Christ's kingdom would have an end. But there the clause remains, a fossilized protest against an extinct heresy. It is of the nature of creeds to freeze contemporary issues into enduring statements long after the issues have become dead. This clause can be regarded as a kind of Tutankhamun of theological controversy.

But though the language of the Nicene Creed may be obsolete, the shape is not. The Arian solution to the question which had been pressing upon the church ever more insistently since the second century was a most unsatisfactory one, though it was, we must now admit, well-intentioned. A high God who is beyond suffering and a lower God who can experience suffering might have had some attraction in the late Roman empire when the word 'God' had many more shades of meaning than it has for us (unconsciously but inevitably influenced by the Nicene Creed) in the twentieth century. The pro-Nicene writers who opposed Arianism were quite right to exclude it as a possible account of the Christian doctrine of God. Jesus Christ is either wholly God or not God at all. There is no half-way house. They were also justified in taking the drastic step of finally excluding the use of the pre-existent Son as a convenient philosophical device, as an explanation of how the supreme Being could come into contact with transience and history and human experience without compromising himself. Athanasius above all recognized that if we take the New Testament seriously we must conclude that Christ is not a safeguard against God the Father involving himself with human affairs, but a guarantee that he has done so.

It was equally necessary to refuse the alternative road of describing God as having three aspects or phases of self-revelation corresponding to Father, Son, and Spirit. This was a possibility which manifested itself, though only sporadically, during the fourth century, in the ideas of Eustathius of Antioch, of Marcellus and of his disciple Photinus. It had little attraction for the people of that day and never won wide acceptance, as the Arian version was able to do. To adopt such a

Sabellian alternative (to use the technical term of the day) would not do justice to the Christian message of redemption, to the drastic nature of God's involvement with history, nor (though the theologians of the fourth century scarcely realized this) to the eschatological language of the New Testament.

The shape of the Trinitarian doctrine finally achieved in the fourth century, then, was necessary, indeed we may say permanent. It was a solution, *the* solution, to the intellectual problem which had for so long vexed the church. Through the ages in the hands of many different thinkers in East and West it has been presented in different ways, by John of Damascus, by Augustine, by Thomas Aquinas, by Gregory Palamas, by John Calvin, by Karl Barth, by Karl Rahner. But the shape has endured, standing the test of time. Christian theology is Trinitarian; Christian worship should be Trinitarian too. But the Fathers of Constantinople in 381 left to posterity another vexing problem, by the very success of their efforts, that of making sense of the Incarnation. The formula of 451, seventy years later, gave a certain shape to the problem, but can hardly be said to have solved it.

NOTE

1 This paper was written before the publication of R. P. C. Hanson, *The Search for the Christian Doctrine of God*, Edinburgh 1988, which is an attempt to fill this gap.

Eunomius: hair-splitting dialectician or defender of the accessibility of salvation?

MAURICE WILES

When I began the study of theology, I did not at first find patristics a particularly attractive branch of the subject. The Trinitarian and Christological controversies, which bulked so large in those initial studies, seemed to me to be a prime example of those 'strifes of words' (or *logomachiai*, to give them their more forceful Greek expression) against which the author of the Pastorals warns us (1 Timothy 6:4). The first step in acquiring a basic sympathy with what was going on in those controversies, essential to any serious engagement with, let alone understanding of, them, was to see how closely they were felt to impinge on the issue of salvation. That is one of the many insights for which I am indebted to Henry Chadwick. So when in my first book I included the sentence 'The concern about Christology was not a barren intellectual concern; it was intimately connected with a concern about soteriology',[1] I gave the sentence a justifying footnote consisting of a reference to an article by Henry Chadwick. In that article, 'Eucharist and Christology in the Nestorian Controversy', he not only emphasizes the soteriological rather than psychological nature of Cyril's concern for the unity of Christ, but also brings out how Cyril's eucharistic doctrine 'strikes at the heart of Nestorius' soteriology'.[2] Soteriological concerns were central to both sides of that debate. Few scholars today would enter on any discussion of those fourth- and fifth-century Christological controversies without that recognition as a basic element in their approach. Certainly it has remained for me a fundamental principle at the heart of my patristic work.

In recognizing that the principle applies to both sides of the controversy, to Cyril and to Nestorius, Chadwick reminds us of the importance of allowing it to guide our understanding of those who were ultimately dubbed 'heretical' as well as of those who were regarded as 'orthodox'. That has been generally accepted in relation to heretics of what might be described as the theological 'right', men like Apollinarius or Eutyches. It is perhaps not unreasonable to see the latter of those two as an example of someone whose heart ruled his head, of someone whose religious conviction about the way of salvation counted for more than reasoned reflection in a cool hour. But the significance of a strong soteriological concern has been less readily accepted with regard to heretics of the 'left'.

This reluctance has been particularly operative in the case of Arianism. It is not surprising that that should be so. In relation to any of the heretics, our evidence is limited and tends to consist mainly of extracts from their writings selected by their opponents for polemical purposes. Citations chosen with such an end in view are highly unlikely to be ones which bring out any religious or soteriological emphases there may have been in the sources from which the citations have been taken. Recognition of the presence of any such emphasis is therefore bound to involve a measure of reading between the lines, and the interpreter is not unlikely to find only what he expects to find. And in the case of Arianism there is a special reason why people may be somewhat reluctant to find such an emphasis. The Nicene Creed continues to play an important role today, not only in terms of ecumenical consensus but also in the lives of large numbers of ordinary worshippers. Its decisive emphases were shaped by the need of the Arian controversy. It is much easier to justify and draw benefit from its contemporary use if it can be presented as protecting saving Christian truth in the face of a challenge that lacks the essential religious and soteriological dimension of true Christian faith. A vivid illustration of this principle at work can be seen in the Lutheran–Catholic dialogue in the United States. The first document to come out of that dialogue was devoted to 'the Status of the Nicene Creed as Dogma of the Church'.[3] The very considerable measure of agreement reached was clearly helped by the fact that both the main spokesmen, one on each side of the debate, unhesitatingly accepted the traditional negative assessment of Arianism. The Catholic spokesman, John Courtney Murray, asserts that 'Arius...felt it necessary to appeal to [the] norm [of the Word of God in the Scriptures], though his doctrinal system owed nothing to Scripture' (p. 19), while the Lutheran spokesman, George Lindbeck, claims that the Arian use of the New Testament subordinationist and adoptionist concepts and images was heretical, because 'it was opposed, so to speak, to the intention of the New Testament usage which was to exalt Christ rather than to lower him' (p. 14). The ecumenical usefulness of their failure to acknowledge a religious or soteriological dimension to the Arian position is only too evident.

Nevertheless, the recognition of a soteriological motif within early Arianism is now beginning to find a fair measure of acceptance in the scholarly world. The book that has done most to heighten awareness of this issue and stimulate discussion of it has been Robert Gregg and Dennis Groh's work, *Early Arianism – A View of Salvation*. Whatever criticism may properly be raised about some of the detail of their arguments, there can be little doubt that the perspective suggested by their title does more justice to early Arianism than Gwatkin's dismissal of the whole movement as 'a lifeless system of unspiritual pride and hard unlovingness'.[4] My own work on the *Homilies* of Asterius, undertaken in collaboration with Robert Gregg as a result of the stimulus of that book, revealed even more clearly a major soteriological emphasis in his preaching – more clearly because of the fuller and more direct nature of the evidence. What is particularly striking is the different form of soteriology detected in the two cases. The soteriological scheme which Gregg and Groh detect in the Arian sources on which they draw is one for which it is what is 'common to us and to the Son' that is significant. It is the fact that his sonship is constituted by his obedience to the Father, by his willing God's will, that enables him to save us into a sonship in the same mode;[5] whereas in the case of Asterius it is the distinctive godhead of the Son that enables him to divinize us by divine self-giving in incarnation and crucifixion.[6] The two schemes may agree in finding it necessary to speak of the Son as divine, but in a sense clearly distinct from the divinity of the Father; in the one case this is to make it possible to speak of a real obedience of Son to Father, in the other to enable us to speak unequivocally of the Son's undergoing of passion and death. But as schemes of salvation, they could hardly be more different. Perhaps both had a place within the Arian movement, which is probably better understood as a loosely allied group of people with overlapping but by no means identical concerns, held together more by their opposition to certain Marcellan and Athanasian tendencies than by a single specific theological platform.

Plenty of work remains to be done in sorting out the various strands within the early Arian movement and in assessing the true force and character of the soteriological concerns that were undoubtedly at work there. But it is not my intention to pursue that task now. For if most scholars have come to admit a soteriological concern among the motives of early Arianism, the same is not true of later stages of the movement.

The derogatory rationalist mantle with which so many earlier scholars clothed the whole Arian movement still sits on the shoulders of the neo-Arian leaders, Aetius and Eunomius. Harnack described them as 'openly proclaiming the conversion of religion into morality and syllogistic reasoning'.[7] And still today the first thing that the student is told about them, at their initial appearance on the pages of a standard text-book such as J. N. D. Kelly's *Early Christian Doctrines*, is that they 'made great play with a hair-splitting pseudo-Aristotelian dialectic, arguing their case in rather specious syllogisms'.[8] The fact that Eunomius was a bishop, even if only for a few months, tends to be greeted with the same kind of incredulity with which a German professor, visiting Oxford at the turn of the century and discovering that the Hebrew scholar S. R. Driver was a canon professor, is said to have exclaimed 'Does Driver preach?'

Is such an account of the neo-Arian leaders justified? Certainly that is how most of our sources present them. There is nothing to match the grudging acknowledgment we find in the case of Arius, that he was a biblical expositor and a man of piety. Nor does a reading of that strange work, the *Syntagmation* of Aetius, with its string of condensed formal proofs of a logical kind, do anything to dispel the impression those hostile sources combine to give.[9] With Eunomius we have a slightly broader base for any attempted reconsideration, even though in his case too the material comes primarily from the setting of formal theological argument. Moreover, there is one particular saying ascribed to Eunomius which is frequently cited as a point of difference between himself and Arius and as significant evidence of his more intellectualist and irreligious stance. Thus Kelly goes on from his initial scathing account of Aetius and Eunomius to speak of two respects in which Anomoean teaching diverged from that of Arius. The second divergence he describes in these terms:

While Arius considered the Godhead incomprehensible, the Anomoeans deduced Its perfect comprehensibility from Its absolute simplicity. So Eunomius could claim, 'God does not know His own being any better than we do; His essence is no more manifest to Himself than it is to us'.[10]

Notwithstanding the fact that simplicity was well established as a characteristic of the divine nature, these words cannot fail to suggest intellectual arrogance and the absence of religious sensitivity. Are they valid evidence in support of the traditional evaluation of neo-Arianism? The first fact to notice is that, despite the way in which Kelly introduces the words, they do not come from an established work of Eunomian authorship. They are quoted by the church historian, Socrates, as a verbatim (*kata lexin*) quotation, though without explicit reference to any particular work of Eunomius.[11] Moreover, a very similar sentiment is ascribed by Epiphanius to Aetius, who is credited with saying: 'I understand God as clearly and as fully as I understand and know myself, so that I do not know myself any better than I understand God'.[12] But once again the words do not come from a specific Aetian writing, although a little later on in the same work Epiphanius supplies us with the full text of the *Syntagmation*. They are described rather as the conclusion which both he and those taught by him were misled into asserting, through following out the implications of their initial heretical error. But it is in the more unacceptable form ascribed to Eunomius, in which human knowledge of God's essence is claimed to be equal to God's own knowledge of it, that the saying so frequently recurs in the tradition. Theodoret ascribes it specifically to Eunomius but in a summary account of his own composition, not as a direct citation.[13] Chrysostom and pseudo-Athanasius give a similar version of the saying but in a much less precise form. In both cases it is knowledge of God, not of God's essence, that is said to be claimed, and the saying is attributed simply to an Anomoean.[14]

The authenticity and accuracy of the words ascribed to Eunomius by Socrates must remain an open question. The most that we can assert with any confidence is that there must have been some characteristic feature of Anomoean teaching concerning the knowability of God, which could plausibly be presented by their opponents in this pejorative light. Is it then possible to conjecture what might be the context and intention of this Anomoean insistence?

One proposal has been put forward by Ronald Heine, who writes:

[The] recognition by Arius that God was incomprehensible gave the orthodox teaching a weapon which, in Diekamp's opinion, was proving embarrassing to the Arians. If one recognizes that human understanding cannot penetrate the divine nature, then one cannot reject the possibility of the eternal generation of the Son having the same essence with the Father. In order to wrest this weapon from the orthodox and to make the Arian teaching secure against their attack, the Anomoean leaders asserted that man can have full knowledge of God's essence.[15]

This account is certainly a plausible one. It represents a pattern not uncommon in the history of theology. If a theologian stresses the mystery of God, it is bound to be more difficult for him to demonstrate that his opponents' beliefs are false. In his desire to exclude what he believes to be false teaching, he is likely to be tempted to claim greater precision (and therefore greater power of exclusion) for his own formulations than the evidence warrants, or even than he himself in his heart of hearts may want to claim. If something like that is in fact what has given rise to the shift in relation to the knowability of God between the earlier and later stages of the Arian movement, we would have to say that the change, however understandable, represents a regrettable narrowing of religious vision on the part of Eunomius.

The evidence of the debate between Eunomius and the Cappadocians certainly suggests that this is the right context for understanding Eunomius' remark, but that the stress needs to be put in a slightly different place. The stress seems to be not so much on 'making the Arian teaching secure' against orthodox attack as on exposing the unacceptable nature of the Cappadocian position. Since those two emphases are so similar, to distinguish between them may appear to be an example of that hair-splitting pseudo-logic of which the neo-Arians are so frequently accused. But putting the matter in this alternative way can help to point towards a more positive evaluation of Eunomius' apparently arrogant intellectualist claim.

It is clear that the Cappadocians appealed to the mysterious nature of the Godhead in defence of their teaching about a co-equal Trinity. They understood both the unity of God and the co-equality of the three persons as data of revelation. *How* the three were one within the simplicity of the divine *ousia* was beyond finite human comprehension. It would not be surprising if some people found difficulty with the claim that there were three distinct persons within the one divine *ousia*, which was agreed to be *haplous kai asunthetos* and regarded an appeal to mystery as too easy an answer to their difficulties. Such an appeal can too readily be invoked to justify any theological proposal whatever. The way in which this objection was pressed home by Eunomius is best understood in terms of the theory of names, which is another distinctive feature of this later stage of the Arian controversy.

Any sensitive theologian must acknowledge the human base, and consequent inadequacy, of the language we use to speak of God. Origen, Arius and the Cappadocians are at one in this. The term *epinoia* plays an important role in the theology of them all. We speak of God not directly but with the aid of human conceptions which enable us to form some notion of God's ongoing activity. Even the word *theos*, the ordinary word for God, refers not to God's nature but, as its etymology was claimed to show, to his oversight of the universe.[16] But what God really is in himself is hidden within the transcendent mystery of the divine being. This approach receives clear delineation in the important distinction between the divine *ousia* and the divine *energeia* which first comes to prominence in this same stage of the Arian controversy. No one gives more emphatic expression to this religiously attractive insistence on the mystery of God's being than Gregory of Nyssa, with his notion of *epektasis*. Even in the life to come, that mystery remains permanently beyond the grasp of finite comprehension. However far we progress in the knowledge of God, there remains a never-ending path of discovery before us as we continue to explore the inexhaustible riches of the mystery of the divine being. No wonder the remark ascribed to Eunomius, asserting his full knowledge of God's *ousia*, sounds contemptible and blasphemous by comparison!

But such a radical stress on transcendence raises a serious problem, with both intellectual and religious implications. If the true God, the God whom it is salvation to know and to be made one with, is, in Paul Tillich's phrase, 'the God beyond God' – the God beyond all that we can say or imagine in speaking or conceiving of him – how can we be sure that our language really does refer to the true God, or, putting the matter religiously rather than intellectually, how can we be confident that we are being brought into living touch with the true God and not with some lesser idol? We seem to be in danger of falling into a Feuerbachian abyss, in which we discover that not only is our language a matter of human invention but so is that to which we believed it to refer. Paul Tillich, whose phrase 'God beyond God' I have just quoted, laid great stress, as did the Cappadocians, on the symbolic nature of all our language about God. He sought to deal with the problem that I have raised by insisting that there is one non-symbolic statement to be made about God, namely that God is being-itself.[17] Although he subsequently modified this claim under the pressure of criticism, he was still anxious to make some sort of comparable claim. Some form of non-symbolic statement (even if in dialectical combination with the symbolic) continued to be regarded by him as vital to the intellectual and religious coherence of his whole scheme. 'It is the condition for man's religious existence and for his ability to receive revelation.'[18]

May not something similar be a significant concern in the case of Eunomius also? Certainly he castigates the Cappadocian understanding of language about God as untrue to scripture and involving a reduction of it to a form of human invention that renders it unable to fulfil its goal.[19] This might be just one more indication that Eunomius does not belong to the category of 'sensitive theologian' to which I referred earlier. But Eunomius is no crude literalist. He has no intention of denying that words when applied to God have to be understood in an appropriately divine sense and do not mean the same as when applied to earthly realities.[20] But that does not give the interpreter licence to understand them as he or she will. The relation of words to things is given by God.[21] And in some cases those words relate directly to the essence of that which they indicate.[22] This more realistic theory of language is important to Eunomius, to ensure that there is an identifiable referent for the language we use and that the language really does apply to it. As Richard Vaggione argues: 'The purpose of his language was surely not to claim an exhaustive knowledge of reality, but to make a knowledge of reality possible at all by guaranteeing the objective reference of words.'[23]

If this is a valid interpretation of the general concern inherent in Eunomius' theory of language, then his notorious remark about the measure of his knowledge of God is likely to have been more limited in scope and patient of a more religious significance than his opponents allow. Eunomius, for his part, taunted them with worshipping what they do not know, like the Samaritans of old (John 4:22),[24] something incompatible, he says, with claiming the name of Christians.[25] That is certainly a polemical parody. But so, surely, is their understanding of his contrasting position as a claim to equality with the divine self-knowledge. It is most unlikely that Eunomius was claiming to know all that there is to be known about God. It is much more likely that he was simply claiming to know enough about the *ousia* of God, about what it is to be God, to be able to exclude what he regarded as Cappadocian mystification and to ensure that our Christian language refers, that our speech about God has a purchase on reality.

The point can be expressed in soteriological terms, which reveal a rough similarity to the soteriological issues at stake in the Christological controversies which I referred to at the outset. There the two principles involved were that the one who saves must be fully divine, since only the fully divine can be the author of salvation, but he must also be one with us, so that salvation can be effectively received.[26] Different schools varied in the effectiveness of the emphasis they put on the two sides of this dual requirement. The church struggled to hold the two together, but never succeeded in doing so fully without strain and conflict. So in this debate one might say that the object of human worship must be radically transcendent because only the fully transcendent is worthy of worship, but must also be available as an object of our real knowledge so that the worship can be properly directed. Eunomius, I want to suggest, was genuinely concerned that the Cappadocian stress on transcendent mystery had lost its hold on that second important soteriological, or perhaps in this context one might better say doxological, principle.

Even if in this kind of way Eunomius' claim can be made to appear less bombastic than it is usually understood to be, the claim is still there and we need to ask what it amounts to. What is the content of this claimed knowledge of the divine *ousia*? It is usually asserted that the fundamental claim that Eunomius wants to make about the divine *ousia* is that it is *agennētos*. That God is the unbegotten is taken to be the crucial non-symbolic statement that Eunomius is determined to make about God, and unbegottenness the true and literal description of what God is. And the fact that it is so philosophical a term which is assigned this crucial role is seen as further evidence of the precedence of the rational over the religious in Eunomius' concerns. But considerable caution is needed at this point. The use of the term *agennētos* to refer to God was no novelty, introduced at a late date into Christian discourse. It was traditional Christian usage of two centuries' standing. Its particular centrality in the thought of Eunomius is certainly evident from the major role it plays in the *Apologia*. Moreover it is unquestionably true that in his controversy with Basil, Eunomius is keen to insist that unbegottenness characterizes the divine *ousia* as such and not just the hypostasis of the Father. The point is vital to his argument with his opponents, and if it is once granted he has an unassailable advantage in the ensuing debate with them. The status of the term *agennētos* is therefore the issue most extensively discussed. Nevertheless, if we isolate that term and see it as providing the primary designation of God in the thought of Eunomius, I believe we are in danger of building up a misleading picture of the underlying character of his theology. It is not *agennēsia*, I want to suggest, that he is tempted to regard as the proper name for God.

The denial that God has a name was well established, both inside and outside Christianity, as a way of emphasizing God's transcendence. It is strongly asserted by Justin, who says that the reason God cannot be named is the fact that he is *agennētos*. 'Father', 'God', 'Creator' and such like terms are not strictly names (*onomata*) but forms of address (*prosrēseis*) derived from divine activities.[27] That particular linguistic distinction can hardly be observed consistently in light of the use of the word *onoma* in scripture. Thus in another, baptismal, context where Justin again asserts the impossibility of naming the ineffable God, he cannot avoid speaking of the 'name of the God the Father and Lord of the Universe' in which the believer is baptized.[28] But his proposed distinction between *onoma* and *prosrēsis* is a way of drawing attention to the variable status of different names or designations, a point of great significance in later discussion. Origen held a high doctrine of the significance of names. They are not, for him, a matter of arbitrary convention, but have an intrinsic relation to the things they describe. It is therefore important that we use the proper names for God, and that means the names given in scripture.[29] On more than one occasion he cites Exodus 3:14 in a form which gives God's words to Moses as: '*ho ōn*, that is my name'.[30] And in his discussion of the clause in the Lord's Prayer, 'Hallowed by thy name', he argues that since God is unchanging so must his name be. He allows that there might be more than one name, provided they all carry the same signification, but the one name that he selects to give (recalling its scriptural source) is *ōn* – being or being-itself.[31]

Origen's discussion (with its assertion of a theory of language akin to that of Eunomius) provides a clue to what may lie at the heart of Eunomius' position. The same text, Exodus 3:14, is of central importance to Eunomius also. It is a recurrent theme in the surviving literary debate between Basil, Eunomius and Gregory.[32] Moreover, in the *Apologia* itself, it is one of two scriptural examples which Eunomius selects to illustrate words that directly refer to God.[33] It is surely more probable that Eunomius should have regarded the scripturally given *ōn* rather than *agennētos* as constituting the true name of God.[34] It is, of course, closely linked with *agennētos* in Eunomius' thought. For Origen it is the unchangeableness of being that is its most fundamental aspect. Thus in his discussion in the *De oratione* it is the terms *atreptos* and *analloiōtos* that are most directly linked with the designation of God as *ōn*. For Eunomius it is the underivedness of being that is most significant, and therefore the term *agennētos* that is most intimately associated with it. *Agennētos* is indeed affirmed to be descriptive of the divine *ousia*. But Eunomius goes on to insist that such a description is to be understood as a way of fulfilling our fundamental duty to 'confess that he is what he is'. Even though the words do not take the form of a direct quotation of Exodus 3:14, the phrase is most naturally to be taken as involving a specific allusion to it. For Eunomius, insistence on *agennētos* as characterizing the divine *ousia* is a way of spelling out what is implicit in the fact that God's name is *ōn*.[35]

But Basil will have none of it. *Agennētos*, he argues, can come no nearer to expressing what God is than can a physical term, like fire; it can express only how God is.[36] But it is not only Eunomius' understanding of *agennētos* that he challenges. He also takes him to task for his interpretation of Exodus 3:14 and denies that it shows *ōn* to be the name of God. In the first place, he argues, the name in view in the passage is the immediately preceding 'God of Abraham, God of Isaac, God of Jacob' and not the earlier 'I am'. And, second the name envisaged is not the name of God's essence; that, as Exodus 6:3 implies, remains unrevealed.[37] Here, too, there is a point of fundamental divergence, perhaps the most fundamental point of divergence, between Eunomius and his opponents. For Eunomius, being or reality (*ōn*) is God's name; for his opponents the really real (*to ontōs on*) is above every name.[38]

To call God 'being' or 'being-itself' sounds to many contemporary ears as discouragingly philosophical in character as to designate him 'unbegotten'. Certainly that objection was vigorously raised against John Robinson's use of 'ground of being' in *Honest to God* (London 1963). But for Eunomius the term came with the sanction of scripture (and God's self-designation in scripture at that), as well as with the support of a long-standing tradition. He had good grounds for rejecting any suggestion that he was replacing Christian language with the language of philosophy. Indeed, in his eyes it was precisely his opponents of whom that was true. It is to claim that God is beyond being, he could argue, that is to succumb to the influence of Platonic philosophizing; to call him being is to stay with scripture and revelation.

Is there any wider evidence that might offer support to this more religious interpretation of Eunomius' basic position? The proposal as outlined so far is a highly tentative one. The nature of the material from Eunomius' own pen, as well as the citations in polemical sources, is singularly ill-suited to reveal any deeper religious concerns. The difficulty of drawing on other sources by way of corroboration is that the Eunomian provenance of other writings cannot itself be more than a matter of conjecture. But it is worth drawing attention to two other writings, the *Clementine Recognitions* and the *Apostolic Constitutions*, although it would require a much more detailed discussion than is possible here to make use of them in anything more than a highly tentative way.

Of the two, the *Clementine Recognitions* is the better established as a potential source of Eunomian teaching.[39] One section (III.2–11) is widely acknowledged to be an interpolation of Eunomian provenance. In general character it is not very promising material for our purpose, but Vaggione points to two passages in that interpolation relevant to our theme.[40] 'Unbegotten' is there stressed as a fundamental attribute of him who is. But it is a human designation indicating that God is without beginning, not made or begotten even by himself. It does not tell us what God is. That is known only to God himself.[41] This might be seen as a correction from within the neo-Arian movement itself to the more extreme claim ascribed by Socrates to Eunomius. It makes very much the same point that Basil makes against Eunomius, despite the fact that the passage as a whole is clearly Eunomian in character.[42] On the other hand, it may be a more accurate presentation of Eunomius' own position than the strong version of it assumed by his opponents for polemical purposes. Mme. Harl speaks of 'la distinction, si souvent reprise chez les pères Grecs, entre savoir que Dieu existe et pouvoir definir son *ousia*: le titre *ōn* renvoie a cette *ousia* divine sans le definir'.[43] It would not be surprising if there were confusion and misunderstanding in the drawing of this distinction. To insist that *ōn* is a name for God, correctly describing the divine *ousia*, need not ever have been intended to suggest a definition of God, in the sense of a full knowledge and comprehension of what God is. It may rather, as I have been suggesting, have been intended as a means of ensuring that the God whom we claim to know is real, or better *the* real, and not a figment of the imaginative power of human words. The *Clementine Recognitions* cannot be used to clarify the issue with any confidence. But they do seem to offer some support, however tentative, to the argument already developed that the Anomoean position did not lay claim to an exhaustive knowledge of God in the way its opponents allege.

Since Vaggione's thesis was written, Thomas Kopecek has given further support to the identification of the final redactor of the *Apostolic Constitutions* as a neo-Arian, with the promise of a fuller statement of his case in the future.[44] In the liturgies of Book VIII, God is addressed as *agennētos* at a number of the most solemn points in the liturgy.[45] However philosophical the word's origins, it is here integrated into the stuff of worship. There is nothing surprising in that. *Homoousios* entered Christian vocabulary as a result of theological controversy, in a way which required even those who most strongly supported it to offer somewhat embarrassed apology for its unscriptural tone. Yet 'of one substance' has become a focal point of devotion in the recitation of the

Creed and 'consubstantial' can stand with powerful effect in the doxologies of hymns. Read one way, the liturgies of the *Apostolic Constitutions* can sound like highly artificial and undevotional constructions; read another way, they can provide an impressive evocation of awe in the presence of the divine majesty. One incidental feature of these liturgies is particularly pertinent to our discussion. The opening words of the long prayer for the ordination of a bishop are *ho ōn*.[46] In this solemn prayer it is *ho ōn*, rather than *theos* or *kurios* or *patēr*, which is the initial form of address to God. That term for the neo-Arians was not only philosophically important. It came to them with the force of scripture and tradition as well. It combined the connotations of 'being-itself' and 'the Great I am'. It was for them the primary name of God, given by God himself and serving to ensure that our worship is directed to the true God, to God as he really is. It could be used not only in talk about God, but in address to God.

It has not been possible in a single paper to discuss every aspect of Anomoean faith or practice – indeed, I have not touched at all on many of those areas, such as Christology, baptism or eucharist, which have most obvious links with the theme of salvation. I have chosen to look rather at the issues of debate for which the neo-Arians were most strongly criticized at the time and which have been the basis of subsequent evaluation of them as even more unspiritually minded logic-choppers than Arius himself. And I have ventured to claim that even there it is not unreasonable to see a deeply felt religious and soteriological concern – how to affirm the true and transcendent God in such a way that we may know him and worship him as he really is. Knowledge of the true God has an intellectual dimension, but it is not an exclusively intellectual matter; it is essential to worship in spirit and in truth. And it is essential to the way of salvation, since it is knowledge of the only true God which is life eternal (John 17:3).[47] To present the arch-heretic, Eunomius, in such a light is not to ask for a reversal of the judgment made in favour of Cappadocian orthodoxy. It is only to insist that, even in this most unpromising of cases, the line between orthodoxy and heresy is not the line between a soteriological and a rationalist concern, between a religious and a philosophical spirit. Rather, it is a line which separates two understandings of the faith, both of which were equally concerned to offer a reasoned faith as a way of salvation.

NOTES

I am grateful to Thomas Kopecek and Anthony Meredith for helpful comments on an earlier draft of this paper.

1 M. F. Wiles, *The Spiritual Gospel*, Cambridge 1960, p. 147.

2 H. Chadwick, 'Eucharist and Christology in the Nestorian Controversy', *JThS*, n.s. 2 (1951), 152–3 and 157.

3 Paul C. Empie and T. Austin Murphy (eds.), *Lutherans and Catholics in Dialogue I* (Minneapolis, n.d.). The date of the meeting at which the document was agreed was 1965.

4 H. M. Gwatkin, *Studies of Arianism*, Cambridge 1882, p. 266.

5 See R. C. Gregg and D. E. Groh, *Early Arianism*, Philadelphia and London, 1981. See especially pp. 50–70 under the sub-heading 'Adoption as Salvation: "Common to us and to the Son"?'

6 See M. F. Wiles (in collaboration with R. C. Gregg), 'Asterius: A new Chapter in the History of Arianism?', in R. C. Gregg (ed.), *Arianism: Historical and Theological Reassessments*, Philadelphia 1985, pp. 111–51, esp. pp. 138–40. Since the publication of that article, questions have been raised about the reliability of Richard's ascription of those Homilies on the Psalms to Asterius. While the difficulties are serious, I still think the balance of probability is in favour of Asterian authorship.

7 A. Harnack, *History of Dogma*, vol. 4, p. 74.

8 J. N. D. Kelly, *Early Christian Doctrines*, London 1958, p. 249.

9 See L. R. Wickham, 'The Syntagmation of Aetius the Anomean', *JThS* n.s. 19 (1968), 532–69, esp. 534–6.

10 J. N. D. Kelly, *Early Christian Doctrines*, p. 249. I have kept Kelly's translation, but it should be noted that both 'being' and 'essence' correspond to an original *ousia*.

11 Socrates, *HE* IV.7.

12 Epiphanius, *Panarion* 76,4,2.

13 Theodoret, *Haereticarum fabularum compendium* 4,3.

14 Chrysostom, *De incomprehensibilitate* II (*SC* 28, p. 154, lines 158–9); ps.-Athanasius, *Dialogus de sancta trinitate* I. 1.

15 R. E. Heine, *Perfection in the Virtuous Life*, Philadelphia Patristic Foundation 1975, p. 135.

16 See Gregory of Nyssa, *Contra Eunomium* II (ed. Jaeger, vol. 1, pp. 268–9); *Ad Ablabium* (ed. Jaeger, vol. 3, pp. 44–5).

17 Paul Tillich, *Systematic Theology*, vol. 1 (London, 1953), pp. 264–5.

18 Ibid. vol. 2 (1957), pp. 10–11. Perhaps similar critical pressure may be one reason for the varied forms in which the Anomoean saying we are considering has come down to us.

19 Eunomius, *Apologia apologiae* (in Gregory of Nyssa, *Con. Eun.*, ed. Jaeger vol. 1, pp. 315.31–316.4); *Apologia* 8.

20 Eunomius, *Apologia apologiae* (in Gregory of Nyssa, *Con. Eun.*, ed. Jaeger, vol. 1, pp. 46.21–47.15); *Apologia* 16.

21 Eunomius, *Apologia apologiae* (in Gregory of Nyssa, *Con. Eun.*, ed. Jaeger, vol. 1, p. 282.5–7).

22 Eunomius, *Apologia* 9 and 24.

23 R. Vaggione, 'Aspects of Faith in the Eunomian Controversy', unpublished D Phil dissertation, Oxford 1976, p. 278. I am much indebted to Dr Vaggione for my understanding of Eunomius, through his thesis and through subsequent studies. His recent book, *Eunomius: The Extant Works* (Oxford 1987) is an invaluable aid to Eunomian studies.

24 Gregory of Nyssa, *Contra Eunomium* III, 1 (ed. Jaeger, vol. 2, p. 39. 13–14); Basil, *Epistula* 234,1.

25 Gregory of Nyssa, *Contra Eunomium* III, 9 (ed. Jaeger, vol. 2, p. 284. 16–18).

26 See my 'Soteriological Arguments in the Fathers' in F. L. Cross (ed.), *StPatr*, 9 (1966), 321–5.

27 Justin, *II Apologia* 6,1–2.

28 Justin, *I Apol.* 61,10–11.

29 Origen, *Exhortatio ad martyrium* 46.

30 Origen, *Com. Jn.* II, 13, 95; *Comm. Matt.* 17.36.

31 Origen, *De oratione* 24.2. Koetschau, the *GCS* editor, emends the MS reading *ōn* to *ho ōn* in line with the Exodus text, but the emendation is unjustified. Cf. the use of *ōn* by Basil of Ancyra in Epiphanius, *Panarion* 73.12 (*GCS*, p. 285 1.20) and by Eunomius, in *Apologia* 17.

32 Gregory, *Contra Eunomium* III, 8 and 9 (ed. Jaeger, vol. 2, pp. 251.16–279.23).

33 Eunomius, *Apologia* 17. (Cf. n. 31 above.)

34 Cf. Gregory of Nazianzus's affirmation that *ho ōn* is uniquely indicative of God's essence, because unlike other basic titles, such as *theos*, it is not derived from some aspect of the divine activity (Gregory of Nazianzus, *Orationes* 30,18).

35 Eunomius, *Apologia* 7–8. The Greek phrase is *tēn tou einai ho estin homologian*.

36 Basil, *Adversus Eunomium* I, 14–15 (*PG* 29. 546AB).

37 Ibid. I, 13 (*PG* 29. 542C–544A).

38 Gregory of Nyssa, *Contra Eunomium* III, 9 (ed. Jaeger, vol. 2, p. 279. 22–3).

39 See Vaggione, *Aspects of Faith*, pp. 116–20.

40 Ibid., pp. 270–80.

41 *Clementine Recognitions* III, 3,5–8; III, 7,3–9.

42 See n. 37, above.

43 M. Harl, 'Citations et Commentaires d'Exode 3:14 chez les Pères Grecs des quatre premiers siècles', in *Dieu et l'Etre* (Paris 1978), pp. 87–108.

44 T. A. Kopecek, 'Neo-Arian Religion', in R. C. Gregg (ed.), *Arianism:*

Historical and Theological Reassessments, Philadelphia Patristic Foundation 1985, pp. 153–5.

45 *Apostolic Constitutions* VIII, 5,1; 6,8; 6,11; 12,6; 14,3; 48,3.

46 Ibid. VIII, 5,1.

47 John 17:3 was a text of great importance to the Arian movement as a whole. And *monos alēthinos theos* stands alongside *ho ōn* in the *Apologia* of Eunomius as the other scriptural phrase illustrative of titles referring directly to God (cf. n. 33 above).

Some sources used in the *De Trinitate* ascribed to Didymus the Blind

ALASDAIR HERON

For some two hundred years following its mid-eighteenth-century discovery by Mingarelli in a manuscript lacking title page and the opening chapters, the *De Trinitate*[1] was regarded as the chief surviving work of Didymus the Blind (313–98), the last really distinguished leader of the catechetical school in Alexandria. Mingarelli based his ascription in part on the numerous and striking verbal parallels between this work and Didymus' *De Spiritu Sancto*, which survives only in Jerome's Latin translation.[2] The last generation, however, has seen a remarkable shift in scholarly opinion on the matter: the discovery of the Toura papyri in 1941 and the ascription to Didymus of a series of extensive biblical commentaries contained in them has led in turn to comparisons of these works with the *De Trinitate* which seemed to support the conclusion that Didymus could not also have been the author of the latter.[3] If correct, this conclusion not only requires a radical revision of the entire picture of Didymus and his theological teaching developed before the discovery of the Toura papyri; it also leaves the *De Trinitate* – a major work by any standards – floating in the void of anonymity. In recent years, study of Didymus has concentrated on the Toura commentaries;[4] the *De Trinitate* has received relatively scant attention, though it is arguably more theologically substantial and significant than the commentaries, whether or not Didymus is the author.

One issue calling for consideration in this context is that of the sources used by the author of the *De Trinitate*. Some years ago I laid out the evidence for his use of several of the pseudo-Athanasian *Dialogues*, arguing at the same time that he was not himself their author.[5] I would like here to carry the matter a stage further by summarizing some of the available evidence for his use of three other sources: Didymus, *De Spiritu Sancto*; pseudo-Athanasius, *De Trinitate et Spiritu Sancto*;[6] and pseudo-Basil, *Adversus Eunomium* iv–v. The parallels obtaining between *De*

Trinitate and these writings are both numerous and strikingly extensive, making it impossible seriously to avoid the conclusion that it has made direct use of them all. It is not merely a matter of occasional turns of phrase, but very often of long and complex arguments, of identical or very similar combinations of biblical texts, of points argued in the same or remarkably similar terms. Some of these parallels have of course been known of for a considerable time, especially some of those between *De Trinitate* and the *De Spiritu Sancto* and *Adversus Eunomium* IV–V respectively;[7] but, if I see aright, they are even more numerous than previous published studies have shown. I would also hazard the guess that the *De Trinitate* has drawn on yet other sources as well, which have not yet been explored.[8] It is, after all, a vast compendium of exegetical and theological arguments dating from around the end of the Arian controversy and therefore very likely to have drawn on a whole host of sources.

The parallels here presented between *De Trinitate* and the other three works were detected by an analytical comparison under three heads:

1 Correlations and combinations of biblical proof-texts
2 Refutations of heretical exegesis
3 Distinctive orthodox arguments

Within the compass of a short essay it is not possible to quote the passages verbally, though it is only when they are laid out side by side that it becomes apparent how many close resemblances there are, as well as that the *De Trinitate* has indeed drawn on the other works rather than vice versa.[9] For published illustrations of the method of source-analysis used I must refer to my articles on the pseudo-Athanasian *Dialogues* and the *De Trinitate et Spiritu Sancto* and the *De Incarnatione et contra Arianos*. Suffice it to say here that the cumulative evidence that *De Trinitate* is the terminus of this group of writings is overwhelming.

One further point of potential significance is that many (though by no means all) of the parallels also obtain to some degree between the other three writings. It is not impossible that the *De Trinitate et Spiritu Sancto* has itself been influenced by Didymus' *De Spiritu Sancto* and that both works have in turn influenced the *Adversus Eunomium* IV–V – this quite apart from the use of all three as sources for the *De Trinitate*. But there is sufficient material independently common to each of these and the *De Trinitate* to indicate that it drew directly on all of them, as the following tables show. In the tables the references are given, for the sake of consistency and convenience, to Migne, *PG* ; the *De Trinitate* (*DT*) is

Table 1. *Correlations and combinations of proof-texts*

Texts correlated	DSpS	DTSpS	AE	DT
Isaiah 6:8–11 John 12:39–41 Acts 28:25–8	1059 Bf	1207 Bf	{ 721 Cf 756 AB	{ 364 Af 657 AB
Matthew 12:28 Luke 11:19–20	1051 BC	1216 BC	716 Cf	565 A
I Kings 2:25 Matthew 12:32 Hebrews 10:29	{ 1033 B 1085 Af	1218 Af		749 Bf
Proverbs 9:1 Matthew 1:18–20 Luke 1:35	1062 AB	1203 Af		569 Cf
I Corinthians 12:6 I Corinthians 12:11		1195 B	{ 717 AB 729 AB	{ 368 C 601 Cf
Isaiah 29:24 I Corinthians 7:34	1081 A			525 Df
Matthew 7:11 Luke 11:13	1035 Df			532 A
Isaiah 44:3 Romans 14:7 Colossians 1:9–10	1042 Af			532 Bf
Acts 11:17 Acts 15:8–9	1043 Bf			{ 456 B 533 A
John 5:43 John 14:26	1060 AB			732 Cf
Psalm 94:9–11 Acts 7:51 Hebrews 3:7		1204 Df		365 BC
Deuteronomy 10:9 Psalm 15:5 Jeremiah 10:16 Ephesians 1:13–14		1210 C		368 BC
Romans 6:10–11 2 Corinthians 5:15 Galatians 5:25		1202 Df		376 A
Psalm 36:31 Romans 8:2 I Corinthians 9:20–1		1199 B		376 B

Table 1. (*cont.*)

Texts correlated	*DSpS*	*DTSpS*	*AE*	*DT*
I Kings 13:1–2		1199 Cf		376 Cf
I Kings 17:18; 24				
2 Kings 4:9				
Psalm 89 title				
Acts 11:26				
I Corinthians 2:14–16				
I Corinthians 12:1–3				
Matthew 22:21		1199 C		377 Cf
Philippians 2:21				
I Corinthians 2:14				
Isaiah 63:13–14		1199 B		365 Cf
Jeremiah 2:6				
Isaiah 1:18			717 Bf	577 Cf
Isaiah 43:25				
Mark 2:5				
John 20:22–3				
Deuteronomy 32:12			709 B	365 Cf
I Corinthians 10:4				
Matthew 11:27			753 Df	497 A
I Corinthians 2:11				
Romans 11:36			756 AB	924 Af
I Corinthians 8:6				
Matthew 10:20			721 A	373 B
2 Corinthians 13:3				

to be found, like Didymus' *De Spiritu Sancto* (*DSpS*), in volume 39; the *Adversus Eunomium* IV–V (*AE*) in volume 29; the *De Trinitate et Spiritu Sancto* (*DTSpS*) in volume 26.

Table 1 lists passages containing similar or identical correlations or combinations of biblical proof-texts. By 'correlation' is meant a technique of mutual interpretation of two or more texts by each other, as when Matthew 12:28 and Luke 11:19–20 are brought together to show that the 'finger of God' is the Holy Spirit. By 'combination' is meant a rather looser use of a whole series of texts in more or less the same constellation, employed to make the same point or points. It should be added that in the majority of cases listed in this table the passages using the same or similar biblical correlations or combinations

Table 2. *Refutations of heretical exegesis*

	DSpS	DTSpS	AE	DT
Proverbs 8:22			704 A	817 B
			704 AB	824 AB
			704 B	816 Cf
			704 B	816 A
			704 C	813 Cf
Amos 4:13	1046 Cf	1215 BC		949 Cf
	1047 C			952 Cf
	1048 A			952 Cf
		1215 CD	693 A	340 Cf
Matthew 26:39			697 AB	905 Bf
Mark 10:18			700 Cf	352 A
			700 C	353 Bf
Mark 13:32			696 B	920 AB
			696 C	917 B
John 14:26	1056 Af			977 C
	1058 B			972 Cf
	1057 Df			973 C
John 14:28			696 A	332 C
			693 Cf	332 Cf
John 15:1f.			700 AB	849 BC
John 16:13	1065 A			984 A
	1065 C			981 C
	1066 A			981 Cf
	1064 C			888 BC
Acts 2:36			704 Df	841 Bf
	1077 C		704 C	844 AB
			705 AB	844 Cf
I Corinthians 2:10			765 Cf	969 Cf
I Corinthians 15:28			693 B	893 B
Colossians 1:15			701 BC	832 A
			701 C	836 A
			701 CD	832 CD
			701 Df	833 Af

turn out to be similar in other ways as well, even down to subtle points of argument; it is not, for the most part, merely a matter of similar use of the same or similar combinations of texts, but of wider ranging resemblance in style and content, in the conclusion aimed for and the opponents envisaged. This is not to say that every parallel passage listed necessarily includes *all* of the texts indicated or *only* these; but the texts mentioned are the substantive core of the argument as it is finally developed, and some or all of them appear in each of the passages mentioned, and in such a way as to indicate a literary connection.

Table 2 lists parallels discovered by comparing the ways in which heretical exegesis of controverted texts is handled in the four writings. Book III of the *De Trinitate* is devoted entirely to this subject, as is the second half of *Adversus Eunomium* IV – though *De Trinitate* III is incomparably fuller and more extensive. (It is indeed the fullest single contemporary orthodox catalogue of Arian, Eunomian and Macedonian exegesis.) The evidence here is particularly clear that *De Trinitate* has drawn upon *Adversus Eunomium*, integrating its material in a wider and fuller arsenal of argument; but it also draws here and there on *De Spiritu Sancto* and *De Trinitate et Spiritu Sancto*. Here, too, the literary dependence of *De Trinitate* on all these sources is apparent.

Table 3 is concerned with passages in which particular, distinctive orthodox arguments are presented. Here too the evidence indicates that *De Trinitate* has drawn on all three other works: the similarity extends repeatedly to details of terminology and argument permitting of no other conclusion.

But what, it may be asked, does all this comparison of texts prove? Does it help to show that Didymus was, after all, the author of the *De Trinitate*? It may do so, but that question is a large one which cannot be opened up here.[10] But a couple of hints and nods may be in order:

(1) The *De Trinitate* seems beyond all reasonable doubt to date from late fourth-century Alexandria. If Didymus is not the author, it is hard to imagine who else could have been. There is, quite simply, no other known Alexandrian theologian of that period who would have been able to produce a work of this calibre.

(2) The current fashion for interpreting Didymus solely through the lens of the Toura commentaries with their penchant for Origenist allegory is in danger of forgetting Jerome's evidence that Didymus was indeed Origenist in his exegesis – but catholic in his teaching on the Trinity. It also tends to ignore the *De Spiritu Sancto*, and with it, Didymus'

Table 3. *Distinctive orthodox arguments*

	DSpS	DTSpS	AE	DT
God is unchangeable; creatures changeable		712 AB	512 Bf	
God is substantially good etc., creatures by reception	1036 A		712 C	
			713 A	524 A
			697 C	860 B
	1039 AB			528 A
			729 C	481 BC
Only God can indwell a rational soul	1044 D			369 B
	1082 C		713 A	529 A
	1054 Cf			369 Bf
				636 A
	1055 C			369 BC
	1082 C			372 Bf
The Son is Image of the Father's Being			676 A	336 B
The Son and Spirit possess free-will			697 C	604 CD
The Spirit does not worship God		1192 B		545 A
		1192 C		544 Cf
		1209 B		545 AB
Worship in the Spirit is worship of the Spirit		1206 Df		741 Af
The Spirit is 'living water'		1214 AB		556 B
		1213 A		{ 553 C 556 BC
The Spirit is 'oil of anointing'		1210 AB		556 Cf

concern to defend Trinitarian orthodoxy. The author of the *De Spiritu Sancto* could certainly have been capable in later years (and with access to numerous additional sources) of compiling the *De Trinitate*. Future research on Didymus would perhaps do well to include the *De Spiritu Sancto* within its purview instead of concentrating so one-sidedly on the Toura commentaries as has recently been the practice. That in turn might lead to a surprising new consensus that Mingarelli was right after all.

Finally, whether or not the *De Trinitate* can eventually be reclaimed for Didymus, this kind of comparative analysis of the work and its sources has its own modest contribution to make towards a better understanding of the evolution of orthodoxy in the Nicene and post-Nicene era. It can put us on the track of some trajectories of exegetical and dogmatic argument in the controversial theological literature of the late fourth century; it can help us to see more clearly and precisely how biblical and theological material was developed, applied and adapted in the course of that controversy; and it can assist us in tracing how, alongside and accompanying the contributions of such first-rank theologians as Athanasius and the Cappadocians, others too laboured to build up a rich stock of orthodox biblical and dogmatic argument. The evolution of orthodoxy did not only depend on the insight of theological genius; it was supported and enabled by efforts many times more modest and pedestrian, yet also laborious and deserving of respect. These authors too are our ancestors in the faith. The study of their writings, the analysis of their sources and their development of them, the detection of the principles and arguments they felt to be of fundamental and decisive importance – all this is part of that ongoing conversation between past and present to which Henry Chadwick has contributed so richly and without which the church today and tomorrow would be the poorer.

NOTES

1 *PG* 39.269–922. Part of the text is now available in critical editions: Jürgen Hönscheid, *Didymus der Blinde*: *De Trinitate, Buch I* and Ingrid Seiler, *Didymus der Blinde*: *De Trinitate, Buch II, Kapitel 1–7* (both Meisenheim am Glan 1975).

2 *PG* 39.1033–86. The parallels to *De Trinitate* discovered by Mingarelli are given in his edition of the latter, reproduced in *PG* 39.

3 Cf. for example the surveys by Bärbel Kramer, 'Didymus von Alexandrien', *TRE* vol. 8, Berlin 1981, 741–6, and Frances Young, *From Nicea to Chalcedon*: *A Guide to the Literature and Its Background*, Philadelphia 1983, pp. 83–91.

4 Most recently, Bart D. Ehrman, *Didymus the Blind and the Text of the Gospels*, Atlanta 1986. Pp. 4–29 offer a useful survey of other recent work, but marred by being out of date in the discussion of the *de Trinitate*, the *adversus Eunomium* iv–v and the pseudo-Athanasian *Dialogues*.

5 Alasdair Heron, 'The Two Pseudo-Athanasian Dialogues against the Anomoeans', *JThS*, 24.1 (1973), 101–22, here especially 118f.

6 My reasons for believing (against Martin Tetz) that the *De Trinitate et Spiritu Sancto* is both prior to and more significant than the other pseudo-

Athanasian work, *De Incarnatione et contra Arianos*, and that *a fortiori* the latter cannot safely be ascribed to Marcellus of Ancyra, are given in my contribution, 'The Pseudo-Athanasian Works *De Trinitate et Spiritu Sancto* and *De Incarnatione et contra Arianos*: A Comparison', to G. D. Dragas (ed.), *Aksum-Thyateira*: *A Festschrift for Archbishop Methodios of Thyateira and Great Britain*, Athens 1985, pp. 281–98.

7 The first list of parallels between *Adversus Eunomium* iv–v and *De Trinitate* was presented by F. X. Funk, 'Die zwei letzten Bücher der Schrift Basilius des Grossen gegen Eunomius', in his *Kirchengeschichtliche Abhandlungen*, vol. 2, Paderborn 1899, pp. 291–329.

8 Cf. e.g. the striking similarities between *De Trinitate* iii. 21–2 and Epiphanius, *Ancoratus* 31–9.

9 Most of the parallel passages here listed are presented in detail and analysed for indications of literary dependence in pp. 91–166 of my 1972 Tübingen dissertation, *Studies in the Trinitarian Writings of Didymus the Blind: His Authorship of the Adversus Eunomium IV–V and the De Trinitate*.

10 The matter is discussed extensively in pp. 196–230 of my dissertation (cf. n. 9 above). The considerations there offered do not appear to have been overtaken or rendered out of date by any more recent research. My conclusion was then (and remains today) that the evidence *against* Didymus' authorship is much weaker, and that *for* it is much stronger than the scholarly opinion of recent years would imply.

The rhetorical schools and their influence on patristic exegesis

FRANCES YOUNG

To honour Henry Chadwick is to honour the great tradition of British scholarship to which Edwin Hatch belonged. The work of Edwin Hatch was the inspiration of this paper, and it may be regarded as a celebration of the centenary of the publication of his Hibbert lectures of 1888, as well as a tribute to one who, like him, has achieved international acclaim for his erudition.

Some of what Hatch pioneered in those lectures on *The Influence of Greek Ideas on Christianity* has become commonplace, but not all.[1] It was the content of the first three lectures which provided the starting point of this study, those on Greek education and its legacy, on the influence of Greek methods of exegesis on Christian exegesis, and on the debt Christian preaching owed to Greek rhetoric.

By the Christian era, there was long established a system of education based upon the study of literature and practical exercises in speech-making.[2] As Hatch explained, literature from the distant past was powerful speech preserved from a Golden Age, which could act as a model for those who produced literary exercises to be declaimed. The teaching of the grammaticus and the rhetor in each city's gymnasium was the principal agent for the spread of Hellenistic culture throughout the then known world, and for its ongoing transmission through approximately 800 years.[3]

Hatch stressed the hold the educational system had upon the society into which Christianity came, and showed how inevitably it would affect the emerging church. He then went on to explore Greek and Christian exegesis. His conclusion that Christian allegory derives via Philo from the way Greeks treated Homer is now commonplace. Sensitively he helps us to appreciate how the ancients were affected by the mystery of writing, reverence for antiquity and belief in inspiration, as a prelude to describing the place Homer had in Greek culture: literature, especially ancient and revered literature, was assumed to be universal, to be wisdom for all time. Drawing moral lessons from literature was normal practice.

But Hatch made little of the fact that the humanistic thrust and this-worldly ideals of rhetorical education were frequently in conflict with the ideals of philosophy[4] – tension between two opposed educational ideals is already there in Plato's disputes with the Sophists and his reservations about poetry. It is true that Aristotle and his successors regarded all areas of research as open to the philosopher, and literary criticism, linguistic analysis and rhetorical techniques were placed on the philosopher's agenda. Indeed, the Stoics pioneered the classification and analysis of grammar and figures of speech which was used in the Hellenistic schools. Undoubtedly each had a profound effect upon the other and some important figures would have claimed both traditions: Cicero, Plutarch, Dio Chrysostom, for example. Nevertheless, tension and accommodation oscillated in the relationship between philosophy and rhetoric: philosophy accused rhetoric of being merely an empty technique with no moral purpose, practised by those who wanted to get ahead in the world; rhetoric countered by emphasizing its moral aspects, its aim being to prepare the pupils to play an active and effective role in civic and political life. On rhetoric's side, philosophy was sneered at as withdrawal from the world, or as useless speculation, the profound disagreement between philosophical schools only reinforcing the criticisms. Indeed, rhetoric was certainly the more pervasive and influential: philosophy was the crown of education for a few, but many studied rhetoric, and over those 800 years the character of education changed only in the proliferation of technical terms and more refined formal analyses.

Hatch tends to imply that nearly all interpretation was affected by the search for symbolical meanings. Certainly everyone looked for the moral of the tale, but symbolical allegory was not universal. The tracing of doctrines, or universal truths, or metaphysical and psychological theories by means of allegorical reading was characteristic of the philosophers, especially the Stoics, but was not, I suggest, the universal way of reading literature in the ancient educational system – indeed, hardly characteristic of the grammar and rhetorical schools. Symbolic allegory was characteristic of a philosophical approach to literature; the rival rhetorical approach sought to derive moral principles, useful instruction and ethical models from their study of literature. This approach, I suggest, informed Antiochene exegesis of the Bible with its reaction against Origenist allegory.

EXEGESIS IN THE RHETORICAL SCHOOLS

What then were the methods of exegesis practised in the schools? The biggest problem is the dearth of direct evidence about what went on in the grammaticus' classroom, or indeed how the rhetor would comment on literature. It was, like school teaching in every age, an oral medium. By contrast we know a lot about how speeches were constructed and how school exercises were set and composed, both from papyri and from text-books. Systematic studies of style and construction are readily available. Inevitably it is on the acquiring of such formal rhetorical techniques that most modern studies of Greek education have focussed, because that is what we have evidence for.[5] Apart from some scholia and marginalia, we do not have notes on texts.[6]

But we can glean some information. Quintilian is one of our most informative sources.[7] True he was not a Greek rhetor, but in his position as first official state rhetor in Rome, he certainly practised Greek rhetoric in a Latin medium, and after his retirement wrote a massive book on rhetorical education. Cross-checks with Greek sources where they can be effected confirm that his methods and aims were essentially the same as those that had been and would be practised for centuries. The chief value of Quintilian's work for our purposes is that he does not assume we know what went on in the elementary stages, as most sources do. So he provides the only summary account we have of the use of literature in the school classes of the grammaticus.

Correct reading precedes interpretation, says Quintilian. It is important to remind ourselves that correct reading was itself a process of exegesis, since words were not divided, there was no punctuation and not all hand-written copies in the class would be identical. Teachers had to begin by establishing an agreed text and rejecting spurious material, and by discussing how a text was to be read. All reading in the ancient world was reading aloud. A text was a form of speech which had to be realized to make sense, rather as a musical score means little to many until it is played.

But more than correct reading is involved in interpretation. The linguistic aspect requires considerable scholarship: much literature being very ancient and containing unfamiliar archaic words and forms, vocabulary and parsing is bound to occupy the class. Quintilian himself dwells upon the problem of distinguishing the consonantal use of the semivowels 'u' and 'i' in Latin, as well as conjugation, parts of speech, the construing of sentences, etc. The situation with respect to the Homeric dialect of Greek would be even more acute. Much of school comment on literature was clearly concerned with basic linguistic correctness. But the good teacher also expounded the origin and meaning of names as part of this grammatical instruction. Tracing etymologies was certainly a very important activity in commenting on texts in schools.

Quintilian regrets that many teachers do not pay enough attention to these preliminary mechanical foundations, but rush on to display the more interesting aspects of their act. Of these, style was clearly of supreme importance. By noticing how great authors produced stylistic effects, the pupil was prepared for producing his own stylistic compositions under the rhetor. Quintilian recognizes that there is a literary vocabulary which in itself gives the impression of the 'sublime', but he insists that it is the combination of appropriate words in connected speech that also produces real excellence. Teachers therefore need to be discriminating as they note barbarisms, grammatical solecisms and ugly combinations of syllables – not the sort of thing to be imitated, unless a particular kind of effect is required. Comment will be made on foreign words, their origins and how to decline them. The use of metaphor and archaisms will be carefully and judiciously considered. 'Language is based on reason, antiquity, authority and usage', says Quintilian. Coining new words or forms or metaphors is less acceptable than following literary usage. Adopting current speech habits, especially those of the uneducated, is to be frowned upon. So noting proper stylistic usage is a most important function of studying literature.

So what the teacher does, as he reads in class with his pupils the great corpus of classical literature Quintilian recommends, is to analyse a verse into parts of speech, metre, etc., to note linguistic usage, especially commenting on acceptable and unacceptable usage and style, to discuss the different meanings which may be given to each word, to expound unusual words, to elucidate figures of speech or ornamental devices, and to 'impress on the minds of the pupils the value of proper arrangement and of graceful treatment of the matter in hand'. In addition to this he will explain the stories – unpack allusions to classical myths, gods, heroes, legends, histories – not in too much detail, advises Quintilian, nor in too many versions. The mind must not be swamped.

Commentaries are full of such erudition. Nevertheless, the exploration of these background points is important, and these two aspects of exegesis are called *methodikē* and *historikē*.

The study of literature with the rhetor became even more pragmatic, as the great orators and prose-writers were used principally as models for rhetorical composition. We are now told more about curriculum than method. Yet there are some clues, and the very technicality of the rhetor's analysis of how a speech should be composed is a good indication of the kind of thing they would be looking for in studying literature. Quintilian passes rhetorical judgment on the classical authors he lists, and in the literary essays of Dionysius of Halicarnassus, the search for standard *aretai* and the application of technical rhetorical distinctions provide criteria for critical assessment.[8]

The principal categories are *ho pragmatikos topos* (or *res*), that is the subject-matter; the area determined by the author's *heuresis* or *inventio*, his skill in presenting and manipulating the material; and *ho lektikos topos* (or *onomata*, *verba*), that is, the style and vocabulary, which the rhetor tended to treat not as integral to the subject but as a separate matter. Undoubtedly the latter interest was predominant: whether a thing was in a plain style, a grand style or a middle style would be carefully computed according to choice of words, their arrangement, the figures of speech and the presence or absence of certain *aretai*, which included purity of language, lucidity, brevity, vividness, character-drawing, emotional power, magnificence, vigour and effectiveness, charm and permissiveness, and propriety.[9] Still, for all the emphasis on style, it is clear that the rhetor was also interested in how the author chose, delimited and handled his theme, how he divided up and arranged the subject-matter, how he drew his characters and produced his effects, how the thrust or intention was actually conveyed or concealed by the adoption of certain techniques.[10] If the exegesis practised in the schools appears at first sight to be piecemeal, and principally concerned with the outer dress of diction and style, the commonplace that language was mere clothing meant that the thought enunciated also needed distinguishing. The author, it was assumed, had a subject to cover or thesis to propound, like those set as exercises for the budding rhetor. So comment included discerning this. Rhetorical criticism, however, was always 'audience-orientated': it always looked for the effect produced, and this was one of many features which blocked the development of historical criticism, or an awareness of the difference between what the author intended and what the interpreter might discern. There was some gossipy biographical interest, but no true historical sense.[11] So all interpretation would tend to be anachronistic.

So, as we can confirm from other sources too,[12] school exegesis consisted of: (i) *diorthōsis* – the establishment of agreement about the text to be read; (ii) *anagnōsis* – the construal and correct reading of it; (iii) *exēgēsis* – the *methodikē* and *historikē* described earlier, comments on language and explanatory notes on all kinds of narrative references, not just what we would call history: places, dates, genealogies, characters, actions, events, whether historical or mythological; (iv) *krisis* – the discernment of the good, the judgment of the poets.

Now *krisis* clearly needs more discussion, though our main source, Quintilian, does not treat it. It apparently included literary, or perhaps we should say rhetorical, evaluation; and questions of authenticity, relative dating, etc., were certainly raised.[13] Yet *krisis* seems on the whole to have been less aesthetic or critical in our sense, than moral, the search for *aretē*, virtue, not just for *aretai*, stylistic excellences. The educator sought moral lessons in literature.

As is well known, Plato had raised doubts about the moral influence of the poets, and literature had to be defended against these charges. Plutarch is one of many who advised various methods of extracting moral advice from literature and neutralizing its potentially adverse moral effect.[14] Poetry he regarded as a seductive form of deception: but prospective philosophers he advises to use poetry as an introductory exercise, and to develop their moral sense by exercising critical judgment. The poets tell lies, so text must be weighed against text, and the poet's real intention thus uncovered. Admonition and instruction is implied in the invention of tales and myths as examples of good and bad conduct. Context and circumstances may modify our apprehension of the sense of the words, as may careful attention to the kind of alternative meanings taught by the grammaticus. Poetry is 'true to life' in its inextricable mixture of good and evil: so moral judgment is important, and the young should be urged to emulate the virtuous. Plutarch advocates a kind of moral 'pruning' which lays bare the profitable things that are hidden under the prolific foliage of poetic diction and clustering tales. This kind of moral criticism was adopted by the rhetorical schools enthusiastically, and the discussion of moral virtues was included among the themes adopted for practice declamations. Thus as Plutarch recommended, the student of poetry with the grammaticus would be used to bringing poetry out of the realm of myth and impersonation through discussing ethical doctrines, and moral philosophy would not come as a shock at a later stage in his education.

So the study of literature critically meant the discernment of moral good as much as aesthetic good. Such procedures, and indeed the search for etymologies too, could be conducive to the development of allegory. But symbolic allegory of the kind practised by the Stoics, seems not to have been characteristic in the schools of the grammaticus and rhetor, except in so far as they came under the influence of philosophical schools. Plutarch expected the teachers of literature to discover moral lessons, not cosmological or mystical meanings. He was hostile to Stoic allegorizing of the poets, in spite of his own use of allegory in religious and philosophical treatises. Perhaps we should conclude there was allegory and allegory – reading texts symbolically and mystically was philosophical whereas reading texts to tease out a moral was rhetorical.

So in spite of the mutual influence of rhetoric and philosophy, it seems likely that there were two overlapping yet distinct traditions when it came to treating literature. They had linguistic, textual and etymological interests in common, and philosophy built upon and embraced the techniques of school exegesis. Yet there were two distinct attitudes to a text's fundamental meaning and reference and how these were to be discerned. Where philosophy found abstract doctrines or virtues through verbal allegory, rhetoric looked for concrete ethical examples in a narrative, and for models of excellence both stylistic and moral in the construction and presentation of the whole. Plutarch's discussion also demonstrates, by the way, that when Basil, in his *Address to young men on how they might profit from pagan literature*,[15] advised parents and young people to allow the usual education curriculum to train the mind while discriminating between the morally useful and the harmful, he was drawing upon an ancient commonplace, and not devising some peculiar Christian double-think.

ANTIOCHENE EXEGESIS

The basic thesis being presented is that the Origenist tradition adopted the allegorical techniques of the philosophical schools, and the Antiochene reaction was the protest of rhetoric against such a way of handling texts. In view of what has been said about the absence of interest in history, this suggestion may appear incompatible with the standard characterization of Antiochene exegesis, emphasizing its concern with the 'literal' meaning and historical reference of the Bible.

But this characterization has introduced all kinds of problems into understanding what the Antiochenes were doing. If we look at their work, we find a profoundly dogmatic exegesis, and in most cases, an attitude to typology and prophecy which sits very uncomfortably with their so-called historical approach. Rowan Greer has tried to explain it in exclusively theological terms.[16] What makes the difference between Antiochene and Alexandrian exegesis, he claims, is their different fundamental theological frameworks, rather than a particular methodology: 'theology...shapes exegesis in the sense that it determines the questions asked of the text'. There is a great deal in this. But my suggestion that the exegetical debate reflected a difference within Greco-Roman culture about how to treat texts, means that the question of method remains relevant, and also accounts for those features of Antiochene exegesis which sit so ill at ease with attempts to characterize it as if it were the precursor of modern historico-critical method. There was no genuine historical criticism in antiquity. The Antiochenes do take *historia* seriously, but in the sense of *to historikon*.

Is there any plausibility in the basic idea that rhetoric influenced the Antiochenes? What do we know about their education?[17] Well, John Chrysostom studied with the famous pagan rhetorician, Libanius, who claimed he would have been his successor if the Christians had not stolen him. He received the nickname 'Golden-mouth', like a famous rhetorician before him, and his reputation was for public speaking. Theodore of Mopsuestia is probably to be identified with John Chrysostom's student friend, Theodore, in which case he had the same education. Their Christian biblical teacher was Diodore: let his enemy Julian the Apostate characterize him:

Diodore, a charlatan priest of the Nazarene...is clearly a sharp-witted sophist of that rustic creed...For he sailed to Athens to the detriment of the public welfare, rashly taking to philosophy and literature, and arming his tongue with rhetorical devices against the heavenly gods.

No wonder Julian banished Christians from the schools – much to the fury of educated church leaders like Gregory of Nazianzus. Diodore was a Christian Sophist, and a dangerous opponent of his pagan revival in Antioch. As for Theodoret, he may insist that he received all his education from monks, he may describe Diodore and Theodore as his teachers, but every word he writes proclaims his training in the classical *paideia*; he quotes Homer, Sophocles, Euripides, Aristophanes, Demosthenes and Thucydides, and his correspondents include distinguished sophists. The Antiochenes had a rhetorical education. Evidence of formal philosophical training is less apparent.

Turning to their exegesis, what do we find? Characteristic of both commentaries and homilies are opening chapters or paragraphs discerning the *hupothesis* of the book to be studied, or of the passage to be treated. Details of the text are then examined point by point. Details commented upon range from discussion of alternative readings and their relative merits, questions of correct punctuation and how the sentences are to be construed, together with problems of translation where applicable, to etymologies, explanations of foreign and unfamiliar words, attention to metaphor and other figures of speech, and mini-treatises, with masses of scriptural cross-references, on the special biblical flavour of particular words or phrases. What is this but the *methodikē* of the schools? The commentaries further explore the context and sequence of thought, test text against text, as Plutarch recommended, and explain or debate the reference of the text, by outlining what is known of the time of the prophet or, say, the events of Paul's life. Here they speak of the *historia*, and they are concerned to get it right: Theodoret maintained that Paul had visited and knew the church at Colossae, though Theodore had denied this. Yet what is this but the *historikē* of the schools? To jump to the conclusion that they had the same kind of historical interest as modern critics is perhaps understandable, but it is not always convincing. After all, Theodore in commenting on the Psalms recognized that 'By the waters of Babylon, there we sat down...' referred to the exile, but that did not mean drawing critical historical conclusions in our sense. The Psalms were all written by David, so David must have been prophesying. Of course, they usually assumed that the reference was to facts – unless the text was metaphorical, parabolic, clearly intended as a fable, or to be taken as prophetic – in which case the text refers to what it prophesies however veiled the reference. It is quite misleading to view their work as some kind of historical criticism, and to assume that it was a historical concern which produced the protest against allegory. What they were concerned to do was to take the thrust of the text seriously, rather than dissipate or distort it in word-by-word allegory. So much is this the case that many readers both ancient and modern have commented upon the dull and pedestrian character of Antiochene commentaries, which rarely rise above the commonsense 'nitty-gritty' of exegesis or simple paraphrase.

Summary and paraphrase is a persistent Antiochene technique for bringing out the gist of the argument, and the *hupothesis* usually includes this, together with historical or circumstantial introductory material. This technique ensures that context and thrust were not lost under the mass of detailed commentary. Without doubt the discussion of subject-matter in the schools, which included the *hupothesis* and sought to discern the underlying 'idea' dressed up in the words of the text, lies behind this. Theodore in particular was concerned with what he called the *skopos* of the text – its aim or intent, setting this up as a principle against piecemeal interpretation, and insisting that a text has only one *skopos*. This had some notorious consequences, like his denial that Psalm 22 referred to the Passion, despite its appearance on the lips of Jesus in the Gospels, on the grounds that the speaker refers elsewhere in the Psalm to his sins. I have not been able to document the use of *skopos* as a technical term in the schools,[18] but certainly the practice of providing *hupotheseis*, which often outline the *skopos*, appears to have its background in the school treatment of literature.

The use of typology by the Antiochenes may well have some background in literary theory, as well. Theodore accepts that Jonah prefigures Jesus because the extraordinary events of his life signify by *mimēsis* Christ's rejection, resurrection and conversion of the Gentiles. Now *mimēsis* was a key term in ancient literary criticism,[19] and carried implications very different from the fables and fantasies of allegorical interpretation. Literature imitates life, and can therefore be instructive, particularly in the moral sphere. This view, coupled with the long-standing Christian tradition of seeing everything in the Old Testament as prophetic, gave Theodore a method of appropriating some typological exegeses, in spite of his very radical views on the difference between Old and New Testaments. Key Old Testament narratives prefigured by *mimēsis* the events of the New. As for dogmatic exegesis, Hatch noted that ancient texts were universally assumed to contain abiding truths, to be useful and instructive. As we have seen, there was no real awareness in antiquity of the difference between what an author intended and what the interpreter might discern, still less of historical distance. Is it surprising that fifth-century theologians could discern no difference between the theology of Paul and their own doctrine, or that Theodore believed that the purpose of a commentary was to deal with problem texts, particularly those twisted by the heretics?

As is well known, Theodore was somewhat extreme in his exegetical principles, even among the Antiochenes. Theodoret allows a text more than one *skopos*, and permits a far greater range of traditional prophetic and typological meanings – indeed, you might call some of them

FRANCES YOUNG

allegorical, like his acceptance from Origen (against Theodore) that the Song of Songs referred to the marriage of Christ and the Church. But there is allegory and allegory – and on the whole the *theōria* he employs is far removed from the kind of thing Alexandrian allegory produced. His methods are fundamentally akin to those of Theodore. It is the 'nitty-gritty' of exegesis which exercises him – the *methodikē* and the *historikē* – the latter embracing more prophetic references. Furthermore, Theodoret generally focusses on morals drawn from the text, rather than imaginative or mystical speculations.

The propensity to draw morals from the text is most dramatically evidenced in Chrysostom's homilies. Chrysostom shares all the methods described, but he is preaching, and he tends not to burden his congregation with too much *methodikē*. However, expounding the *historia* is important, though not because it is historical, but because it becomes exemplary. Whatever he is commenting upon is turned into a moral lesson, an example, an exhortation. The anhistorical character of Chrysostom's exegesis is evident in another feature, namely the way he collapses the time-gap between, say, Paul's church at Corinth and his own congregation, by reading between the lines to bring out the tone of Paul's voice and his use of tactics to win over his hearers.[20] The preacher makes Paul address his own congregation as he elucidates what response he wished to draw out of his readers. Paul's oscillation between praise and blame, severity and tenderness, humility and assertion, is part of his subtle handling of the Corinthians in their disunity, immorality, pride and disloyalty: that one minute Paul scares them and the next minute softens his words to win them belongs to the 'economy' of his discourse – the term 'economy' being one of the terms of rhetorical criticism for 'arrangement' of the subject-matter. What is this then but the audience-oriented criticism of the rhetor, used now not to train budding declaimers to manipulate an audience, but to facilitate the appropriate moral response from the congregation? And where else did the constant moralizing come from but the educator's search for morally edifying examples? It was, after all, morals that Plutarch thought the poets taught.

This moralizing is of a very different flavour from the moral and spiritual meanings discerned by Origen. Chrysostom sees morality in terms of exemplary deeds not abstract virtues, and, whether it is Paul or Abraham, it is to their exemplary character and practice to which he draws attention. A good example of the kind of difference in interest between someone like Chrysostom and someone like Origen can be found in comparison of their respective comments upon Matthew's Feeding-story. Origen,[21] in his Commentary, takes the story as symbolical of spiritual feeding, seeing the desert-place as representing the desert condition of the masses without the Law and the Word of God, and explaining that the disciples are given power to nourish the crowds with rational food. The five loaves and two fish are interpreted in terms of scripture and the Logos. Chrysostom,[22] however, turns the story into proofs of dogma and moral lessons – Christ looks up to heaven to prove he is of the Father, and he uses the loaves and fish rather than creating food out of nothing to stop the mouths of dualistic heretics like Marcion and Manichaeus. He let the crowds become hungry and only gave them loaves and fish, equally distributed, to teach the crowd humility, temperance and charity, and to have all things in common. He wanted to ensure that they did not become slaves of the belly – and that comment allows Chrysostom the chance to preach detachment from worldly pursuits. This is no more historical or literal than Origen's allegory. It has its basis in the search for morals in literature characteristic of the rhetorical schools.

THE REJECTION OF ALLEGORY

So neither literalism nor an interest in history stimulated the Antiochene reaction against Origenist allegory, but rather a different approach to finding meaning in literature which had its background in the rhetorical schools. This suggestion is confirmed by the one complete surviving work of Eustathius of Antioch, *On the Witch of Endor and Against Origen*.[23]

Quasten remarks, 'Eustathius rejects not only Origen's interpretation of this particular passage but his entire allegorical exegesis, because it deprives scripture of its historical character.' To look at the treatise is to discover very quickly that that is a most misleading statement. It is true that Eustathius begins by attacking Origen for paying attention to *onomata* (names, terms) rather than *pragmata* (deeds, events), but the ensuing discussion proves that what he means by the distinction is analogous to the categories *pragmatikos topos* and *lektikos topos* (or *onomata*) that we found in Dionysius of Halicarnassus. Eustathius objects to Origen's verbal or lexical approach to the text, without paying regard to the subject-matter. Origen is in this case *too literal*!

It appears that Origen has made certain deductions about the resurrection on the basis of the statement that the Witch summoned up

Samuel from Hades. Eustathius argues that only God can raise up the dead, therefore the Witch cannot have done it. Samuel was not raised at all: rather the devil used the Witch to play upon the mad mind of Saul and induce him to believe he saw Samuel. The whole treatise is a series of rationalistic arguments to prove that Origen's literal reading of the text is totally along the wrong lines, and so everything he deduces from it is unacceptable. According to Eustathius, the thrust of the whole tells against Origen's view. It is Saul who *thinks* he sees Samuel – there is no statement anywhere that he actually did.

And so it goes on: rationalistic arguments and scripture parallels justifying a more satisfactory but less literal interpretation than that of Origen. Every detail of the conversation between Saul and the Witch is exploited to show that it represents the dissimulations of the devil and makes sense no other way, and the scriptural laws against sorcery and consulting mediums confirm that the words of the Witch must be treated as false. Eustathius even justifies his non-literal interpretation by giving examples of other scriptural narratives where details are not spelled out verbally but left to commonsense inference.

Now clearly we cannot explore every detail of Eustathius' argument, but there are some points worth noting: Eustathius is really worried about the doctrines Origen deduces from the text, not about his allegorical method. He does, in a long aside, object to the fact that Origen allegorizes Moses' accounts of creation, paradise and many other things, including gospel-narratives which Eustathius thinks should be taken literally, but his point is that it is scandalous to allegorize those things and then treat this story literally, especially when it leads one into blasphemous conclusions. Eustathius is objecting to methods which ignore the sequence of the story, the intention of the story-writer and the coherence of the narrative with the rest of scripture. He argues that the very word *eggastrimuthos* shows that the story-writer meant to imply the Witch was false. It is at this point that he takes a particularly interesting line. He refers to the definition of 'myth' in rhetorical textbooks as a fiction made up for pleasure and also for a purpose. Fiction is a plausible *mimēsis* of reality, like painting, but it creates unreal things. Myths are a way of educating children (and Plato's advice to parents is here quoted), but Greek children are eventually taught to distinguish between truth and fiction. Eustathius' purpose is to prove his basic point: the *eggastrimuthos* has myths created in her inward parts, her stomach rather than her mind, by the devil. In the process he uses standard etymological techniques, explicitly refers to literary-critical observations about art being a *mimēsis* of life, makes a learned reference to Plato as any well-educated teacher would, and actually mentions rhetorical textbooks.

Clearly the source of his methods lies in the schools. All through the piece he insists on looking for the actual *historia* of the *gramma*: this is surely not 'history' in the modern sense, but something like the narrative logic of the text – making sense of the whole sequence of events described, is more or less his own phrase. He is looking for a coherent account of things. His objection to Origen is that, whether he takes a text literally or allegorically, he is too concerned with the verbal level of the text, and not with its thrust or subject-matter.

Doubtless Eustathius assumed a correlation between this 'thrust of the text' and 'what really happened'. But he was no historical critic. He was simply using standard literary techniques deriving from the treatment of texts in the rhetorical schools to protest against esoteric philosophical deductions being made in what he regarded as an arbitrary way. One thing he was keen to show is that Origen appeals to other scriptures which were inappropriate and unconvincing while ignoring genuinely relevant passages. In other words Origen's methods were arbitrary and his conclusions unreliable: this story is not about the resurrection. To prove this Eustathius attempts to interpret instead by *methodikē* and *historikē* – not historically in the modern sense, nor literally, but according to the rationalistic literary-critical methods current in the contemporary educational practice of grammaticus and rhetor. In this he was the precursor of Diodore, Theodore, Chrysostom and Theodoret, and perhaps the successor of that shadowy but influential biblical scholar, Lucian of Antioch.

CONCLUSION

If this line of approach is accepted, then it helps to explain some other puzzles about patristic exegesis. Why is it so difficult to 'place' the exegesis of people like the Cappadocians? Often it has been stated that they are closer to the Antiochenes in method than to Origen – yet they were great admirers and students of Origen, and occasionally used allegory in a distinctly Origenist way. How can their exegesis be explained? We now have the key. They had all been trained according to the classical *paideia*, and naturally used rhetorical techniques in commenting upon literature, in spite of their philosophical interests. Basil even taught as a rhetor before abandoning a lucrative career to become a monk and eventually a bishop. In the *Hexaemeron* he discusses and mocks the various theories of philosophers in true rhetorical style. His brother, Gregory of Nyssa, also had a rhetorical career, until rescued by his pious and domineering sister; and Rosemary Ruether has characterized the vacillating career of their friend, Gregory of Nazianzus, as a constant battle between the ideals of rhetoric and philosophy in Christianized forms.[24] It is in the preaching of the Cappadocians that Christian panegyric flowers, orations celebrating saints and martyrs which follow all the stylistic techniques and devices of the rhetorical text-books.[25] It was a form later embraced and perfected by Chrysostom. Is it not clear that their exegetical work came under the same rhetorical influences?

How far back in the history of the church does this influence from the schools go? To take up Hatch's third Hibbert lecture on Greek and Christian rhetoric is scarcely possible at this stage, and must await another occasion. But perhaps I may conclude by hazarding the suggestion that from a very early date the homily was the bishop's lecture on the literature that really mattered, namely the scriptures. Everyone studied week by week with the Christian 'grammaticus'. Origen was an innovator, not because he was the first rhetorical exegete, as Hatch supposed, but because he was the first philosophical exegete, offering higher education somewhat in competition with the bishop's 'school'. The Antiochenes belonged to the older tradition, and in reaction to Origen, deepened it and refined it.

NOTES

1 Edwin Hatch, *The Influence of Greek Ideas on Christianity*, Harper Torchbooks, New York 1957: reprinted by arrangements with Williams and Norgate, London. Note the foreword with notes and bibliography by Frederick C. Grant to be found in this reprint edition.

2 On ancient education see H.-I. Marrou, *L'Education dans l'Antiquité*. Paris 1948, ET New York, 1956; Werner Jaeger, *Paideia: the Ideals of Greek Culture*, 3 vols.; ET Gilbert Highet, Oxford 1943–5; George Kennedy, *The Art of Persuasion in Greek*, Princeton 1963, *The Art of Rhetoric in the Roman World*, Princeton 1972, *Greek Rhetoric under Christian Emperors*, Princeton 1983, and *Classical Rhetoric and its Christian and Secular Tradition from Ancient to Modern Times*, University of North Carolina 1980; R. W. Smith, *The Art of Rhetoric in Alexandria*, The Hague, 1974; D. L. Clark, *Rhetoric in Greco-Roman Education*, New York 1957.

3 On Hellenization see Moses Hadas, *Hellenistic Culture*, New York and Oxford 1959; Martin Hengel, *Judaism and Hellenism*, London 1974; Emil

Schurer, *The History of the Jewish People in the Age of Jesus Christ*, vol. 2, rev. and ed. by Geza Vermes, Fergus Millar and Matthew Black, Edinburgh 1979; A. H. M. Jones, *The Greek City from Alexander to Justinian*, Oxford 1940.

4 On the conflict between rhetoric and philosophy see: Jaeger, *Paideia*; Marrou, *L'Education dans l'Antiquité*; Kennedy, *The Art of Persuasion in Greek*; Rosemary Radford Ruether, *Gregory of Nazianzus. Rhetor and Philosopher*, Oxford, 1969. The classic study is the Introduction, 'Sophistik, Rhetorik, Philosophie, in ihrem Kampf um die Jugendbildung', to H. von Arnim, *Leben und Werke des Dio von Prusa*, Berlin 1898, pp. 1–114.

5 On rhetoric and rhetorical handbooks see: Marrou, *L'Education dans l'Antiquité*; Kennedy, *The Art of Persuasion*, *The Art of Rhetoric*, *Greek Rhetoric*; Smith, *The Art of Rhetoric in Alexandria: Menander Rhetor,* ed. with trans. and commentary D. A. Russell and N. G. Wilson, Oxford 1981. Useful texts include Aristotle, *Ars rhetorica*; Cicero, *De oratore, et al.*; Demetrius, *On Style*; Longinus, *On the Sublime*; Quintilian, *Institutio oratoria*; *Rhetorica ad Herennium* – all accessible in the Loeb Classical Library. Marrou is the exception to my comment that modern studies focus mainly on rhetorical composition. George Kennedy, like Hatch, has only a brief couple of paragraphs in *The Art of Persuasion*, and a summary of what Quintilian says in his *Quintilian*, New York 1969. More helpful are the accounts of ancient literary criticism, but these tend to be based on treatises like Aristotle's *Poetics* and Longinus, *On the Sublime*. Exegetical practice in the schools is barely discussed, largely for lack of evidence. See D. A. Russell, *Criticism in Antiquity*, London 1981, and the selection of texts in D. A. Russell and M. Winterbottom, *Ancient Literary Criticism*, Oxford 1972. Good evidence is probably provided by the critical essays of Dionysius of Halicarnassus: see further below.

6 H.-I. Marrou, *L'Education dans l'Antiquité*, p. 229: the scholia in manuscripts and papyri may provide an echo of the classroom, but the evidence is meagre. For examples of scholia, comment and lexica, see *Sammlung griechischer und lateinischer Grammatiker*, ed. Klaus Alpers, Hartment Erbse and Alexander Kleinlogel. Vol. 3 contains *Die Fragmente des Grammatikers Dionysios Thrax. Die Fragmente der Grammatiker Tyrannion und Diokles Apions Glōssai Homērikai*. This confirms an interest in alternative readings, definitions, synonyms, etymologies and other lexicographical points.

7 *Institutio oratoria* 1.iv–ix – text in Loeb Classical Library. See also George Kennedy, *Quintilian*.

8 Quintilian, *Inst. orat.* x.i and ii; Dionysius of Halicarnassus, *On Literary Composition*, Introduction, translation, and notes by W. Rhys Roberts, London 1910, and *Critical Essays*, vol. 1, Loeb Classical Library 1974 – see especially the *De Thucydide* (the translation and commentary by W. Pritchett, University of California Press 1975, is also useful). The interest in

FRANCES YOUNG

classification, and ultimately *mimēsis*, pervades these works. Dionysius also
wrote a treatise on *mimēsis*, now lost, but known through epitomes and his
own description in his letter to Ptolemaeus: see Dionysius of Halicarnassus,
The Three Literary Letters, ed. and trans. by W. Rhys Roberts, Cambridge
1901.

9 A useful table will be found in S. F. Bonner, *The Literary Treatises of
Dionysius of Halicarnassus*, Cambridge 1939, p. 24.

10 Ibid., 84ff., commenting on the *De Thucydide*. Also Pritchett, *De Thucydide*,
p. xxxvi, for summary table of the rhetorical system of Dionysius. The
pragmatikos topos involved discussion of *hupothesis, diairesis, taxis* and
exergasia.

11 See particularly D. A. Russell, *Criticism in Antiquity*, especially ch.8 on
rhetoric, and ch.11 on literary history.

12 See H.-I. Marrou, *L'Education dans l'Antiquité*, pp. 230ff, and particularly
Dionysius Thrax, *Ars grammatica*, ed. G. Uhlig, Leipzig 1883. This treatise
is principally about grammar in the technical sense, but in the opening
paragraph Dionysius distinguishes six components of *grammatikē*, which is
defined as '*empeiria tōn para poiētais te kai suggrapheusin hōs epi to polu
legomenon*':

anagnōsis entribēs kata prosōdian;
exēgēsis kata tous enuparchontas poiētikous tropous;
glossōn te kai historiōn procheiros apodosis;
etunologias heuresis;
analogias eklogismos;
krisis poiēmatōn, ho dē kalliston esti pantōn tōn en tē(i) technē(i).

13 See e.g. Dionysius of Halicarnassus, *Epistle to Ammaeus* 1, in Rhys Roberts
(ed.), *Three Literary Letters*.

14 Plutarch, *Moralia* 1, Loeb Classical Library, 1927. N.B. *On the Education of
Children* and *How the young man should study poetry*.

15 Ed. N. G. Wilson, *St Basil on the value of Greek Literature*, London, 1975.
Trans. in Basil of Caesarea, *Letters*, vol. 4, Loeb Classical Library.

16 Rowan A. Greer, *The Captain of our Salvation. A study in the Patristic Exegesis
of Hebrews*, Tübingen, 1973.

17 For evidence and bibliography, see my *From Nicaea to Chalcedon*, London
1983.

18 George A. Kennedy, *Greek Rhetoric under Christian Emperors*, pp. 126–32
notes the use of *skopos* in fifth-century neo-platonic Commentaries on Plato.
The search for the *skopos* of the dialogue is linked with the theory that the
whole work should cohere like a living organism, since the literary artist is
analogous to the demiurge and creates a microcosm of reality through the
use of symbols. The commentator's function is to discern the artist's
unifying intention, or *skopos*. Clearly this is the same usage as we find in

Theodore. Theodore certainly did not get his idea of the *skopos* of the text from later philosophical commentaries. Neo-platonist and Christian are more likely independently to have taken over what was a technical usage in the schools and each adapted it to their own dogmatic concerns.

19 D. A. Russell, *Criticism in Antiquity*, especially ch.7.

20 See my paper 'Chrysostom on I & II Corinthians' delivered at the 1983 Patristic Conference in Oxford, to be published in *Studia Patristica*.

21 *Commentary on Matthew* Book XI. Text in *GCS*. Origen vol. x, pp. 34ff. Trans. Ante-Nicene Christian Library, additional volume, p. 431ff.

22 *Homilies on Matthew* xlix. Text in Migne, *PG* 58.495ff. Trans. *NPNF*, Series 1, vol. x, pp. 303ff.

23 Migne, *PG* 18.613–73. The remark quoted is from J. Quasten, *Patrology*, vol. 3, p. 303. Rowan Greer, *The Captain of our Salvation* recognizes the true nature of this work.

24 *Gregory of Nazianus, Rhetor and Philosopher*.

25 *Menander Rhetor* (See above, n. 5). A number of doctoral theses on the influence of the Second Sophistic on various Greek Fathers have been published by the Catholic University of America, Washington D.C. For the influence of rhetorical forms on the Cappadocians, see also R. C. Gregg, *Consolation Philosophy*, Patristic Monograph Series no. 3. Cambridge, Mass. 1975.

Pelagianism in the East

LIONEL WICKHAM

Church councils at any level are improbable organs of the Holy Ghost, subject, as they are, to the same failings and mischances as beset annual general meetings of amateur dramatic societies, the proceedings of Faculty Boards and even more august assemblies. They are composed of the few who speak much, and the many who sit silent save when roused to chorus approval or outrage. When they meet, some members will turn up late; most will have only an imperfect understanding of the business; and none will remember what they collectively did at the meeting, till the minutes are later circulated. Indeed 'remember' is too strong a word, since the chairman and secretary will have drawn up the record and decreed a corporate memory of what was said and done.

The Council of Ephesus (AD 431) is an excellent example of the genus at its worst. It was, effectively, run by the bishop of Alexandria, Cyril, in the absence of a substantial portion of the membership which turned up late and set up its own assembly; the Roman delegates, whose presence validated Cyril's assembly as the genuine Ecumenical Council, were only very badly informed about the question of Nestorius which was the main business; and the subsequent accounts of the proceedings were, at least partly, edited by Cyril who veiled, so far as he could, some damaging items. So, did the Council actually condemn 'Pelagianism' (as it is usually said to have done)[1] and, if it did, did it know what it was doing? In view of the way the Council met and functioned, you might want to return a negative answer to both questions. But at least there are what purport to be a General Synodal Letter decreeing excommunication against those who hold the opinions of Celestius,[2] and a letter to Pope Celestine saying that the minutes of the deposition of Pelagius, Celestius, Julian and four others were read and that the Council upheld 'the validity of the decrees issued by your holiness and are in unanimou accord in holding them as deposed'.[3] Something was, then, pretty certainly done; and there was certainly, too, at least one Greek-speaking bishop (Cyril himself, as we shall see) who had thought about the issues. The casualness of the condemnation, though, makes it clear that the council under Cyril did not debate 'Pelagianism' in detail. It condemned, surely, because Cyril and the Roman delegates insisted it should; and it acted in the way that a church council usually will: the majority following the persuasive voices which urged something like 'the need for a show of solidarity with our Western brethren in expelling the evil errors of Celestius'.[4] As for the rival assembly under John of Antioch, knowledge at first hand was more widely spread amongst them, since Celestius and Julian had thrown themselves upon the mercies of leading churchmen, including Nestorius, in that group, and he had shown them some favours. But their malicious report that Cyril and his party had admitted to communion lawfully excommunicated Euchites (Messalians) who held the same views as Celestius and Pelagius,[5] showed they were prepared to recognize 'Pelagianism' as an error, odious to Rome, of course, but odious in itself. If they had been required to 'gratify the West' with a public gesture of condemnation there is little doubt that they would have done so.[6]

What, then, was the 'Pelagianism' the Greeks were prepared to condemn and how far was that condemnation real and not simply a genuflexion towards Rome? Did contact with 'Pelagianism' produce any changes of attitude? And is there any connection between 'Pelagianism' and 'Nestorianism'? Before I attempt answers, some disclaimers are in order: I bring forward no evidence not found in ordinary printed texts; I shall not attempt a connected narrative; and I will not look at any antecedents of 'Pelagianism' or say anything about Rufinus the Syrian, who might have inspired Celestius. For even granted that 'Pelagianism' was an Eastern virus, it returned from the West in a mutated form and it is that form I propose to examine.

To the first question, then: the definition and the understanding of Pelagian error. I look initially at Cyril of Alexandria. What did he know about it when he condemned it, what did he think it was and what did he really care about it?

There is, so far as I can see, no record that Cyril publicly disowned Pelagianism *expressis verbis* before the onset of the Nestorian controversy. His first explicit statement is given in a *diamarturia* recorded in the minutes of the session of the Council of Ephesus, (Friday) 17 July 431.[7] Here he makes an avowal of personal orthodoxy, unusual for him, anathematizing Apollinarius, Arius, Eunomius, Macedonius, Sabellius,

Photinus, Paul, Manichaeus, Nestorius and his associates and those who held the views of Celestius or Pelagius. The first name was the most important to his audience, for everybody knew he was accused of being Apollinarian. The last two names might well have surprised, for, so far as I know, he had not shown much concern about the matter before. At any rate I have not found anything in his writings prior to the council. You might well imagine that Cyril only became aware that he had been an anti-Pelagian all along when he realized that the pope, Celestine, had not recovered from a traumatizing experience of his earlier years: he had been suspected of favouring the losing side when imperial authority took Zosimus by the scruff of his neck and forced him to retract his papal acquittal of Celestius. Celestine could be easily roused on the matter. That was all that Cyril knew or cared.

That can only be partly true. For Cyril was well-informed, certainly about the issues in the phase of the controversy before the entry of Julian into it. We know, in the first place, that Cyril, whatever may have been his knowledge about Celestius' condemnation in Carthage in 412 (before he came to the throne, in any case) was aware of Pelagius' acquittal at the Synod of Diospolis (415) soon after it took place and hence of the origin of the controversy. We know this now from the newly published *Epistle 4**[8] of Augustine to Cyril, to be dated after the publication of Augustine's *De gestis Pelagii* early 417. In this letter Augustine writes (§2): 'Your Sincerity will recall, I think, that you sent us the ecclesiastical proceedings in the province of Palestine, at which Pelagius, deemed a Catholic, was acquitted, when he took cover in a cunning den of words and deceived our brothers, the presiding bishops, in the absence of an opponent from the other side to rebut him.' From these lines, coupled with the general tone of the first paragraph, we may gather that Augustine was writing a full letter only for the first time to Cyril. Why Augustine should have got his copy of the *Acta* of the Synod of Diospolis from Cyril we are not told. We could guess (but it would only be a guess) that Pelagius was now in Egypt, had got the ear of Cyril and put him up to it to embarrass Augustine. Busy bishops do not necessarily read the documents that pass through their hands, especially one like Cyril, deeply troubled by his diocese and its discords. But I cannot believe that Cyril had not noted the contents of the *acta*, and, if so, he was aware of the substance of the dispute. Augustine goes on, in *Epistle 4**, to speak of the reply he had written to the Synod of Diospolis in his *De gestis Pelagii*, summarizing the case he put there and elsewhere with such assiduity that it came to be the standard judgment on that assembly: Pelagius pulled the wool over the eyes of his accusers and was acquitted because his own views were deliberately dissembled and the prosecution case ineffectively made. A copy of the *De gestis Pelagii*, we are told, has been in circulation in Alexandria at the hands of Justus, the bearer of the letter. The *De gestis Pelagii* has given offence to certain parties because of the passage where Augustine argues that not all sinners are punished by eternal fire. Augustine makes clear the reason for the claim: it is directed against the Pelagian assertion that a sinless life is possible and that therefore in the after-life no hope is left for those who are conscious of daily sin and the daily need for forgiveness. Justus has been accused of tampering with Augustine's words and has brought his copy to Augustine to inspect. He is returning with Augustine's confirmation of the correctness of the copy and Cyril is invited to protect Justus against the accusation of forgery and to take appropriate measures against two unnamed Latins who, Augustine suspects, are Pelagians and who may be lurking amongst Greeks, where their errors are less clearly understood, and may escape detection and rebuttal.

Cyril did not, I think, take Augustine's over-bold advice. Why, after all, should he interfere with the verdict of a local council he had nothing to do with? Some objectionable propositions had been put forward purporting to be Pelagius' views, but he had denied them to the satisfaction of his judges. Moreover, Pelagius had managed to make the charge of Origenism stick on those who had objected to his view of an equality of punishment for all sinners. The prosecution case looked weak and there was something suspicious about the text of Augustine's book, never mind its arguments. It would have been quite improper to take any measures against Pelagians in Egypt on such a flimsy basis.

Augustine did not leave Cyril alone. He wrote again. The letter has not survived, but Julian refers to it and reveals, incidentally, that Cyril may very well have known Jerome's *Dialogues against the Pelagians* (a work I shall be referring to again in connection with Theodore of Mopsuestia). Julian writes: 'On the subject of this book [of Jerome] you boast in the letter you addressed to Alexandria that Pelagius, overcome by the weight of Scripture, was unable to establish free will. But a stop was put to that book by the Catholic man who had been attacked.'[9] The 'Catholic man' is, of course, Pelagius and the stop put to Jerome's work was Pelagius' *De libero arbitrio*. The implication of these lines seems to be that Cyril knew Jerome's book and Pelagius' reply and, furthermore, that he found Pelagius' words more to his taste than Jerome's.

So when in 418 Zosimus sang his notorious palinode, routed by the state and the African church, and despatched his *Epistula tractoria*,[10] condemning Pelagius and Celestius, to Egypt, Constantinople, Thessalonica, Jerusalem and elsewhere,[11] Cyril will have known from a variety of sources what the issues were. His attitude to the pope's letter was lukewarm. We find a certain Eusebius writing to reprove him for sitting on the fence and continuing to harbour Pelagians: 'Why at this present time, though Innocent of blessed memory condemned the Pelagian and Celestian heresy along with its heads, and all the Easterns exclude them, is the church of Alexandria alone in accepting them into communion, Alexandria which uniquely and first amongst its conprovincials should have rejected such people?'[12] Eusebius goes on to complain that, as he had informed Cyril in a letter of a year before, a certain Valerian,[13] who is a standard-bearer and ally of Pelagians, has found leisure in Alexandria to propagate his views. This belly-talker (*ventrilocus*) and gormandizer is no free man, but a slave of the count Valerius and ought to be returned to his owner;[14] only respect for Cyril kept Eusebius from making this request before. Perhaps this Valerian was one of the two Pelagian suspects mentioned by Augustine. The date of Eusebius' letter is not quite clear, but I think it is best placed in the spring of 419 and the earlier letter to which he refers in 418. Plainly, then, Cyril was slow to disengage himself from Pelagians, even after the Roman denunciation. It was a tricky matter. A few intelligent, and probably useful, refugees had turned up (I suggest) and promised not to be a nuisance and to keep quiet. The arguments against them did not look strong and different courts had given different verdicts on them. The *Epistula tractoria* made a great difference, of course. No more Pelagians would be allowed to feel at home in his diocese (the exiled Julian did not go to Egypt) but those already there were not to be harassed. Something like that, I suggest, is what happened.

A decade later, Cyril was no longer on the fence. He certainly used 'Pelagianism' as a means of stirring up Celestine against Nestorius and during the controversy was moved to write some lines on his attitude to Pelagianism in a letter to Theodosius, the emperor. They are summarized by Photius (*Bibliotheca* 54).[15] Cyril identifies Nestorianism and Celestianism: Celestians ascribe the salvation of Christians not to God the Holy Ghost who gives faith and all that leads to life, true religion and salvation, to each individual as he wills, but to man's fallen nature, alienated from God and doomed to death, which by its own choice invites or repels the Holy Ghost; Nestorians similarly ascribe man's salvation to his own act and make of Christ not the Son of God born of Mary but one who was united by his choice to the eternal Son whose name he shares in a metaphorical sense. This is not much, of course, and I surmise that Photius saw not a whole letter of Cyril dealing with the relation of Nestorianism and Pelagianism, but only a *testimonium*. But at least it shows that Cyril had made up his mind about what the issues were and where he stood.

These lines, this *testimonium*, are the sole remains of any explicit rejoinder to Pelagianism. But there is a hint of Pelagian issues (without mention of names) in the two sets of answers Cyril gave on different occasions after 432 to a group of Palestinian monks led by Tiberius, the *Answers to Tiberius* and the *Doctrinal Questions and Answers*. Questions about the possibility of a life without concupiscence and the sinlessness of Christ,[16] on the relation of our sin to Adam's and its remission in baptism[17] (a peculiarly Pelagian-sounding question this) were raised and suggest to me souls troubled by some of the Pelagian arguments. More than that one cannot say, since the majority of the questions are quite unconnected with that controversy. I will not detail Cyril's answers. It is enough to say that: a life without concupiscence is impossible; Christ did not sin and it is a foolish question to ask if he *could* have sinned; Adam's guilt belonged to him alone but his death, which was his punishment, he transmitted to his successors. On other points relevant to the Pelagian controversy, he asserts (as usual) the absolute freedom of the will and the necessity of God's help to fulfil the good. It goes without saying that we are here a long way removed from the controversial positions of Augustine or even Jerome. But I would submit that they are the responses of a man, who, as we have seen, was well acquainted with the Pelagian question; who knew that it was about divine help and human incapacity; about the damage done to human nature by Adam's transgression; about sexuality and the possibility of sinlessness. He thought of Pelagianism as a twin of Nestorianism, in that it viewed grace as superfluous and salvation as a matter of man's choice. He sincerely condemned the views that Adam's death was not a punishment for sin and affected only himself (the first and second of the items in Zosimus' list) and that just as Adam's fall did not bring universal death so Christ's resurrection does not bring universal resurrection (the fifth in that list). On the other items (the state of the new-born children and the fate of unbaptized children), I suspect his assent to the *Tractoria*, and so his official condemnation, to be more notional than real.

What reception had been given further East, and in particular at

Constantinople, to Pelagianism? The new *Epistle 6*[*18] of Augustine to
Atticus sheds a bit more light on that subject. The date of the letter is
not entirely plain, but it connects so closely with the fresh issues which
were to emerge in the controversy with Julian's entry into the debate
and Augustine's publication of *De nuptiis et concupiscentia* in 419/420 that
a date about then is required. What is new is the emphasis of the debate
upon concupiscence and the mode of inheritance from Adam and it is on
these themes that Augustine writes. Atticus has 'acted with a pastor's
care, so that the crookedness of certain Pelagians might be straightened
and their cunning guarded against'. So we may assume that the Western
condemnation of Pelagianism holds good in Constantinople. The
burden of Augustine's letter is that his views are being misrepresented
by Pelagians who are saying that he vilifies marriage and sexual relations
by recognizing concupiscence as inherently evil. Atticus is given an
exposition of sexual relations as they might ideally be and as they
actually are, and is invited to distinguish (as Pelagians do not) between
the properly controlled desire which exists in marriage and the
indiscriminate desire of the flesh. How well this distinction, and indeed
the whole letter, went down with Atticus we do not know. I would
suggest that this long and complicated letter would do nothing for
Augustine's cause and was more likely to raise doubts than to assuage
them. Atticus is not given the sorts of argument he needs to deal with
contumacious Pelagians – something hard-hitting with plenty of biblical
quotations.[19] At any rate, I think we may deduce from the letter that the
Pelagian case is beginning to have an effect in the Eastern capital, despite
repressive measures from the bishop.

Away from the capital, Julian's polemic found a ready listener in
Theodore of Mopsuestia, with whom Julian took refuge. Theodore
eventually disowned Julian but not before he had written a work against
certain Western theologians who 'say that men sin not by will but by
nature'. The leader of the party attacked by Theodore was Jerome
('Aram' he is called by Theodore) of whom Theodore gives a
slanderous, but true, account: as a Westerner who had gone to live in
the East and had composed books about the new heresy which he had
despatched to his native country; as one who claimed to have found a
fifth gospel in the library of Eusebius of Palestine; who had rejected the
translation of the New and Old Testaments and composed a new one,
though his qualifications in Hebrew did not come from speaking it
naturally but by having learned it from a low-born native speaker. The
reference to Jerome's fifth gospel fits so well with Jerome's *Against the*

Pelagians III. 2 that it must be very likely that Theodore had read the book. But Jerome was perhaps not the only target for Theodore. The compiler of the collection in which fragments of this work of Theodore's seem to be preserved says it was directed against *Augustine*,[20] and the five points of heresy that Theodore (according to Photius' *Bibliotheca*, 177) attacked, though they can be found in Jerome, sound especially characteristic of Augustine as strained through Julian's sieve. Moreover, Theodore writes:

But the extraordinary proponent of original sin could see none of these points because he had never been trained in the divine Scriptures or 'learned', as blessed Paul says, 'the sacred writings from infancy', but making frequent utterance whether on the meaning of scripture or on doctrine he has often and shamelessly exhibited to large numbers many particular or general ineptitudes on the subject of the scriptures themselves and [their] teachings. For fear of [his] power permitted nobody to contradict him but those who had knowledge disparaged him in silence only.[21]

That, I should suggest, fits Augustine better than Jerome. However that may be (and why should he not have attacked both?), the five points of heresy are: (1) that men sin by nature not by will, and by nature is meant the fallen nature of man; (2) that infants are sinful and (3) this is proved by their baptism and admission to the eucharist; (4) that not even Christ our God was free from sin since he took fallen nature; (5) that sexual relations are the works of men's evil nature. The fragments of Theodore's work preserved in the *Collectio Palatina* do not deal with any of these five points, except tangentially with (4), so we do not know how he resolved them in his book. Importantly though, they do show him arguing in favour of the view that Adam was created mortal – the old point urged against Celestius and condemned in the *Tractoria* – and trenchantly repudiating the idea of death as a punishment for sin; he speaks, too, of the righteous of the Old Testament and of future punishment as purgative and finite. The most revered theologian of the Eastern Greeks, then, accepted the main features of Julian's case and took no notice of the condemnation of Pelagianism by the West.

Theodore died in 428 and some time in his last years, and after Julian's departure, he was moved to condemn Julian's doctrines at a synod. We do not know why or in what terms. That same year his pupil, Nestorius, ascended the throne of Constantinople. He was promptly approached by the group of Pelagian exiles headed by Julian and Florus, and including Celestius, who hoped for his help to re-establish their cause. Nestorius encouraged them. He wrote a sympathetic letter to

Celestius. 'Do not take it ill, respected [friend] (*venerabilis*)', he writes,

that you are bearing assaults greater than men ought to bear, especially when they defend the truth and shun the communion of the defiled and polluted, because to the saints too who lived before our era, tribulations were pleasing...Do not betray the truth by lapsing from it. Since both the letters of the council sent to the bishops of the West and to the bishop of Alexandria and the replies to many thoughtful men of the same orthodox persuasion have made clear to you our view. For it may be with the Lord's help, that something productive of right faith will appear for the Church. We greet the whole brotherhood.

The letter ends: 'And in another hand: safe and sound, strong in heart and interceding greatly on our behalf, may you be given to us, most devout brother.'[22] From the postscript it is clear that Nestorius is expecting a visit from Celestius, and from the main text that he has been writing round for him. The advocacy, though, was unavailing, and in 429 first Julian and his associates and then Celestius were expelled from Constantinople by decree of Theodosius. Nestorius, then, having failed, abandoned the cause.

Formally Nestorius condemned Pelagianism and was sound on the subject of original sin. So Celestine's clearly nervous response to Nestorius affirms. But is that the truth? Marius Mercator, who takes the credit for securing the rout of the Pelagians in Constantinople,[23] quotes some sermons by Nestorius directed, according to him, against the heresy and proving Nestorius' orthodoxy. The first, he says, was delivered in the presence of Julian and his associates in Constantinople.[24] It is for a feast,[25] the time for baptism is approaching and the candidates are told (in a surely very odd way) not to die before baptism lest they lose its benefits and are submerged by the evils attendant upon Adam, taking away with themselves the sentence of punishment pronounced against (human) nature. This sentence of punishment is apparently not death itself, but the ills attendant upon the present human condition. Though marriage is good in itself, the anxieties of conception and the pains of labour (from which the Blessed Virgin Mary was free) are the consequence of the divine curse. So are the toils of extracting a living from the soil. Christ's birth annihilates the curse in both its aspects; how, he does not say. The style of argument is close to Theodore, and Julian, listening in the congregation, will surely have warmed to the declaration on marriage – nothing about the evils of concupiscence. It is not obviously anti-Pelagian. Extracts from other sermons on Christ's temptations are more easily interpreted in that direction. There we read that human nature became mortal as a result of sin and the devil's machinations, in two aspects, physical and spiritual: loss of physical life, loss of knowledge.[26] Nestorius pursues the Irenaean theme of Christ's reversal of Adam's sin by his obedience in temptation. Human nature, having Adam as its foundation, collapsed along with its foundation and came under the devil's sway. The devil held out Adam's sin as a note of hand, but Christ strove for the nullification of the debt in his sinless flesh. By Christ's resurrection what is mortal is re-created and restored, free now from the devil's power. There is nothing about the need for grace, but Nestorius clearly does not teach that man was made mortal from the beginning or that Adam's sin affected only himself. Two prominent Pelagian theses are denied and the solidarity of mankind in Adam asserted. If Celestine knew these passages, as he probably did, he could not complain that Nestorius was a Pelagian.

And in truth he was not. For his Christological 'dualism' is determined by his sense of Christ's solidarity with us. It comes out clearly in a couple of other sermon passages. In his sermon for Friday 12 December 430,[27] he interprets Christ's being made a curse for us as Christ taking upon himself the whole curse owed by us: all the punishment due to us he bore in his guiltless flesh. In the other sermon he uses the curious image of our sinful nature pleading the sinless Christ in its cause against the devil.[28] He distinguishes the two perfect natures in Christ just because our own nature, which is to be redeemed, is under the curse of Adam. And that being so his rejection of the main plank of Pelagianism is as real as Cyril's. It may well be that he approved of certain features in the Pelagian critique of Augustine (its rejection of Manichaeism in any form he will certainly have applauded); he betrays no sympathy for notions of inherited guilt and says little of continuous divine grace; he certainly did not follow Augustine on the subject of concupiscence. But he was sound on original sin: we are involved in Adam's condemnation as we are liberated by Christ's incarnation and saving work. In this way, I suggest, Nestorius' rejection of Pelagianism will have been typical of the general rejection of it amongst his friends and supporters at Ephesus in 431. It was perhaps a narrower rejection than Cyril's; it had more overt sympathy with aspects of Pelagianism outside the limits of what it rejected, but the rejection was genuine. Nobody simply followed Rome's lead without examination or irresponsibly.

At the beginning of this essay I raised three questions. I have attempted to answer the first: the content of what was condemned by Greeks generally by 431. Let me turn briefly to the other two. First, did contact with Pelagianism produce any changes of attitude? The explosion was small and far less momentous for Greeks than the Christological question which engaged them, but some fall-out, at least, might have been expected. I have found very little beyond the queries addressed to Cyril, mentioned above. It may be that a few striking affirmations of man's solidarity with Adam's fall by the celebrated preacher at Jerusalem in the early decades of the fifth century, Hesychius, reflect concern with the controversy.[29] He belongs to a milieu where that is to be expected. It may be, too, that in the dialogue which appears in Nestorius' *Liber Heraclidis* and is most plausibly taken, I believe, to come from some other hand, there are indications of someone who has attended to Julian's critique: the author tells of a Christ who has assumed a fallen nature like ours, capable of sin and subject to all men's natural passions including concupiscence; the saints fight against the devil like Christ and apparently with the same degree of success; divine grace figures little and it is an effortful, active view of the spiritual life which predominates.[30] Amongst the Eastern Greeks a sort of 'Pelagianism' may have continued to allure. But the conclusion that I at present draw is that neither 'Pelagianism' nor its disavowal had any obvious or enduring effects in the East. When the mind of the Eastern church was directed to issues germane to the Pelagian controversy (the nature of fallen man, of the finite to the infinite will, and the consciousness of Christ), as it was in the controversy between Severus of Antioch and Julian of Halicarnassus in the sixth century, and in later monothelete and agnoete controversies, the issues were raised and resolved in ways which had nothing to do with Pelagian controversy.

To my last question: is there any connection between 'Pelagianism' and 'Nestorianism'? The connection was proposed by Cyril (as we have seen) and in different ways by Cassian and Prosper.[31] There is Charles Gore's dictum, too: 'The Nestorian Christ is the fitting saviour of the Pelagian man'.[32] It would be foolish to reject these testimonies to an apparent connection of ideas out of hand. Cyril was surely quite right to say in effect that if Christians are like runners in a race who merely need encouragement in order to run successfully, then it is logical to think that Christ is just the front-runner showing the way for the rest. Furthermore, you might allow that Pelagius' picture of Christ emphasizes the distinction of natures in him and that Nestorius seems to stress man's efforts to achieve virtue. There is, for sure, the historical connection between Theodore and Julian, Celestius and Nestorius. And, finally, it is a striking coincidence that Pelagianism and Nestorianism appear at the same time, too striking to allow the phenomena to be unrelated. Must we not look for a link or a common source: a Pelagio-Nestorianism traceable to Origen (who else?), who somehow produced the conditions which gave rise to the two kindred patterns of ideas? Are Pelagianism and Nestorianism akin because both Pelagius and Nestorius were ascetics, keen on effort, impatient of the need for grace in ordinary Christians?

I would allow these considerations some weight and nothing in this essay forbids, as it were, the attempt to answer those questions I have just put so rhetorically. Yet I would suggest it makes no sense to pursue them by the method of historical investigation. At the level of ideas abstracted from the minds that speak them there may be a connection between 'Pelagianism' and 'Nestorianism'. But in life Nestorius and the Eastern Greeks rejected the Pelagianism they were confronted with. They did it a bit grudgingly to start with. But then so did Cyril of Alexandria. We do not know what Celestius made of Cyril's *Third Letter* to Nestorius with its anathematisms. No doubt he would have thought it replete with blasphemy, but so would the then Archdeacon Leo if he had read it, and he was not a Pelagian. If Nestorius was, in some sense, as a pupil of Theodore, anti-Augustinian, Cyril was certainly not an Augustinian. And so one can go on, raising insuperable objections to an analysis which would link the phenomena historically. Perhaps one might put it another way: the thinkers church historians write about are neither as logical, as truthful or as edifying in their morals as the devout usually expect. And that is a truth that Dr Chadwick has taught wisely, wittily and with warm humanity over many years and in many books. I am deeply grateful for the lesson.

NOTES

1 H. Denzinger, *Enchiridion Symbolorum Definitionum et Declarationum de Rebus Fidei et Morum*, 36th edn by A. Schönmetzer, SJ, Freiburg, i. Br. 1976, pp. 267–8, quoting the General Synodal Letter, mentioned below, under the heading *Condemnatio Pelagianismi*.

2 *ACO* 1.1.3 pp. 26ff., especially p. 27. See Schwartz' *Praefatio* for a note on these so-called 'canons' of the Council. It is a General Letter addressed to 'bishops, priests, deacons and all the laity of each province', and denounces thirty-four bishops (beginning with John of Antioch) who represent the

opinions of Nestorius and Celestius, and proceeds to appoint penalties against Celestians.

3 *ACO* 1.1.3 p. 9. There is no record in the minutes of the council of this having taken place. The 'minutes of the deposition of Pelagius etc.' and the 'decrees issued by your holiness' would presumably be Zosimus' *acta* of 418 (so Schwartz, *ACO* 1.1.8 p. 10, lines 3ff). But how vague the whole thing is!

4 Care is taken to smear the rival body with the tar-brush of Pelagianism. Cf. the Council's report to Theodosius, *ACO* 1.1.3 p. 12: John of Antioch is left with approximately thirty-seven supporters *of whom some are Pelagians* (line 5).

5 *ACO* 1.1.3 p. 42. The alleged connection of 'Messalianism' (for the sources see Kmosko's Introduction to the *Liber graduum* in *PS* III) and 'Pelagianism' lies, presumably, in the common emphasis on human effort to attain serenity and perfection of life. The same connection is made by Jerome in the Prologue to *Against the Pelagians* (*ad init.*).

6 I filch a phrase from Dr Chadwick's *The Early Church*, p. 198.

7 *ACO* 1.1.3 p. 22.

8 Edited by J. Divjak, *CSEL* 1981.

9 As quoted by Augustine in *Opus imperfectum contra Julianum*, PL 44 col. 1389.

10 The fragments are conveniently collected in Otto Wermelinger's *Rom und Pelagius* (vol. 7 in the series *Päpste und Päpsttum*), Stuttgart 1975, pp. 307f.

11 *ACO* 1.5 p. 67 (Marius Mercator, *commonitorium super nomine Caelestii*).

12 *collectio Avellana*, edited by O. Günther, *CSEL* 35, pp. 113–15.

13 Wermelinger, *Rom und Pelagius*, p. 251, note 178, says that he was accepted by Cyril into the ranks of the clergy. But the passage does not necessarily mean that.

14 The distinguished addressee of Augustine's *de nuptiis et concupiscentia*, and instrumental in securing Celestius' condemnation in Rome.

15 It [that is, the copy of some Western *acta* against Nestorianism] uses Cyril as a witness [to the identity of Nestorianism and Celestianism], writing to the emperor Theodosius that the Nestorian heresy is identical with the Celestian. Clearly, he says, for Celestians make bold to claim of the body or members of Christ (that is, the Church) that it is not God (that is, the Holy Ghost), who imparts to each individually their faith and all that pertains to life, true religion and salvation, as he wills, but that it is the subordinated nature of man, fallen from bliss, sundered from God by transgression and sin, committed to death, this nature it is that according to the merit of its choice invites or repels the Holy Ghost. Nestorians, on the other hand, have the same outrageous opinion about the body's head, Christ. They say that since Christ is of our nature, God wills that all men should be saved in the same way, should correct their fault by their own choice and make themselves worthy of him; and so it is not the Word which was born but the one born of Mary who

through the merit of his natural choice had the Word accompanying him, sharing the condition of sonship only in dignity and in a common name with the Word. Cf. also M. Aubineau's important review of Henry's edition in *Revue de Philologie* 93 (1967), 232ff. (I owe the reference to Wermelinger's fine book, *Rom und Pelagius*.)

16 *Answers to Tiberius*, nos. 12f.

17 *Doctrinal Questions and Answers*, no. 6.

18 Edited by J. Divjak, *CSEL* 1981.

19 Augustine ends with an apology: 'Pardon me for burdening your sainted feelings by the prolixity of my letter. I intended to rebut their misrepresentations to you, not to make you more of a scholar.' He perceived that it might all sound too much like a lecture, which it does: a good, but strenuous and over-subtle treatment of the points. I would invite the reader to test this by a look at the long paragraph 7, for example.

20 *ACO* 1.5 p. 173.

21 *ACO* 1.5 p. 174, lines 27ff.

22 *ACO* 1.5 p. 65.

23 *ACO* 1.5 p. 65.

24 *ACO* 1.5 p. 60.

25 Probably Lady Day.

26 *Collectio Palatina* nos. 32–4. *ACO* 1.5 pp. 62–5.

27 *Collectio Palatina* 23. *ACO* 1.5, pp. 39–45.

28 *Collectio Palatina* 21. *ACO* pp. 31–7.

29 Edited and translated by M. Aubineau, *Les Homélies Festales d'Hésychius de Jérusalem*, subsidia Hagiographica. Société des Bollandistes, Brussels, no. 59, 1978/9, Homilies I, 7:14ff. and VII, 4:1–5. Cf. the observations on p. LXXI.

30 In the translation by F. Nau, *Le Livre d'Héraclide de Damas*, Paris, 1910, especially pp. 59ff.

31 See Cassian, *De incarnatione Christi* II, 3–5 (*PL* 50, cols 20ff.); Prosper (in an ironical poem) *PL* 31, col. 153.

32 In 'Our Lord's Human Example', *Church Quarterly Review*, 16 (1883), 98.

The legacy of Pelagius: orthodoxy, heresy and conciliation

R. A. MARKUS

Two images of heresy and orthodoxy prevailed in Christian antiquity. One had been canonized by Eusebius and was generally accepted until the seventeenth century, that orthodoxy is primary and heresies are deviations, corruptions of a previously pure, virgin orthodoxy. Its echo is distinctly audible in the edict issued by the court of Ravenna in 418 condemning the teaching of Pelagius, Celestius and their followers: they were confounding the 'light of catholic simplicity shining forth with permanent radiance'.[1] This image represented orthodoxy as a given constant: a rock buffeted by the waves, the light of the sun hidden by the clouds. Held often alongside it, there is another, equally common, belief with an even more venerable ancestry (1 Corinthians 11:19): that heresy serves to bring orthodoxy to light.[2] Compared with the first model, this treats heresy as creative: orthodoxy is the product of faithful response to heresy. Both models invite us to see the conflict of heresy and orthodoxy in the perspective imposed on it by the 'orthodox'. The besetting temptation for any historian is to take the past at the valuation of those who emerged as the victors; and nowhere more so than in the study of what councils, theologians and ecclesiastical historians have come to label as 'heresy' and 'orthodoxy'. What is 'heresy', what is 'orthodoxy', and what constitutes 'progress', are all determined by the victors, that is to say by those who were, by their own definition, the 'orthodox'. Not until our own century has this version of ecclesiastical whiggery been seriously questioned.[3] The historian's task – especially in an investigation of the evolution of orthodoxy – must begin with divesting himself of the perspective imposed on the past by the victors, to enter the perspective of the defeated.

Henry Chadwick has taught us, among many other things, the delicacy of the task of peeling away the accumulated overlay of 'heresy' which has come to cling to some of the defeated in the conflicts of the early church, such as, for instance, Priscillian of Avila. The views Priscillian was accused of holding had long been condemned by all right-thinking Christians and by the laws of the emperors. The case of Pelagius and his followers in the second decade of the fifth century was different. They were not branded as 'heretics' for rejecting an established and recognized 'orthodoxy'. They were breaking rules not yet made. The orthodoxy they were thought to have offended was only defined in the course of the conflict with the African church between 411 and 418. Until then, 'orthodoxy' and 'heresy' were indistinct, conflicting doctrinal traditions upheld by the North African church on the one side, and by a group of theologians, mainly Italian, who could count on a good deal of sympathy outside North Africa, on the other. What crystallized from this conflict was not only a new 'heresy': it was also a new 'orthodoxy'.

The orthodoxy of Augustine and his African colleagues certainly seemed a novelty to Pelagius's followers, such as the Italian bishop, Julian of Eclanum.[4] In his eyes, the doctrines he and his friends affirmed and which the government condemned in 418, were the received orthodoxy of the church. The North African orthodoxy was not that of the Italian church. Opinion in Italy was more divided, orthodoxy and heresy less sharply distinct. In 418 a number of Italian bishops, Julian among them, went into exile rather than comply with the government's edict. More than ten years later, Julian and the deposed bishops who had remained faithful to him were 'complaining tearfully' that they were being subjected to persecution 'as orthodox, in orthodox times'.[5] Only official pressure could secure the consent of the Italian episcopate. A pagan prefect of the city was threatened with the death penalty if he failed to put an end to the dissensions within the Christian community in Rome by delaying the expulsion of Celestius from the city.[6] In Gaul, too, the government – or was it the personal piety of the Empress Galla Placidia, just re-established in Italy? – felt it necessary in 425 to instruct the praetorian prefect to get Patroclus, the metropolitan bishop of Arles, to secure professions of orthodoxy from his fellow bishops, many evidently reluctant, on pain of deposition and banishment.[7] Even so, Prosper, who tried to give Augustine's late and extreme views on predestination a foothold in Gaul, feared a recrudescence of the heresy under new disguises.[8] Britain is a shadowy land at this time, where the emperor's writ had ceased to run. What little evidence there is for the state of public opinion in the island does not, however, suggest that Augustinianism met a readier reception here than on the European continent.[9]

The Eastern churches were scarcely touched by the controversy. True, the origins of Pelagian theology had been shaped by an obscure Syrian residing in Rome at the same time as Pelagius,[10] and both Pelagius and Celestius had been exonerated from the charge of heresy by a synod in Palestine. This does not, however, mean that Pelagius' teaching expressed the orthodoxy of the Eastern churches. In the 420s the Eastern churches stood aside from the controversies around the teaching of Pelagius, Celestius, Julian and Augustine. The theology deployed by Augustine and his African fellow-bishops was at least as foreign to them as was that of their opponents. Although two patriarchs of Constantinople appear to have complied with Western wishes, Nestorius gave shelter to the bishops exiled by the government of Ravenna after the proscription of the teaching of Pelagius and Celestius in 418. Marius Mercator, in his history of the conflict, remarked, of the favour shown by Nestorius towards the heretics, that 'whether he did this from malice or from folly, it is hard to know'; and he was careful to dissociate Nestorius – who had troubles enough with his own heresy – from the views of Celestius and Julian of Eclanum, on which matters, he says, Nestorius 'thought and taught correctly'.[11] Nowhere is the distance between the Roman concern about the questions at issue and the Constantinopolitan incomprehension more apparent than in the exchange of letters on the matter between Pope Celestine and the patriarch, Nestorius.[12] It does seem that Pelagian teaching was condemned at Ephesus; but the matter was clearly a side-issue, mentioned to cater for Western susceptibilities, but – despite Julian of Eclanum's attempt to rally some support – of insufficient interest to most of the participants to leave more than a trace in the council's Acts.[13] The conflict which divided the Western church bypassed Eastern Christendom almost entirely.

Such a lack of enthusiasm for the orthodoxy enforced by the court and endorsed by Pope Zosimus gives some substance to Julian's view that the church was being threatened by an African take-over bid. Was the Pelagian controversy another case of conflict between a provincial Christian tradition and the universalism of the imperial church? The widespread lack of enthusiasm for the whole body of North African doctrine reveals how little agreement on the nature of orthodox doctrine could be taken for granted. Another hundred years were to elapse before the point of equilibrium would be found between the extremes represented by the Augustinian theology of the North African church and the Pelagian theology of Julian of Eclanum. It has long been widely agreed that the doctrine on grace defined at the second Council of Orange in 529 fell well short of the full-blooded Augustinian teaching on grace and predestination. The aim of the present study is not to investigate the nature of the orthodoxy which emerged in 529, but, rather, to trace the nature of the process, during the century between Augustine's death and the Council of Orange, which led to that clarification. Two aspects of this process of clarification are of particular interest: the parts played in it by the papacy, and by the churches of the African provinces with their distinctive theological standpoint.

Modern scholars have often been inclined to take Pope Zosimus at the estimate of the African churchmen: as weak and indecisive in the troubled years of 417–18. It seems, rather, that he was seeking to keep a freedom of action for the papacy in face of the African churches. His predecessor, Innocent, had, he thought, perilously compromised this freedom of action. He had been too ready to fall in with peremptory African initiatives in condemning Pelagius and Celestius. Zosimus had to defend himself against African remonstrations that he was going back on his predecessor's endorsement of their views and injuring the accord between themselves and Innocent. Zosimus gave them a firm reminder of the Roman See's authority, and went on to express his reluctance to proceed too fast, without wider discussions in the church. The pope's circumspection was, however, overtaken by the court, acting in response to African lobbying. The pope acted on the principle of joining those he could not beat. In his *Tractoria* (of which only fragments have come down to us) 'he bowed to [the Africans], and in order to dress up better his defeat in the proud garments of grandeur, he took a solemn and categorical stand'. In reality, however, it was 'an African triumph: a real victory in the face of the pontifical procedure, a considerable success in so much as the Roman See now proclaimed against Pelagius and Celestius, without reserve, the faith of Aurelius, Augustine and their episcopal colleagues'.[14]

With the pope coming into line with the African Councils, the solidarity of the Western church now seemed assured. His retreat even assisted – with African help – in raising his see's prestige. There was little hope of *rapprochement* while the struggle continued between the protagonists, the aged Augustine and Julian of Eclanum, on whom the mantle of Pelagius and Celestius had fallen. But by 431 Augustine was dead and many of Julian's supporters had bowed to official pressure and, denouncing their errors, were received into communion.[15] Prosper, assisted by his friend Hilary, continued to keep up the Augustinian pressure in Gaul;[16] but here, too, the temperature of the conflict was falling rapidly in the 430s. In 431 or 432 Prosper and Hilary visited Rome, with a view to enlisting the pope's support against Cassian and other Gallic detractors of Augustine. At this time, however, Cassian's prestige stood high at Rome. Prosper and Hilary could hardly count on the unambiguous support against him that they had been hoping to receive, and the pope's 'evasive' response must have done much to prevent a deep and lasting split between Cassian and Prosper and their partisans.[17] Moreover, whether through the influence of the Roman deacon, later pope, Leo, or for whatever reason, Prosper's own theological opinions mellowed with the passing of the years. Indeed in his late work, *The Calling of All Nations*, he shows a pronounced streak of universalism of a kind which his earlier intransigent stand by the full rigour of Augustine's late views on predestination would have made difficult to express, and which he owed, in all probability, to the influence of Leo.[18]

Prosper had given the credit for the zeal shown by Pope Sixtus in dealing with remnants of Pelagian heresy to his deacon, Leo (*Chronicon*, *ann.* 439, 1336). When Leo succeeded Sixtus in the Roman see, his pontificate certainly saw a flurry of activity against heretics. His efforts to clear Rome and elsewhere of Manichees are well known; and the Manichees continue to turn up in the catalogues of heresies which adorn so many of his sermons, and even letters.[19] From 449, Christological error came to take a dominant part; but Manicheaeism, Arianism and so forth recur in the catalogues of heresies. Pelagianism and its adherents are, by contrast, absent from his sermons and, with one exception, his letters; nor did Leo intervene in the controversies on grace and predestination in Gaul, or anywhere else. Even when preaching on the subject of grace, he does not mention any errors such as those of the Pelagians. The matter had clearly ceased to be topical. The only exception to this unruffled consensus appears to have been in the province of Aquileia. At the beginning of his pontificate Leo received a complaint from the bishop of a neighbouring see about Pelagian heretics among the clergy of Aquileia: their activities within the congregations were unchecked by any concern about their orthodoxy. The pope's correspondence on this matter leaves much entirely obscure, but strongly suggests that the charge of heterodoxy was a by-product of clerical jealousies, apparently kindled by controversial, perhaps irregular, promotions among the local clergy and consequent ill-feeling.[20] At any rate, once Leo dealt with the matter, we hear no more about Pelagianism during his pontificate.

Leo demanded an unambiguous denunciation of heresy from the suspect clergy of Aquileia – 'let there be nothing obscure in their words, let nothing ambiguous be found in them'.[21] Leo, it appears, was content with the denunciations of Pelagius, Celestius and Julian of Eclanum by his predecessors and he was uninterested in theological refinements of a sort around which the debate about grace and predestination had come to revolve since the time of Cassian and Prosper. What a later age would call 'semi-Pelagianism' was of no interest to him, so far as his sermons or letters allow us to see. His own views on these matters are ill-defined. Studies of Leo's views on grace have come to divergent conclusions: some find nothing specifically Augustinian in them, while others have seen his teaching as 'semi-Augustinian', a simpler, more optimistic, more universalistic and less passive version of Augustine's.[22]

Leo's apparent indifference to the finer points at issue between upholders of the Augustinian doctrines and their opponents is in line with the tradition established by his predecessors. There could be no going back on the condemnations of 418. Leo insisted on unambiguous adherence to this, exacted it at Aquileia, and resisted attempts to rehabilitate Julian of Eclanum.[23] But he did not wish to encourage further and, in his view, unnecessary divisions in the church. His reticence in this respect is striking, especially for a pope with such an interest in safeguarding the true belief.

Controversy continued in Gaul, though with Prosper's departure for Rome, probably in or soon after 433, it was continued at a lower pitch of intensity. Treatises were now produced which took up a mediating position between the theology associated with the monastic milieu of Marseilles and the proponents of Augustinian views.[24] Attempts were still being made, as for instance by the author of a pseudo-Augustinian *Hypomnesticon*, to identify adherents of 'semi-Pelagianism' with Pelagianism;[25] but they carried little weight. Prosper made little impact on Lérins.[26] Opponents of the extremer forms of the predestinatarian theology of Augustine's old age were no longer battling against being branded as heretics. Vincent of Lérins, for instance, who (if he can be identified, as he almost certainly can be, with the Vincent whose objections Prosper dealt with in his *Responsiones*) had raised far-reaching objections to Augustinian theses some years earlier, set himself a new task. Though his *Commonitorium* is clearly aimed against 'small Augustinian conventicles',[27] he was not attacking the views of his Augustinian opponents on grace and free-will here, or defending his own. He was now groping for criteria of what should be regarded as falling within the scope of faith, and hence subject to questions about orthodoxy. The application of his criteria would imply that outside the limits of what constituted the universally and traditionally received content of faith, theological discussion could proceed without necessarily raising questions about heresy and orthodoxy. His own old objections to Augustinian views are here quietly bypassed by his central argument: some of Augustine's teaching would simply not pass muster as among the doctrines taught *semper, ubique, ab omnibus*.[28] But they need not be refuted; indeed they are not touched upon – the parody of Augustinian views in the notorious chapter 26 of Vincent's book is deliberately crude, to avoid the risk of bringing Augustinian theology within the scope of the discussion. And that is precisely what Vincent wished to avoid, for the thrust of his argument was that beyond the restricted area of what was universally received as the traditional faith, opinions might be right or they might be wrong; but, inasmuch as they lay outside the area in question, error here need not be heresy. 'Orthodox' was no longer co-extensive with 'true'. Pope Celestine's letter to Gaul was thus (somewhat tendentiously) made to assert Vincent's central principle: 'not that tradition should cease to crush novelty, but that novelty should cease to attack tradition'.[29] This conception of orthodoxy seems to be echoed by the bishops at the Council of Vaison in 442 when they agreed that there was no need to enquire into the views of their colleagues 'for it will suffice if none of them refuse communion to another'. Vincent's view that faith was not directly at stake in the controversy was not new; but his careful essay in defining the scope of faith was a creative, new and important contribution, which could have lifted the debate on to a different level.

But the debate did not continue. From about 440, the time of Pope Leo's intervention at Aquileia, until the pontificates of Felix III and Gelasius I half a century later, and in Gaul – with one exception – until more than thirty years later still, we hear no more about any controversy over the subject which had generated so much heat in the debates between Prosper and his friend Hilary, and their opponents, Cassian, Vincent and the monastic circles of Marseilles and Lérins. It was not for lack of interest in the matter. Rather, it seems, Prosper's attempt to drive a wedge into current ways of thinking about grace had been forgotten. The church in Gaul settled into its accustomed ways as if he had never tried to rally it to the doctrine of 'that illustrious preacher of grace',[30] Augustine. Augustine's prestige and influence had, in fact, always remained high among the theologians of Provence, and for Pelagius they had no more sympathy than had Cassian. Their resistance was to the views Augustine came to formulate in the course of the debate of the last decade of his life. A Gallic chronicler writing soon after 452 could refer with cool impartiality both to the 'insane Pelagius' who tried to stain the churches with his 'execrable teaching', and to the 'heresy of the predestinatarians, which is said to originate with Augustine' (who, as he drily remarks, 'has treated several subjects in innumerable books').[31] At about the same time Salvian is a fine example of a writer whose work resists being drawn into the 'sterile antithesis' of Pelagian or Augustinian;[32] and the biographer of Hilary, the bishop of Arles,[33] could write that had Augustine come after him, he would have been judged his inferior![34] Augustine continued to be read in Provençal intellectual circles. His *Confessions*, especially, served to mould ascetic ideals at Lérins, and disagreement was limited to the specific issues raised in the time of Prosper.[35] The priest Lucidus, whom Faustus of Riez set out to refute (at the request of the bishop of Arles, and with the approval of a council of bishops at Arles and at Lyons) in his *On Grace*, is the only known propounder of 'predestinatarian' doctrines. Avitus of Vienne, who defended the need for grace in a letter to the Burgundian king, was more interested in presenting the Gallic church as united in doctrine than in assessing Faustus' teaching, about which he may, anyway, have been confused or ill informed. His attitude indicates not an exceptional degree of sympathy with predestinatarian teaching, but a shift towards the unity imposed a decade or two later at Orange. Gennadius, whose own position had much in common with Faustus', not only admired him, but clearly had no doubts about his own orthodoxy, which he confidently asked Pope Gelasius to approve.[36] The preaching of Valerianus, bishop of Cimiez, shows strong affinities with the views propounded by Faustus. Some scholars have detected Pelagian leanings in it; but others have stressed its affinities with pre-Pelagian Eastern orthodoxy. It stands in the central Lérins tradition and is significant testimony of the survival of an ancient theological and homiletic tradition untouched by the conflicts of the 420s and 430s.[37] Faustus' teaching on grace and predestination has been described as pre-

Augustinian in character and akin to the doctrine generally current in the Greek church.[38] Something like it was the Gallic church's orthodoxy in the last decades of the fifth century.

Two questions demand an answer: how did this all-but-undisturbed consensus come about during the period between Prosper and Faustus? And how can we account for its swift ending, in the time of Caesarius of Arles and the second Council of Orange in the following generation? We may approach an answer to the first question by considering the state of the Gallic church during this period; for the second, we shall need to look further afield, to Italy, to North Africa and even Constantinople.

One reason for the emergence of a Gallic 'orthodoxy' crystallized on the lines of Cassian's teaching is quite simply the prestige of Lérins. Prosper's initiative never succeeded – despite the general respect for Augustine – in launching an 'Augustinian movement' in Gaul which could take root in more than small isolated communities, whereas the influence of Lérins and Arles was growing. In the insecurity since the end of the fourth century, Lérins became a haven for refugees from all over Gaul, and emerged as a seminary for aristocratic monk-bishops. It was the origin of a great part of the episcopate and of the literature produced in fifth-century Gaul.[39] Moreover, concern about the niceties of the doctrine of grace was unlikely to be acute in a period when most bishops and clergy were preoccupied – if they had any interest in matters of heresy and orthodoxy – with the heresy of the Arian Burgundians and Visigoths on their doorsteps. This problem largely disappeared in the decades after 500, with the conquest of most of Gaul by the Franks and their conversion to Catholicism, followed soon by that of the Burgundian kingdom and the re-entry of the Gallic church into the mainstream of what was left of the intellectual life of Western Christendom. This must be at least part of the answer to our second question.

It has been said that the doctrinal consensus which obtained in Gaul at the end of the fifth century 'could not but provoke a reaction'.[40] But when we turn to Italy, the inevitability of such a reaction is not at all apparent. In the years around 490 the Popes Felix III and Gelasius I gave their attention to Pelagianism, for the first time since Leo's intervention in Aquileia fifty years before. Their attention was drawn to two separate cases, neither in Gaul: the first was in Dalmatia, where some were reported to have been sowing 'revived weeds' of the heresy. They were to be firmly recalled – just like Leo's Aquileians – to the condemnations previously issued by popes and emperors alike. A second letter on the same subject sheds an intriguing sidelight on this case: the pope's intervention was evidently resented in Dalmatia; the suspect clergy, though willing to comply, indignantly professed themselves to have been orthodox all along. To meet this circumstance the pope composed a lengthy statement of the teaching approved by his predecessors.[41] The other case was nearer home: in the province of Picenum a 'miserable old man' called Séneca was reviving the heresy. To judge by Gelasius' exposition of Seneca's three principal errors, he appears to have been a Pelagian of the old stamp, denying original sin, infants' need of baptism and the insufficiency of free-will to attain salvation. The likeliest conjecture is that what we have to do with here is a relic from the age of Julian, rather than a serious and large-scale revival: the feeble autumnal attempts of a 'fly about to die', as the pope thought, to obscure the bright lights of the church's summer, Jerome and Augustine.[42]

The pontificates of Gelasius and his predecessor do, however, seem to be a turning point in the tolerance hitherto shown to views of a semi-Pelagian kind. It was probably at this time and in Rome that a collection of canons on this subject was made; and it rests on an African dossier. Gelasius was anxious to reassure himself of the orthodoxy of more distant bishops.[43] This marks the beginning of a second conversion of the Roman see to the theological standpoint represented by the African church. It would henceforth be more difficult to take a standpoint simultaneously anti-predestinatarian and anti-Pelagian, such as that taken by most of the Gallic writers and the probably Italian writer of *Praedestinatus* (whose admiration for Augustine combined with an attack on his late, predestinatarian, views need not be as disingenuous as is usually believed) and Arnobius the Younger.[44] But it was the next episode in the encounter of Italian with African theological traditions that would be crucial for the future.

This was the result of a combination of circumstances in the course of the theological *rapprochement* between Rome and Constantinople which began in 519. The issues at stake at this time had arisen from the unresolved Christological problems in the wake of Chalcedon. A group of Scythian monks, fanatical champions of orthodoxy intent on hunting down any traces of Nestorianism, did not flinch from creating trouble in Constantinople or in Rome. Grace and predestination were drawn into the debate almost by accident, and, paradoxically, as a result of the intervention of an African bishop, Possessor, living in exile in Constantinople. Possessor had invoked Faustus of Riez against the

Scythian monks. In doing so, he inadvertently alerted them to his dubious orthodoxy on the matter of grace. They put to good use the heresy on grace which they detected here. With a view to rallying support at Rome, the Scythian monks appealed to the African bishops exiled by the Vandal regime to Sardinia. They asked for confirmation of their views 'so that the mouths of those speaking iniquity may be stopped'. They consulted the Africans on two points: the incarnation of the Lord, the central issue under debate; and the grace of Christ, a second issue, the consequence of their recent discovery of Faustus and his heresy, whose potential as a bonus in their struggle they were quick to see and to exploit. They received a reply embracing both subjects. It was the work of one of the African exiles, Augustine's distinguished disciple, Fulgentius of Ruspe. But the Africans were clearly more interested in the secondary issue, to which they devoted more than half of their long letter. Fulgentius' biographer recalled only his reply to the 'brothers in Constantinople offended by the two books composed by the Gallic bishop Faustus against grace, masquerading as a Catholic but secretly favouring the Pelagians'.[45] The letter was a re-statement of the grand Augustinian theses on grace, infant baptism and predestination.

Fulgentius had already written on this subject. His Carthaginian friend Monimus had difficulty with Augustine's teaching on pre-destination. Fulgentius wrote at length, expounding the doctrine which he would, before long, transmit, on behalf of his episcopal colleagues, to the Scythians.[46] Like many African Christians, Monimus and Fulgentius had been nourished on Augustine's writings. They inherited an unbroken tradition, not least concerning grace. The work of Augustine's disciple Quodvultdeus, bishop of Carthage, shows the degree to which even under the rule of Arian Vandals the Pelagian heresy remained a principal preoccupation of African catholics in the 440s and 450s.[47] In Africa, unlike Gaul or elsewhere, Augustine continued to be synonymous with orthodoxy. It is not, therefore, surprising that the Scythian monks' request for support should have been deflected by the direction of the Africans' interests. Two or three years later another appeal reached the African bishops from the same group. But this time the centre of gravity of the query had shifted: grace was now the sole issue at stake. The bishops again commissioned Fulgentius to write at length, commending his zeal and knowledge and his (lost) refutation of Faustus' work *On Grace*. They rallied to the support of the Scythians against their opponents' attempts 'to elevate the freedom of man's choice above God's grace', and bade them to get their brothers of doubtful orthodoxy to study 'the blessed Augustine's books written in response to Prosper and Hilary'.[48] Fulgentius' answer was the long work, full of the most authentic Augustinian teaching, *On the Truth of Predestination and Grace.*

Recommending the study of Augustine's books in their letter to the monks, the bishops referred to the letter Pope Hormisdas had written (in 520) to Bishop Possessor in Constantinople. The pope had mentioned a set of propositions (*capitula*) from the works of Augustine concerning this question which was kept in the papal archive, and could be sent to them if needed.[49] Hormisdas evidently did not wish to be drawn into yet another controversy. He hoped to allay Bishop Possessor's fears of heresy and to settle the matter with the aid of documents in his archive which seemed adequate for the purpose. If these are identical with the *capitula* used by Caesarius in compiling the first eight canons of the Council of Orange (529), they must have been available in the papal archive before 520. Their theological orientation has been well described as 'un augustinisme intermédiaire', lying midway between the views of Augustine and Prosper and those of Faustus of Riez. They have been attributed to the enlargement of the horizon given to the debate on grace by the 'evasive' intervention of Hormisdas, and the far more decided contribution of the Africans.[50] Their authorship has been much debated. Their latest editor has rightly dismissed the suggestion that they might be the work of the Scythian monks, or of one of their number, Maxentius; or even that they were composed under Scythian influence. We need not accept his conjecture (which is actually impossible) that their author was Prosper; but the evidence certainly points to Gaul as their home country. Whatever their origin, the Acta of the Council of Orange say that Caesarius had at his disposal 'a few *capitula*' – which can hardly refer to anything other than this document – from the Apostolic see, to which he demanded his fellow-bishops' assent. His own orthodoxy would at the same time be vindicated: it had been called in question very recently in the neighbouring province of Vienne, whose relations with Arles were not always happy.[51] How did Caesarius come by the document, and why did it commend itself to him as the basis for his first eight canons?

The answer to these questions must remain in doubt. If the *capitula* were already in existence and in the papal archive in 513/14, when Caesarius visited Rome, he might well have obtained them long before the council. He might have received them more recently, perhaps in preparation for the council; or he might have found them in his own cathedral archive at Arles and inferred, as has been suggested, from the indication he read in their title that they had been 'sent to Rome', that they must first have been received at Arles from Rome; or, finally, he might have been using a new document – that now known to us – concocted by himself.[52] However he came by the document, he would already have been disposed to adopt a more Augustinian approach to the problem of grace than most of his Gallic episcopal colleagues. The influence of his teacher, the African émigré Julianus Pomerius,[53] and his own cosmopolitan experience could well have combined to make him adopt views on grace that the bishops of the neighbouring province would regard as suspect. It is of the utmost significance, however, that these views fell far short of a full-blooded Augustinianism.

The work of Caesarius of Arles and of the second Council of Orange are the final act in the dramatic encounter of traditions which began with the struggle between Pelagius and Augustine. It has been, and will continue to be, much studied. To assess its significance in the evolution of the orthodoxy on the nature of grace it needs to be set in the context of the whole development of the Gallic church over the preceding century. Fifty years before Orange, the Gallic church had closed ranks almost solidly behind a theology which, looked at from an Augustinian perspective, would have looked highly dubious. Now, Faustus of Riez, Gennadius, the whole tradition of Provençal theology, began to look anachronistic, if not downright heretical. During the ten years preceding the council, powerful theological pressures were again active at Rome. The agitation of the Scythian monks combined with the theological learning of the African exiles to expose the Roman church, once again, after a hundred years, to a strong current of the Augustinian theology of grace. But neither the Roman nor the Gallic church allowed themselves to be carried away by it. The popes, Hormisdas supremely, were determined to stand by the traditional orthodoxy, sufficiently defined, in their view, by the condemnations of Pelagius, Celestius and Julian of Eclanum. Their aim was to restrain further speculation and controversy on the matter, and they resisted trouble-makers who disturbed the peace of the church. Caesarius belonged to the world of Lérins and Gaul, and wished to re-establish its ancient links with Rome and the Latin church as a whole. His concern in 529 was to achieve this integration without surrendering the native traditions of his own church: he had to restrict the influence of the African theological revival, mediated through Sardinia, as much as he had to restrict the scope for views which could be seen as crypto-Pelagian. The doctrine of grace that issued from the council succeeded in both.[54] The faith of Orange was neither Pelagius' nor Augustine's; it was the product of a century's thought, debate, preaching and ascetic discipline, shaped and provoked by the two great innovators, and – no less! – by the Gallic churches' resistance to innovation.

No living scholar has done more than Henry Chadwick – and not only by his published work – to help us understand our common Christian past, and to help us to heal our present divisions. To him this study is gratefully dedicated.

NOTES

1 'ad conturbandam catholicae simplicitatis lucem semper splendore radiantem' (*Collectio Quesnelliana* 14, *PL* 56. 490–2).

2 E.g. Augustine, *De civitate Dei* xvi.2.1. A. Trapé, 'Un libro sulla nozione di eresia mai scritto da sant' Agostino', *Augustinianum*, 25 (1985), 853–65 discusses the reasons why Augustine found it difficult to define 'heresy'. The *profectus fidei, non commutatio* of Vincent of Lérins (*Commonitorium* 23), and his conception of heresy and orthodoxy (esp. *Comm.* 19–23; 32) need more careful discussion than they have received since Newman's time. I touch on Vincent below, pp. 219–20.

3 W. Bauer, *Rechtgläubigkeit und Ketzerei im ältesten Christentum*, 1930; ET *Orthodoxy and Heresy in Earliest Christianity*, London 1972. Discussion by H. W. Turner, *The Pattern of Christian Truth*, London 1954; R. A. Markus, 'The Problem of Self-definition: From Sect to Church', in *Jewish and Christian Self-definition*, ed. E. P. Sanders, vol. 1, London 1980, pp. 1–15; 217–19 (= R. A. Markus, *From Augustine to Gregory the Great*, London 1983, 1) and R. L. Wilken, *The Myth of Christian Beginnings*, New York 1970; London 1979.

4 On what follows, see my paper 'Pelagianism: Britain and the Continent', *JEH*, 37 (1986), 191–204 and references there given to other studies. I here single out only Peter Brown's two fine papers, 'Pelagius and His Supporters: Aims and Environment', *JRS*, 51 (1961), 1–11 and 'The Patrons of Pelagius: The Roman Aristocracy Between East and West', *JThS*, n.s.21 (1970) 56–72 (both reprinted in *Religion and Society in the Age of Saint Augustine*, London, 1972, pp. 183–207 and 208–26).

5 Mansi, *Concilia* iv. 1021 (*ACO* 1/2 p. 12, 65). The extent of dissent in Italy cannot be gauged. The *Libellus fidei* generally known as the 'Aquileian manifesto' (G. de Plinval, *Pélage: ses écrits, sa vie et sa réforme*, Paris 1943, pp. 336–41; cf. O. Wermelinger, *Rom und Pelagius* (Päpste und Papsttum 7 (Stuttgart 1975), pp. 220–6) is in fact likely to pre-date the deposition of Julian, and may have no reference to Aquileia: cf. C. Pietri, *Roma christiana*,

BEFAR 224, Rome and Paris 1976, pp. 940–4, with references; G. Bouwmann, *Des Julian von Aeclanum Kommentar zu den Propheten Osee, Joel und Amos, Analecta biblica,* 9, Rome 1958, pp. 4–5, and Y.-M. Duval, 'Julien d'Eclane et Rufin d'Aquilée: du Concile de Rimini à la répression pélagienne. L'intervention impériale en matière religieuse', *REAug.*, 24 (1978), 243–71, at 254.

6 *Coll. Quesn.* 19 (*PL* 56.499–500). For the date (418, not 421), cf. A. Chastagnol, 'Le sénateur Volusien et la conversion d'une famille de l'aristocratie romaine au Bas Empire', *REA*, 58 (1956), 241–53; *La Préfecture urbaine à Rome sous le Bas Empire,* Paris 1960, 170–1.

7 *Constitutiones Sirmondianae* 6, which seems to form part of a batch of similar legislation issued in the summer of 425: cf. *Codex Theodosianus* 16.5.62, 63 and 64.

8 *Contra collatorem* 21.4; *Epistula ad Rufinum* 1.2.

9 The case of Britain has been most recently studied by E. A. Thompson, *Saint Germanus of Auxerre and the End of Roman Britain,* Studies in Celtic History, 6, Bury St Edmunds 1984. For my re-assessment of the problem of Pelagianism in the light of Thompson's work, see my study referred to above, n. 4. I do not here consider the case of Britain further, except to note that the case for the view I defend there, that the Pelagian controversy made little or no impact in Britain, has been further strengthened by evidence that Britain was a principal route for the transmission of Pelagius' writings, and that they continued to be read in Wales. See D. Dumville, 'Late seventh- and early eighth-century evidence for the transmission of Pelagius', *Cambridge Mediaeval Celtic studies,* 10 (1985), 31–52.

10 Fundamental: B. Altaner, 'Der "Liber de fide": ein Werk des Pelagianers Rufinus der "Syrer"', *ThQ*, 130 (1950), 432–49 (= *Kleine patristiche Schriften,* Berlin 1967, 467–82); H. I. Marrou, 'Les attaches orientales du pélagianisme', *CRAI*, 1968, 459–72. The important studies by G. Bonner, 'Rufinus the Syrian and African Pelagianism', *AugStud*, 1 (1970), 31–47 and his *Augustine and Modern Research on Pelagianism* (Villanova 1973) have further clarified Rufinus' part in the development of Pelagianism. E. TeSelle, 'Rufinus the Syrian, Celestius, Pelagius: Explorations in the Prehistory of the Pelagian Controversy', *AugStud*, 3 (1972), 61–95 has brought the problem into relation with the Origenist controversy. That Augustine knew Rufinus' work has been established by F. Refoulé, 'Datation du premier concile de Carthage contre les Pélagiens et le *Libellus fidei* de Rufin', *REAug*, 9 (1963), 41–9. I have not been able to take account of F. G. Nuvolone, 'Pélage et Pélagianisme', *DSp*, 12 (1986), 2889–942.

11 'rectissime sentiebat et docebat' (*PL* 48.186A; *ACO* 1/5 p. 60).

12 Celestine, *Epistula* 13.8 (*PL* 50.480–2; *ACO* 1/2 p. 11).

13 After anathematizing a number of other heretics, of more immediate relevance, Cyril added 'those who follow the opinions of Celestius and

Pelagius, which we have never received' – Mansi, *Concilia* IV.1320 (*ACO* I/
1.3, p. 22; 1/2, p. 80); Celestius is mentioned in Canons 1, 2 and 5 (Mansi,
canons 1 & 4, IV.1472–3; *ACO* I/1.3, pp. 27–8; 1/4, p. 243). The
deposition of Pelagius, Julian and their followers is said in the synodal letter
to Celestine, Mansi, *Concilia* IV.1324 (*ACO* I/1.3, pp. 5–8; *PL* 50.522) to have
been read out to and approved by the council. Marius Mercator reports that
they were condemned by the Council – see his *Commonitorium* V.2 (*PL*
48.108A; *ACO* I/5 p. 65); and in his preface to Nestorius' sermons: *iterum
iterumque damnati sunt* (PL 48.186A; *ACO* I/5, p. 60).

14 Pietri, *Roma christiana*, 1241. For a full account, cf. pp. 1212–44. Zosimus'
cautious approach: his letter in *Coll. Avell.*, 50 (*CSEL* 35.115–17).

15 *ACO* I/5, p. 70.

16 Among modern accounts, see D. M. Cappuyns, 'Le premier représentant
de l'augustinisme médiéval, Prosper d'Aquitaine', *RThAM*, 1 (1929),
307–37. Cf. also the introductions by P. De Letter to his translations of
Prosper, *The Call of All Nations*, *ACW* 14, Westminster, Maryland 1952,
and *Defense of St Augustine*, *ACW* 32, 1963; R. Lorenz, 'Der Augustinismus
Prospers von Aquitanien', *ZKG*, 73 (1962), 217–52; J. Chéné, 'Que
signifiaient "initium fidei" et "affectus credulitatis" pour les semi-
pélagiens?', *RSR*, 35 (1948), 566–88 and the same author's 'Le semi-
pélagianisme du midi de la Gaule d'après les lettres de Prosper d'Aquitaine
et de Hilaire à saint Augustin', *RSR*, 43 (1955), 321–41, on the roots of the
controversy in Gaul.

17 Cf. O. Chadwick, *John Cassian*, 2nd ed, Cambridge 1968, pp. 131–2;
Cappuyns, *RThAM*, 1 (1929), 318–19, 326–7; 'evasive': 326 (Chadwick, p.
132, calls it 'this ambiguous decree'). De Plinval, *Pélage*, p. 370 speaks of 'un
esprit de détente généreuse' after Celestine's initial severity; 'less papes
désiraient l'apaisement' – on Leo, p. 373.

18 Doubts on the Prosperian authorship of the *De vocatione*, serious and long
held, have been laid to rest by Dom Cappuyns' study, 'L'auteur du De
vocatione omnium gentium', *RBen*, 39 (1927), 198–226. For a survey of
subsequent views, see Lorenz, *ZKG*, 73 (1962), p. 233, n.129. The dating
of the work, however, remains uncertain: Lorenz (following an unpublished thesis by Gaidioz which I have not been able to consult) inclines
to *c*. 440 rather than the date favoured by Cappuyns and most others, *c*. 450.
For discussion of the extent to which Prosper's views on predestination
represent a retreat from hard-line Augustinian views, see de Plinval, *Pélage*,
p. 369; and the same author's 'Prosper d'Aquitaine, interprète de saint
Augustin', *RechAug.*, 1 (1958), 339–55, at 351–2. cf. also Cappuyns,
RThAM, 1 (1929), esp. 327–37; De Letter, *Call*, 164–5, n. 52; for an
important reservation to the view that Prosper's later work represents a
substantial retreat from the Augustinian position, see Lorenz, *ZKG*, 73
(1962), 237–51. On the universalism of the *De vocatione* and Leo's influence,

see my study 'Chronicle and Theology; Prosper of Aquitaine', in *The Inheritance of Historiography*, ed. T. P. Wiseman and C. Holdsworth, Exeter 1986, pp. 31–43.

19 On Manichees: *Sermones* 9.4; 16; 24; 34; 42; 76 (Ballerini; Chavasse, *CC* 138, 138A), *inter plura*; *Epistulae* 7, 8, 16, 52, 59. Catalogues: *Sermones* 28.4; 47.2; 96.2; *Epistula* 165.2.

20 *Epistulae* 1, 2 and (perhaps) 18. On their recipients and dating, see the Ballerini brothers' *Admonitio* prefixed to the letters in their edition. The preoccupation with regular canonical procedure in clerical promotions both in *Epistula* 1.5 and in *Epistula* 18 (where in fact Pelagianism is not mentioned at all, but some of the heretics appear to have been rebaptized, and, therefore, not to be Pelagians) suggests that some problem about clerical rivalry and ill-feeling lay at the root of the Aquileian difficulties.

21 *Epistula* 1.2.

22 P. Hervé de l'Incarnation, 'La grâce chez Léon le Grand', *RThAM*, 22 (1955), 17–55; 193–212; and A. Lauras, 'Etudes sur saint Léon le Grand', *RSR*, 49 (1961), 481–499.

23 Prosper, *Chronicon, ann.* 439 (ed. Mommsen, *Chronica minora* 1, *MGH.AA* 9) 1336. The attribution to Leo is absent from some of the manuscripts.

24 A. Zumkeller, 'Die pseudo-augustinische Schrift "De praedestinatione et gratia": Inhalt, Überlieferung, Verfasserfrage und Nachwirkung', *Aug.*, 25 (1985), 539–63.

25 See J. E. Chisholm, *The Pseudo-Augustinian Hypomnesticon Against the Pelagians and Celestians, Paradosis*, 20–1, Fribourg, 1967, 1980, vol. 1, 39; idem, 'The Authorship of the Pseudo-Augustinian *Hypomnesticon* Against the Pelagians and Celestians', *StPatr* 11 (*TU* 108, 1972), 307–10 suggests Prosper as the likely author.

26 Cf. H. Koch, 'Vinzenz von Lerin und Gennadius. Ein Beitrag zur Literaturgeschichte des Semipelagianismus', *TU* 31/2, Leipzig, 1907. Koch, however, argued that Augustinian pressure caused Vincent to adopt a measure of secrecy. See additional note on p. 234.

27 E. Amann, 'Semi-Pélagiens', *DThC*, 14/2 (1941), 1796–1850, at 1821. The anti-Pelagian *Hypomnesticon* transmitted among the Augustinian pseud-epigrapha probably belongs to such a milieu: cf. Chisholm, *The Pseudo-Augustinian Hypomnesticon*, pp. 17ff. Against whom the *Commonitorium* is and is not aimed, see E. Griffe, 'Pro Vincentio Lerinensi', *BLE*, 62 (1961), 26–31, who, however, overstates his case in writing that the *Commonitorium* 'se situe au dehors de cette controverse' (p. 26).

28 *Commonitorium* 2, 20 etc.

29 'ut non vetustas cessaret obruere novitatem, sed potius novitas desineret incessere vetustatem' – Comm. 32. This had evidently been the attitude of Prosper's opponents from the beginning: see Prosper, *Epistula ad Augustinum*, 8; they did not think faith was involved in the differences of

opinion under discussion; Prosper wanted Augustine's help in convincing them that their views constituted a danger to faith. In *C.coll.* 1.1 (*PL* 51.215) he implied that his opponents' views fell short of heresy, for they 'are within the fold, but favour the wolves'. Cf. 1.2 (*PL* 51.217): they are 'nostri concorporales et comparticipes gratiae Christi'.

30 *Responsiones ad excerpta Genuensium*, 'ipse insignis gratiae praedicator' (*PL* 51.197).

31 *Chronicon Gallicum ann. cccclii*, n. 44, 81, 47 (ed. Mommsen, *Chron. min.* 1, *MGH. AA* 9, 650, 656, 652). The second entry has secured a firm place in popular mythology in the mistranslated form, 'In this year [418] Augustine is said to have invented the heresy of Predestination.' Cf. Ennodius, *Epistula* 2.19 (ed. Vogel, LVI; *MGH.AA* 7.72) on predestinationism as *lybicae pestis*.

32 J. J. O'Donnell, 'Salvian and Augustine', *AugStud*, 14 (1983), 25–34.

33 O. Chadwick, 'Euladius of Arles', *JThS.*, 46 (1945), 200–5, has shown that the reference to the bishop whom Prosper numbered among Augustine's admirers on every subject save that of grace and predestination in his *Epistula ad Augustinum*, 9, was not Hilary but his predecessor.

34 *Vita Sancti Hilarii Arelatensis*, 11.14 (*PL* 50.1231); ed. S. Cavallin, Lund, 1952, 93.

35 P. Courcelle, 'Nouveaux aspects de la culture lérinienne', *REL*, 46 (1968), 379–409 and C. Tibiletti, 'Libero arbitrio e grazia in Fausto di Riez', *Aug*, 19 (1979), 259–86.

36 Lucidus: cf. Faustus, *Epistulae* 18, 19 (*MGH. AA* 8, 288–91), and *Concilia Galliae*, ed. C. Munier (*CC* 148) 1, 159–61. Avitus, *Epistula* 4 (*MGH. AA* 6/2, 31–2). Cf. I. N. Wood, *Avitus of Vienne: Religion and Culture in the Auvergne and the Rhône Valley, 470–530*, unpublished DPhil. dissertation, Oxford 1979, 56–61. Gennadius on Faustus: *De viris illustribus*, 86; his own orthodoxy, ibid., 99 – which may well be a response to Gelasius' concern about orthodoxy in distant quarters (cf. below, n. 43). On Gennadius, see also P. Courcelle, *Les lettres grecques en Occident de Macrobe à Cassiodore*, Paris 1948, pp. 221–3. His orthodoxy has been convincingly vindicated by S. Pricoco, 'Il *De viris illustribus* di Gennadio', in *La storiografia ecclesiastica nella tarda antichità*, Messina 1980, pp. 241–73.

37 On Valerianus of Cimiez, see J. P. Weiss, 'Valérien de Cimiez et Valère de Nice', *SE*, 21 (1972–3), 109–46; idem, 'La personnalité de Valérien de Cimiez', *Annuaire de la Faculté des Lettres et Sciences humaines de Nice*, 11 (1970), 141–62 (who observes, p. 155, that the controversies of the 420s were now forgotten, but is inclined to find some affinities with Pelagius); and C. Tibiletti, 'Valeriano di Cimiez e la teologia dei maestri Provenzali', *Aug*, 22 (1982), 513–32, who shows how little Provençal theology owes to Pelagius and rightly brings out its affinities with pre-Pelagian and Eastern theological traditions.

38 A. Koch, *Der heilige Faustus Bischof von Riez. Eine dogmengeschichtliche Monographie*, Stuttgart 1897, p. 48. C. Tibiletti surveys the modern literature on the whole subject in 'Rassegna di studi e testi sui "semipelagiani"', *Aug*, 25 (1985), 507–22.

39 For details, see F. Prinz, *Frühes Mönchtum im Frankenreich*, Munich, Vienna 1965, pp. 47–58 on 'Flüchtlingskloster'; pp. 60–2 on school for bishops; 452–561 on learning and letters; and also S. Pricoco, *L'isola dei santi*, Rome 1978, pp. 59–73.

40 Amann, *DThC*, 14/2 (1941), 1837.

41 *Collectio Avellana* 96, 98 and 97. The traditional attribution to Gelasius (Thiel, *Epistulae* 4, 5 and *Tractatus* v) has been rejected by P. Nautin, *DHGE*, 16, 889. His arguments in favour of Felix III as the author of the letters to Honorius and the treatise seem convincing. We shall need to await Nautin's fuller study to accept his estimate of Felix III as 'ce pape autoritaire et vindicatif', and of Gelasius as 'un esprit sans grand envergure, hostile à toute recherche théologique', who could only continue his predecessor's proud and sterile policies (*DHGE*, 20, 294). It may, of course, still be the case that Felix's letter was drafted by Gelasius before he became pope: see H. Koch, 'Gelasius im kirchenpolitischen Dienst seiner Vorgänger, der Päpste Simplicius (476–83) und Felix III (483–92)', *SBAW. PPH.*, 1935–6 (Munich 1936); cf. E. Caspar, *Geschichte des Papsttums* 2, Tübingen 1933, pp. 750–1.

42 *Epistula* 6 (= *C.Avell.* 94). W. Ullmann, *Gelasius I* (Päpste und Papsttum 18, Stuttgart 1981), 255 assigns *Tract.* v to this occasion, I think without grounds and contrary to the evidence of *Epistula* 5.2 and 6. If the attribution of *C.Avell.* 98 and 97 to Felix III is accepted, the matter would be settled. *C.Avell.* 94 (= Thiel, *Ep.* 6) would be the only Gelasian document of the Pelagian dossier.

43 On the origins of the *Collectio Quesnelliana*, see O. Wermelinger, *Rom und Pelagius*, Päpste und Papsttum 7, Stuttgart 1975, pp. 166–7, and n.153 for details. On Gelasius' concern about unorthodoxy cf. Photius, *Bibliotheca* 54 (John, bishop of Alexandria) and Gennadius, *Vir.ill.*, 99 (Honoratus). Cf. n. 36 above on Gennadius.

44 On the controverted and obscure question of the authorship and date of the *Praedestinatus*, fundamental is H. von Schubert, *Der sogenannte Praedestinatus*, *TU* 24/4, Leipzig 1903. See also G. Morin, 'Arnobe le Jeune', in *Etudes, textes, découvertes*, Paris 1913, pp. 304–439; Bouwmann, *Des Julian von Aeclanum Kommentar*; and M. Abel, 'Le "Praedestinatus" et le pélagianisme', *RThAM*, 35 (1968), 5–25, whose conclusion that the author is an Italian 'semi-Pelagian contaminated by some errors held by Julian of Eclanum' (p. 24) I find convincing.

45 The Scythians' letter *Inter epistulas Fulgentii* (*CC* 91–91A, Fraipont; = *CC* 85A), 16, and the *Rescriptum*, 17. Fulgentius, the Scythian monks and

Faustus' alleged crypto-Pelagianism: see Ferrandus, *Vita Fulg.*, 28.54. For discussion and chronology, see E. Schwartz, *ACO* IV/2 (1914), praef.; V. Schurr, *Die Trinitätslehre des Boethius im Lichte der 'skythischen' Kontroversen*, *Forschungen zur christlichen Literatur und Dogmengeschichte* 18/1, Paderborn 1935, 142–80; E. Amann, 'Scythes (Moines)', *DThC* 14/2, (1941), 1746–53; F. Glorie, Prolegomena to his edition in *CC* 85A (1978); and H. Chadwick, *Boethius*, Oxford 1981, 185–8.

46 See especially *Ad Monimum*, prol.; 1.2; 3; 7–12: 17–20, etc.

47 On dating and authorship, see R. Braun's introduction to his edition (*SC* 101–102, Paris, 1964). For the preoccupation with Pelagianism, *Liber promissionum et predictorum Dei* II.vi.10–11 (Pelagianism is the leprosy which covers the whole body); II.xxxvi.82; *Dimidium temporis in signis Antichristi*, VI.12. *Sermo* 5.8 (*PL* 40.685–6); 7.6 (*ibid.*, 693).

48 *Epistula* 15.19, 2, 18.

49 *Epistula* 15.18, quoting *Epistula Hormisdae* (*c.Avell.* 231), 14. The *Capitula Sancti Augustini ad urbem transmissa* are edited by F. Glorie, with introduction, in *CC* 85A, 243–73.

50 D. M. Cappuyns, 'L'origine des "Capitula" d'Orange, 529', *RThAM*, 6 (1934), 121–41, at 126–40.

51 *Canones Arausicorum*, prol. (*Concilia Galliae* 2, *CC* 148A, 55); *Vita Sancti Caesarii Arelatensis*, 1.60 (ed. Krusch, *MGH.SR Merov.* III.481; ed. Morin, 321). J. J. O'Donnell, 'Liberius the Patrician', *Traditio*, 37 (1981), 31–72, casts a powerful sidelight which throws unaccustomed contours into sharp relief, esp. pp. 52–60.

52 See C. Fritz, 'Orange, deuxième Concile d', *DThC*, 11/1 (1941), 1087–103; for the relation between Canons 1–8 of Orange and the *capitula*, Cappuyns, *RThAM*, 6 (1934), 121–411; for the Gallic origins of the *Capitula* and Caesarius finding them in Gaul, P. Nautin, 'Orange 529', *Ecole Pratique des Hautes Etudes*, *Annuaire* 1959–60, Paris 1960, 86–87; and Glorie's prolegomena to his edition (see above, n. 49), who rejects Nautin's suggestion that their composition depended on the work of the Scythians. J.-P. B[ouhot], in his review of Glorie's edition, *REAug*, 25 (1979), 377–9 makes a case for Caesarius' authorship. If this suggestion is accepted, at least one other set of *capitula* must have circulated previously.

53 The Augustinian influence on Pomerius has been established by e.g. J. C. Plumpe, 'Pomeriana', *VigChr*, 1 (1947), 227–39 and A. Solignac, 'Julien Pomère', *DSp* 8 (Paris 1947), 1594–600. C. Tibiletti, 'La teologia della grazia in Giuliano Pomerio', *Aug*, 25 (1985), 489–506, has confirmed this indubitable influence and also shown its limits: the absence of polemical intent and the doctrine of predestination and the stress laid on aspects of Augustine most acceptable to the Lérinese milieu.

54 Much more work on the state of public opinion in the Gallic church and on the immediate background to Caesarius and the Council of Orange will

have to be completed before a fully elaborated judgment can be made. My summary owes a great deal to the advice of a number of scholars whose work has done and will undoubtedly do much to illuminate various aspects of the study of the Pelagian controversy, of its impact on Gaul and its resolution: Gerald Bonner, Roger Collins, William Klingshirn, John Moorhead, Mark Vessey and Ian Wood, all of whom I wish to thank for advice on one or another point.

ADDITIONAL NOTE

In the light of W. O'Connor, 'Saint Vincent of Lérins and Saint Augustine', *Doctor Communis* 16 (1963), pp. 123–257, which was not available to me at the time of writing. I would now wish to revise the view I expressed in the text (above, p. 219 and n. 26) concerning the identification of Vincent of Lérins with the author of the *Objectiones Vincentiahae*.

Augustine and millenarianism

GERALD BONNER

Augustine's disavowal, in Book xx of *De civitate Dei*, of a materialistic understanding of the thousand-year reign of Christ with His saints, as prophesied in Revelation 20:4, is undoubtedly a symbolic gesture in the intellectual history of Western Christendom. 'He marks...a decisive moment of western thought, in which it frees itself from a paralysing archaism and turns to an autonomous creation', is the verdict of Jean Daniélou.[1] Nevertheless, the effect of Augustine's change of mind should not be exaggerated. Millenarian eschatological hopes and ideas survived, to find expression in the prophecies ascribed to Joachim of Flora and, later, in the ideology of the Anabaptist movement, thereafter to find their way, in a secular and anti-religious guise, into philosophies like Marxism and anarchism, as a consequence of the apparently ineradicable human longing for a state of perfection to be enjoyed upon this earth by the elect, however the elect may be defined. It is, of course, undeniable, given the influence of Augustine's theology on mediaeval thought, that professional theologians would have followed his lead in rejecting a literal understanding of the thousand-year reign; but a doubt remains. Was Augustine's rejection of millenarianism as uncompromising as is generally assumed? The fact that in the *de haeresibus*, written a year or two after Book xx of of *De civitate Dei*, Augustine attributes millenarian beliefs to the heretical Cerinthians might seem to be decisive, but the millenarianism of the Cerinthians was only part of a wider and more general Judaizing theology, which represented a much greater challenge to right belief than did millenarianism.[2] It is possible that Augustine's attitude to millenarianism was less absolute than is commonly asserted, and that the end of millenarian expectations in the Christian church was due to other factors than his influence. The purpose of this article is to consider the evidence afresh, without any preconceptions, as Henry Chadwick has done in more majestic fashion in his *Priscillian of Avila*.

The point of departure must be Augustine's own words in *De civitate Dei* xx, 7:

Some people have assumed, in view of this passage [Revelation 20:1–6], that the first resurrection will be a bodily resurrection. They have been particularly excited, among other reasons, by the actual number of a thousand years, taking it as appropriate that there should be a kind of Sabbath for the saints for all that time, a holy rest, that is, after the labours of the six thousand years since man's creation, when in retribution for his great sin he was expelled from paradise into the troubles of this mortal condition... This notion would be in some degree tolerable (*utcumque tolerabilis*) if it were believed that in that Sabbath some delights of a spiritual character were to be available for the saints because of the presence of the Lord. I also entertained this notion at one time. But in fact those people assert that those who have risen again will spend their rest in the most unrestrained material feasts, in which there will be so much to eat and drink that not only will those supplies keep within no bounds of moderation, but will also exceed the limits even of incredulity (*sed modum ipsius incredulitatis excedent*). But this can only be believed by materialists; and those with spiritual interests give the name 'Chiliasts' to the believers in this picture, a term which we can translate by a word derived from the equivalent Latin 'Millenarians'.[3]

Augustine's objection to millenarianism, then, at least as stated in *De civitate Dei*, is essentially determined by its materialism. In itself the concept was admissible, even though Augustine had personally discarded it.

Among those scholars who have particularly influenced the modern understanding of Augustine's abandonment of millenarianism three names particularly stand out: Heinrich Scholz, in his *Glaube und Unglaube in der Weltgeschichte* (1911), who linked it with the influence of the Donatist Tyconius; Jean Daniélou, in *Bible et liturgie* (1951); and Georges Folliet, in an article, 'La typologie du sabbat chez S. Augustin', in *Memorial Gustave Bardy*.[4] More recently Martine Dulaey, in a very learned essay,[5] has raised serious questions about the alleged Tyconian influence on Augustine's thought in the years before he came to complete the *De civitate Dei*. Folliet, in his article, brought together a collection of eleven passages which appear in Augustine's writings between 389 and 400, in which the saint speaks of the symbolism of the sabbath rest and interprets it in an eschatological sense – *pas toujours orthodoxe d'ailleurs, comme il le reconnaîtra lui-même* is Folliet's comment (p. 371). Most of these passages occur in the course of anti-Manichaean polemic. Thus, in *De Genesi contra Manichaeos* I, 22, 23 and 25 (written about 389), Augustine is concerned to show that the idea of the sabbath is not to be understood *either* in the material sense of the Jews *or* in the crudely literal sense forced upon it by the Manichees, who affected, for controversial purposes, to understand that Genesis 2:2 implied a cessation of activity by God Himself on the seventh day. Augustine refutes such an exegesis by interpreting the sabbath of God as a symbol of the rest which will be enjoyed by the saints with Christ in the seventh age of the world, after His Second Coming:

then those to whom it was said: *Be ye perfect, as your Father who is in heaven is perfect* [Matthew 5:48] will rest with Christ from all their works. For such people perform works that are truly good; and after such works peace may be hoped for, on the seventh day which has no evening.[6]

This is, no doubt, as Folliet says, millenarianism;[7] but it is millenarianism of a very moderate kind, which does no more than regard the sabbath rest as something literal, and not figurative.

A brief reference to the seventh age of the world as eternal repose in the *De vera religione* (xxvi, 49) is irrelevant to our discussion, as is likewise *De diversis quaestionibus LXXXVIII*, q.58. However, in Question 57, 2 of the same work, Augustine expounded millenarian doctrine unambiguously. Discussing the eschatological significance of the 153 fishes of John 21:11, which he regards as signifying the elect, he speaks of the intermingling of the good and bad in the church in the present age and declares:

separation takes place at the end of the age, just as it did on the edge of the sea, that is, on the shore [Matthew 13:47, 48], when the righteous reign, at first in time, as it is written in the Apocalypse [Revelation 20:4, 6], and then for ever in the city which is there described [Revelation 21:10–27].[8]

Here, as in *De Genesi contra Manichaeos* I, 23, 41, Augustine teaches millenarianism, but avoids going into details, contenting himself with a bare statement of belief.

The two primary documents, however, for assessing Augustine's millenarian theology are Sermons 259 and Mai 94. The date of these two sermons is not clear. Sermon 259 was assigned by Kunzelmann to about 393; more recently Suzanne Poque has argued for a date around 400. Martine Dulaey is convinced that only a date of 393–5 is admissible, on the ground that by 400 Augustine had abandoned millenarianism.[9] The crucial passage is as follows:

The eighth day therefore signifies the new life at the end of the age; the seventh day the future quiet of the saints upon this earth. For the Lord will reign on earth with His saints as the Scriptures say [Revelation 20:4, 6], and will have His Church here, separated and cleansed from all infection of wickedness, where no wicked person will enter, as those one hundred and fifty-three fishes signify, about which, as I recall, I have already spoken previously.[10]

The date of Sermon Mai 94 cannot be satisfactorily established, but its general tone suggests that it was probably preached about the same time as Sermon 259:

What is this *peace upon peace* [Isaiah 57:19] which He promises elsewhere by the prophet, if not the Sabbath, signified by the seventh day, which although it is comprehended in the same temporal cycle as the other days, undoubtedly implies the repose promised upon this earth to the saints, where no tempest of this age disturbs them, taking rest in their God after their good works? And in order to give a sign of this long before, after he had made all things very well [Genesis 1:31] God Himself rested on the seventh day [Genesis 2:2]. Or is there any other reason for what is written in the book of Job: *Six times from thy necessities have I delivered thee, and in seven evil shall not touch thee* [LXX 5:19]? But because that day has no evening, because it is without any incursion or overshadowing of sadness, which often at the present time stems from converse with evil men, it causes the saints to pass over to the eighth day, that is to eternal blessedness. For it is one thing to rest in the Lord while time itself endures, which is the state signified by the present day, that is, by the Sabbath, and another to transcend all time and to be at peace for ever with the maker of time, which condition is signified by the eighth day which, by not revolving with the rest, declares itself to have the image of eternity.[11]

These two sermons represent Augustine's most extended exposition of a millenarian understanding of the apocalyptic reign of Christ with His saints on earth, and it is significant, as Folliet has pointed out, that in Mai 94 it is not the Apocalypse which provides the text for the earthly rest of the saints but Isaiah.[12] Augustine is already spiritualizing the doctrine of the sabbath rest for the saints of God. In *Contra Adimantum* 2,2 (written in 394–6) Augustine again identifies the sabbath with the seven-day rest promised to the faithful after this life, that is, with the last age of the world ('sic requiem quae nobis promittitur post opera quae in hoc mundo habemus, si iusta fuerint, consequemur, septima scilicet eademque ultima parte saeculi, de qua longum est disputare'). Here again Augustine's theology is millenarian only in a very moderate fashion. Finally, in Letter 55, x, 19 (AD 400), the seventh day is said to signify the rest which will be given to the saints after their good works, though this rest is not to be confused with the eighth day, the day of Christ's resurrection (xiii, 23).

The distinctive feature of all these millenarian passages is Augustine's disinclination to speculate about the nature of the life of the saints during the thousand-year reign with Christ, beyond declaring it to be a state of rest. He regards the reign of the saints as a prophecy of a future event which will take place within time, but declines to define its character. In so doing he has already separated himself from the earlier millenarian tradition going back to Papias and including among its exponents Irenaeus of Lyons, which understood the thousand-year reign not only literally, but also in material terms.[13] Are we to understand Augustine's reticence as a deliberate action, perhaps designed to reject the older millenarian tradition by tacitly ignoring it?

This question raises another: was Augustine aware of the old millenarian tradition through Irenaeus? Daniélou implies that, in his early days, Augustine inherited Irenaeus' opinions, at least to some degree.[14] This seems to be simply wrong – Augustine's millenarianism, as Folliet points out, is quite different from that of Irenaeus.[15] But had Augustine actually read Irenaeus? It would appear that he was familiar with him as early as 396/7, since he apparently draws upon him (*Adversus haereses* IV, 30) in *De doctrina Christiana* II, xl, 60 and subsequently appealed to him against Julian of Eclanum (*C.Iul.* I, iii, 5). One cannot, however, positively affirm that he knew of Irenaeus' teaching on the millennium at first hand, since he nowhere cites the relevant Irenaean passage (v, 33–6 esp. 35, 1). However, Berthold Altaner, in a characteristically careful study of Augustine's debt to Irenaeus, came to the conclusion that Augustine knew the *Adversus haereses* from the Latin translation and not from a citation from some other author.[16] Yet even if we assume that Augustine knew about millenarianism from Irenaeus – and he may have known of the doctrine from Tertullian, whom he certainly had read[17] – it is noteworthy that he made no attempt to reproduce Irenaeus' teaching. On the other hand, assuming that Augustine had known Irenaeus' doctrine, he would have been reluctant to reject it openly, in view of Irenaeus' reputation as a champion of Catholic orthodoxy. Even the anti-millenarian Jerome, at the end of his life, was constrained to admit that belief in a material New Jerusalem could not be condemned, because so many churchmen and martyrs had maintained it.[18] Augustine did not go as far as that. Millenarianism might be acceptable, but it must be purged of any materialistic elements, and by the time he came to compose Book xx of *De civitate Dei*, Augustine had himself abandoned even moderate millenarian beliefs.

In this context it may be noted that when discussing the pseudo-Sybilline writings in Book xviii of *De civitate Dei* Augustine acknowledged his indebtedness to the *Divine Institutes* of Lactantius (iv, 18–19) as a source for his knowledge, but made no reference either there or in Book xx to Lactantius' millenarian expectations of a thousand-year reign of the saints in which Satan would be bound and the Holy City established in the midst of the earth, when the sun would shine with seven times its present brightness, the rocks ooze honey and the streams run with wine and the rivers with milk[19] – a picture drawn from the Sybillines and expressing precisely the sort of materialistic millenarianism which is to be found in Papias. Of all this Augustine, understandably, says nothing.

We are therefore faced with two questions: when, and why, did Augustine cease to be a millenarian? The answer as to when seems to be fairly straightforward: it would seem to have been not later than 397–8, when he composed the *Contra Faustum*.[20] The reason for Augustine's change, so far as he himself was concerned, was the replacement of a theology of world history in six ages, each of a thousand years, by one in which the sixth age is of unknown duration, and the acceptance of a spiritual sabbath without an evening – an idea which is already to be found in the undated millenarian Sermon Mai 94, which may therefore represent a state of transition in Augustine's thinking from literalism to symbolism.[21]

Since the researches of Heinrich Scholz, it has been widely assumed that Augustine's change of mind was brought about by a study of the *Commentary on the Apocalypse* by the Donatist Tyconius, which appeared about 380. 'Ticonius ist der Theologe gewesen', declared Scholz confidently, 'der Augustin von seinen chiliastischen Träumen geheilt hat.'[22] Martine Dulaey has, however, recently argued that there is no positive evidence for Augustine having read the *Commentary* – as opposed to *The Book of Rules*, which he commends in the *De doctrina Christiana* (iii, xxx, 42-xxxvi, 56) – at any date much earlier than 427, when he was composing the final section of *De civitate Dei*.[23] If she is right – and her questioning is persuasive – it would seem reasonable to regard Augustine's abandonment of millenarianism as a personal belief as being due, not to a sudden intellectual illumination, such as he experienced with regard to the character of divine grace when replying to Simplicianus of Milan in 396/7, but rather to a general theological development, not unaffected by pastoral considerations, which left him reluctant to attempt to define too exactly the manner in which biblical prophecy would, in the future, be fulfilled. His debate with Faustus had come about as a consequence of the discovery that, however inadequate the Manichaean bishop might have been in defending his own beliefs, he was an alarmingly formidable critic of any too-literal understanding of Catholic scripture. This did not result in Augustine's abandoning a literal exegesis of scripture – on the contrary, his interpretation of the creation narrative of Genesis became increasingly literal with the passage of time – but in his discovering that a crudely literal sense was not only inadequate for understanding what was past, but was also to be avoided as a guide for anticipating the future, as also for explaining the phenomena of the physical world which were capable of being explored by natural science.[24]

Such a development of outlook would explain why Augustine was eventually unable to tolerate a material understanding of the millenial passage of Revelation, even though it had been accepted by many devoutly orthodox Christian exegetes in the past. But beside this intellectual development there existed a very practical reason for reservation on this particular issue in the North Africa of Augustine's day, where the occult and bizarre, not to say the frankly pagan, continued to exercise a fascination for many of the catholic faithful, as they did in other parts of the Christian world. For those attracted by such things there existed a rich corpus of literature, both in the gnostic tradition, made famous by the Coptic library of Nag Hammadi, and in the eschatological–apocalyptic, for which a quantity of apocryphal scriptures catered. In the latter category comes the *Apocalypse of Paul*, denounced by Augustine in the ninety-eighth sermon on St John's Gospel, preached at some time between 414 and 418.

Empty-headed persons with a most stupid presumption have even forged an Apocalypse of Paul, which the sober Church does not accept, a work full of fables, and asserting that this was the cause of Paul saying that he had been rapt into the third heaven.[25]

One of the fables in the *Apocalypse of Paul* is the teaching that the damned in hell enjoy a sabbath-day's respite through the prayers of the saints. Augustine refers to this belief in a sermon preached some time after 418;[26] in the *Enchiridion ad Laurentium*, composed in 421 or 422; and in Book XXI, 23 of *De civitate Dei*, which is to be assigned to 426/7. From what Augustine says in the *Enchiridion* it would appear that this particular doctrine of the *Apocalypse of Paul* enjoyed considerable popularity in Africa:

It is therefore in vain that some persons – or, indeed, a great many – feel pity for the eternal punishment of the damned out of human feelings, and refuse to believe that this will indeed be the case. However, there is no harm in their thinking that the penalties of the damned are at certain seasons somewhat relaxed, if this gives them pleasure.[27]

Augustine's rather grudging concession to belief in a sabbath-day's respite for the lost is conditioned by the fear that it may lead to belief in their eventual liberation at the intercessions of the saints,[28] a belief to which he refers in *De civitate Dei* xxi, 24, and which actually appears in one of the later recensions of the *Apocalypse of Paul*.

In addition, however, to belief in a sabbath-day's respite for the damned, the *Apocalypse of Paul* also preaches a millenarian doctrine in the most uncompromisingly materialistic terms.

The angel answered and said to me: When Christ whom you preach comes to reign, then by the fiat of God the first earth will be dissolved and this land of promise will be shown, and it will be like dew or a cloud; and then the Lord Jesus Christ, the eternal king, will be revealed, and He will come with all His saints to dwell in it and He will reign over them for a thousand years, and they will eat of the good things which I shall show you. And I looked round that land and I saw a river flowing with milk and honey; and at the edge of the river were planted trees full of fruit. And each tree was bearing twelve fruits in the year, various and different. And I saw the creation of that place and all the work of God. And I saw there palm trees, some of twenty cubits and others of ten cubits. Now that land was brighter than silver. And the trees were full of fruit from root up to tree-top. From the root of each tree up to its heart there were ten thousand branches with tens of thousands of clusters [and there were ten thousand clusters on each branch] and there were ten thousand dates to each cluster. And it was the same with the vines. Each vine had ten thousand branches, and each branch had on it ten thousand bunches of grapes. And there were other trees there, myriads and myriads of them, and their fruit was in the same proportion. And I said to the angel: Why does each single tree yield thousands of fruits? And the angel answered and said to me: Because the Lord God of His abundance gives gifts profusely to the worthy, for they, while they were in the world, afflicted themselves of their own will and did everything for His holy name's sake.[29]

The passage quoted provides a good reason for Augustine's objection to any material understanding of the thousand-year reign: the saints of the *Apocalypse of Paul* are to enjoy 'the most unrestrained material feasts, in which there will be so much to eat and drink that not only will those supplies keep within no bounds of moderation but will also exceed the limits even of incredulity' – Augustine's language in *De civitate Dei* xx, 7 applies most appropriately here, while 'Paul's' reference to the vines, each having ten thousand branches, and each branch bearing ten thousand grapes, seems like an echo of the language ascribed to Christ by the Elders and reported by Irenaeus (v, 33, 3). One can well understand Augustine's distaste, and suspect that if he had read such things in Lactantius, or even in Irenaeus, he would have personally rejected them; but just as he was prepared to tolerate the idea of a sabbath-rest for the damned, provided that it did not lead to belief in universal salvation, so Augustine was prepared to tolerate a moderate millenarian doctrine even after he had himself abandoned it. What had to be recognized, in his view, was that both doctrines – that of a sabbath respite and of a literal understanding of the millennium – unless they were carefully controlled, could lead to superstition or to downright false belief, and were therefore best avoided.

Augustine's reference to the *Apocalypse of Paul*, in the ninety-eighth tractate on John, bears witness to his distaste for a materialistic millenarianism by the period 414–418. This distaste is expressed again in *De civitate Dei*, Book xx, when he had himself wholly discarded millenarianism, but was still prepared to tolerate it, if understood in a spiritual fashion, such as he had himself formerly entertained. Did he change his opinion shortly afterwards, when he came to compile the *De haeresibus* in 428/9? For here he reports that the Cerinthian heretics tell fables about a thousand-year reign after the resurrection, with carnal delights of feasting and lust, for which reason they are called Chilistae.[30] The sources of the *De haeresibus* are difficult to establish; but we know that Augustine made use of the work of Filastrius of Brescia, which appeared between 385 and 391, in which the millenarians, called Chiliontaetitae, are denounced in language which could well have inspired Augustine's remarks in *De civitate Dei* xx, 7, for holding that, during the millennium, life will continue in a carnal fashion, with reproduction and eating, as in the present age;[31] and it is possible, though not certain, that he also consulted the *indiculus* of pseudo-Jerome, where similar information is given about the Chiliastae.[32] To these two sources may be added a reference in Rufinus' Latin version of the *Ecclesiastical History* of Eusebius, with which Augustine was acquainted by 424/5,[33] and which he specifically mentions in *De haeresibus*,[34] to an Egyptian bishop named Nepos who, *Iudaico intellectu,* held that the saints would reign with Christ for a thousand years enjoying corporeal pleasures, basing this belief on the Johannine Apocalypse.[35] All these three sources speak of millenarianism in the materialistic form which Augustine rejects in Book xx of *De civitate Dei*. None of them actually denounces millenarianism – considered simply as a literal understanding of Revelation 20:4 – as heretical.

It is therefore reasonable to hold that, despite the passage relating to the Cerinthians, Augustine never actually condemned millenarianism, in itself, as a possible type of scriptural exegesis, but only its abuse, when it led to a materialistic and Judaizing understanding of the biblical text. Here, unlike Jerome, Augustine was not deterred by the fact that earlier theologians of accepted orthodoxy had entertained materialistic views. In this, as in other matters, he was prepared to follow his own convictions.

The reasons which led Augustine to change his mind and to prefer a symbolic interpretation of the millennium to the literal understanding which he had once held invite closer examination. Martine Dulaey had mentioned as factors determining Augustine's mental evolution his rejection of a notion of a world history of six thousand years' duration and the acceptance of the idea of a sabbath without an evening which ushers in the eighth day. There is, however, another factor, noticed by William Cunningham in his Hulsean Lectures more than a century ago,[36] and subsequently developed by J. N. Figgis in his last published work, *The Political Aspects of Saint Augustine's 'City of God'*:[37] Augustine's attitude to the church militant as already, in some sense, constituting the millennium, expressed in the phrase: 'et nunc ecclesia regnum Christi est regnumque caelorum' – 'The Church is *even now* the Kingdom of God'. Behind this declaration lies a number of differing, but cohering, trains of thought: that the first resurrection of Revelation 20:4 is a spiritual, not a bodily, resurrection, since it refers to the martyrs and to those whose sins have been forgiven in baptism (*De civitate Dei* xx, 6); that the martyrs are to reign with Christ for a thousand years, that is, in the present age of this world, when they are not, as yet, restored to their bodies (xx, 9); and that the souls of the faithful dead are not separated from the church, which is the Body of Christ.

But this reign after death belongs especially to those who struggled on truth's behalf even to death; and that is why it is only the souls of the martyrs who are mentioned in the Apocalypse.[38] Nevertheless we take the part as implying the whole, and interpret it as meaning that the rest of the dead also belong to the Church, which is the kingdom of Christ.[39]

Augustine, in his reference to taking the part as implying the whole, draws upon Tyconius' fourth rule for understanding scripture, *De specie et genere*, in order to understand the rule of the martyrs with Christ as including the pious dead, who are commemorated at the offering of the Eucharist. Similarly, he makes use of Tyconius' second rule, *De Domini corpore bipartito*, to resolve the problem of how the church militant, which contains both the elect and the reprobate, can be the kingdom of Christ:

we must understand the kingdom of heaven in one sense as a kingdom in which both are included, the man who breaks what he teaches and the man who practises it, though one is the least and the other is great in the kingdom; while in another sense it is a kingdom into which there enters only the man who practises what he teaches. Thus where both are to be found we have the Church as it now is; but where only the one kind will be found, there is the Church as it will be, when no evil person will be included. It follows that the Church even now is the kingdom of Christ and the kingdom of heaven. And so even now His saints reign with Him, though not in the same way as they will then reign; and yet the tares do not reign with Him, although they are growing in the Church side by side with the wheat.[40]

Figgis has suggested that Augustine's ground for rejecting millenarianism was that it postulated an absence of earthly trials for the church in this life,[41] which was precisely the assumption which Augustine was seeking to controvert when he embarked upon the composition of the *De civitate Dei*, and to which he gave special attention in his Letter 140, *De gratia Novi Testamenti*: that the grace of the New Testament is not material prosperity in this world but the hope of eternal blessedness in the next. No doubt considerations of this nature played a part in Augustine's rejection, but it is hardly less likely that it was the idea of the eucharistic church, the Body of Christ, which is offered at the altar by Christ, the high priest, which would have been for Augustine a decisive consideration.

The souls of the pious dead are not separated from the Church, which is even now the Kingdom of Christ. Otherwise they would not be commemorated at the altar of God at the time of the partaking of the Body of Christ.[42]

In dictating these words Augustine could hardly have been unmindful of his mother's dying request to be remembered at God's altar; and it is here, if anywhere, that the contradictions between the church militant and the church triumphant are resolved: in the Eucharist, time impinges on eternity and Christ reigns with His saints both now and for ever.

Furthermore, this view of the role of the church was already implicit in Augustine's earlier, millenarian view of the reign of Christ, when in Sermon 259 he declares that

> the Lord will reign on earth with His saints as the Scriptures say, and will have His Church here, separated and cleansed from all infection of wickedness, where no wicked person will enter.

The problem facing Augustine in adopting the symbolical exegesis of the thousand-year reign in place of his own former millenarian understanding, and identifying the church with the kingdom of Christ, was how to preserve the purity, which had been an axiomatic attribute of the church in Sermon 259, in the context of practical pastoral theology, when controversy with the Donatists required the acceptance of the proposition that the church militant is a mixed body, in which the tares grow side by side with the good grain until the harvest. Augustine could find a solution, assuming that he had not already evolved it on his own account, in the second rule of Tyconius, regarding the true and the mixed body of Christ. So the church becomes the 'apocalyptic kingdom ... [T]he millenial kingdom is already in existence'.[43]

It has been argued that, momentous as was this change in interpretation for Augustine's theology, and for that of his disciples in later centuries, it did not constitute a condemnation of millenarianism in itself, but only of the exaggerated and sensual forms in which it appeared in works like the *Apocalypse of Paul*. Yet, from the fifth century onwards, millenarianism became increasingly unfashionable among serious theologians. Eschatological expectations survived, and a practical administrator like Gregory the Great could be haunted by a sense of impending doom and the approaching dissolution of the secular order, but this was not to usher in the millennium, for Gregory had fully absorbed the realized eschatology of the later Augustine. '[T]here is a peculiar tension at the heart of Gregorian eschatology; the sense of an imminent, indeed already present, doom hanging over the world seems to co-exist with a surprising assurance and confidence about the life of the Church.'[44]

It was not, however, Augustine's personal rejection of millenarianism which brought about this changed outlook, for Augustine had condemned millenarianism only in its gross and extravagant form. No doubt the influence of his personal change of mind was important – the *De civitate Dei* was one of the most popular books in mediaeval reading, and Emile Mâle has shown how Augustine's treatment of the resurrection and last judgment, as mediated by such authors as Honorius Augustodunensis and Vincent of Beauvais, influenced mediaeval sculpture,[45] but it is significant that belief in millenarianism dies out in the late patristic age, not only in the West, but in the Greek East as well, where Augustine's change of mind was unknown. The abandonment of millenarianism as an acceptable theological opinion seems to have occurred over the whole Christian world at approximately the same period.

This change of outlook, it may be suggested, was not due to the influence of any one theologian, however eminent, but rather to the changed circumstances brought about by the establishment of the Christian Roman empire by Constantine and his successors. One of the most remarkable developments in European history is the manner in which the catholic church adjusted herself to the revolution which made her first the most favoured and subsequently the official religion of the Roman empire in the course of the fourth century. In such a privileged condition it might well seem to the Christians that the millennium had begun.[46] The raptures of Eusebius of Caesarea – who, significantly, found Papias, the exponent of millenarianism, a man of very mean intelligence (*Historia ecclesiastica* III, 39.13) – over the new order are well known, and his delight was shared by others less famous and less vocal than he. Millenarianism is an attitude of mind best suited to the underprivileged and excluded, and continued to be so for many centuries, as Norman Cohn's famous study has shown; for millenarianism is not primarily a matter of exegesis, but of outlook. It is not surprising that Victorinus of Poetovio, one of the last orthodox exponents of a millenial reign of Christ upon earth before the Judgment, died a martyr under Diocletian,[47] and that Lactantius composed the seventh book of the *Divine Institutes* in the shadow of the same persecution; for millenarianism, whether sacred or secular, will always have an appeal for the underdog, for the wretched of the earth, together with those recruits from the privileged classes who, either by generosity or by calculation, choose to throw in their lot with the oppressed.[48] Considered as a theological proposition, belief in a thousand-year reign is an open question. The mind which longs to be dissolved and to be with Christ, *which is far better*, is not likely to be attracted by the hope of earthly millenial delights; but there are others who, however sincerely they may believe the message of the gospel, yet desire to be vindicated in this world, to postpone the eternal for temporal domination and felicity. Hence the appeal of the apocalyptic millennium when

GERALD BONNER

Christianity was an unpopular, and sometimes persecuted, minority in the Roman empire. When, however, things changed, and the church basked in the sunshine of imperial favour, no longer persecuted but able to persecute, it was easy enough for those who benefited from the new state of affairs to feel that the millennium had indeed arrived, without having read Tyconius, Augustine, or any other theologian; and it was among the masses, for whom the change had been less obviously beneficial, that the millennial hope survived.

This did not mean that the Christian mediaeval world ceased to be eschatologically minded. On the contrary, in East and West alike men and women retained a lively sense of an approaching end of the world and of the Last Judgment. The apparent stability of the Byzantine world, an orthodox Christian society ruled by an emperor who was God's vicegerent upon earth, was tempered by an urgent apprehension of the end. The Eusebian Platonic view of the Empire was always tempered by the biblical conviction that time must have a stop: *Little children, it is the last hour*. The West was equally conscious of the question: 'What if this present were the world's last night?' Reference has already been made to Gregory the Great being haunted by a sense of impending doom in the concluding years of the disastrous sixth century but also sustained by a sense of confidence in the victory of the church. A similar assurance is to be found in Bede: the world is near its end and yet – or in spite of this – the church is prevailing; the dark night of heathendom is passing away, and we may look with confidence to the coming of Christ.[49] The almost lyrical note of Bede's commentary on the Song of Songs helps to explain how he could entertain the notion of an identification of the thousand-year reign of the saints with the church militant without ceasing to have an urgent expectation of the approaching end of the world.

Bede, in his *Commentary on the Apocalypse*, was much influenced by Tyconius' earlier commentary, which was also used by Caesarius of Arles, Apringius of Beja, Primasius of Hadrumetum, Ambrosius Autpertus, and Beatus of Liebana, the last of whom provided the inspiration for a famous cycle of manuscript apocalypse-illustration.[50] It is possible that Tyconius' exposition of the apocalypse 'in a wholly spiritual fashion'[51] had ultimately a greater influence on the mind of early mediaeval interpretation of the apocalypse than had the views of Augustine; but it is difficult to regard either of them as having been responsible for ending millenarian belief in the Middle Ages. The crucial fact is that millenarianism became unfashionable, not only in the Latin West but also in the Greek East where, so far as we know, the thought of Tyconius and Augustine exercised no influence. In the face of such evidence it seems best to explain the change as being due to the altered circumstances of the church, rather than to any particular theologian. The canon of Christian orthodoxy is determined in a variety of ways, and while we must never ignore the influence of the individual thinker, we would be well advised to ascribe the sea-change brought about by an altered environment as the principal factor determining the development of biblical and theological thinking regarding the nature of the millennium.

NOTES

1 *Bible et liturgie. La théologie biblique des sacrements et des fêtes d'après les Pères de l'Eglise*, Paris 1951, p. 374: 'Il marque...un moment capital de la pensée occidentale, celui où elle se détache d'un archaïsme qui la paralysait et s'oriente vers un construction autonome. C'est le moyen âge qui commence.'

2 *De haeresibus* 8: 'Cerinthiani a Cerintho idemque Merinthiani a Merintho, mundum ab angelis factum esse dicentes, et carne circumcidi opportere, atque alia huiusmodi legis praecepta servari; Iesum hominem tantummodo fuisse, nec resurrexisse, sed resurrecturum asseverantes. Mille quoque annos post resurrectionem in terreno regno Christi, secundum carnales ventris et libidinis voluptates, futuros, fabulantur; unde etiam Chiliastae sunt appellati', *CCL*, xlvi, 294.

3 *De civitate Dei* xx, 7, tr. by Henry Bettenson, *CCL*, xlviii, 709.

4 G. Folliet, 'La typologie du sabbat chez S. Augustin', in *Memorial Gustave Bardy*, *REAug*, 2 (1956), 371–90.

5 'L'Apocalypse. Augustine et Tyconius', in *Saint Augustin et la Bible*, ed. A.-M. la Bonnardière, Bible de tous le temps 3, Paris 1986, pp. 369–86.

6 *De Genesi contra Manichaeos* 1, 23, 41: 'tunc requiescent cum Christo ab omnibus operibus suis ii quibus dictum est, *Estote perfecti, sicut Pater vester qui in caelis est*. Tales enim faciunt opera bona valde. Post enim talia opera speranda est requies in die septimo, qui vesperam non habet', *PL* 34.193.

7 *REAug*, 2 (1956), 373: 'Augustin situe d'emblée ce repos sabbatique dans une perspective millénariste, quelque peu indéfinie sans doute, mais dont il nous fait connaître l'élément essential: la vie des saints avec le Christ revenu pour un nouvel âge.'

8 *De diversis quaestionibus* 57, 2: 'Fit autem separatio in fine saeculi tamquam in fine maris, id est in litore, cum regnant iusti primo temporaliter sicut in Apocalypsi scriptum est, deinde in aeternum in illa civitate quae ibi discribitur', *CCL*, 44 A, 101.

9 A. Kunzelmann, 'Die Chronologie der Sermones des hl. Augustinus,' *Miscellanea Agostiniana*, vol. 2, Rome 1931, p. 490; S. Poque, *Augustin d'Hippone: Sermons pour la Pâque*, SC 116, Paris 1966, p. 87; Dulaey, 'L'Apocalypse', p. 373 note 12.

10 *Sermo* 259, 2: 'Octavus ergo iste dies in fine saeculi novam vitam significat; septimus quietem futuram sanctorum in hac terra. Regnabit enim Dominus in terra cum sanctis suis, sicut dicunt Scripturae, et habebit hic Ecclesiam, quo nullus malus intrabit, separatam atque purgatam ab omni contagione nequitiae; quam significant centum quinquaginta tres illi pisces, de quibus iam, quantum memini, aliquando tractavimus', PL 38.1197.

11 *Sermo Mai* 94, 4: 'Quid est enim quod et alibi per prophetam promittit *pacem super pacem*, nisi quia et sabbatum, quod septimo die significatur, quamvis eodem dierum temporali contineatur volumine, habet utique requiem, quae in hac terra sanctis promissa est; ubi eos nulla huius saeculi procella sollicitet, post opera bona requiescentes in deo suo? Quod ut tanto ante significaret, postea quam fecit omnia bona valde, die septimo etiam ipse requievit. An propter aliud in libro sancti Iob scriptum est, *sexies de necessitatibus erui te, et in septimo non te tangit malum*? Sed propterea ille dies iam non habet vesperam, quia sine ullo incursu et obnubilatione tristitiae, quae plerumque de hominum malignorum permixta conversatione suffunditur, traicit sanctos in octavum diem, hoc est beatitudinem sempiternam. Aliud est enim, inter ipsa adhuc tempora requiescere in domino, quod die septimo id est sabbato significatur; aliud autem, transcendere omnia tempora, et in artificem temporum sine ullo iam fine componi, quod octavo significatur die, qui non volvendo cum ceteris, aeternitatis indicium se habere declarat', PL Supplementum 2, 485–6.

12 Folliet, REAug, 2 (1956), 377.

13 See J. Daniélou, 'La typologie millenariste de la semaine dans le Christianisme primitif', VigChr, 2 (1948), 1–16.

14 *Bible et liturgie*, 380: 'Nous retrouvons, rejoignant d'admirables profondeurs, le vieux millénarisme d'Irénée.'

15 Folliet, REAug, 2 (1956), 389.

16 Altaner, 'Augustinus und Irenäus', ThQ, 129 (1949), 162–72, reprinted in *Kleine patristischen Schriften herausgegeben von Günter Glockmann*, TU 83, (1967), pp. 194–203.

17 See Dulaey, 'L'Apocalypse,' pp. 370–1, notes 4 and 5.

18 Jerome, *Commentarius in Ieremiam* 19, 10: 'Iudaei auream atque gemmatam Ierusalem restituendam putent...et regnum in terris Domini Salvatoris. Quae licet non sequamur, tamen damnare non possumus, quia multi ecclesiasticorum virorum et martyres ista dixerunt', PL 24.833 A.

19 *Divinae institutiones* VII, 24: 'tunc auferentur a mundo tenebrae illae quibus obfundetur atque occaecabitur caelum, et luna claritudinem solis accipiet nec minuetur ulterius, sol autem septies tanto quam nunc est clarior fiet.

terra vero aperiet fecunditatem suam et uberrimas fruges sua sponte generabit, rupes montium melle sudabunt, per rivos vina decurrent et flumina lacte inundabunt; mundus denique ipse gaudebit et omnis rerum natura laetabitur erepta et liberata dominio mali et impietatis et sceleris et erroris. non bestiae per hoc tempus sanguine alentur, non aves praeda, sed quieta et placida erunt omnia. leones et vituli ad praesepe simul stabunt, lupus ovem non rapiet, canis non venabitur, accipitres et aquilae non nocebunt, infans cum serpentibus ludet. denique tum fient illa quae poetae aureis temporibus facta esse iam Saturno regnante dixerunt'. *CSEL* 19, 660.

20 See *Contra Faustum* XII, 8 (*CSEL* 25, 336) and XII, 19 (*CSEL* 25, 347), cited by Dulaey, 'L'Apocalypse', p. 373 note 13.

21 Ibid. pp. 373–5.

22 *Glaube und Unglaube in der Weltgeschichte*, p. 117.

23 'L'Apocalypse,' pp. 375–6.

24 *De Genesi ad litteram* I, xix, 39: 'Plerumque enim accidit ut aliquid de terra, de caelo, de caeteris mundi huius elementis, de motu et conversione vel etiam magnitudine et intervallis siderum, de certis defectis solis ac lunae, de circuitibus annorum et temporum, de naturis animalium, fructicum, lapidum, atque huiusmodi caeteris, etiam non christianus ita noverit, ut certissima ratione vel experientia teneat. Turpe est autem et perniciosum ac maxime cavendum, ut christianum de his rebus quasi secundum christianas litteras loquentem, ita delirare quilibet infidelis audiat, ut, quemadmodum dicitur, toto caelo errare conspiciens, risum tenere vix possit', *CSEL* 28 (1), 28–9.

25 *In Joannis evangelium tractatus* 98, 8: 'Qua occasione vani quidam Apocalypsim Pauli, quam sana non recipit ecclesia, nescio quibus fabulis plenam, stultissima praesumptione finxerunt, dicentes hanc esse unde dixerat raptum se fuisse in tertium caelum, et illic audisse ineffabilia verba *quae non licet homini loqui*', *CCL* 36, 581.

26 *Enarrationes in Psalmos* 105, 2. *CCL*, 40, 1554. For a discussion of the date, see A.-M. la Bonnardière, *Recherches de chronologie augustinienne*, Paris 1965, p. 149.

27 *Enchiridion ad Lausentium* xcii, 112: 'Frustra itaque nonnulli, immo quam plurimi, aeternam damnatorum poenam et cruciatus sine intermissione perpetuos humano miserantur affectu, atque ita futurum esse non credunt... Sed poenas damnatorum certis temporum intervallis existiment, si hoc eis placet, aliquatenus mitigari', *CCL*, 46, 109.

28 It was in this context that Augustine was to show himself so inflexibly opposed to Vincentius Victor's suggestion that the soul of the unbaptized Dinocrates had been released from hell by the intercession of his sister, St Perpetua. See *De anima et eius origine* I, x, 12; II, x, 14; xii, 16; III, ix, 12; IV, xvii, 27. *CSEL* 60, 312; 349; 351; 370; 407.

29 *Visio Pauli* 21, 22. Tr. in E. Hennecke, *New Testament Apocrypha*, ed. W. Schneemelcher, ET by R. McL. Wilson, London 1965, vol. 2, pp. 772–3. The Latin text, which is defective, and has to be supplemented from the Coptic, has been edited by M. R. James, *Texts and Studies*, vol. 2, 3, Cambridge 1893 and Th. Silverstein, *Visio Sancti Pauli*, Studies and Documents, ed. Lake, vol. 4, London 1935, p. 137.

30 *Haer.* 8, quoted above, note 2.

31 Filastrius Brixiensis, *Diversarum hereseon liber* 59: 'Alia est heresis Chiliontaëtitarum, id est mille annorum: quae docet ita: cum venerit Christus de caelo, inquit, mille anni illi erunt nobis iterum carnaliter ad vivendum, generandum et manducandum, sicut fit in hoc saeculo cottidie; ignorantes escam caelestem, id est immortalitatis illud praemium adfuturum, non hoc caducum et transiens, cum et dominus in evangelio Iudaeis quibusdam hoc suspicantibus: *Nescitis*, inquit, *scripturas et virtutes earum ignorantes*', *CSEL* 38, 31.

32 Pseudo-Jerome, *Indiculus de haeresibus Iudaeorum* 43: 'Chiliastae dicunt regnum sanctorum in carne carneum futurum, nolentes carnem nostram innovatam recipere spiritalem, sed bona terrae carnalia carnaliter per mille annos asserunt manducanda', *PL* 81.643 AB. See G. Bardy, 'Le "De Haeresibus" et ses sources', in *Miscellanea Agostiniana*, vol. 2, Rome 1931, pp. 397–416.

33 Altaner, 'Augustinus und Eusebius von Kaisareia', *ByZ*, 44 (1951), 1, reprinted in *KpS*, 253–4.

34 *Haer.* 83: 'Cum Eusebii historiam perscrutatus essem, cui Rufinus a se in Latinam linguam translatae subsequentium etiam temporum duos libros addidit', *CCL* 46, 337.

35 Rufinus/Eusebius, *HE* VII, 24: 'Episcopus quidam erat in partibus Ægypti Nepos nomine. hic Iudaico intellectu de futuris repromissionibus sentiebat easque corporaliter exhibendas docebat et mille annis in deliciis corporalibus in hac terra sanctos regnaturos esse cum Christo, huiusque sui dogmatis probamenta sumptis ex revelatione Iohannis testimoniis conabatur adserere, de quibus etiam libellos edidit interpretationes huiusmodi continentes', *GCS Eusebius*, Bd. 2, Teil 2, 686–7.

36 *St Austin and his Place in the History of Christian Thought*, London 1886, p. 116.

37 *The Political Aspects of Saint Augustine's 'City of God'*, London 1921, pp. 68–80, esp. 73–5.

38 Had Augustine in mind Tertullian's assertion (*de anima* 55.4) that Perpetua (an error for Saturus) saw only martyrs in Paradise?

39 *Civ.* xx, 9: 'Sed ideo tantummodo martyrum animas commemoravit, quia ipsi praecipue regnant mortui, qui usque ad mortem pro veritate certarunt. Sed a parte totum etiam caeteros mortuos intellegimus pertinentes ad ecclesiam, quod est regnum Christi', *CCL* 48, 718.

40 Ibid.: 'Alio modo igitur intellegendum est regnum caelorum, ubi ambo sunt, et ille scilicet qui solvit quod docet, et ille qui facit; sed ille minimus, ille magnus; alio modo autem regnum caelorum dicitur, quo non intrat nisi ille qui facit. Ac per hoc ubi utrumque genus est, ecclesia est, qualis nunc est; ubi autem illud solum erit, ecclesia est qualis tunc erit, quando malus in ea non erit. Ergo et nunc ecclesia regnum Christi est, regnumque caelorum. Regnant itaque cum illo etiam nunc sancti eius, aliter quidem, quam tunc regnabunt: nec tamen cum illo regnant zizania, quamvis in ecclesia cum tritico crescant', *CCL* 48, 716.

41 *The Political Aspects*, p. 73.

42 *Civ.* xx, 9: 'Neque enim piorum animae mortuorum separantur ab ecclesia, quae nunc etiam est regnum Christi. Alioquin nec ad altare Dei fieret eorum memoria in communicatione corporis Christi', *CCL* 48, 717.

43 Figgis, *The Political Aspects*, pp. 72, 73.

44 R. A. Markus, 'The sacred and the secular from Augustine to Gregory the Great', *JThS*, n.s. 36 (1985), 93.

45 Emile Mâle, *The Gothic Image. Religious Art in France of the Thirteenth Century*, ET by D. Nussey, New York 1958, ch. 6.

46 See the remarks of Joseph Vogt, *The Decline of Rome: The Metamorphosis of Ancient Civilisation*, ET by J. Sondheimer, London 1967, 116: 'The arguments advanced by Hilary and Lucifer struck a blow at the roots of ecclesiastical policy as conducted since the time of Constantine. But these were in the nature of lightning revelations descending upon individual protagonists, who had suffered much themselves. For the Church as a whole there was no question of returning to the age of the martyrs; on the contrary, from now on the Christian empire found its justification in a new type of political theology, while the Christian Church, in an age which could conceive of no separation between Church and State, kept its place as part of the God-given political order.'

47 Jerome, *De viris illustribus* 74, *PL* 23.719–20. See Pierre de Labriolle, *Histoire de la littérature latine chrétienne* 3rd edn, Paris 1947, vol. 1, pp. 318–20.

48 It may be noted that the credulity of Western intellectuals in the 1930s about the coming of the socialist state, foreshadowed in Soviet Russia, which would be an earthly paradise, fully equalled anything in the extravagances of Papias or the *Apocalypse of Paul*. Cf. Arthur Koestler, *The Invisible Writing*, London 1954, p. 158: 'At a Writers' Congress in Moscow, after listening to countless speeches promising universal happiness in a brave new world, André Malraux asked suddenly: "And what about the child run over by a tram car?" There was a pained silence; then somebody said, amidst general approbation: "In a perfect, planned socialist transport system there will be no accidents."'

49 See, for example, Bede, *In canticum canticorum* 11: '*Iam enim hiems transiit*, etc.

Hoc est quod Apostolus ait: *Nox praecessit, dies autem appropinquavit. Abiiciamus ergo opera tenebrarum, et induamus nos arma lucis* [Romans 13:12]. Sicut enim tenebras noctis, sic etiam recte per austeritatem hiemis et imbrium, tempestas exprimitur infidelitatis, quae totum orbem usque ad tempus agebat Dominicae incarnationis. At ubi Sol iustitiae mundo illuxit, abscedente mox ac depulsa prisca brumalis infidelitatis perfidia, flores apparuerunt in terra, quia initia iam nascentis Ecclesiae in sanctorum fideli ac pia devotione claruerunt' (*PL* 91.1110 CD); ibid. VI: 'Et bene dictura, *Surgamus ad vineas*, praemisit *Mane*; Mane enim dicit ipsum verae lucis exortum, per quem de potestate tenebrarum mundus ereptus est. *Mane* ergo, inquit, *surgamus ad vineas*: ac si patenter dicat: Quia nox priscae infidelitatis abscessit, quia lux Evangelii coruscantis iam apparere incipit, *surgamus*, quaeso, *ad vineas*, id est, ad Ecclesias per orbem Deo instruendas operam damus' (*PL* 91.1202 A). Cf. G. Bonner, 'Bede and Medieval Civilization', *Anglo-Saxon England*, 2 (1973), 84.

50 W. Neuss, *Die Apokalypse des hl. Johannes in der altspanischen und altchristlichen Bibel-Illustration*, Spanische Forschungen der Görresgesellschaft 2–3, Münster in Westfalen 1931, 2 vols.; John Williams, *Early Spanish Manuscript Illumination*, London 1977.

51 Gennadius, *De scriptoribus ecclesiasticis* 18: 'Exposuit et Apocalypsin Iohannis ex integro nihil in ea carnale, sed totum intelligens spiritale', *PL* 58.1071.

Divine simplicity as a problem for orthodoxy

CHRISTOPHER STEAD

'The evolution of orthodoxy' might easily be understood as a process which belongs wholly to the past: the development of Christian doctrine, on which Henry Chadwick has shed such a graceful and penetrating light, would then be contrasted with a complete and stable construction in which Christianity has come to rest. But to call it complete and stable need not mean that further progress is excluded; at the very least, new challenges are likely to arise, and old truths will need to be re-stated. And most of our generation, and of our juniors, will think this programme far too tame: in their eyes, only an obstinate and secluded mind will persist in defending an orthodoxy that is purely static. I for one would certainly wish to see its evolution as a continuing process, in which established positions need to be clarified and some false steps retracted, in the faith that a better grounded and better articulated consensus of belief may be attained.

From such a standpoint one can turn with a rueful admiration to a handbook which has given invaluable service to a succession of beginners in theology, the *Enchiridion Patristicum* of M. J. Rouet de Journel, completed in 1911 and appearing in its twenty-fourth edition in 1969. The learned author has collected over 2,400 brief passages from the Fathers, and offers a guide to his selection in an 'Index Analyticus', arranged so as to suggest that the Fathers prospectively uphold the entire structure of modern catholic orthodoxy as defined in the tradition of St Thomas Aquinas. As article 97, we find the heading *Deus est simplicissimus, ita ut nullum omnino admittat compositionem*. The authorities cited include Tertullian, Athanasius, Basil, Gregory of Nyssa, John Chrysostom, Ambrose, Augustine and Cyril: and most of them, it must be said, are consonant with the author's formulation and seem to have no reservations about the black-and-white antithesis, simple or composite, on which it is based.

I shall submit that this is an over-simplification: we must not think that simplicity is itself a simple notion. But how else can one explain the fact that the theme of divine simplicity has been so little discussed? It figures, no doubt, in text-books of dogmatic theology: but I cannot discover that much detailed attention has been given to the actual usage of the key words *haplous* and *haplotēs* or to their Latin equivalents. The entry in H. J. Sieben's *Voces* makes it appear that simplicity has been examined only in its guise as a moral virtue, in which a modest disposition is expressed in truthful unaffected language and unassuming reliability of conduct. The article 'Einfalt' in the *Reallexikon für Antike und Christentum* surveys much the same ground. Nevertheless there are some unexpected features in the philosophical use of the words for simplicity, and some transitions of thought which I believe cannot bear the weight that has been put upon them.

We may begin by taking an example of the standard exposition from Gregory Nazianzen's *Second Theological Oration (Oratio 28)*, 7 (not included in the *Enchiridion*):

For what will you conceive the Deity to be, if you rely on all methods of reason?...A body? How then is he infinite and boundless and formless and intangible and invisible?...For how shall he be an object of worship if he be circumscribed? Or how shall he escape being compounded out of elements and resolved into them again, or indeed totally dissolved? For composition is a source of conflict, and conflict of separation, and this again of dissolution; and dissolution is totally foreign to God and to the first nature. So there can be no separation, to exclude dissolution: no conflict, to exclude separation; no composition, to exclude conflict; and therefore He is not a body, to exclude composition. So the argument is established by going back from the last to the first.

The rhetorical and allusive style which Gregory adopts, while addressing a largely uninstructed congregation, shows that he takes his argument to be thoroughly established and familiar. The word *haplous* does not in fact appear in this passage, but Gregory makes his point clearly enough by saying that God is 'not compounded of elements' (*ek stoicheiōn sugkeisthai*) and is immune from composition (*sunthesis*); composition would imply conflict (*machē*). The mention of conflict suggests that Gregory is using 'elements' in the fairly precise sense to indicate the traditional four, earth, air, fire and water, which were thought to display contrary qualities, hot and cold, wet and dry: it was a favourite topic of Christian apologetics to say that God's wisdom is manifested in the art with which he combined potentially discordant elements into an harmonious world order.[1] One feature of the traditional construction which Gregory omits is the doctrine that God is strictly immutable: but this is commonly based on a rather different understanding of 'composite being', in which change is explained as a rearrangement of the minute particles, atoms or otherwise, of which material things are composed: thus also they would come to an end when their constituents lose their cohesion and are absorbed into the surrounding matter. Conversely, if God is not composed of such particles, he is immune from change. This argument can easily be illustrated (e.g. Athanasius *Contra gentes* 41, *De decretis* 11); but it is not easy to see why change or dissolution should result from *conflict* among minute bodies such as atoms: one would rather think of a failure to cohere or to maintain their orderly disposition. This may already suggest that the orthodox case is not quite so simple and straightforward as appears at first glance.

The origins of this train of thought are clearly pre-Christian, and illustrations can be found in Philo; but for the moment I will postpone this enquiry, and consider some other, and less rigorous interpretations of simplicity which entered the Christian tradition.

(1) First of all, a student of Aristotle cannot read far without encountering the phrase 'simple bodies', *hapla sōmata*. 'Simple' in this connection means that they do not consist of other elements which could exist separately. The last four words are important, since the four elements, which are simple bodies in this sense, were thought to result from the imposition of qualities on formless matter (see e.g. Hippolytus, *Refutatio omnium haeresium* 1.19.1 for a doxographic account): but this is a purely theoretical analysis, as one cannot actually find matter existing without qualities, or vice versa, to use as ingredients which could actually be combined or compounded. Further, 'simple bodies' have no structure or pattern; or more exactly, to say that they are simple makes no stipulations about their location or distribution. It follows that things which are simple in this sense need not be indivisible; the element fire, for example, appears in a multitude of separate places, in the stars, for instance, and in a modified form in animal bodies. Arius Didymus mentions the division of simple bodies.[2]

Within the Christian tradition this usage is best illustrated by Tertullian, who of course makes use of stoic teaching on matter and its qualities. The Stoics held that the elements can change one into another (*SVF* 2.413 etc.), so that none of them is imperishable except the fire from which they originate and to which they return; while in the short run it is admitted that fire itself can be extinguished and 'die' (ibid. 430, 446). The whole process is controlled by 'spirit', *pneuma* (ibid. 416), whose status is unclear; it is sometimes identified as a separate element (ibid.), sometimes as fire (ibid. 421–3) or a compound of air and fire (ibid. 439–41); but in each case it functions as the rational directive process in the universe, or God (ibid. 1045). God, then, is in some sense simple (*suneches*), but is not unchangeable.

These doctrines appear with some variation in Tertullian's teaching about the soul. He takes it for granted that the soul is immortal; but if indissoluble, it must be indivisible, and therefore simple (*singularis et simplex*, *De anima* 14). But it is only simple in a very large and loose sense; Tertullian immediately notes that it is commonly divided into 'parts'; though these are more properly called 'faculties' or 'powers' (*huiusmodi autem non tam partes animae habebuntur quam vires et efficaciae et operae*, ibid. 14.3). On the other hand he believes that the soul is corporeal and has a shape conforming to that of the body (ibid. 9); it is hard to see how it can fail to have 'parts' in the sense of limbs and other members; and if so, it is 'simple' in a much weaker sense even than 'simple bodies' like fire or spirit. Moreover Tertullian, while repeating that the soul is *substantia simplex* (22.2), also insists that it is subject to change (21); otherwise there could be no possibility of human free will. One might compare the stoic doctrines that both God and the soul are 'spirit' (*SVF* 2.1035) and that God is subject to change (ibid. 1045, 1049ff.); though on the latter point Tertullian dissents and takes the normal view: only God is unchangeable (*De anima* 21.7).

In other respects, however, Tertullian stands apart from the main tradition, and I am not clear that the Fathers commonly understood the simplicity of God on the analogy of simple bodies. It might certainly have provided an answer to anthropomorphic theories; the idea that God had man-like limbs and features could be contradicted by picturing him as uniformly distributed through the universe, and Augustine tells us that he came to rest for a time in a conception of this sort (*Confessiones* 7.1.1–2). Again it might seem a natural deduction from the statements that God is light, and fire, and spirit (1 John 1:5, Deuteronomy 4:24, John 4:24); but in a well-known passage (*De principiis* 1.1.4) Origen explains that these words are not to be interpreted in physical terms, and he could probably count on general agreement. Some suggestion of the 'simple bodies' interpretation might be found in Eusebius, who argues (*Demonstratio evangelica* 4.15.16) that God's simple, uncompounded and unmixed nature may be symbolized by the simple 'oil of gladness' with which Christ is anointed (Psalm 44:8 LXX) whereas God's many powers and functions are suggested by the composite ointment (*muron*) prescribed for the priests in Exodus 30:22ff. But the physical implication is not to be taken seriously, any more than the suggestion that God's will is, so to speak, the matter and substance from which the universe is derived. In Eusebius' view God is a unity, *monas* – indeed he surpasses the monad as the source of all creation (ibid. 4.1.5); and in a later work, the *Ecclesiastical Theology* (2.14.6) Eusebius insists on the absolute simplicity of the divine being.

(2) Tertullian's opinion that the soul is a simple substance but is also subject to change could be endorsed by many thinkers, both Christian and pagan, who would not accept his peculiar doctrine of a corporeal soul. It seems likely, in fact, that the whole argument about the simplicity of God begins with a debate about the soul, in which Plato played the leading part. In the *Phaedo* 78a, he draws a distinction between composite things and those that are uncompounded (*axunthetos*), and argues that it is the former that are liable to change, whereas absolute essences, for instance of beauty or equality, persist unchanging. But the soul is akin to these realities; it is 'most like the divine and immortal and intellectual and uniform (*monoeidēs*) and indissoluble and unchanging' (ibid. 80b). The natural inference would be that the soul can properly be described as simple. On the other hand, in the *Phaedrus* and the *Republic* he introduces the well-known theory of three elements in the soul: it can be compared with the 'composite force' (*sumphutō(i) dunamei*) of a pair of winged horses and their charioteer, which represent desire, impulsiveness and reason (*Phaedrus* 246A). Plato is very sparing with technical terms; he does not refer to 'parts' of the soul, but to 'natures' (*phuseis*) or 'forms of being' (*eidē*) which are not 'identical in nature' (*homophuēs*: *Republic* 439e, 440e, 441a). However, since he introduces the discussion by asking whether we learn and lust and rage with three distinct 'things' (*trisin ousin*, cf. *tritō(i) tini*) or with the whole soul – 436a – it was natural to represent him as analysing it into three parts. Finally, a perplexing passage in *Republic* 10, 611a–d suggests that the description of the soul as simple only applies to its ideal condition or 'truest nature' (*tē(i) alēthestatē(i) phusei*); in its actual state, as manifested in disorderly characters, it is truly described as composite, and not even well compounded (611b and c).

Aristotle makes it clear that in his day there was a debate as to whether one should refer to 'parts' of the soul (*merē*, *moria*) or regard it as

CHRISTOPHER STEAD

undivided but exercising a variety of functions, *dunameis*.[3] The latter opinion seems to have gained ground; at any rate Galen reports that both Aristotle and Posidonius preferred to speak of 'powers' in the soul rather than 'parts';[4] but arguments about 'parts' of the soul continued, at least in the doxographic literature,[5] and are frequent in Philo.[6] Posidonius accepted Plato's threefold analysis and claimed the support of Cleanthes,[7] whereas Chrysippus apparently adopted an intellectualist theory which regarded emotions as judgments[8] and so thought of all the operations of the soul as proceeding from a single source. Posidonius complains that Chrysippus' language is confused, but Tertullian is probably mistaken in saying that he reckoned eight parts in the soul; this was a common Stoic opinion, but not that of Chrysippus himself.

In the later tradition opinion seems to have veered to the view that is it correct to speak of 'powers' of the soul rather than 'parts'; so Tertullian, as noted above: Galen, Alexander of Aphrodisias, Calcidius 223, Porphyry and Severus, in Eusebius, *Praeparatio evangelica*, 13.17.6, all noted by J. H. Waszink[9]; Iamblichus is inconsistent, but on the whole prefers 'powers'.[10]

Meanwhile it had become customary to apply the same principle to the divinity; Philo draws a parallel between our mind and the divine one (*ho huper hēmas*), explaining that both are without parts and undivided (*quis rerum divinarum heres?* 234–6); but this apparently applies to our mind only, as distinct from other 'parts' of the soul.[11] Philo seems to speak of such 'parts' without embarrassment; but his enumeration of these parts can be precisely paralleled in terms of 'powers', seven lower powers plus the reason (*De mutatione nominum* 110–11). But God is a whole in which there are no parts (*De posteritate Caini* 3–4, *Mut. nom.* 184); moreover to speak of parts would suggest the picture of a God in human form, which the scriptures introduce only as a concession to human weakness (*De somniis* 1.234–6). It follows that God must be seen as operating through his powers.

A similar parallel between God and the human mind could be drawn by considering not their constitution but their operations. It is a commonplace that the mind does not impair its own power by expressing itself in words or by making an act of will (so e.g. Philo, *De gigantibus*. 25). In the same way Christian theologians could argue that the divine Logos proceeds from the Father without any loss or division, as spoken Word or as expressing the Father's will (Justin, *Dialogus* 61 and 128, Tatian, *Ad Graecos* 5.1, Theophilus, *Ad Autolycum* 2.22 etc.) 'without cutting off any part of the mind' (Origen, *De principiis* 1.2.6).

This notion of 'undiminished giving', accepted also by neo-Platonist philosophers,[12] has been much discussed, and probably needs no further illustration.

From the above reflections it would seem that there are radical defects in the neat antithesis of simple and compound which is presupposed by Gregory and has been adopted by orthodox Christian theologians. For, in the first place, an object which has no parts need not be wholly undifferentiated; it might have distinguishable features, like the colours of a rainbow, which could not properly be described as parts (whether we think of the colours themselves, or of the coloured areas which merge one into the other). Again, if an object consists of parts, it does not follow that it is constructed by assembling those parts: a tree has a trunk, branches, and twigs, but it is not brought into being by taking those parts and putting them together, as a house is built by collecting and then assembling bricks, beams and roofing tiles in the appropriate order. And the converse is also probable; it is not intuitively obvious that physical objects can only perish by the separation of their parts; why should not some things simply fade away, like a spark? Again, a tree may die without its branches falling apart from the trunk; this will occur later, it may be, when both have begun to rot; the *total* dispersal of its constituent atoms will take still longer.

Where the soul is concerned, it seems reasonable to use the comparison of a natural organism; and the Stoics may have partly seen this possibility, even though they expressed it in the rather absurd form (as we would think) that the universe is a rational animal;[13] for they represented the cosmos as an organic whole whose parts reacted one upon another by 'sympathy',[14] and taught that there is an analogy between the cosmos and man, who can be called a 'little universe' or 'microcosm'.[15]

On the other hand it would seem that a soul which exercises a variety of powers cannot be simple in any very rigorous sense; for if they are to be powers *of* the soul, rather than autonomous agencies that just happen to sympathize with its activities, there must be modifications in the soul which explain why it exercises one power rather than another on a given occasion or towards a particular object. This will be true, I think, whether the powers are seen as truly intrinsic to the soul or as semi-independent auxiliaries; if such auxiliaries merely go into action on behalf of a rigorously simple soul, the soul itself is not acting.[16] And the same should be true of God, whose action is sometimes seen as delegated to quasi-independent powers or even to angels, who can act on a lower level (Philo, *De opificio mundi*. 74–5!), misunderstand their instructions or even rebel (*Gig.* 6.17). There is of course the alternative of supposing that all God's powers are mutually compatible, and that he exercises them all perpetually.[17] And this view can be advocated in impressive terms; God confronts us in a single undifferentiated blaze of majesty and mercy by which we are both humbled and uplifted. But this can only be made convincing if stated as a generality; we have no grounds for believing that 'God opposes the proud but gives grace to the humble'; we have to say that the proud are frustrated because they miss their way to the goal which would truly satisfy them, and, more sadly, that the humble are uplifted if they can find the confidence to overcome their dejection. The identity of God's attributes and powers cannot be combined with a genuine doctrine of particular providence.

(3) One reason why simplicity is easily misconstrued is that it is one possible interpretation of the notion of unity, and is liable to be influenced by its neighbours. In my book *Divine Substance*, pp. 180–93, I referred to three interpretations of unity which can be labelled by the catchwords *unicus*, *simplex*, *constans* (or *immutabilis*). It might have been helpful to have added a fourth, namely *primus*, to take note of the view, probably Pythagorean in origin, that the structure of the universe can be explained in terms of numbers, and that numbers derive from the One, which is therefore the origin of all things.

Why 'probably' Pythagorean? Because Aristotle, our most reliable witness, represented them as teaching that the One is derivative; see *Metaphysica* A 5, 987 a 13ff. – they reach *two* first principles – and *Ethica Nicomachea* A 4, 1096 b 5, they place the One in the column of goods (and so not at its head). But contrast *Metaphysica* A 6, 987 b 23ff: Plato said, like the Pythagoreans, that numbers are to other things the cause of their being, but differed from them in postulating a dyad *instead of the unlimited as a unity*. Probably, then, some members of the school reckoned the monad as the first principle. Among later critics, Aetius seems to make them teach two principles, of which however the monad has the active and formative role and is identified as God;[18] in Hippolytus' account the monad is the sole source (*Refutatio omnium haeresium* 1.2.6). Philo refers to God as monad (e.g. *quod Deus immutabilis sit*, 11, *heres* 183), but also teaches that the monad merely symbolizes God (*Legum allegoriae* 2.3, *De specialibus legibus* 3.180, cf. *De praemiis et poenis* 40); the dyad is, or symbolizes, created and divisible matter (*Somn.* 2.70, *Spec. leg.* 3.180) and is given a radically inferior dignity.

To resume: if we now consider a scheme involving four members, *primus, unicus, simplex, constans*, it will be difficult to resist the claims of two other candidates, namely *bonus* and *verus*, since these constantly figure in ancient discussions in conjunction with the notion of unity. Plato for instance argues that a god must be both simple and unchanging, and sees immunity from change as a sign of goodness (*Rep.* 2.380 d–e). Aristotle discusses the relation between unity and truth, without it seems reaching a final conclusion. On the one hand he asserts that knowledge implies an identity – at least an identity of form – between the mind and its object (*De anima* 3.5, 430 a 20 etc.); on the other hand *both truth and falsity* entail a composition of thoughts into a unity (ibid. 3.6, 430 a 27–8); or, with a different emphasis, both truth and falsehood involve a combination of notions (432 a 12).

In theory, it would be an admirable project to consider the logical relations between the six attributes we have named. In practice, it would be an impossibly complex task. A set of six members exhibits $6 \times 5 = 30$ possible combinations, and each of these would have to be tested in both directions; if a, then b; but also, if b, then a. But what finally puts this project out of court is the fact that several, and possibly all, of the attributes in question have been understood and explained in different ways by different writers. We have been considering simplicity; but this is a minuscule discussion compared with the vast literature devoted to the nature of goodness, and to theories of truth.

It is possible, however, to say something about the logical links which were thought to connect simplicity in particular with its neighbours; and I would begin by observing that most of them are pre-Christian, and can be illustrated from Philo. Some further precision may have accrued in later discussion; but in the main they belong to the inheritance, rather than to the evolution, of Christian orthodoxy. It hardly needs repeating that Philo takes over the Pythagorean teaching that a simple unity is the source of all reality; at *Heres* 190 he recalls the purely arithmetical doctrine that the monad is not a number (i.e. plurality) but the source of all number; at *Somn.* 2.70 he applies this doctrine to theology, so as to equate the monad with the Maker. It might seem otiose to maintain that the monad is unique; but the Pythagoreans exploited the verbal similarity of *monas/monos/monimos*, and Philo in turn observes that the monad is like God because of their singularity, monōsis (*Heres* 183, *Spec. leg.* 2.176). At *Somn.* 2.221 Philo speaks of the constancy of the ultimate source; at *De confusione linguarum* 180 he associates 'the eldest of things that are' with 'the most perfect good'; at *De praemiis et poenis* 40 'better than the good' is coupled with 'older than the monad' cited above. Finally the monad is absolute reality (*Immut.* 11), and *De ebrietate* 45 refers to 'the one true God'. In terms of our catchwords, therefore, the monad is *simplex, primus, unicus, constans, bonus, verus*.

The source of these connections must be looked for in a region of ancient philosophy which remains obscure despite intensive discussion: the Pythagorean philosophy before the time of Plato, and the Pythagorean teaching which Plato adapted in his theory of ideal numbers, and above all in his enigmatic lecture on 'the One and the Good'. We are not concerned at present with the question, how Plato thought the numbers are derived from the One;[19] nor with the connections of thought which Plato must have tried to establish between individual numbers and basic concepts (of which the traditional example is that four = justice, invoking the 'four-square' right-angle as the basis of exact division, of equality, and of stable constructions). Our main interest is the One itself; and I suggest that we can trace back to these early discussions two principles which came to form part of the Christian tradition. The first is that the One is the ultimate source of a multiplicity of Forms which provide the permanent structure of the universe and also the pattern of its values. These Forms themselves exhibit both unity and goodness, but in a lesser degree and a relative mode compared with their source; they are each of them a unity relative to their multiple instances, but they are distinct from each other as contrasted with its absolute unity; and they are each of them the source of goodness, or pattern of goodness, for some class of beings, 'a good so-and-so', rather than being the sole source of all goodness. The second principle is that the One is the highest reality and absolute truth, since it holds the key to the Forms on which all true predication must be based; but it is a truth which is inconceivable and inexpressible, certainly to us men, and possibly to any being other than itself; the reason being that true statements were conceived on the model of a synthesis of two notions (and, for that matter, knowledge was seen as the identification of the mind with its object); but in neither case was pure and absolute unity achieved; a true statement could only be significant if two distinct notions were brought together (a theory opposed to the view put about by Antisthenes that the only unquestionably true statement was the unqualified identity 'X is X'); and the mind's 'identity' with its object could only be an identity of form, not a wholesale coalescence. It followed that the One had to be exhibited as, on the one hand, good, being the source of all goodness; but contrariwise as unknowable and indefinable; not simply devoid of qualities (e.g. sense-qualities) but unconditioned by any attribute whatsoever, since any statement about it could not be true unless it was in formal correspondence with its object (i.e. simple) and could not be significant unless it were composite, attaching a predicate which was distinguishable from its subject.

Within the Platonic tradition, Plotinus made the most sustained and coherent effort to work out these principles, concluding *inter alia* that the ultimate source could not have knowledge even of itself, since even self-knowledge implied a distinction between the mind as Knower and the mind as Known; thus the traditional 'scale of being', ascending from inanimate nature to conscious minds and upwards through progressively purer and more penetrating intelligences, was apparently interrupted; not simply lost in the clouds of heavenly glory, but brought to a stand by the paradox of a Being who is the source of all goodness but cannot be good.[20] Christian thinkers, inheriting a richer though far more complex tradition, struck out new lines of thought which were never (I think) connected in a logically coherent whole, but which, if pursued, should have exhibited the notion of wholly undifferentiated divine simplicity as an unwanted survival.

Within the compass of this essay, there are only two critical principles which I have space to develop. One of these might be labelled 'the diminishing returns of unification'; the other I take to be simply an application of a fairly recent movement in philosophy, namely the rejection of the picture theory of meaning.

However, no originality is claimed for the first principle either. It relates to a proposal made by Leonard Hodgson,[21] which perhaps never attracted as much attention as it deserved. Hodgson contrasted 'mathematical' with 'organic' unity, explaining that 'Approximation to the ideal of mathematical unity is measured by a scale of…absence of multiplicity; but approximation to the ideal of organic unity is measured by a scale of intensity of unifying power' (p. 94). Hodgson considers the case of human character, in which a divided mind or a split personality is a grave disadvantage. 'In the case of the human self, the unity is by no means always perfect…But in whatever measure it is achieved, this is not affected by the cancellation of factors until nothing is left but an undifferentiated unity…far more intense is the unity manifested in a life which unifies a wider range.'

One might, alternatively, consider the role of unity in personal relationships, taking a single pair of friends to deputize for the more complex interrelations of a group or of our whole society. Clearly there must be some correspondence or similarity of interests, fortune or temperament if any personal relationship is to begin; and the process of growing together, of assimilating another's experience and imitating his judgments and values, can be exciting and rewarding. But the partnership needs refreshing by the maintenance of outside interests and the bringing in of fresh experience by each of the partners and ideally by a love shared by both partners but directed on to another person or cause; for however attractive initially the recognition of an *alter ego* provided by fortune, or the attempt to realize it as an ideal, the project is self-defeating: to make one personality an exact replica of the other is to reduce by one the number of distinct moral agents; and a mutually monopolizing partnership has no great advantage over a self-absorbed individual.

Hodgson used his concept of unity to formulate a doctrine of the Trinity in social terms. 'The true pattern of unity for men who are made in the image of God is one in which there is a place for all our different selves, so far as they are good selves, a unity in which each is to remain its own self in order that it may play its part in enriching the whole' (p. 185). I would not follow him at every point: the sentence just quoted could easily provoke the reply that there can be no analogy of this kind with a God who needs no enrichment, since he is himself the source of all good things. But the alternative seems to be that we treat the substance or inner being of the Godhead, characterized by mysterious and incomprehensible but absolute simplicity, as something totally unrelated to the Trinity of Persons in which we believe it is deployed. And I would think also that there is no escaping the conclusion drawn by Plotinus: an absolutely simple Godhead cannot understand or control the influence and attraction that he exerts.

My second point is that it is a mistake to think that a descriptive sentence can only be true if it is in a structural correspondence with the reality or state of affairs which it describes. Like so many philosophical theories, the picture theory of meaning is a Cinderella's glass coach so long as one is content to go along with it and accept it on its own terms, but collapses into dust and cobwebs when the spell is broken.[22] It seems beneath the dignity of a serious objection if one observes that, on such a theory, to state that there are four people in this room one would have to formulate a sentence embodying four identical symbols. And of course the theory can be developed so as to escape such simply conceived objections: we have to incorporate conventions in which 'four' replaces a symbolism of the form a, b, c, d, and 'in the room' is a conventional equivalent for an ideal symbolism in which the symbols for the four people would be actually enclosed by the symbol for 'room'.

Theories of this kind, however, seem to have affected ancient discussions on the nature of God; it could be argued, for instance, that God cannot be known because he cannot be defined; he cannot be defined because that would involve assigning him to a genus within which he is distinguished by a differentia; and this would mean he consisted of two distinct elements, and was no longer simple.[23] The answer, reduced to its simplest terms, is that there is no reason to think that a correct description mirrors the structure of the thing described. If we describe man as a rational animal, we cannot point to the two elements named by this phrase; and if we tried to do so – perhaps by saying that he has an animal body *plus* a directing intelligence – we can only make this plausible by ignoring the relatedness of the two components. Man lives his animal life in a way prescribed by reason, but conversely the exercise of his reason is qualified and sometimes interrupted by his animal nature. Why not then ignore the attempt to conform him to his definition, refer to him as a psycho-physical unity and be done with it?

It is a mistake of this order which I take to be a peculiar weakness of the Cappadocian theology of the Trinity: the three Persons are defined as possessing the same simple undivided divine substance qualified by three distinguishing peculiarities. But this is not presented only as a way in which they may be conceived; the definitions are supposed to conform to their inner structure, so that the undivided Godhead which they share is not so much manifested in three personal beings or modes as contradicted by the imposed characteristics by which they are distinguished. On the other hand the Cappadocians most opportunely, though unexpectedly, insist that the simplicity of the Godhead does not preclude a multiplicity of descriptions, *epinoiai*. These, however, were thought to relate to the energies and relationships of the Godhead, leaving his simple substance unaffected; a position which I have given reason to reject.

To return, in conclusion, from the intricacies of exact theology to the burdens imposed on our mortality by faith in a transcendent spirit: the concept of divine simplicity should present a challenge to an over-simple faith. One cannot help feeling that there is some force in the sceptics' objection to 'God-bothering'; it is less easy for us than it was for an earlier generation to assert without misgivings that 'the eyes of the Lord are over the righteous and his ears are open unto their prayer'. If we claim that our prayers are heard and answered, does this mean that we expect God to give us his undivided attention? Not, surely, in the sense that we ask him to neglect all other petitioners. Can we then imagine a mind whose capacities are so vast that it can respond to the individual needs of men whose numbers are multiplying beyond all imagination? The problem here is that this is more easily imagined if we note the capacity of our own minds to control many complex movements and activities without a conscious effort of attention; we might suppose that in some similar way God automatically distributes his bounty, 'making the sun to rise upon the evil and upon the good', or more personally and creatively, distributing to each man the help or correction that his condition requires. But this still does not suggest a God who stands in a caring relationship; and it may prove that the only way in which this can be upheld is by giving full weight to the doctrine that the Father exercises this condescending grace through his expression in the incarnate Christ made man for us. To suggest this puts the orthodoxy of Nicaea and Chalcedon under the severest strain;/we wonder whether it can support the union of infinite, all-regarding majesty with the intimacy of a man-to-man relationship; so that the operations are undivided, the majesty unimpaired by an unlimited distribution, the intimacy preserved without distraction over a cosmic extension of concern. This is a problem on which even the Arians, if given their due, might have something to teach us; and on which the evolution of orthodoxy might bring much-needed light.

NOTES

1 Methodius, *De resurrectione* 2.10; Eusebius, *Laus Constantini* 11.13, 12.11; Constantine, *Ad sanctos* 7.1–2; Athanasius, *Contra gentes* 27 fin, 36–7; cf. Severus in Eusebius, *Praeparatio evangelica* 13.17.2.
2 Diels, *DG*, p. 449, fr. 5.
3 See *De anima* 1.5, 411b 1–19, 2.2, 413b 13ff., 28, cf. 2.3 *init.*; *De iuventute* 1, 467b 17; *Ethica Eudemia* 2.1, 1219b 32.
4 Posidonius, fr. 142–6 Edelstein.
5 Diels, *DG*, Index, p. 781b.
6 See J. Leisegang's index (vol. VII. 2, Berlin 1936), 868b 869a, to L. Cohn and P. Wendland's edition of Philo.
7 Fr. 32 = *SVF* 1.571.
8 Fr. 34, cf. *SVF* 2.283.
9 *Tertullianus de anima*, Amsterdam 1947, p. 215.
10 A.-M. Festugière, *La révélation d'Hermès Trismégiste*, vol. 3, pp. 194–5.

11 For which see *Quis rerum divinarum heres?* 232; *De opificio mundi* 117; *Legum allegoriae* 1.11; *Quod deterius potiori insidiari soleat* 168; *De agricultura* 30 etc.

12 R. T. Wallis, *Neoplatonism*, London 1973, pp. 34, 62.

13 *SVF* 2.92, 633–5, 638, etc.

14 *SVF* 2.475, 534, 546, 1023, 1211 (= Posidonius fr. 106); Philo, *migr.* 178–80; Marcus Aurelius, 6.38.

15 Philo, *Heres* 155, cf. *Migr.* 219–20.

16 Cf. W. Pannenberg, in *Basic Questions in Theology*, vol. 2, London 1971, pp. 170–1.

17 Irenaeus, *Haer.* 2.13.3, see my *Divine Substance*, Oxford 1977, pp. 187–9; Pannenberg, *Basic Questions*, p. 167.

18 Diels, *DG* 281a 6–12, 302a 7–10.

19 For which consult, e.g., W. D. Ross, *Plato's Theory of Ideas*, Oxford 1951, and the passages collected by C. J. de Vogel, *Greek Philosophy. A Collection of Texts*, vol. 1: *Thales to Plato*, Leiden 1950, under the heading 'The Ideal Numbers'.

20 Plotinus himself did of course identify the first principle as 'the Good', as well as 'the One'.

21 *The Doctrine of the Trinity*, London 1943, pp. 89ff., esp. pp. 94–5.

22 I use the phrase rather loosely, without specific reference to Wittgenstein's theory, for which see G. H. R. Parkinson, *The Theory of Meaning*, Oxford 1968, p. 5.

23 Cf. Pannenberg, *Basic Questions*, p. 132.

The origins of monasticism

J. C. O'NEILL

Henry Chadwick, once fellow of Queens', Cambridge, student of Christ Church, Oxford, and Dean, returned to Cambridge and became the most junior fellow of Magdalene. As he humbly performed the duties of the most junior fellow in the combination room after dinner, he would delight to tell a stranger that he was following the rule handed down from monasticism of old. In a volume devoted to the evolution of orthodoxy I offer him my hunch that the tradition is even older than he thinks. He will find the rule he followed in Magdalene explicitly stated in Philo's book *On the Contemplative Life*, §67. Ideas may evolve, but practice remains stubbornly the same, and I offer this essay as grateful tribute to a teacher and friend who passed on to me by precept and example the ancient practices of scholarship without which truth would soon be choked with weeds. I argue that, if orthodoxy evolved, the practice of the orthodox did not.

Everyone says that monasticism began with Antony and Pachomius in Upper Egypt, that is, at the end of the third century and the beginning of the fourth, and the case is certainly impressive. Athanasius' *Life of Antony*, and the *Life of Pachomius* are massive literary evidence of a popular movement, first of disciples around the great hermit Antony, and then of settled monasteries governed by an abbot according to a definite Rule, a Rule formulated by Pachomius. Upper Egypt was visited by Christians from other parts of the world, who went home and founded monasteries after the pattern they had seen flourishing there.

I want to argue that monasticism did not begin with Antony and Pachomius, did not begin with their allegedly less-well-organized predecessors. I want to argue that monasticism was always simply there in the life of the church. More than that. I want to argue that Christian monasticism was a continuation of Jewish monasticism, and that Jewish monasticism reached back to the communities of the sons of the prophets. The Carmelites, who traditionally claimed to live in unbroken continuity with the prophet Elijah, had a point.[1]

There are two massive facts of Christian history that need to be explained if the usual view of the origin of monasticism is right: two impossibilities, I should say. The first is the preservation by the church of more than sixty different classical Jewish writings, some of them in more than one manuscript, together with all the works of Philo.

Take, for example, the preservation of the manuscripts and versions of the *Testaments of the Twelve Patriarchs*. This was a Jewish collection which has come down to us in 14 Greek manuscripts (representing probably 2 text-types), about 56 manuscripts of the Armenian version, 6 manuscripts of the Slavonic (3 of the long version, 3 of the short), and some relatively modern versions. Aramaic fragments of the *Testament of Levi* have been found in caves at Qumran, and there are Aramaic fragments from the Cairo Geniza at Cambridge and Oxford.

As far back as we can trace these manuscripts, they were preserved in monasteries, in bishops' libraries, or in synagogues. The safest of these three institutions for preserving books would have been monasteries, for monasteries are remote, stable places, with facilities for copying and recopying books that have begun to wear out. The bulk of the manuscripts of the *Testaments of the Twelve Patriarchs* were, in fact, preserved in monasteries. Is it likely that the other two possible institutions for transmitting books, the cathedral library and the synagogue or church library, preserved this Jewish collection for the Christian church in the turbulent three hundred or so years when there were, so we are told, no monasteries? Is this how the *Martyrdom* or the *Ascension of Isaiah*, the *Testament of Abraham*, the *Assumption of Moses*, the *Books of Adam and Eve*, the various books of *Enoch* and of *Baruch*, *Joseph and Asenath*, the *Psalms* and *Odes of Solomon*, and a host of others came down to us? I doubt it. If there were no continuing monasteries, I doubt if any of these books would have survived.

Perhaps another institution, the catechetical school, might have served to collect and transmit this literature, but how fragile an instrument for preserving books this proved to be. Clement of Alexandria's *Protrepticus* and *Paedagogus* survive in one manuscript, the Arethas codex (from a monastery?) in Paris, and his *Stromateis* in one manuscript (from a monastery?) in the Laurentian Library in Florence; most of his other works are lost. Origen, his successor, who worked and wrote in Caesarea as well as in Alexandria, has hardly survived in the original Greek at all, and Origen was a librarian; but libraries are easy to burn. For Origen we have actual evidence of the existence of two of his books in a third-century Egyptian library from the catalogue that has survived – and the catalogue is very probably the catalogue of a monastic library.[2]

The one institution that was good at preserving books before the rise of the great libraries of Christian princes and prelates and before the foundation of university and college libraries was the monastery. Had there been no monasteries in the first three Christian centuries, we may well doubt that any Jewish books would have survived at all; certainly the Jewish school and synagogue could not preserve the great heritage of Jewish books in Greek that we now possess. Many of these Jewish books are secret books of Jewish communities rather than books meant for public reading to the synagogues. Are we to believe that these secret books were taken into Christian churches, kept safe there for two centuries, and then removed again to monastic libraries? Is it not more likely that Jewish communities with libraries became Christian and preserved the secret books there, in the one place, until modern scholars discovered them, still in monasteries where they had always been?

The second massive fact that would need explaining if the usual view of the origin of monasticism is right is a massive silence. If monasteries originated at the end of the third century and the beginning of the fourth century, where is the great monastic protest against a church that had proved so dangerous a place in which to attain salvation that men and women had to flee the cities and towns in which she was now so firmly established and take to a common celibate life, without private possessions, in the desert? If, on the other hand, the ancient established churches saw so many of the sons and daughters of their leading families and so many new converts suddenly leaving a settled existence to go out to find salvation in newly created monasteries, why did they not protest? On the contrary, the monastic leaders and members always behaved as obedient children of the church, remained dependent on the church's priests for the sacraments, and honoured the bishops; the church leaders, in their turn, seemed happy that monasteries existed, and bishops like the orthodox Bishop Arius asked Pachomius to found monasteries around Panopolis, his diocesan town.[3] When the Synod of Gangra (c. 340) condemned the break-away celibate groups led by Eustathius of Sebaste, they specifically labelled the theory that underlay these moves as the introduction of novelties (canon 31); they fully recognized the asceticism that existed alongside secular Christianity, which did not abandon the ordinances of the church. In short, the church preached the monastic ideal and seemed glad when Christians took the gospel demands literally. Isn't this strange, doesn't it beggar belief, if monasticism were a new unheard of thing? Harnack, in his famous long address on the ideals and history of monasticism, expresses astonishment at the equanimity with which the church accepted the new institution and at the lack of ambition among the monks to reform the church. All he can say, in explanation, is that the church could do no other than accept the inevitable, and that somehow the church had already so firmly lodged herself in the minds of men that it was inconceivable her power should be challenged.[4] These do not seem to me very compelling arguments. The lack of ecclesiastical protest at the flourishing of the monasteries and the lack of root-and-branch criticism of the church by the monasteries seem to me to have a much simpler single explanation: the monastery was not a new institution; there had always been monasteries since the days of the apostles.

When we turn to the *Lives* of Antony and Pachomius we discover not only evidence that neither man ever claimed to be doing anything startlingly new, but also many incidental pieces of evidence that the monastery was a venerable institution stretching back into the early days of the Christian church.

In the *Life of Antony*, it is true, we read that when Antony proposed to an old monk that they should go together to live in the desert he declined for two reasons, his age and 'because as yet there was no such custom' (chapter 11). But this incident merely confirms what the rest of the story abundantly testifies, that there were already a great number of solitary ascetic Christians outside the towns, that they did live together at least in pairs, and that Antony was notable for one thing alone, his zeal to face the devil in a severer test by living among the tombs and going out into the desert itself. There is no claim and no suggestion that the solitary life was the precursor of the common life of those who gave up marriage and private possessions to live in community under an abbot or abbess; on the contrary, strict solitariness seems dependent on an existent community ascetic life. When Antony first sold his great possessions to follow his calling, he put his sister, for whom he was responsible, into a convent (chapter 3).[5]

Pachomius, the alleged originator of community life for monks, was a disciple of an older man, Palamon. When Pachomius set up his own monastery, Palamon came to visit him and they resolved to keep in touch with each other by visits – but the older man, Palamon, was an abbot, too, surrounded by a community, like Pachomius himself (chapters 12, 13: Palamon is advised in his last illness *by some brothers* to eat better food). The existence of other monasteries not under Pachomius's jurisdiction is quietly assumed (e.g. chapter 27: 'And if a monk from another place is ordained to the priesthood, again we do not despise him as power hungry... ')

When Pachomius drew up a simple rule for his communal house, it is stated specifically that he drew on old traditions: 'and so [Pachomius] drew up for them a convenient rule and traditions helpful to their souls, prescribing out of the divine writings the proper measurement of their dress, the equal sharing of their food, the seemliness of their sleeping arrangements' (chapter 25). I doubt very much whether Pachomius thought he was prescribing regulations about habit, food, and sleeping arrangement out of the public and canonical Bible: the 'divine writings' are more likely to be ancient holy writings about the common life of those who had left behind marriage and private property in order to devote themselves to prayer and fasting.

The *Life of Pachomius* contains at least one reference to the earlier existence of monasteries. In chapter 2 the author casually states that notable abbots, fathers of their communities, had arisen ever since the Incarnation of the Blessed One who blesses all, in every region; although not many in Egypt and the Thebaid until after the persecution of Diocletian and Maximian (AD 284–305). This sort of statement could be dismissed with the remark that all such institutions as monasteries in the church always assume that they go back to apostolic days, but we should not be so hasty. There do exist scraps of evidence to suggest that the author of the *Life of Pachomius* was assuming to be true what in fact was true.

Cassian reports the same tradition in his conference on his visit to Abbot Piamon (XVIII. 4–6). Abbot Piamon said that the coenobites began in the days of the preaching of the apostles (Acts 2:45; 4:32, 34, 35) and moved out into the country when the church began to wax cold and to make concessions to the Gentiles. Abbot Piamon asserted that these communities had a continuous existence until the time of Abbot Paul and Antony. He also taught that the anchorites were first trained in the coenobium and then went on to harder things alone in the desert.

What is the evidence that these traditions were right? Firstly, let us call Eusebius. Eusebius never seems to mention monasteries explicitly, and so has been assumed to support the ruling view that monasteries began with Antony and Pachomius. But his witness is not so simple.

In Book II, chapters 16 and 17, of the *Ecclesiastical History* Eusebius argues that Philo's book *On the Contemplative Life or Suppliants* was really a description of the life of Christian ascetics in Alexandria. His argument rests on the doubtful tradition that Philo spoke to Peter when he came to Rome at the time of Claudius; but his argument rests also on the assumption that Philo's book 'obviously contains the rules of the church which are still observed in our time'. He argues that Philo's is 'a very accurate description of the life of our ascetics...apostolic men who were, it appears, of Hebrew origin, and thus still preserved most of the ancient customs in a strictly Jewish manner'.[6] Eusebius assumes that the church rules governing communities of ascetics had continued unbroken to his own day from the time of the apostles.

The same assumption underlies his description of the two kinds of Christian life preserved in the *Gospel Demonstration*, Book I, chapter 8.[7] One is the extraordinary type which is beyond the common and human way of life, which does not accept wives, children, property or surplus goods, which completely and utterly escapes the common customary life of all men, and, for the utmost heavenly love, is devoted only to the worship of God. These Christians are transported in soul to heaven, leaving their mortified mortal bodies on earth. This is the perfect type of the way of life according to Christianity. The lower, more human, type allows sober marriage and childbearing, land and possessions, fighting righteously and fulfilling civic duties, agriculture and commerce for one's own benefit.

Eusebius' plain exposition of the two sorts of Christian life simply assumes that the two ways are ancient and traditional; there is no suggestion that the higher way is the least bit novel.

Origen in his commentary on Matthew 19:21, Jesus' call to the rich man: 'If you would be perfect, go sell your possessions and give to the poor and you will have treasure in heaven and come follow me', cites in support Acts 2:44ff., 47; 4:32, 37 and 5:1ff., the story of Ananias and Sapphira. He thinks that rich well-born Christians should be ready, at the bishop's request, to sell all and set up communities of the common life and persuade others to join them. The story of Ananias and Sapphira was a definite image of the concord of the life of believers as the apostles wished it to be. Origen simply assumes that the bishops will be on the look-out for opportunities to found new monasteries.[8]

There is evidence from other parts of the church besides Egypt that the ideal of a celibate common life without private possessions was fully alive in the first three centuries. The Syrian church seems to have been distinguished by celibate communities of men and of women calling themselves Sons of the Covenant or the Daughters of the Covenant (*bnay Qyama*; *bnath Qyama*).

The interpretation of the seventh *Demonstration* of Aphrahat is controversial,[9] but it does not seem likely that either Aphrahat or the tradition he is passing on regarded celibacy as the condition of baptism. The liturgical text certainly calls men and women to take part in the spiritual war and warns those who would marry to do so before baptism, but the married will be baptized. The spiritual war is for the few who are unencumbered by thought of wife or the planted vineyard or the house that is building. Gideon's small army was fighting for all Israel; there is no suggestion that the army *is* Israel. There are traditions that the Syriac church was founded by the Thaddaeus sent by the Apostle Thomas to Edessa to King Abgar.[10] That tradition probably dates the foundation of the church too early, but it seems likely to me that the Christian faith spread rapidly to the Jewish community in Edessa and found a ready hearing. And as far back as we can go in the history of that church we find the tradition that some Christian men and women are to volunteer for celibacy and renunciation of possessions in order to engage in the contest with evil; these men and women are especially devoted to the love of Christ, the Bridegroom.

So far I have kept to orthodox churches, but when we turn to look carefully at movements that eventually were excluded from the orthodox church (or excluded themselves) we again find the same pattern: some, but not all, are called to abandon marriage and property in the service of God.

The Montanists are supposed to have demanded celibacy from all, and Tertullian, who says they only prohibited second marriages, is regarded as a witness to a later form, but is this likely?[11] Montanus and Prisca certainly preached celibacy but they also went to established churches to gather funds from them, a sure sign they expected Christians who accepted their new revelation to continue to work and raise families in the normal way. The Montanist church that persisted in the fourth century had a patriarch at Pepuza, *koinonoi*, and bishops, presbyters and deacons.[12]

Or take Hieracas of Leontopolis. He gathered an ascetic community around him about AD 300. He certainly taught celibacy as the one new thing Christ came to teach, but I think Neander was right to maintain that he did not exclude the married from the Kingdom of God. He accepts Hebrews as scripture, where it says 'marriage is honourable in all' (Hebrews 13:4), and only prefers St Paul's advice later on (in the canon) that he wished all men were celibate like him (1 Corinthians 7). In support of his teaching that Melchizedek was the Holy Spirit, an idea that could have been derived from the Qumran Melchizedek fragment, he cited the Jewish apocalypse, the *Ascension of Isaiah*.[13]

But surely, you will say, there exists definite evidence that the church of the second century did not countenance monasticism and rejected the very idea. The theory that monasticism began in Upper Egypt in the late third century seems to be confirmed by three explicit denials that monasticism existed earlier.

Tertullian's *Apology*, chapter 42, assures the authorities of the Roman empire that there is no truth in the charge that Christians make no contribution to the economic wealth of the state.

For we are no Brahmins or Indian gymnosophists, living in woods, and exiles from life... So we live with you in this world not avoiding the forum, not avoiding the market, not avoiding your baths, bazaars, workshops, inns, fairs and other places of commerce. We sail with you and we fight alongside you and we farm with you, and likewise we unite with you in trade: our skills and our abilities we use for the common good.

Put alongside that the similar statement in chapter 5 of the *Epistle to Diognetus*, which emphasizes that Christians follow local customs, and the direct command in the *Epistle of Barnabas* 4.10 not to retire apart and live alone as though already made righteous, and we seem to have a watertight case that Christian monasticism was a new creation, which only arose when earlier prohibitions were forgotten.

Certainly we hear of wandering prophets in the *Didache*, but why silence about ascetic communities, if ascetic communities existed? Surely persecutors would have destroyed such communities, if they existed to be destroyed. There were Pythagorean communities which men entered only after they had sold all their property and given it to the community. Surely critics of Christianity would have noticed the parallel, if parallels existed.

We must be cautious. It is true that the *Didache* seems silent about the existence of monastic communities, although it has much to say on wandering prophets, yet the *Didache*, like Eusebius, assumes that there are two distinct types of Christian life. 'For if you can bear the whole yoke of the Lord, you will be perfect; but if you are not able to: what you can, this do' (6.2). Is not this sufficient charter for monasticism?

The *Epistle to Diognetus* does not seem to contain anything that definitely rules out monasticism: his entirely general points that Christians share all things as citizens and marry as all men do (5.5f.) would not be affected by the existence of celibate communities whose members did not marry or own property, any more than the rule that pagan citizens took part in civic affairs and married would be affected by the existence of Pythagorean communities.

Barnabas' warning not to enter into a solitary life as if you were already made righteous is possibly not a warning against monasticism but a warning against the solitary life; the remark, 'come together to seek together concerning what is fitting in common' (4.10) seems to be recommending the common life for those who are especially called to be spiritual. The 'as far as in us lies' of 4.11 seems to imply the two sorts of life we have already noticed in the *Didache* and in Eusebius.

Tertullian's *Apology* seems a more formidable barrier to my thesis. But is it really so? To be sure he specifically denies that any Christians are Brahmins or Indian gymnosophists, but that is a specific reference to a practice his educated reader would know all about from Strabo's *Geography* and other sources. What *this* excluded was the life of the single wise man who went into the woods outside the city and attracted individuals who came to hear his wisdom. I doubt if Tertullian would have regarded Elijah and John the Baptist as excluded by this description, men who went into lonely places and attracted disciples, but who did not expect people to come out from the towns with food and drink offerings in return for wisdom.

Tertullian's insistence that Christians took part in commerce and ordinary life would hardly be weakened by the existence of communal houses of men and women who devoted themselves to prayer and fasting, having renounced marriage and private property. In fact these communities would probably have fitted into the economic life of their areas: they would probably have farmed or grown fruit for sale, or traded in salt or minerals as their settlements gave opportunity.

Wherever we look, the evidence that there was no monasticism before the time of Antony and Pachomius melts away under our eyes. There are positive traces that monasticism was universally accepted as a higher way to serve God for the few, which existed alongside the ordinary way of salvation for the many.

Where did this assumption that there were two distinct types of the righteous life come from, and was it present in the teaching of Jesus and the New Testament as a whole?

There is no doubt that the crucial assumption upon which

monasticism depends was already made in Judaism by the Essenes. The Damascus Document and one crucial reference in Josephus' description of the sect in the *Jewish War* xiii.160f. show that there were married Essenes who did not sell all their property and give it to the community. They were nevertheless in full agreement with the Essenes who gave up marriage and property in order to live in communities devoted to work, prayer, and study of the sacred books. This is implicit in the fragment from Philo's *Apology* preserved by Eusebius in *Praeparatio evangelica* VIII.1.1: the Essenes 'inhabit many towns of Judaea and many villages and great and populous camps' (if we may translate the *homiloi* as 'camps'). The Damascus Document tells us that the villages and camps are organized under an overseer of all the camps (CD.XIV.8f.), and that each camp has its own overseer. In some at least of the camps there are slaves, maidservants and day labourers employed by members of the community (XI.12) and the members of the community keep what they make, but have to pay over at least two days' wages a month to the overseer and the judges (XIV.12f.). They have children, and the sons who reach the age of twenty have to pledge themselves by the oath of the Covenant (CD XVI.5f.; IQSa 1.6–18).

Since fragments of the Damascus Covenant have been found at Qumran, we must conclude that the Qumran community felt itself to be in communion with the married communities. It is just possible that married Essenes even settled around the celibate houses: the main cemetery of about 1,100 graves is male, but there are females buried in the two secondary cemeteries near the buildings.[14] Similarly the cemetery at the smaller Qumran-type monastery at 'En el-Ghuweir, about 15 km south of Qumran, contains female skeletons.[15]

We must conclude, I think, that the Jewish Essenes had already made the crucial move: they had already discovered that married communities where private property continued and celibate communities, whose members surrendered all their property, could exist side by side among people who lived according to God's covenant. It is very likely that all the various communities were linked together in one organization under one overseer.

The two monastic sites we know, at Qumran and 'En el-Ghuweir, were both destroyed during the Jewish war, but there must have been others. The Therapeutae in Egypt were not attacked and destroyed, as far as we know. Philo tells us that the Therapeutae of Egypt were typical of communities of men and women (Greeks and barbarians as well as Jews) who withdrew from the common life and lived in gardens and lonely places, and that this type of life was to be found 'everywhere in the world' (*De vita contemplativa* 21). What happened to them? Outsiders who report on the Essenes, like Pliny the Elder and his successors, seem to assume that the monasteries continued.

I suspect that some simply faded away for lack of recruits, but that some became Christian. Unless some became Christian, I find it hard to see how so many secret Jewish books survived to be transmitted to us by Christian monasteries. The books never wandered; only the allegiance of the monks changed, from the nameless Teacher of Righteousness to the named Messiah, Jesus Christ.

But surely Jesus and the apostles would not have assumed that monasticism on the Essene model was a possible way of life for true followers? It is true the Essenes are never mentioned explicitly in the New Testament, but surely Jesus was against their spirit?

One warning. We must not be misled by the large monasteries at the flowering under Antony and Pachomius and Basil of Caesarea and their successors. A monastery does not have to be large to be a monastery. The crucial requirements are the acknowledgment that there are two possible types of Christian life, and that one of these types involves giving up property and marriage to live together under a 'father' or a 'mother' in regulated community, which could be of men only or women or of men and women.

Did Jesus and the apostles reject the possibility that some of the followers of the way might live in monasteries? I very much doubt it. On the contrary, there are many indications in the New Testament that not all the commandments are for all. We naturally apply injunctions like 'Take up your cross' to all Christians, although it must originally have been a call to be prepared for actual martyrdom. I have always understood Luke's 'Take up your cross *daily*' as a spiritualizing interpretation, but now I wonder whether it is not a call to the daily martyrdom of life in a celibate community devoted to prayer, fasting and study of the Bible. Even this version might not have been meant for all the righteous in Israel.

Matthew, of course, has a specific reference to voluntary celibacy, but commentators are used to dismissing this as a late idiosyncratic addition: 'there are eunuchs who have made themselves eunuchs for the sake of the Kingdom of heaven. Let him who can be separate be separate *or* Let him who can make room in his life [for this] make room [cf. Justin *Apologia* 1.15]; *or* Let him who can hear, hear' (19:12).

We do not ever take the injunction to the rich young man or ruler

literally when we apply it to all Christians, but should we not accept that
Christ meant it literally, for some? Matthew's 'if you would be perfect'
may well be an appeal to an agreed theology that some of the faithful
were called to monastic perfection while others were not (Matthew
19:16–22, especially 21; Mark 10:17–22; Luke 18:18–23).

Rewards are promised to those who have left all – in Luke, even wife;
but we must not assume that all were called to that complete
renunciation (Matthew 19:23–30; Mark 10:23–31; Luke 18:24–30).

In Luke's version of the call of the tax collector we read that he left
all. Jesus came to the house to eat with him and with many tax collectors
and sinners who Mark says also followed Jesus (Matthew 9:9–13; Mark
2:13–17; Luke 5:27–32). I had always assumed this was a single festive
meal for friends and relations, but now I wonder. The house looks like
a settled refuge for converted sinners who have to learn to live the new
life together, without possessions and power.

I even wonder if Jesus did not give extensive particular instructions
to those who were called to live the common life, instructions that were
not meant to apply to all who believed. Perhaps much of the material in
the Sermon on the Mount and the Sermon on the Plain is drawn from
this special body of teaching. The absence of most of this type of
teaching in Mark may be no accident: Mark could well have been the
collection of teaching and deeds meant for the church at large, people
who went on marrying and having children and owning property.

Even in Mark, though, there is the recognition of two sorts of
Israelites, those taught in parables, and those to whom the mysteries are
revealed. Surely Mark implies that those outside are well taught and
sufficiently taught for salvation, even if there are others who come to
understand more (Mark 4:33f.).

The Acts of the Apostles described for us quite clearly not one but
two forms of the Christian life. Some Christians live in houses and have
servants, 'named Rhoda', for example (Acts 12:12–17); these sort of
Christians contribute gifts of money, which are gathered together and
sent to Jerusalem. Christians of the other sort sell their possessions, in
order to live together in communities. Not all Christians have to do
this – their property remained their own when they became Christians,
but if they decided to join the second group and came to live in a
community they had to sell everything and bring all the proceeds
(though even then it remained in a blocked account and still in their
name until they took their final vows, exactly as at Qumran, Acts 5:4;
1QS 6.16–23, Josephus *BJ* ii.122).[16] When Ananias and Sapphira tried to

deceive the apostles, they were punished with death, and their bodies were carried out by the young men to the community cemetery. Another example: Philip and his four virgin daughters who prophesied may well have constituted a community of the common life of prayer, fasting and withdrawal from the world (Acts 21:8f.).

The usual view of Acts is that all Christians at first sold their possessions and gave them to the new community, and that later this practice died out (Acts 2:44–7; 4:32). But this is sheer speculation. Luke says nothing about such a change in practice; he simply assumes that the two forms of life existed side by side. His sources about the community of goods do, I concede, seem to imply that all believers sold everything, but perhaps we misunderstood the sources; Luke can report the property-owner Mary, the mother of John Mark, who had *not* sold her house, without embarrassment (Acts 12:12). Perhaps the answer is that 'the believers' spoken of in 2:44 and 4:32 are not all Christians, but the Christians who are called to the perfect way. They, 'the perfect trusters', must sell everything; 'Christians' as such need not. The 'poor' in Jerusalem may not have been the whole Jerusalem church but the monastic communities in the area of the holy city. The expression 'the poor of the saints' in Romans 15:26 hardly refers to the Jerusalem church as a whole, and may well indicate definite communities rather than some indefinite part (cf. Galatians 2:10).

There are other traces of celibate communities in the New Testament, particularly in the Pastoral Epistles, where the widows seem to be a distinct order.

We cannot rule out the possibility that complete books were addressed to celibate property-less communities of Christians in the first instance. Colossians, with its emphasis on being in the heavenly places with Christ, is easier to understand as addressed to a monastic community than to an ordinary congregation, and parts at least of Ephesians sound the same.

1 John, with its fierce command not to love the world nor the things in the world and to flee the lust of the flesh and the lust of the eyes and the pride of life (1 John 2:15f.) might well have first been written for a monastic community. Note that the community is male, and consists perhaps of three grades, children, men and fathers (2:12–14).

Perhaps the Epistle to the Philippians was written originally to a small group of Christians who had renounced property and marriage to live in a community. The epistle opens with a greeting to all the saints, with the bishops and deacons, but perhaps this is a later universalizing of the epistle. The epistle itself seems to be directed to people who are to be blameless, pure, unblemished, shining as lights in the world, ready to suffer for Christ (3:15f.; 2:29f.); these people, at the end of the epistle, are told to greet every saint, which perhaps implies that they lived close to other non-monastic Christians (4:21).

The precise meaning of the church in a house has always been obscure. Is the individual's family and servants meant, or is the house an assembly place for one part of the larger church in Rome or Corinth or Colossae or the place where Philemon, Apphia and Aristarchus lived (Romans 16:5; 1 Corinthians 16:9; Colossians 4:15; Philemon 2)? The use of the word *ekklēsia* seems to rule out the second possibility, and the mention of three people (Philemon, Apphia and Aristarchus) seems to rule out the first. Perhaps the house church was a small monastic community. Justin Martyr lived in such a house church in Rome and did not visit any other congregations; pupils came to him and he did not go to them.[17]

The final great obstacle in the way of believing that monasteries always existed from the beginnings of Christianity is that no writer seems ever to have mentioned or described them. Why is no martyr said to have been a member of a community and no community said to have been persecuted as a community; why does no leader emerge from a community to become bishop of a place and why is no promising young man, no daughter of a prominent Christian household, described as leaving the world to enter a monastery?

Against the objection represented by these questions there seems at first no defence. But perhaps there is a defence; perhaps not one, but three. The first is the perfectly general and undisputed fact that celibacy was always highly regarded in the church. Justin Martyr mentions with pride the 60- or 70-year old men and women who have remained celibate as Christians (*apol.* 1.15.6). Detached outside observers of the church like Galen noticed celibacy as a striking feature of the lives of some Christians.[18]

The second is that the widows seem to have been regarded as a distinct group in the church; from earliest times there are regulations for entry to the 'order', if 'order' is the right word – yet they were not ordained like the orders of clergy (1 Timothy 5:3–16; *Apostolic Constitutions* VIII.24.2). *The Shepherd of Hermas* describes virgins who live in a community and spend their nights in prayer (*Similitude* IX.11.7 *et passim*). It seems likely that whenever we hear of widows (and orphans?) we may be hearing of small communities bound by a rule devoting themselves to prayer and good works. Again, an outside observer, the hostile Lucian, notes the widows and orphans as a distinguishable group who gather at the prison door where Peregrinus Proteus is held, when he was going through his Christian phase (Lucian, *Peregrinus* 12). Tertullian notes that the widows have a special place assigned to them in church (*De pudicitia* 13).

But what of the men? Male celibacy is certainly honoured in the earliest records, but I can find almost no trace of male celibate communities. Yet we must be cautious. We know a great deal about some male celibate communities which caused a great deal of trouble to the church in the first two or three centuries, namely the communities gathered round the gnostic heretics. These were sometimes rival churches, but more often they appear as communities drawing off Christians from the churches and promising them superior illumination.

Perhaps some of them were what we should call monasteries. Certainly they possessed secret books with secret teaching. I wonder if there were not similar communities who were not unorthodox – even though they, too, would have their own libraries of teachings about the more perfect way – who lay low. Irenaeus once, in an admittedly obscure passage attacking ascetics, seems to give grudging recognition to the teacher who really renounced all commerce with the world: who had nothing to do with other people's goods, but was literally naked, barefoot, homeless in the mountains, like one of those animals that feed on grass. In attacking the pretensions of the celibate communities to have withdrawn from the world – when they in fact did own property and wanted to enlarge their bequests – he admits the existence of a genuine denial of the world.[19] It would always have been more difficult for male celibates to live in community than female celibates, when the empire was hostile to Christianity and on the look-out for centres of disaffection and rebellion; but the bishops and other leaders of the church may also have been uneasy about communities of educated men who embraced not only a more perfect life (*that* they would recognize), but also a more perfect way with its own teaching (which was far more difficult to acknowledge). Yet such male communities must have existed; if my arguments hold, they must have been continuations of pre-Christian Jewish communities; and they must have proved their antiquity and worth to such notable church leaders as Athanasius, so that, when the conditions were ripe, they could multiply and flourish and spread as an honoured and accepted form of life alongside the congregations of married Christians who lived their life in the world.

We are slowly learning to connect gnosticism with Judaism, but we must now learn to take a second step and connect gnosticism not just with Judaism but also with monasticism. The Jewish doctrine that God delivered to his servants secret writings as well as open writings entailed the founding of communities of disciples where the secret writings could be preserved safe until the day of their publication. The Essene monasteries were, among other things, libraries with a scriptorium; the pots in which to hide the secret writings were no accident of the existence of the skill to make pots at Qumran: it was already laid down in the tradition that rolls were to be anointed with the oil of cedar to preserve them and that the rolls were to be stored in jars (*Assumption of Moses* 1.17f.).

The thirteen Nag Hammadi books of collected documents were almost certainly preserved in a monastery, possibly an orthodox monastery.

Inasmuch as the gnostic books became the scriptures of sects that regarded the ascetic way as the only way to salvation, they were condemned by the church Fathers, but we should not regard the intention of these ancient mystical systems to be necessarily exclusive in their aims: the secret access to the highest vision of God could well have been vouchsafed to a few who were fitted by their renunciation of marriage and property and their discipline of prayer and fasting to go on the spiritual journey for the sake of all Israel, to be the army of Gideon.

How did the idea arise that monasticism began with Antony and Pachomius? The main reason is that historians forgot that the cessation of persecution and the recognition of the rights of the church not only made monasticism more respectable and more popular, but it also allowed documents to be published which were before kept hidden. The ideas, organization, and writings must have been much older. What strikes us about Pachomius is his constant appeal to tradition – principally the tradition of the Old Testament: the names of Abraham, Moses, Miriam, Samson, Elijah and Elisha often appear and David, Isaiah and Jeremiah are constantly quoted and appealed to. His community even treasures old Jewish riddles like: who was not born but died, who was born but did not die, and who died but did not see corruption (§82)?

Historians forgot that institutions can exist underground, unnoticed for centuries, only to appear with startling suddenness in great power. But the historians of monasticism also worked with a prejudice, a

J. C. O'NEILL

prejudice against the possibility of monasticism in primitive Christianity, the prejudice that God requires the same obedience from all. Even the discovery of the Dead Sea Scrolls has not entirely dispelled the prejudice for surely, they have assumed, Jesus and the apostles were against the hierarchy and the monasticism of the Essenes.

I have tried to question all these assumptions. I have argued that the essentials of monasticism were present among the Essenes; that Jesus and the apostles carried forward the same tradition of how the faithful were divided into two sorts; that there were monastic communities in the church from the first; and that they continued, little noticed but simply assumed to be always possible, until the great flourishing at the end of the third century and the beginning of the fourth. Christianity always had its monasteries, as did the Judaism from which it sprang.

NOTES

I am grateful to Dr Christopher Armstrong, Professor Gerhard Wallis (Halle/Saale) and Professor Rowan Williams for advice, criticism and suggestions.

1 See the Cambridge controversy between John Stokes OP who challenged this claim in 1374 and the Carmelite who answered him, John de Hornby, Victoria County History, Cambs., vol. 2, p. 284.
2 Pap. Ash. Inv. 3, Oxford, 13.9 × 8 cm published by C. H. Roberts, Carl Schmidt Festschrift, ZNW, 37 (1938), 184–8. The list of parchments contains The Shepherd (of Hermas), two works of Origen (one on John), Leviticus, Job, Acts of the Apostles, Song of Songs, Exodus, Numbers (?), and The Great Book (the Four Gospels). Line 11 lists very clearly a book Apa Bal. There is no Christian writer whose name begins Bal… I wonder if this is not a book by an unknown abbot of the community. I owe this reference to Professor Henry Chadwick.
3 Life of Pachomius (Vita Prima Graeca), §81.
4 Adolf Harnack, 'Das Mönchtum: seine Ideale und seine Geschichte: Eine kirchenhistorische Vorlesung', Giessen, 1881, end of §III, 6th edn of 1903 in Reden und Aufsätze, Erster Band, Giessen 1904, pp. 102f.
5 Cf. the reference to the holy virgins and brethren in Athanasius, Apologia contra Arianos, ch. 15.
6 HE II.17.1f. translated by Kirsopp Lake, Loeb Library, vol. 1, London 1926, pp. 145, 147.
7 A point made forcefully by W. Gass, Geschichte der christlichen Ethik, vol. 1, Berlin 1881, pp. 122–5.
8 Kenneth E. Kirk, The Vision of God, London 1931, p. 185. Commentarius in Matthaeum xv.15 (GCS 10.394, line 28–395, line 7).
9 For a survey and discussion, see Robert Murray, 'The Exhortation to

Candidates for Ascetical Vows at Baptism in the Ancient Syriac Church', *NTS*, 21 (1974–5), 59–80.

10 Eusebius, *HE* 1.13.

11 See Lietzmann, *History of the Early Church*, English translation, 2nd edn, London 1950, vol. 2, p. 197.

12 Lietzmann, *History*, vol. 2, p. 198; Jerome *Epistula* 41.3. cf. *Codex Justinianus* 1.5.20.3.

13 Epiphanius, *Panarion* 67. See George Salmon in *Dictionary of Christian Biography*, ed W. Smith and H. Wace, London 1880–7, vol. 3, 24f. Dr Rowan Williams directed my attention to Hieracas' knowledge of Jewish apocalypticism.

14 R. de Vaux, *Archaeology of the Dead Sea Scrolls*, 2nd edn, London, 1973, pp. 45–8, 57f.

15 Pessah Bar-Adon, *BASOR*, no. 227 (Oct. 1977), 1–25.

16 See E. Trocmé, *Le 'Livre des Actes' et l'histoire*, Paris 1957, pp. 194–200; A. Dupont-Sommer, *The Essene Writings from Qumran*, Oxford 1961, p. 87, note 1; Brian Capper, *JSNT*, 19 (1983), 117–31, and his Cambridge dissertation, 1986. Dr Capper discusses Bargil Pixner's thesis that there was an identifiable Essene quarter on the south-west hill of Jerusalem. He proposes the hypothesis that a small group, left behind when the radical anti-establishment Essenes moved to re-establish the Qumran settlement, was later carried into the Christian community, which itself met in the upper room, located in the same quarter. 'ΠΑΝΤΑ ΚΟΙΝΑ: A Study of Earliest Christian Community of Goods in its Hellenistic and Jewish Contexts', PhD dissertation, University of Cambridge (1986), especially pp. 149–202.

17 *Acta martyrii S. Justini* 3; [H. Musurillo, *The Acts of the Christian Martyrs*, Oxford 1972, selection no. 4].

18 *Origen contra Celsum* VII.48; Galen, summary of Plato's *Republic* preserved in Arabic quotations (R. Walzer, 'Galen on Jews and Christians' (1949) p. 15, in J. Stevenson, *A New Eusebius*, London 1957, no. 109).

19 *Adversus haereses* IV.30.3; W. W. Harvey's edn of *Adv. haer.*, Cambridge 1857, II.250.

Artistic idiom and doctrinal development

SISTER CHARLES MURRAY

Over twenty years ago, when 'soundings' were beginning to be taken and doubts raised about the future of theology, Root diagnosed as the most serious problem facing the Christian faith the existence of a secularized imagination for which theology is no longer alive.[1] The problem of the imagination as part of a crisis in the cognitive aspect of theology continues to preoccupy theologians almost two generations later.[2] It is also commonly asserted that we are entering an historical age in which the visual will be paramount as the means of exposition of the truth and the verbal, with its great faith in logic, will no longer be accorded the premium which it has had for so long, particularly in European thinking. But in the early church it was possible to think theologically without cutting oneself off from other ranges of thought and imagination which in our day no longer have contact with theology; and in a volume of essays dedicated to Professor Chadwick it is a matter of happiness to begin with the recognition that there is indeed a way out of the modern impasse because it already exists in the tradition.

In 842 when the church proclaimed the Triumph of Orthodoxy it was talking about art as the visual interpretation of dogma. The ancient church considered that nourishment was to be found for theology and doctrine in the world depicted by artists, which sometimes rejects the conventional ways of theology and religion as they exist in the literary expression. This is clear from the continuous tradition of Christian art which goes back on present evidence to the third century AD, where it appears as a common tradition on the monuments of the East and West.

To many observers however this fact is not immediately apparent; the early church appears only as a world in which faith has been articulated in creeds, definitions and doctrines. Now it is true that the religious attitude of the early church was dominated by the notion of orthodoxy, and detailed studies since the nineteenth century of its theological controversies have made us conscious of the intensity and awareness of doctrine, particularly in its propositional form, as the expression of the orthodox faith. However, disagreement with regard to what ideas were to be held as orthodox depended on the prior notion of orthodoxy itself, the existence and nature of which was taken for granted by the whole church. Orthodoxy was the faith, comprised in the tradition, founded on the historical basis of Christianity. Devotion to orthodoxy in its general sense, and to the specifically orthodox doctrines, was the first duty of every Christian, and from the fourth century it was made by Theodosius I the first duty of every citizen as well. In imposing this duty, Theodosius created the circumstances necessary for the rise and spread of a completely Christian art. And it is from the artistic idiom of doctrinal expression, rather than from the logomachies which occupy so much of the theological literature, that we may learn more of the rounded notion of orthodoxy in the early church, and indeed of the nature of orthodoxy itself.

The artistic idiom is a special point in the evolution of orthodoxy, and it has several unusual features which make it very interesting for the historian of doctrinal development. It shows how in the early church orthodoxy developed in a non-controversial way; for it was not a matter of contention until the eighth and ninth centuries, when it became itself the last in a long life of battles over orthodoxy and heresy. And here the matter becomes even more interesting, as an exceptional and striking application of doctrinal principles to a practical problem which, by the end of the ninth century, has itself become a new formulation of dogma. This raises the very interesting question of what it means for art to be orthodox, for it is not immediately visible as such. To investigate this and to observe the relationship of art to orthodoxy and doctrinal development is therefore the purpose of this essay. The problem has two aspects, the historical and the theological, and we may conveniently explore it under these two heads.

I

Historically speaking the public course of art and its function in the early church suggests that we may begin by making some reflections on the nature of orthodoxy as early Christianity understood it, and as we have outlined it above. One of the primary features of the ancient notion of orthodoxy was that it was the view of the church, and as such a function of the unity of the church. Orthodoxy, thus, on the early church's idea, assumes the continuity of visible Christian unity. It was for this reason that any party to a doctrinal dispute had to show that they represented the true tradition and therefore the visible union of the church. When we study the adoption and use of art by the church we see that this idea lived on despite the doctrinal battles. Art enabled the church to continue to express the historical basis of its belief when the content of that belief was disputed. Since art is of its nature positive, the only disagreement possible in relation to art is aesthetic, not logical. If then art was adopted as a means of expressing belief, the idea of orthodoxy presupposed is that the essence of faith is truths that transcend logically contestable truths. The relation of art and the imagination to questions of doctrine is therefore not a thus-and-thus view of orthodoxy. As expressed through the artistic idiom, orthodoxy is not a matter of anxiety over axioms and propositions; less, that is, of a logical idea than an imaginative apprehension of truth.

As a matter of historical fact, the artistic expression of doctrine seems to have been the only unifying theological force in the early church. The artistic idiom was, until the eighth century, when its use was first seriously questioned, the one visible factor of doctrinal integration and the one form of expression when all else divided, which could still manifest the unity of the church. This art therefore was able to give a considered expression to the mind of the whole church, and not simply to that of any given party. It could set forth the orthodox faith in a way that transcended the barriers; and indeed so powerful a medium was it that, when eventually the positive and negative deliverances of logic had run into the ground, and propositional theology had reached stalemate, it provided the church with its last great means of developing doctrine.

Because images united doctrinally when definitions divided, they could do even more. Visual integration can only be social, and since art and society belong together[3] the visible unity of the church as well as its doctrinal unity was continued during our period by the church's art. What we may call the 'major' heresies concerned the whole life of the church. They conserved social structures, order and creed in a manner identical to that of the 'official' church and were in themselves essentially ecclesiastical.[4] They diverged on dogmatic definitions and they sometimes divided entire provinces of the empire, so that a geographical term could be used simply to designate a doctrinal position. But they all practised art. This paradox of an artistically united and verbally divided church can be most vividly illustrated from the sources by two anecdotes, one from the *pratum spirituale* of John Moschus and one from the *Miracles of Cyrus and John* by Sophronius. In Monidia in Scete, according to John Moschus, a monk was asked by an angel whether he wished to be buried as the monks of Egypt or as those of Palestine. An interpreter of the vision had no difficulty in understanding that the angel was distinguishing between Monophysites and Chalcedonians.[5] Sacramentally too, the churches differed, for questions of heresy inevitably affected the doctrine of the Eucharist. Art, however, could cross all boundaries and was not a matter of rival group loyalties. Sophronius relates that at the Christmas celebration the Gaianite followers of the Monophysite Julian of Halicarnassus waited until the Chalcedonian liturgy in the church of Theonas was finished and then entered the church with a hundred clergy to venerate the image of the Virgin.[6] Further evidence on the same point is provided by the *Acts* of Maximus the Confessor which narrate that, at the end of a theological dispute with Theodosius bishop of Caesarea, Maximus and his opponent both kissed the Gospel Book and the Icons,[7] the visible expressions of the fundamental source of truth.[8]

The literary evidence is confirmed by what can be known of the actual iconography of the various churches as it survives. Study of the general trends in the artistic representations of the three great patriarchates of Jerusalem, Antioch and Alexandria seems to indicate that each group had a shared subject-matter but its own artistic style. Chalcedonian Palestine, as might be expected, leaned towards a figural, including narrative, art and, as the frescoes of Beirut and the sculpture of Antioch show, the same appears to be true of the coastal area of Syria. In the hinterland of the Antiochene patriarchate, however, the favoured wall decoration seems to be non-figural, with perhaps hanging icons, since these appear to have been in use. This use of plain wall decoration in combination with the icon is further developed in the patriarchate of Alexandria and in Nubia, where dogmatic scenes and isolated icons, as opposed to narrative cycles, are depicted on church walls.

The iconographical expression of the faith was then considered to be part of the tradition, and one of the great fears which alarmed the orthodox patriarch, Germanus, at the outbreak of Iconoclasm, a man who had enjoyed a brief period as a Monothelite when bishop of Cyzicus, was that to reject the iconic tradition of the church was to admit that for centuries the church had been in error.[9]

What explains the capacity of art to provide the integrating element in the expression of orthodoxy, while the verbal idiom divides, is the nature of the two media. The verbal tradition, the creed and definition, represents the exact, the record which can be preserved for the future. But, once fixed, the literary expression could and did degenerate into dogmatism and inflexibility, so that even the orthodox solution to a problem could itself become rigid and divisive, as the sorry struggles over the Nicene Creed and the Chalcedonian Definition show. Dialogues could continue among learned theologians who shared a technical vocabulary and a common background, but in written official or clerical theology the needs of the consumers of orthodoxy are given a low priority. This type of expression, which is concerned with precision, tends to be of its nature restrictive; its main purpose is to rule out, and so orthodoxy appears in this idiom as essentially a matter of constraint.

Art on the other hand is allusive, and therefore very free and flexible. Of its nature, it can convey the truth inclusively, and so is much more suited to the expression of orthodoxy as *truth* rather than orthodoxy as *formula*. The points at issue are not in play, and, because art depends for its validity on satisfying the hearts and imaginations of its consumers, it places a means of initiative and power in expressing Christian doctrine into the hands of lay Christian individuals. Because the faith was recognized to be more than the literal, and art caters for the more than literal, the church, by adopting its use, was in this respect recognizing the cognitive role of the imagination in knowing God. For the artistic imagination is above all related to interpretation, and the artistic idiom of the church is where doctrinal understanding and the imagination meet. The need to develop this function resulted in a new artistic style, and the truly doctrinal image is the artistic creation of the early church. In establishing the artistic form as a means of expressing the faith, the church has shown forth the liberating factor which orthodoxy essentially is.

These considerations lead on to the second fact that emerges from our analysis, and to another unusual feature of orthodoxy in this matter. Art is and always has been the tradition and the authentic voice of the laity in the articulation of orthodoxy. And it has always been an area which has been remarkably free from official control. So far as we know, art was introduced into Christianity as a private affair of devotion in the cemeteries of the Roman church and in house churches, such as those of Dura Europos and the villa at Lullingstone in Kent, if this is taken to be such.[10] That the Christian artistic idiom was fashioned from its inception as a means of doctrinal expression is clear from the monuments themselves, which all bear all the marks of a true artistic beginning.[11] Though displayed through the normal forms of late antique art, the way in which the images of early Christian art are constructed shows a difference in the way they are intended to function. As a clear example of doctrinal need creating a new artistic form we may quote the creation of the frieze sarcophagus of the early Constantinian period, where Christian art introduced a new concept into the portrayal of narrative art. The frieze sarcophagus is the first Christian object that is truly original and different from anything previously made; its technique for representing a multiplicity of events has no real forerunner in ancient funerary sculpture. Contrary to current practice, when the subject matter was narrative and the whole front of a sarcophagus was then given over to the narration of a single story, the trough of the frieze sarcophagus is divided (normally) into two friezes containing scenes. The scenes are juxtaposed, and it requires the beholder to read the line of them and so make out the meaning. What holds the scenes together, as also in the Catacomb paintings, is the doctrinal implication, which it is left to the viewer to infer.[12]

The range of themes chosen for illustration on the early monuments is very limited, and the same limitation of content and differing conception of style to fit its interpretation, is observable throughout the history of the Christian art of the period with which we are concerned.[13] The narrative cycles of the early Constantinian period illustrate mostly the Old and New Testaments, and the themes of the icons of the early Byzantine period are restricted to Christ, the Virgin, the saints, especially the apostles, and the angels, as the best and one of the earliest icon collections, that of Sinai, shows.[14] This limited choice of themes, combined with the invention of new techniques, made for the creation of what would eventually become fresh aesthetic values and the vehicle of a fully developed Christian imagination; but they were inspired initially by the function of art as the orthodox faith directed at and imprinting itself on the collective consciousness of the church.

On the face of it, restriction and limitation both in content and style, which are usually negative factors and produced such stalemate in the verbal expressions of doctrine, might not be expected to produce the conditions necessary for art. But limitation can in art be very creative and in this area, by its very function of limiting, Christian orthodoxy proved to be fully creative, and Christian art continued to gain in intensity of expression until it ended in the developed high Byzantine style of the East and in the full mediaeval art of the West. The price of entrusting orthodoxy to the artistic idiom of expression and to the laity might seem high, as Eusebius of Caesarea considered,[15] but distortions in Christian art have been very few.[16] Art continued to be the province of the laity and a matter of mutual co-operation between them and the clergy, as the letter of Nilus to the Prefect Olympiodorus shows,[17] and it was only in the iconoclastic period that the church entered an epoch when it was felt necessary in the name of orthodoxy to control art 'from above' and to exclude the people from it. From the third century the church was never shaken from its belief that there was a place for the artistic idiom in the doctrinal expression of Christianity and that this expression truly represented the collective imagination of the Christian church. That art was natural to the church is reflected in the answer given to his iconoclastic opponent by Nicephorus, the orthodox patriarch of Constantinople who was deposed from his see for his belief. When asked where Christians were commanded to worship icons, he replied by pointing to 'faith, as well as the inward and spontaneous impulse of believers to divine things'.[18] Art would indeed open the mind of non-believers also. According to John Damascene, if a pagan were to say to a Christian, 'Show me your faith so that I too may believe' the Christian would show him the church's art, so that in asking about the figures portrayed he would thus open himself to the Christian message.[19]

Mention of these two great theologians leads to the second part of our consideration: what may be known of the church's theoretical ideas on the relationship of orthodoxy to art. These reflections were basically framed at two points, the third century and the eighth to ninth centuries, both of them critical periods also in social and political development – and both, the fourth century above all, crucial for the development of Christian doctrine. It was the position in which the church found itself with regard to the cultural and institutional changes taking place at both these times which seems to have been the occasion for the rise of theological reflections concerning art. For, so far as we can tell from the evidence, no literary affirmation before 300 would give us any real idea of how the church regarded the matter from a speculative standpoint.

While reflections on images are not large in the fourth and fifth centuries, they increase in what is probably to be regarded as the age after Justinian, since much of the literature is difficult to date.[20] It has been shown that images begin to play a conspicuous role in the accounts of pilgrimages to the Holy Land, and they appear increasingly also in the historians; but the largest body of information comes from the hagiography and popular fiction of the time. However, the full flowering of analysis of the role of doctrine and art is to be found in the polemical literature of the iconoclastic period, when attempts were made to clarify the true understanding of art in relation to orthodoxy and doctrine. Our attempts to understand the church's view on the religious nature and function of art can therefore best be aided by looking more closely at these two periods.

II

As with so much else, art was co-ordinated within the Christian confession by the Cappadocian Fathers. They elaborated a theoretical approach which enabled them to maximize its value within the Christian tradition; and their understanding of the nature and function of religious art is shown in their conception of the Christian image as *graphē siōpōsa*, illustrated scripture, and in their emphasis on the value of the image to the beholder. At its lowest level this meant that for them art was essential to the church as a pastoral tool: the only medium of learning and instruction open to the illiterate members of the faithful. As Gregory of Nyssa said, a painting, even if it is silent, is capable of speaking from the wall and of being of the greatest benefit.[21] But on a deeper level a greater awareness of the artistic idiom itself, as a more powerful means for communicating an idea more completely and more fully than is possible in words, is also contained in the concept. This is shown remarkably by Gregory Nazianzen in his thirty-fifth oration. When searching for an image sufficiently appropriate to describe the evil behaviour of certain heretics, he recalls a mural painting of a Dionysiac revel, which he describes to his audience, and invites them imaginatively to enter the picture and thus share his indignation.[22] In this passage, too, is implicit the recognition of the psychological function of art: its capacity to be the source of the most profound emotional stimulus, and its power to generate deep personal response. This is made explicit by Gregory of Nyssa in a passage in which he speaks of a painting of the sacrifice of Isaac as the source for him of a deeply affective experience.[23]

That the Western church possessed more or less the same convictions is shown by the writings of the African bishop Euodius of Uzala (d. 424), and the celebrated letter of Gregory the Great to Serenus of Marseilles, in which he stated what has become the classic Roman view of the nature of art ever since.[24] Art, then, on this view, was not important merely as an aid within the pastoral context but was part of the psychology of the faith.

When, therefore, the Fathers of the fourth century and afterwards spoke in this manner, they were making more than what is usually regarded as a merely utilitarian case on behalf of the use of art by Christianity. Latent in their argument was the idea that the content of theology itself could be visual as well as verbal. Thus the seventh-century John Damascene would develop Gregory of Nyssa's view of images as illustrating scripture into a doctrine that Christian images are in fact scripture itself in visual form.[25]

That there is a strict relationship between theology and art seems to have been recognized in an inchoate way in the fourth century itself by Eusebius of Caesarea who, in his *Letter* to the princess Constantia, offers restrictive comments of a directly theological nature concerning the use of art, which are at variance with the positive attitudes outlined above.[26] He forbids the making of a picture of Christ, on the grounds not only that these are not customary in the church, but that the practice is forbidden by commitment to the doctrine of the incarnation. This raises the debate to a thoroughly theological level, and Eusebius seems to represent the first attempt to import the criteria of orthodoxy and heresy into a theoretical discussion of images which seems to be arising in the fourth century;[27] and to have linked it to the current state of Christological discussion in the realm of learned theology. His letter was rooted in the same pastoral concern which motivated the other great churchmen of the time, but his view of imagery shows the kinds of legitimate concern with regard to orthodoxy which the use of art by the church could raise. It raises in particular the problems of relativism and of idolatry.

Relativism has always been a problem for thoughtful Christians and the nature of images permits a higher degree of it than does the written word. This difficulty had been put long before to Clement of Alexandria in the matter of the suitability of the iconography of seal rings.[28] But, as Clement's answer shows, one cannot have a true or false image, save in relation to the church. This view also seems to underlie the principle enunciated by Augustine, where he shows how the suitability of a picture of God, shown sitting in heaven with a visible right hand, should be judged on Christian principles. It would be wrong to put such a representation in a church, and worse still to picture God in that way in one's heart, God's true temple; Augustine is ruling out not the art but the content: the anthropomorphic conception of God in the Christian imagination.[29]

Besides the possibility of relativism, the use of images could also encourage, it was feared, an idolatrous worship. This may have been, in part at least, the fear of the Council of Elvira.[30] It turns on the possibility of confusing a religious image with an idol. This is in essence an ethical argument: whether, if such a confusion is able to arise, it is legitimate to go on making artistic representations of a religious nature. The matter became a particularly painful issue during the iconoclastic controversy, but on this point, too, the answer had already been indicated in the earlier period. Speaking on the general problem of the veneration of images, Gregory the Great, in the letter referred to above, pointed out to Serenus, whose zeal for true worship had caused him to destroy some religious images, that he had not thought the problem through sufficiently well. Gregory completely approves the prohibition of idolatrous worship but not the destruction of the images for, he says, it is one thing to adore a picture and another thing to learn from it what should be adored. He adjudicates then that, although adoration is totally forbidden, no one is to be stopped who wishes to make a picture. Beholders are to share in compunction from contemplating it and to prostrate themselves in humility only before the Trinity. Later and more succinctly Nicephorus, starting from a different base, was to argue that anyone with common sense could tell the difference between an idol and an icon.[31] What is being argued in both cases here is that underlying the identification of images with idols is a confusion of thinking. And in replying to assertions of idolatry in its use of art, the ancient church was again showing a more penetrating understanding of the nature of the artistic idiom and its relation to doctrine than did its moral critics. The orthodox comments show an admission that in itself imagery is only a technique, a means of expression. Being in itself impersonal it cannot be idolatrous or otherwise, since idolatry is a matter of personal motivation, not of art itself. Gregory's distinctions also make a second point: for the essence of the distinction between an image *qua* image and an idol is that of its nature an image has the capacity to be a vehicle of transcendence, whereas an idol is of its nature purely immanent.[32]

The perception of the transcendental quality of the image was originally introduced into Christian thought by Basil of Caesarea in speaking of the imperial portrait, when he said that honour offered to an image passes through to its prototype.[33] In the context of his discussion, the triune nature of God, he used the idea to clarify the relationship of the Father and the Son and argued by comparison that worship offered to the Father passed through the Son who is his image. The appropriation of this text by the tradition made it possible for the later iconophiles to argue that it enshrined a principle which also applied to material images and could supply a clear basis for a specific theology of art.

Thus it was by using the idea of the image, a very venerable category of Christian doctrine, and by developing its theology further, that the church was able to change the whole conceptual basis for figurative art. This metaphor, derived from the biblical story of the creation of man in the image of God, and successively and successfully transposed into theology and Christology, became an indispensable feature of the Logos theology of the Nicene faith, and the Logos conception of reality, which was formed from its exposition by thinkers such as Basil. With Basil and the Gregorys was set up an intimate connection between Nicene theology and common expressions of culture which made possible a socially and theologically responsible synthesis of orthodoxy, in which the concept of the image was highly important.[34] The Word, the Image of the Father had become visible in Christ, and the theological themes of God and Christ were bound to raise the artistic tradition of the church newly to consciousness in the development of an evermore autonomous Christian culture. The theological and cultural assumptions of the period coalesced and a decision on behalf of art was therefore inevitable. Eusebius' view was bound to be seen as too inadequate to compete. The espousal of art by outstanding and influential figures of unimpeachable orthodoxy ensured that henceforth art was regarded as orthodox.

From the fifth century on production increased and came to a flowering in Justinianic art, but if imperial patrons such as Justinian and Heraclius could give great stimulation to artistic invention, the content was always controlled by doctrine. From the sixth century, in theoretical discussions, the beholder begins to figure less and arguments concern themselves more and more with the establishment of the dehistoricized, metaphysical relation of the image to its prototype; the image was analysed in its own right with regard to its status within the divine order of reality. Thinking on the problem of images was able to incorporate other ideas as they arose in the tradition affecting the relationship of man to God. An interesting example is Hypatius of Ephesus, who justified the practice of Christian art on the basis of scripture interpreted in the light of the symbolic theology and hierarchical chain of images established by pseudo-Denys.[35]

But it was after the Council of Chalcedon that increasingly dogmatic statements based on its definition were able to be made. The Quinisext Council (in Trullo) insisted on one kind of image: following the orthodoxy of the council it required a representation of Christ in the human form of the incarnation and no longer under the ancient images of the church, such as the lamb.[36] But it was in the eighth and ninth centuries that the doctrinal relationship of art to orthodoxy was fully articulated. The bitterest polemics in the history of the church were reserved for what was ostensibly an issue of the fitting use of art in Christian devotion, but which in essence was about the nature and effects of the incarnation. Before it ended it had become a new account of the Christological debate in which art was no longer merely, as at the Quinisext Council, a representation of the doctrine of the incarnation but had itself become part of the doctrine of the incarnation. The orthodoxy which triumphed in 842 was the application of the orthodox dogma of the incarnation to art, and the theological justification not only of a use of Christian art but of the essentially Christian nature of art.

The debate utilized all the earlier acquisitions of Trinitarian metaphysics and Christological terminology. Indeed the Fathers of the Second Council of Nicaea in 787 considered themselves as linked to that of 325 and their Definition on art as the consummation of its faith.[37] The triumph of Christian art was the triumph of the seven councils, and for the church the practice and veneration of images was the only permissible corollary of the one, holy faith. Doctrinal principles were therefore extrapolated from earlier doctrinal development in such a way that the result was a new formulation of dogma. The external history of the controversy and its doctrinal history also have been frequently described, so that we need here only draw out the points of direct interest to our theme.[38]

When one studies the quarrel over images in its theological aspects, one can see that the Chalcedonian definition lay at the root of the argument, for it was possible where art was concerned to draw up two conflicting orthodoxies on the basis of its language. Orthodoxy required that the two natures of Christ had to be acknowledged without confusion, division or separation, and in one Person. The iconoclast Emperor Constantine V, who had a taste for theology, therefore proposed a nice dilemma, in an argument of which the following is the skeleton. The hypostasis of Christ is inseparable from the two natures; one of these two is divine and therefore cannot be circumscribed. It is always a person who is represented in an icon, Christ's person is divine and cannot be represented, therefore it is impossible to paint the hypostasis of Christ. Once these principles are admitted either iconoclasm or heresy follows. The orthodox have a choice between two forms of heresy: if they hold the unity, they are in their art circumscribing the divine Word with his flesh and are therefore confusing the natures; if they avoid this by arguing that they are merely representing his humanity, they are admitting that the flesh has its own *prosōpon*, which is Nestorianism, and are therefore separating the natures, thus making Christ a simple human being. No wonder therefore that Constantine felt free to say, 'Anyone making the icon of Christ...has not penetrated the profundity of the dogma of the union without confusion of the two natures of Christ.'[39] He added one further clinching point: every image is known to be derived from some prototype, hence the only proper use of the term 'image' in the case of Christ is to describe his relation to the Father.

Constantine intended his theology for the bishops, who seem to have been completely convinced by the purity of the doctrinal vision; and during the whole controversy the entire secular clergy apparently remained iconoclast.[40] The orthodox likewise were dumbfounded and Nicephorus admitted that with the problem of circumscription the iconoclasts had raised a rampart difficult for the orthodox to fight against.[41] It took the best Greek minds of the time, John Damascene, Nicephorus of Constantinople and Theodore of Studion, and almost two centuries of thought, to demonstrate the falsity of the dogmatic principles from which the conclusions had flowed.

Since the Christological conception of the iconoclasts was centred on the conviction that no image of Christ was possible, orthodox analysis began with the image. It was chiefly John Damascene who, by refining the theology of the image, showed that Constantine's initial mistake was one of definition.[42] The consubstantial image of which the emperor had spoken was indeed the only image applicable to the relations of the Trinity, but it was only one in a classification of images. In general, he defines an image as a resemblance which characterizes the prototype, while being in some respects different from it. According to whether this something is more or less great, the image will be more or less perfect; the most perfect image, the consubstantial, is found only in the relation of the Son to the Father. His fifth category of images, those which are memorials of past things, are of two sorts, words engraved in books like the scriptures, and words engraved in pictures like icons. He does not go beyond this analysis and it is left for later theologians to make the fundamental distinction between a natural image and an artificial one.

It was Nicephorus, chiefly, who turned to the problem of circumscription and argued in essence that the term *aperigraptos* was being falsely used twice over, once at the level of painting and again when applied to Christology. He devotes a large part of the second *Antirrheticus*[43] to the notion of *perigraphē*, in which he differentiates the painting of an image (*graphē*) from the idea of circumscription which is a notional concept. Painting can be subsumed under it but not the other way round. Since the image is something purely relational and is relational only by resemblance, the icon cannot circumscribe anything substantially; it only represents the visible resemblance of the model. Turning from art, Nicephorus goes on to argue the Christological point: since the icon can only trace the visible aspect of a person everything stands or falls on knowing whether Christ has a visible aspect which can be represented. This had been assumed for centuries by the church but now needed demonstration. The argument had now moved from the level of painting to an unresolved problem in Christology itself.

Theodore, Abbot of the Studite monastery in Constantinople addressed himself to the problem of circumscribing the divinity in circumscribing the humanity of Christ.[44] Constantine's chief argument had been that since the hypostasis of the Word was invisible, one would introduce a second hypostasis in figuring Christ. Theodore replied with the orthodox doctrine on the points of nature and hypostasis: faith confessed that in becoming flesh the divine Word had become a sharer in human nature, but a common nature can only subsist in individuals. Christ is therefore, according to Theodore, only a man if his humanity is seen in an individual. What constitutes his individuality is the features of Jesus of Nazareth, which distinguished him from other men. Then taking up Maximus the Confessor's doctrine of the composed hypostasis – that is, that the hypostasis is the common hypostasis of the two natures – he applies it to the theory of the icon. The mystery of the incarnation consists in that the divine hypostasis of the Word is not made man in general but *a* man Jesus Christ, and therefore the human traits which the icon portrays are the human traits of the divine Person. Paradoxically, the incarnation means that the divine hypostasis of the Word has become circumscribed in the individual human face of Jesus. The icon, since it is the image of the person represented, necessarily circumscribes what it figures and circumscribes therefore the Divine Word himself. There is therefore a link between *graphē* and *perigraphē* as the iconoclasts had perceived and he who paints does circumscribe. But he does not circumscribe the divine nature, as they feared, but the hypostasis. Thus Theodore is able to bring down the whole iconoclast position by pointing to its fundamental mistake, a bad understanding of the concept of hypostasis.[45]

III

In some ways the modern church faces the situation of its ancient predecessor; it too is in the grip of a crisis concerning orthodoxy. Unity is once more seen as a desirable goal and plurality in theology as the best expression of orthodoxy. If modern orthodoxy feels the need to interpret truth in some sort of continuity with the interpretations of the New Testament and of the Fathers who formed the faith of the church we arrive at the heart of its dilemma: the difficult question of what constitutes an acceptable continuity of content, and when doctrinal development may be considered legitimate.

The history just sketched in, albeit in over-simplified form, would suggest that one of the most interesting features of art as a theological idiom is the way in which it perpetuates orthodoxy. Apart from the scriptures, which are judged to contain the historical facts, history shows that the artistic idiom has remained the most stable vehicle for the transmission of orthodoxy since its inception. History, in this area, has been a medium of growth and not a source of embarrassment; and art has prevented the abstract principles concerning Christ from supplanting his person. It has facilitated the transposition of doctrine from static and objective categories to those of a more dynamic character, and it has made easy the transfer of orthodoxy from one area and milieu and from one age to another in the continuity of the community. An imagery conceived long ago under an imperial court, such as the representations of the Pantocrator and the Theotokos, or under papal patronage like the Sistine decorations of Michelangelo, have left and continue to leave a mark on the imagination of their viewers. For most Christians these images continue, by and large, to answer to our visualizations of God, divine majesty, etc. They all date from a time when art was closely allied with doctrine.[46]

An orthodox theology of art, therefore, by the former standards of the church is one in which the faith of the church, as represented in its imagery, is determined by the church's teaching, both with regard to the nature and content of orthodoxy. As we saw at the outset of this essay, the Western church needs to clarify its mind on the relationship of doctrine to art. It has indeed attempted to do so in recent years in the works of Tillich, Küng and others,[47] but one is forced to conclude that these attempts have all been failures. What seems to be wrong with the thinking here, and with that of the works referred to in the opening paragraphs of this essay, is that the problem is conceived to be a philosophical one and so is dealt with as part of the problem of epistemology. The failure lies in constructing the theory first and then relating it to art, thus turning an intended theological reflection into another philosophy of aesthetics, at least in Tillich's case.[48] The practice of the ancient church is instructive here; conversely it began with the material image and in consideration of this arrived not at a philosophy but a theology of art.

Greek ways of thought, however, are not necessarily acceptable to modern theology, but in the matter under consideration, they are not essential. The religious image indicated by the triumph of orthodoxy was the Byzantine icon, an image fully justified by the tradition, but the confining of the religious understanding of art to the icon is not necessarily a constraint demanded by orthodoxy.[49] The same orthodox tradition justifies a freer and more flexible form of artistic expression, on the basis of the same theological principles uttered long ago by the Fathers, and which will allow for greater doctrinal development. As far as one can tell, further development is impossible in the East because, as we have seen, art became so inseparable from theology that as an idiom of expression it lost its autonomy and became swallowed up by theology. It could no longer retain any neutral function and could leave nothing to the realm of the secular, with a resulting canonicity of imagery, which now, like the propositional theology of the Word has become inflexible and from the point of orthodoxy can only rule out. The orthodox artist is not required to appear in his work and must not modify the tradition in any way. To the extent to which he puts himself into his work, the work is a failure.[50]

But for the Western church there is no dogmatic problem in the sense of the specific canonicity of imagery. Nor is there any sense of the sacramentality of the image. As was said earlier, Western thinking, because it bypassed the iconoclastic controversy, is still rooted in the understanding of the image in the less restricted concept that it had had in the tradition up to and including John Damascene, where it meant more or less a symbol of any type. According to earlier thought, both Eastern and Western, God had revealed himself in symbols. Because these are not considered portraits of God, the typological method of representation was able to continue in the Western cultural tradition until it disappeared at the Renaissance, when dogmatic art became based on the logic of history understood as chronology.[51] So in the Sistine Chapel, in contradistinction to the dogmatic sarcophagi of the early church, God the Father alone can be seen creating Adam without offending against the doctrine of the Trinity, because the underlying logic is that, chronologically speaking, the creation is prior to the incarnation.

If one believes, with the Cappadocians, that the role of religious imagery is essentially to communicate and teach, to remind and provoke thought and emotion, then art is left, within orthodoxy, the necessary degree of autonomy it requires to continue as a religious vehicle. It will be thus left open to the techniques, methods and mentalities of the time and place in which the church is situated. The imagination will again be engaged by the best effective means and the role of the artist will become crucial as the one who translates the faith into a visual representation. On the principles of ancient theology, therefore, the role of the artist is crucial to the church, his talent and creativity are of great significance to orthodoxy, and except for some very general restraints he is free to illustrate the scripture as he sees fit. To the Western church the visual is paradoxically both more and less important than the written word.[52] There is no habit in the West of pursuing unorthodox artists as of pursuing unorthodox theologians, probably because the artistic tradition in the West has been on the whole maintained by the laity. Nevertheless the Western church feels a close relationship between theology and iconography; recent thinking, even in traditionally aniconic Protestant theology, is showing a need to reinterpret Calvin's principles in the light of the modern church's need to rediscover the visual medium.[53]

That the experience of orthodoxy is and always has been one of variety and richness in the church the history of spirituality shows very well. In earlier periods art has been able to capture doctrine correctly, while at the same time paradoxically revealing new aspects of it. Should we not have the confidence that it can do so again?

NOTES

1 See H. E. Root, 'Beginning all over again', in A. R. Vidler (ed.), *Soundings*, Cambridge 1963, pp. 3–19.

2 See J. Mackey (ed.) *Religious Imagination*, Edinburgh 1986.

3 The relationship has been much studied. For an example see A. Forge (ed.), *Primitive Art and Society*, Oxford 1973.

4 See J. Gouillard, 'L'Hérésie dans l'Empire Byzantin des origines au XIIe. siècle', in *La Vie religieuse à Byzance*, London 1981, pp. 299–324.

5 *pratum* 178. PG 87.3048.

6 *Miracula* 12. PG 87.3461. The background is studied by H. Chadwick, 'John Moschus and his friend Sophronius the Sophist', *JThS* 25 (1974), 41–74.

7 *Acta* 11, 18.6.26 PG 90.156, 164.

8 See M. Mundell, 'Monophysite Church Decoration', in A. Bryer and J. Herrin (eds.), *Iconoclasm*, Birmingham 1977, pp. 59–74.

9 On Germanus, see L. Lamza, *Germanos I von Konstantinopel*, Würzburg 1975.

10 For the early Catacombs, see J. Wilpert, *Die Malereien der Katakomben Roms*, Freiburg-im-Breisgau 1903. For the later ones, see A. Ferrua, *Le Pitture della Nuova Catacomba di Via Latina*, Rome 1960. J. Deckers and H. R. Seeliger, *Die Katakombe 'Santi Marcellino e Pietro' Repertorium der Malereien*, Münster 1987.

11 See the discussion of E. Kitzinger, *Byzantine Art in the Making*, London 1977, ch. 1, esp. pp. 19f.

12 Ibid. pp. 22f.

13 See, for example, the list of subjects given in A. Nestori, *Repertorio Topografico delle Catacombe Romane*, Vatican 1975.

14 The collection is published in K. Weitzmann, *The Monastery of Saint Catherine at Mount Sinai. The Icons*, vol. 1, Princeton 1976.

15 See his letter to Constantia, H. Hennephof, *Textus Byzantini ad iconomachiam pertinentes*, Leiden 1969, pp. 42–4.

16 These seem to have occurred mainly in the realm of depictions of the Trinity. While representations of the hospitality of Abraham have always been acceptable, depictions of the Three Persons as a three-headed man were condemned by the Council of Trent. The Tridentine principles for orthodox artistic representation were laid down at the twenty-fifth Session.

17 PG 79.577–80.

18 *Antirrhetici* 3,10. PG 100, 392.

19 *Adversus Constantinum Cabalinum* 10. PG 95, 325. The text is traditionally ascribed to John Damascene but is probably the work of John V of Jerusalem.

20 Kitzinger analysed the literature in detail in 'The Cult of Images in the Age before Iconoclasm', *Dumbarton Oaks Papers*, 8 (1954), 83–150.

21 *Laudatio S. Theodori*, PG 46.737. (Some doubt has been raised concerning the authenticity of the panegyric.)

22 *Oratio* 35,3–4, PG 36.260–1. For the conclusion that the discourse is rightly to be attributed to Gregory, see M. P. Masson, 'Le Discours 35 de

Grégoire de Nazianze. Questions d'authenticité', *Pallas*, 31 (1984), 179–88 and 194.

23 *De deitate Filii et Spiritus Sancti*, PG 46.572.

24 Euodius, *PL* 41.850f. Gregory the Great, *Epistolae* IX.209, XI.10, *CCL* 140A, pp. 768, 873–6.

25 *De imaginibus, passim*, ed. B. Kotter, *Die Schriften des Johannes von Damascus III* Berlin 1975. Cf. Theodore Studites *ref.* 1 PG 99.441. The iconophile case rested on the identity of content between the verbal and pictorial descriptions of the scenes of Christ's history.

26 For the genuineness of the letter, see S. Gero, 'The True Image of Christ: Eusebius' Letter to Constantia Reconsidered', *JThS* 32 (1981), 460–70.

27 See C. Murray, 'Le Problème de l'iconophobie et les premiers siècles chrétiens' in F. Boespflug and N. Lossky (eds.), *Nicée II 787–1987. Douze siècles d'images réligieuses*, Actes du Colloque International Nicée vol. 2 Paris 1987, pp. 39–49.

28 *Paedagogus* III, xi, i. *SC* 158, p.125.

29 *De fide et symbolo* 7. PL 40.188.

30 36th Canon. Text in J. Vives, *Concilios Visigoticos e Hispano-Romanos*, España Cristiana, vol. 1, Barcelona-Madrid, 1963, p. 8.

31 *Imag.* 73 PG 100.789.

32 This point is philosophically considered by H. D. Lewis, 'Worship and Idolatry', in H. D. Lewis (ed.), *Contemporary British Philosophy*, London 1956, pp. 265–86.

33 *De Spiritu Sancto* XVIII, 44f. PG 32.149.

34 On Cappadocian humanism, see P. J. Fedwick (ed.), *Basil of Caesarea, Christian, Humanist, Ascetic*, 2 vols., Pontifical Institute of Mediaeval Studies, Toronto, 1981.

35 On Hypatius, see Kitzinger, 'Cult', p. 137f. Also P. J. Alexander, 'Hypatius of Ephesus. A note on Image Worship in the Sixth Century', *HThR*, 44 (1952), 178–81.

36 The Council was held at Constantinople in 692. Text in Mansi XI, 977–80; XIII, 40–1.

37 Definition in Mansi XIII, 373–80; reproduced in *Conciliorum Oecumenicorum Decreta*, Istituto per le Scienze Religiose, Bologna 1973, pp. 135–7.

38 The most detailed historical studies are those of S. Gero; see in particular *Byzantine iconoclasm during the reign of Leo III*, Corpus Scriptorum Christianorum Orientalium, Orientalia Subsidia t. 41, Louvain, 1973. For the doctrinal history, see C. Von Schönborn, *L'Icône du Christ*, Fribourg, 1976.

39 The text of the questions of Constantine V is transmitted in fragments by Nicephorus, *Antirr. PG* 100. 216f. This remark is from the introduction to the second question, col. 329A.

40 This is plausibly suggested by the evidence as at present available. 338

bishops met in 754 for the iconoclastic Council of Hiereia, which means that almost every bishop of the empire was present. The see of Constantinople was at that time vacant. A good number of bishops were also able to be collected quickly for the Council of 815. The real opposition came from the monks. Florovsky drew attention to the 'Origenist' tendencies of the bishops. Origenism in its spiritual form was an intellectual movement, that of the *logioteroi*, of which Cyril of Scythopolis speaks, *Vie de S. Sabas*, ed. E. Schwartz, Leipzig 1939, p. 188, 18. For Florovsky's view, see 'Origen, Eusebius and the Iconoclastic Controversy', *Church History*, 19 (1950), 77–96.

41 *Antirr*. 1,2. *PG* 100.209. It was to destroy this rampart that he wrote his treatises.

42 John of Damascus (675–749), the first great Eastern theologian to make a synthesis of the theology of the icon, wrote his three discourses against those who reject images *c*. 730. He was dead by 754, but his ideas fed later arguments. He was personally anathematized, along with Germanus and George of Cyprus, by the Council. There are ambiguities in his theology which Nicephorus and Theodore were able to avoid. There is a study by H. Menges, *Die Bilderlehre des hl. Johannes von Damaskus*, Münster 1938.

43 *PG* 100.

44 See, chiefly, his refutations of iconoclasm and his letters. *PG* 99 and J. P. Costa Luzzi (ed.), Nova Patrum Bibliotheca, Rome 1871.

45 Von Schönborn's thesis, *L'Icône du Christ*, p. 223.

46 See A. Grabar, *Byzantium from the Death of Theodosius to the Rise of Islam*, London 1966.

47 See P. Tillich, in J. L. Adams (ed. and transl.) *What is Religion?* 'Essay on the Idea of a Theology of Culture' (London 1969), pp. 155f. and ⁶Art and Ultimate Reality', *Cross Currents*, 10, no. 1 (winter, 1960) 1–13. For H. Küng, see *Art and the Question of Meaning*, London 1981.

48 Tillich's work is discussed in M. Palmer, *Paul Tillich's Philosophy of Art*, Berlin 1984.

49 For the text see J. Gouillard, 'Le Synodikon d'Orthodoxie: édition et commentaire', *Travaux et Mémoires*, vol. 2 (1967), pp. 1–316.

50 For an interesting discussion on Eastern and Western attitudes see S. R. Bigham, 'The Image of God the Father in Orthodox Theology and Iconography', *Sacred Art Journal*, 5 (1984), 1–132, 67f.

51 Ibid. pp. 77–8.

52 Ibid. p. 71 The same attitude may be illustrated currently in the case of Liberation Theology. Latin American writings are scrutinized with regard to orthodoxy; the associated art escapes unnoticed. See, as an example of this art, the crucifix on the cover of R. Gibellini, *Frontiers of Theology in Latin America*, London 1975.

53 I am indebted to the author of an as yet unpublished paper on Calvin and imagery for this information.

Index of modern names

Index of ancient and medieval names

Diodore, bishop of Tarsus 189, 195
Diodorus Siculus 109
Diogenes Laertius 58fn4, 59n9, 59n11
Diogenianus, epicurean 118n26
Diognetus 20n25, 22n49, 277f
Dio Cassius 109, 110
Dio Chrysostom 183
Dionysius, bishop of Alexandria 12f
Dionysius, bishop of Corinth 12
Dionysius of Halicarnassus 186, 193,
    197n5, 198n9, 198n10, 198n13
Dionysius Thrax, grammarian 197n6,
    198n12
Diospolis, Synod of (415) 202
Docetism 152
Donatism 28, 29f, 31, 35, 39n44, 106,
    246
Dracilianus 111

Ebionism 39n44, 50
Elijah 271, 278, 285
Elisha 285
Elkesaites, Christian sect 33
Elvira, Council of (c. 306) 297
Encratites, sect 37n4
Ennodius, bishop of Pavia 231n31
Ephesus, Council of (431) 200, 201, 209,
    210, 229n13
Ephraim Syrus 39n38
Epictetus, stoic 42
Epicurus, Epicureans 40–2; see also
    Atomists, Greek
Epiphanius, bishop of Salamis 65, 70, 72,
    85n9, 89n46, 149, 153, 161, 170n12,
    171n31, 181n8, 287n13
Essenes 279f, 285, 286, 286n16
Euchites, see Messalians
Euclid 42
Euladius, bishop of Arles 221
Eunapius, sophist 119n37
Eunomius, bishop of Cyzicus 148,
    157–72, 173, 174, 178, 180n4, 181n6,
    181n9, 201
Euodius, bishop of Uzala 295
Euripides 189
Eusebius, anti-pelagian 204
Eusebius, bishop of Caesarea ix, 12, 13,
    14f, 21n29, 24f, 38n15, 45, 65,
    94–123, 124–41, 144f, 214, 243f, 247,
    248, 258f, 260, 268n1, 274f, 277,
    278, 279, 287n10, 294, 296, 298,
    307n10
Eusebius of Palestine 206
Eusebius, bishop of Vercelli 147

Eustathius, bishop of Antioch viii, 71,
    146, 155, 193ff
Eustathius, bishop of Sebaste 272
Eutropius, historian 119n42
Eutyches 157f
Euzoius, deacon, associate of Arius 115,
    150
Evagrius, praetorian prefect 122n79
Eve 64, 67, 68, 72–9 passim, 84n2, 84n3

Fabius Rusticus 110
Fasir 38n26
Fausta, empress 99, 119n43
Faustus of Milevis 25, 240, 241
Faustus, bishop of Riez 221f, 223f, 225,
    226, 231n35
Felix III, pope of Rome 220, 222, 223,
    232n42
Ferrandus 232n45
Filastrius, bishop of Brescia 243
Flacillus, bishop of Antioch 102
Flavius Dalmatius 118n24
Florus 207
Fulgentius, bishop of Ruspe 224f

Gaianites, sect 291
Galen 260, 287n18
Galerius, emperor 99, 107, 112
Gangra, Synod of (c. 340) 272
Gelasius I, pope of Rome 220, 221, 222f
Gennadius of Marseilles 221, 226,
    230n26, 232n43, 254n51
George of Cyprus 307n42
Germanus, bishop of Auxerre 228n9
Germanus, patriarch of Constantinople
    291, 307n42
Gideon 276, 285
Gnostics, Gnosticism 2, 3, 9, 14, 17,
    21n34, 31, 32, 33, 35, 40f, 44, 45, 51,
    53, 60n40, 62, 63, 241, 285
Goths 105
Gratian, emperor 147, 159
Gregory I, 'the Great', pope of Rome
    227n3, 246, 248, 253n44, 295f, 297
Gregory, bishop of Nazianzus 102, 152f,
    162–5, 169, 171n34, 180, 189, 195f,
    197n4, 256f, 261, 267, 295, 298
Gregory, bishop of Nyssa 62, 148, 152,
    162ff, 166, 170n16, 171n38, 196, 255,
    295, 296, 298
Gregory Palamas 156

Helena, empress 100, 104
Heracleides, bishop 86n25

Index of sources